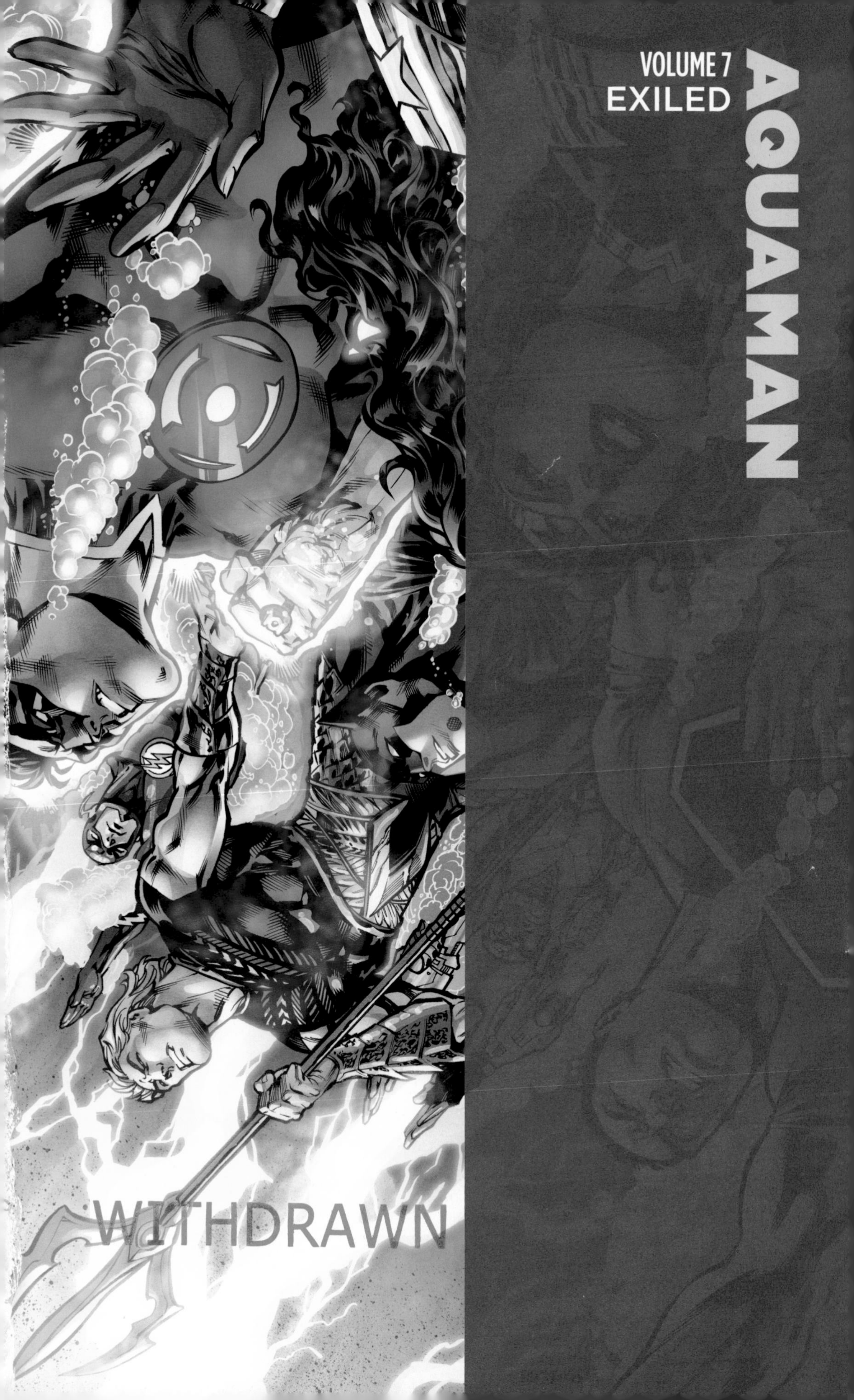
AQUAMAN
VOLUME 7
EXILED

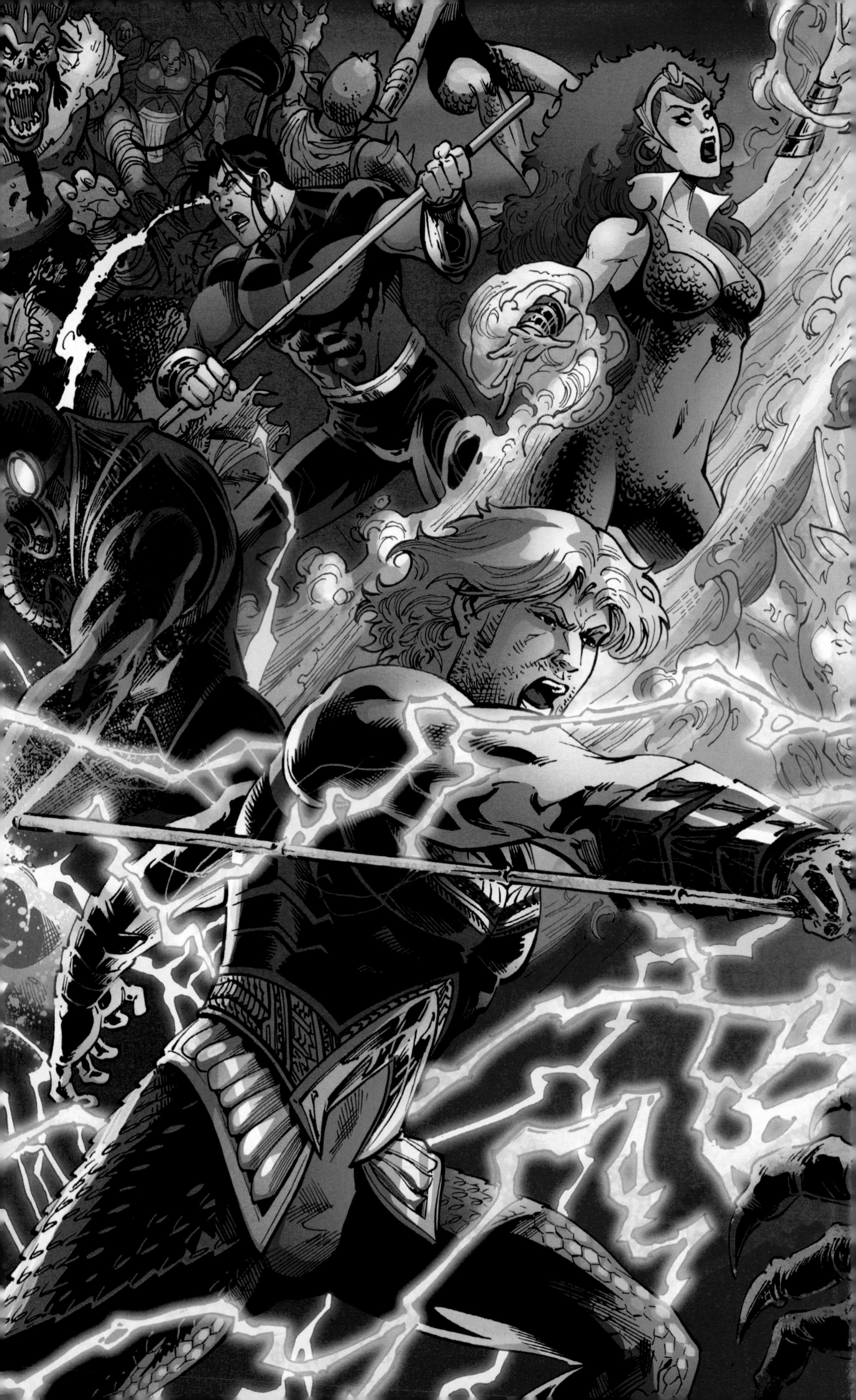

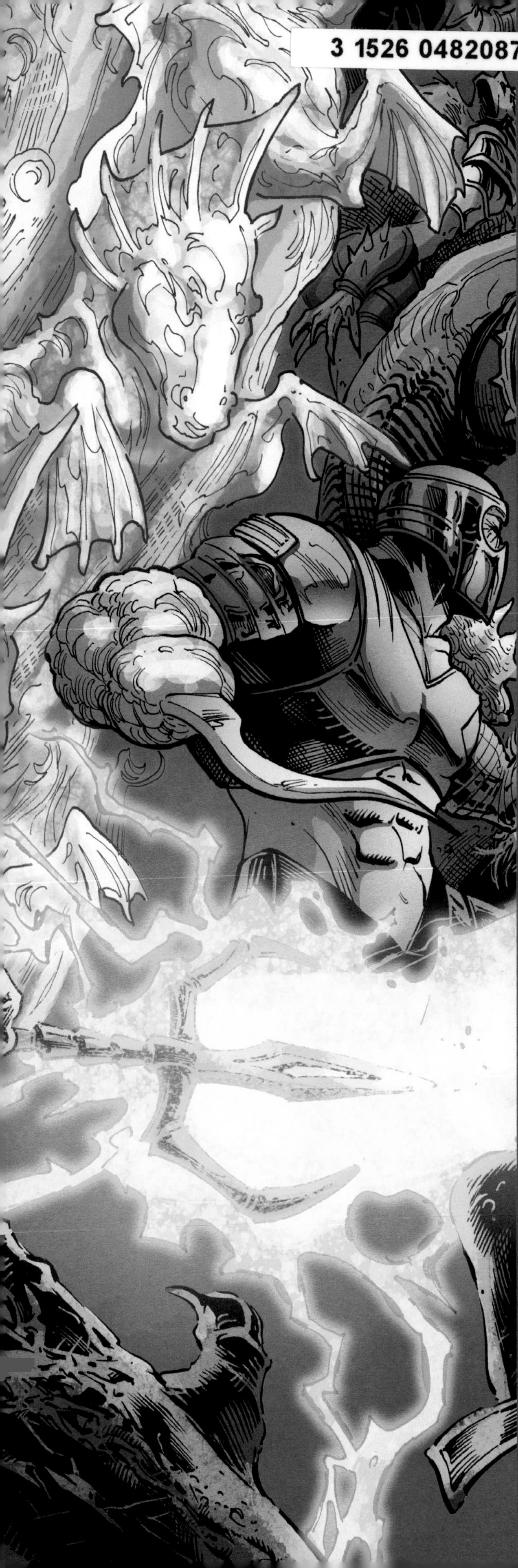

AQUAMAN

VOLUME 7

EXILED

WRITTEN BY
CULLEN BUNN

ART BY
TREVOR MCCARTHY
VICENTE CIFUENTES
JESUS MERINO
WALDEN WONG
ALEC MORGAN
ART THIBERT
JOHN DELL
JOHN LIVESAY
MARC DEERING
DON HO
MARK IRWIN
JUAN CASTRO

COLOR BY
GUY MAJOR

LETTERS BY
TOM NAPOLITANO

COLLECTION COVER ART BY
TREVOR MCCARTHY
& GUY MAJOR

AQUAMAN CREATED BY
PAUL NORRIS

SUPERMAN CREATED BY
JERRY SIEGEL AND
JOE SHUSTER
BY SPECIAL ARRANGEMENT
WITH THE JERRY SIEGEL FAMILY

WONDER WOMAN CREATED BY
WILLIAM
MOULTON MARSTON

BRIAN CUNNINGHAM Editor – Original Series
AMEDEO TURTURRO Assistant Editor – Original Series
JEB WOODARD Group Editor – Collected Editions
LIZ ERICKSON Editor – Collected Edition
STEVE COOK Design Director – Books
DAMIAN RYLAND Publication Design

BOB HARRAS Senior VP – Editor-in-Chief, DC Comics

DIANE NELSON President
DAN DIDIO and JIM LEE Co-Publishers
GEOFF JOHNS Chief Creative Officer
AMIT DESAI Senior VP – Marketing & Global Franchise Management
NAIRI GARDINER Senior VP – Finance
SAM ADES VP – Digital Marketing
BOBBIE CHASE VP – Talent Development
MARK CHIARELLO Senior VP – Art, Design & Collected Editions
JOHN CUNNINGHAM VP – Content Strategy
ANNE DEPIES VP – Strategy Planning & Reporting
DON FALLETTI VP – Manufacturing Operations
LAWRENCE GANEM VP – Editorial Administration & Talent Relations
ALISON GILL Senior VP – Manufacturing & Operations
HANK KANALZ Senior VP – Editorial Strategy & Administration
JAY KOGAN VP – Legal Affairs
DEREK MADDALENA Senior VP – Sales & Business Development
JACK MAHAN VP – Business Affairs
DAN MIRON VP – Sales Planning & Trade Development
NICK NAPOLITANO VP – Manufacturing Administration
CAROL ROEDER VP – Marketing
EDDIE SCANNELL VP – Mass Account & Digital Sales
COURTNEY SIMMONS Senior VP – Publicity & Communications
JIM (SKI) SOKOLOWSKI VP – Comic Book Specialty & Newsstand Sales
SANDY YI Senior VP – Global Franchise Management

AQUAMAN VOLUME 7: EXILED

DC Comics, 2900 West Alameda Ave., Burbank, CA 91505
Printed by RR Donnelley, Salem, VA, USA. 3/18/16.
First Printing.
ISBN: 978-1-4012-6098-9

Library of Congress Cataloging-in-Publication Data is available.

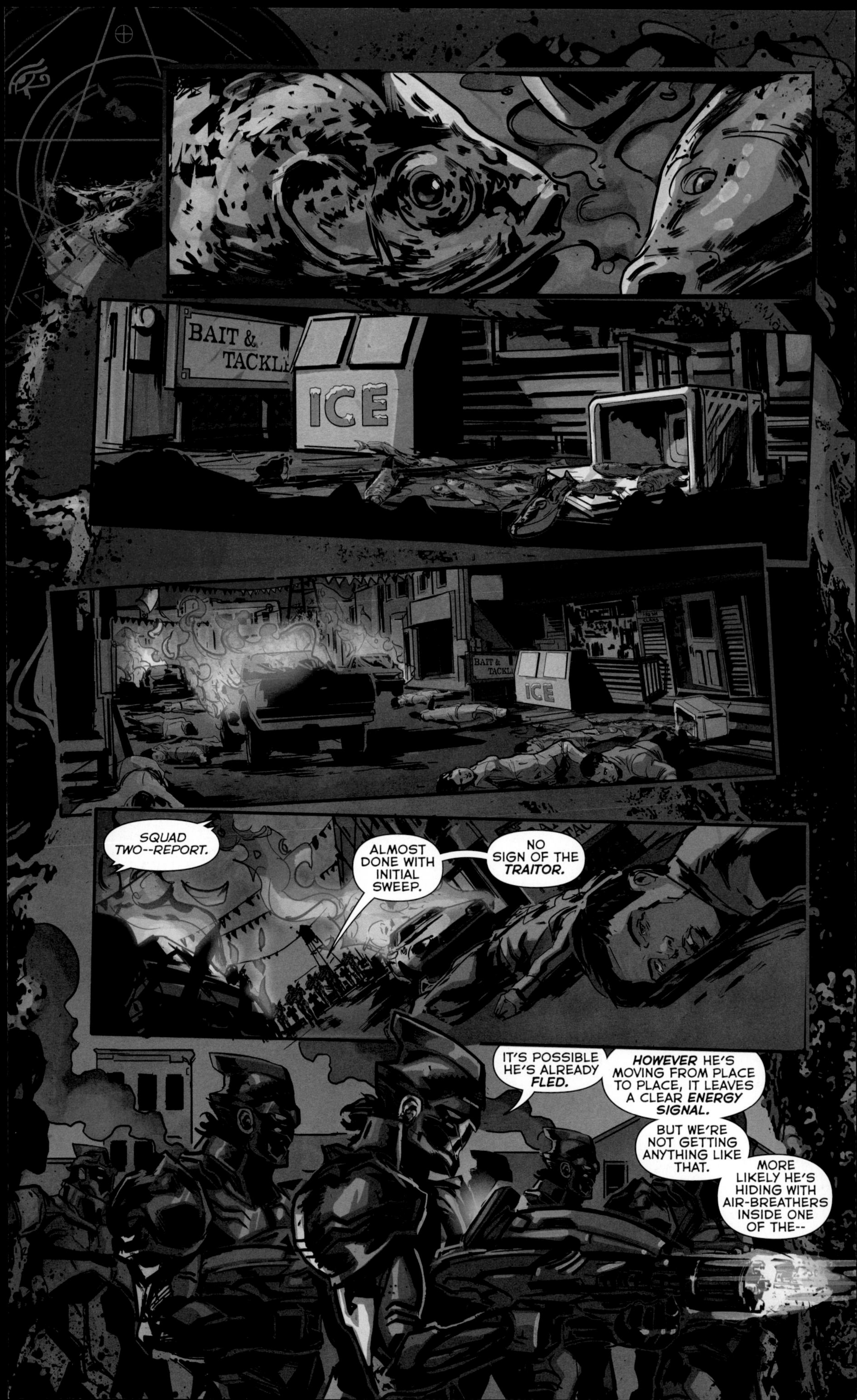
BAIT & TACKLE
ICE
SQUAD TWO--REPORT.
ALMOST DONE WITH INITIAL SWEEP.
NO SIGN OF THE TRAITOR.
IT'S POSSIBLE HE'S ALREADY FLED.
HOWEVER HE'S MOVING FROM PLACE TO PLACE, IT LEAVES A CLEAR ENERGY SIGNAL.
BUT WE'RE NOT GETTING ANYTHING LIKE THAT.
MORE LIKELY HE'S HIDING WITH AIR-BREATHERS INSIDE ONE OF THE--

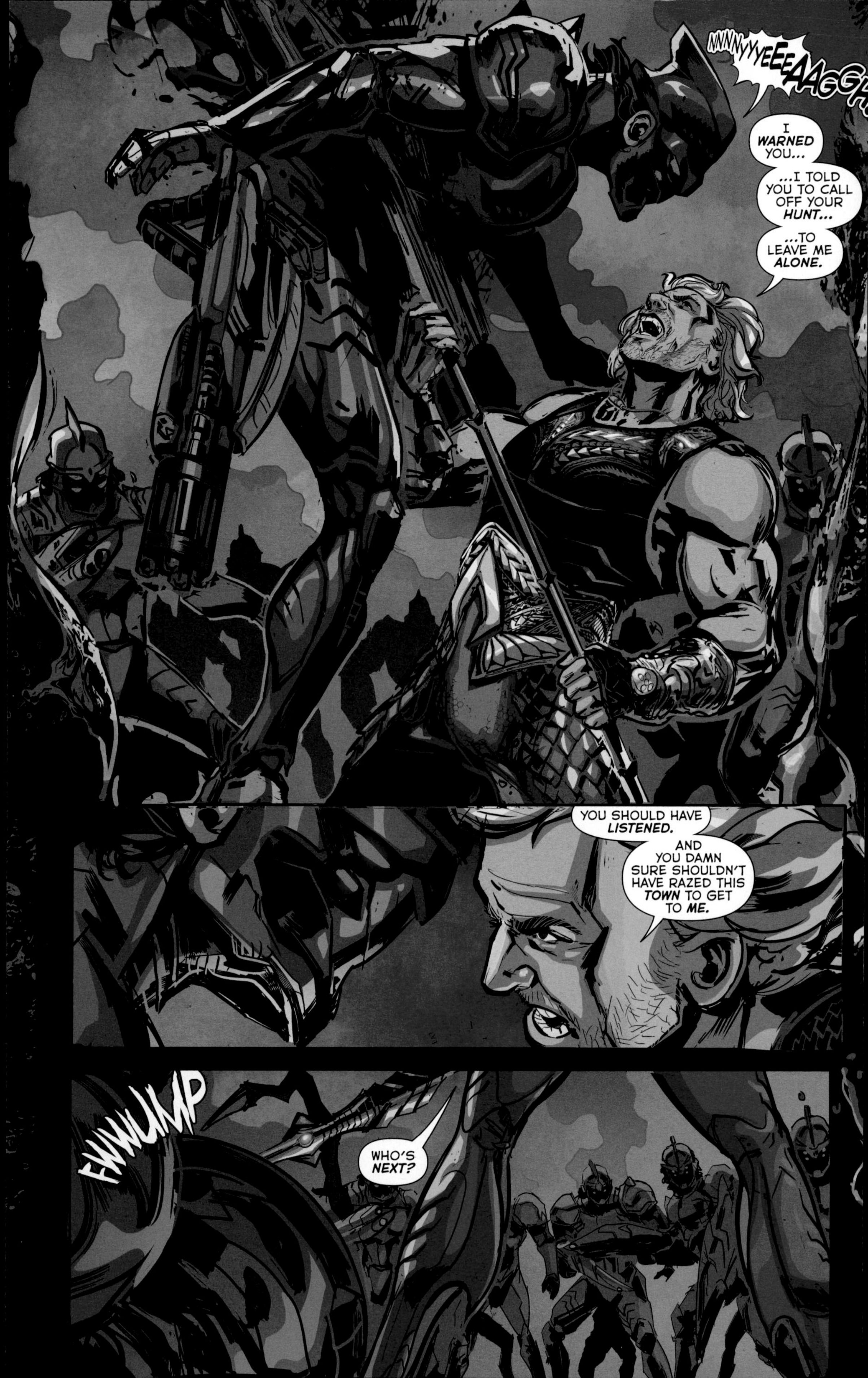
NNNNyyyEEAAGGH
I WARNED YOU...
...I TOLD YOU TO CALL OFF YOUR HUNT...
...TO LEAVE ME ALONE.
YOU SHOULD HAVE LISTENED.
AND YOU DAMN SURE SHOULDN'T HAVE RAZED THIS TOWN TO GET TO ME.
FWUMP
WHO'S NEXT?

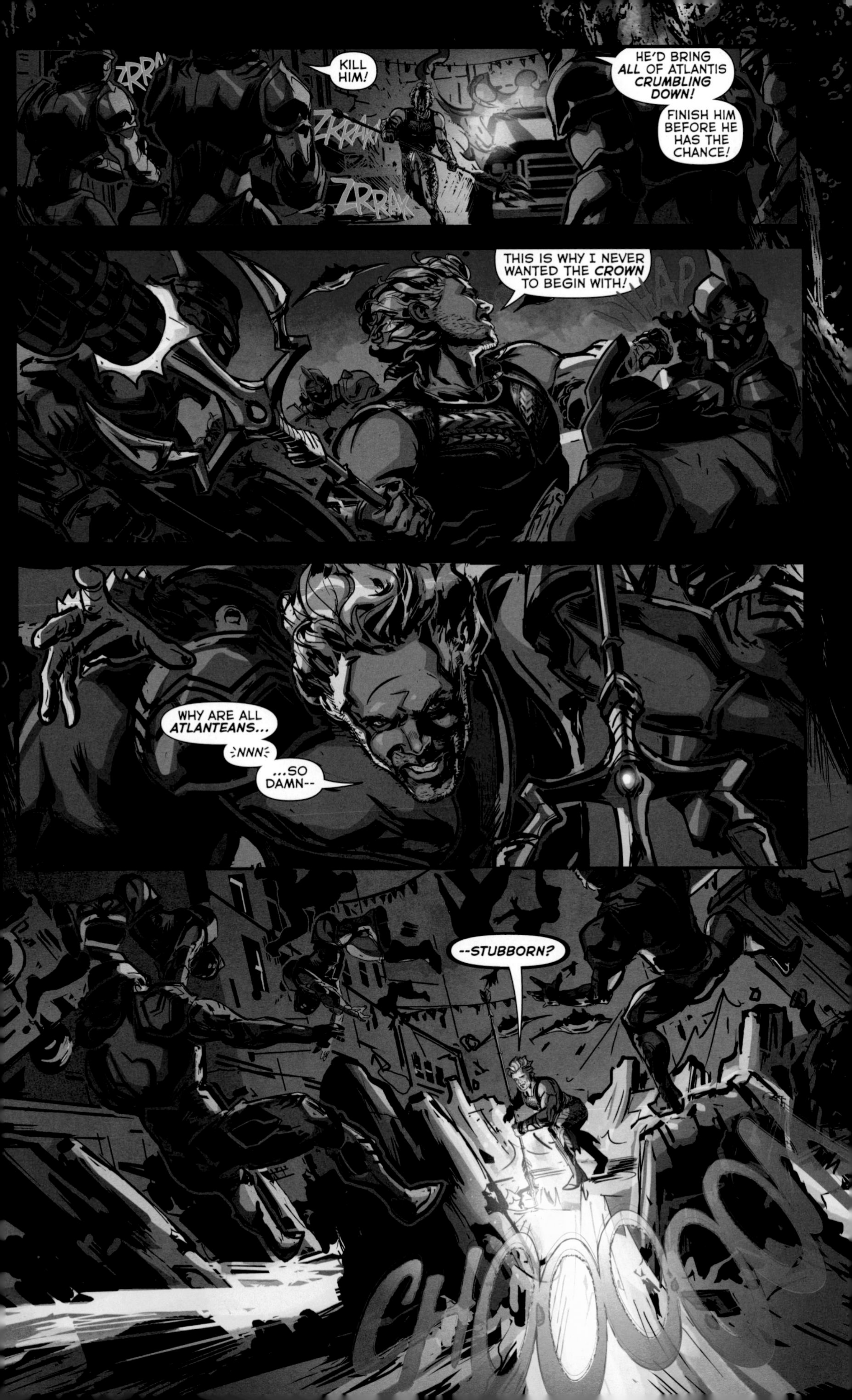
ZRRAK
KILL HIM!
ZKRAK
ZRRAK
HE'D BRING ALL OF ATLANTIS CRUMBLING DOWN!
FINISH HIM BEFORE HE HAS THE CHANCE!
THIS IS WHY I NEVER WANTED THE CROWN TO BEGIN WITH!
WHY ARE ALL ATLANTEANS...
NNN
...SO DAMN--
--STUBBORN?

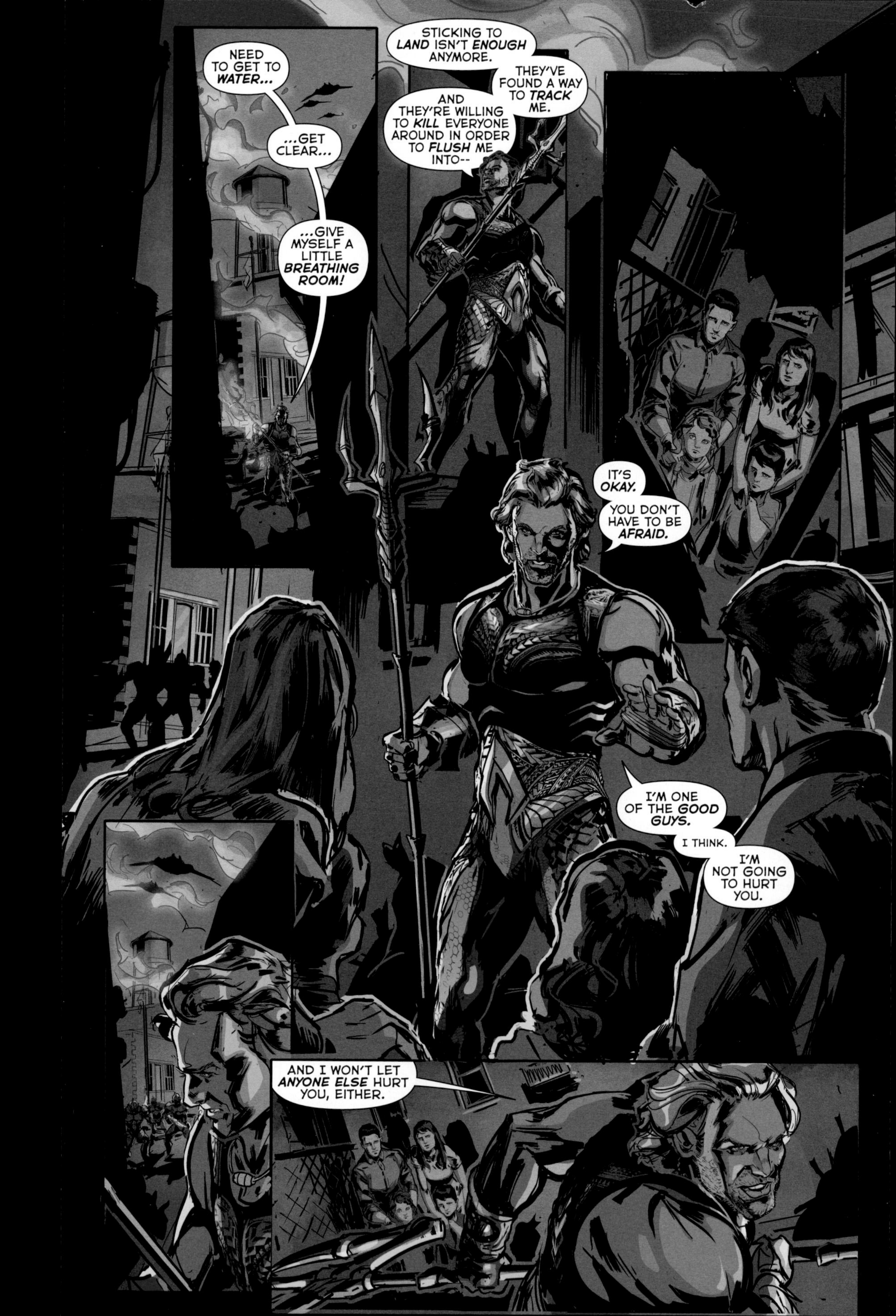
NEED TO GET TO WATER...
...GET CLEAR...
...GIVE MYSELF A LITTLE BREATHING ROOM!
STICKING TO LAND ISN'T ENOUGH ANYMORE.
THEY'VE FOUND A WAY TO TRACK ME.
AND THEY'RE WILLING TO KILL EVERYONE AROUND IN ORDER TO FLUSH ME INTO--
IT'S OKAY.
YOU DON'T HAVE TO BE AFRAID.
I'M ONE OF THE GOOD GUYS.
I THINK.
I'M NOT GOING TO HURT YOU.
AND I WON'T LET ANYONE ELSE HURT YOU, EITHER.

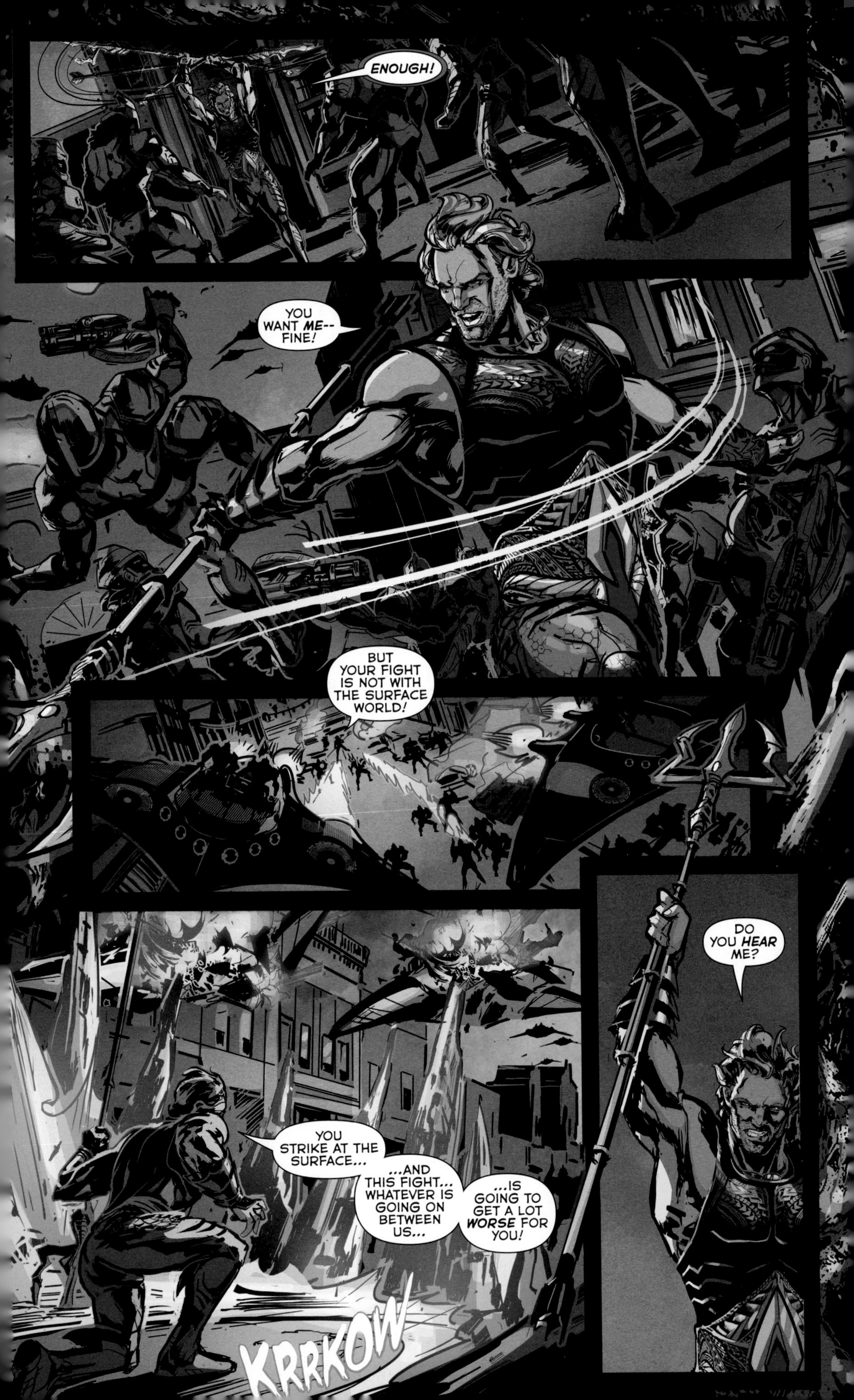
ENOUGH!
YOU WANT ME-- FINE!
BUT YOUR FIGHT IS NOT WITH THE SURFACE WORLD!
DO YOU HEAR ME?
YOU STRIKE AT THE SURFACE...
...AND THIS FIGHT... WHATEVER IS GOING ON BETWEEN US...
...IS GOING TO GET A LOT WORSE FOR YOU!
KRRKOW

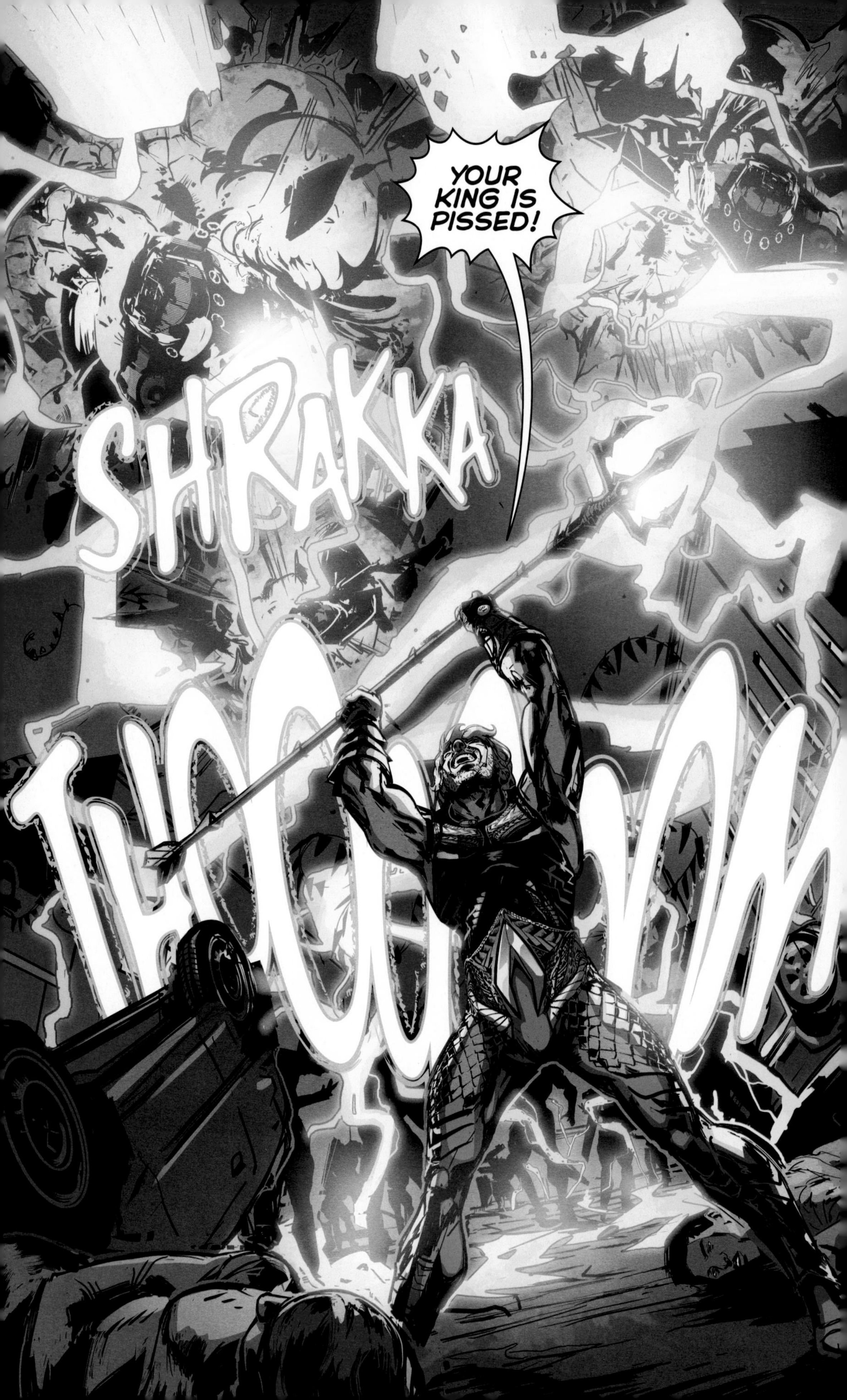
YOUR KING IS PISSED!
SHRAKKA
THOOOOM

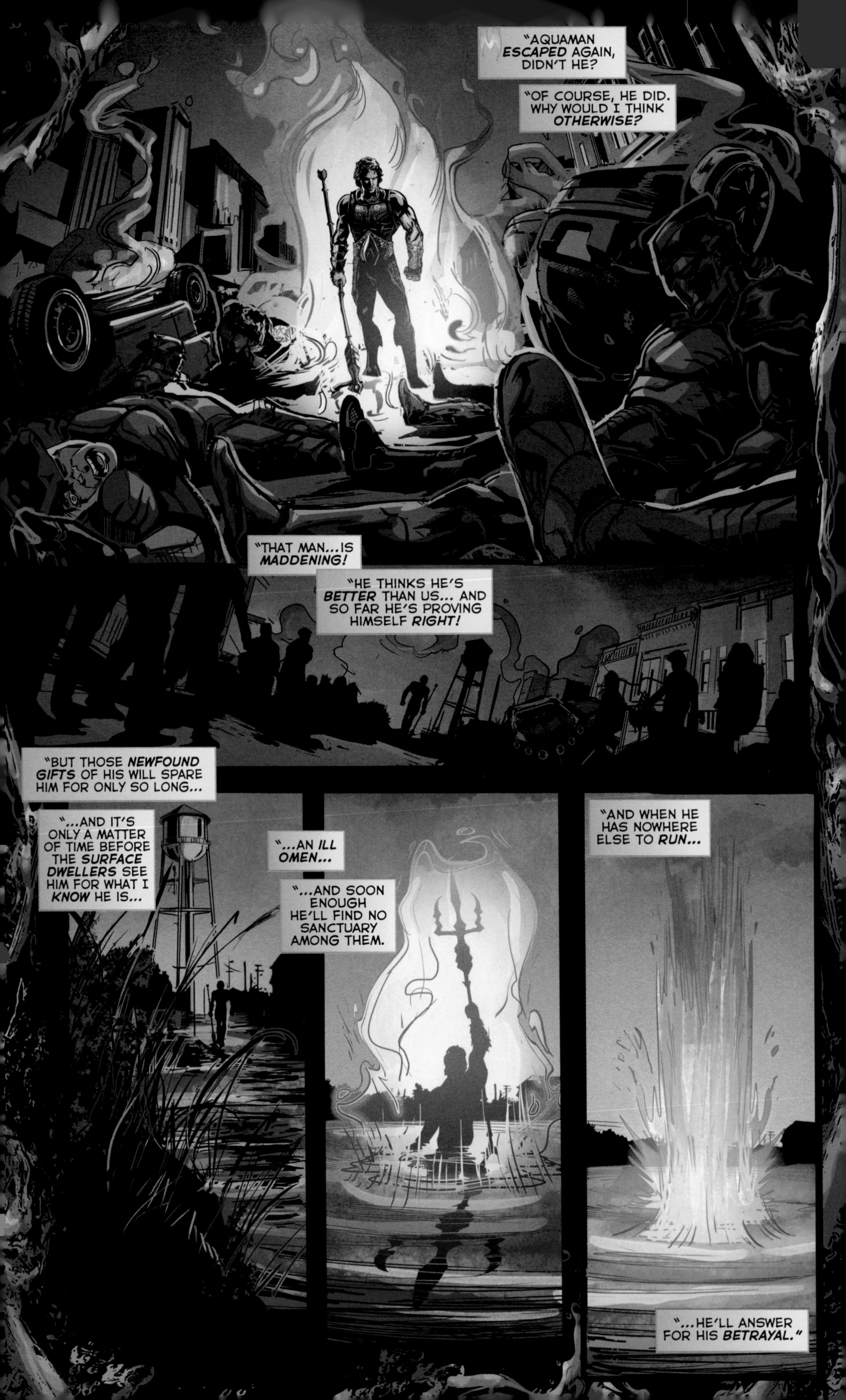
"AQUAMAN ESCAPED AGAIN, DIDN'T HE?
"OF COURSE, HE DID. WHY WOULD I THINK OTHERWISE?
"THAT MAN...IS MADDENING!
"HE THINKS HE'S BETTER THAN US... AND SO FAR HE'S PROVING HIMSELF RIGHT!
"BUT THOSE NEWFOUND GIFTS OF HIS WILL SPARE HIM FOR ONLY SO LONG...
"...AND IT'S ONLY A MATTER OF TIME BEFORE THE SURFACE DWELLERS SEE HIM FOR WHAT I KNOW HE IS...
"...AN ILL OMEN...
"...AND SOON ENOUGH HE'LL FIND NO SANCTUARY AMONG THEM.
"AND WHEN HE HAS NOWHERE ELSE TO RUN...
"...HE'LL ANSWER FOR HIS BETRAYAL."

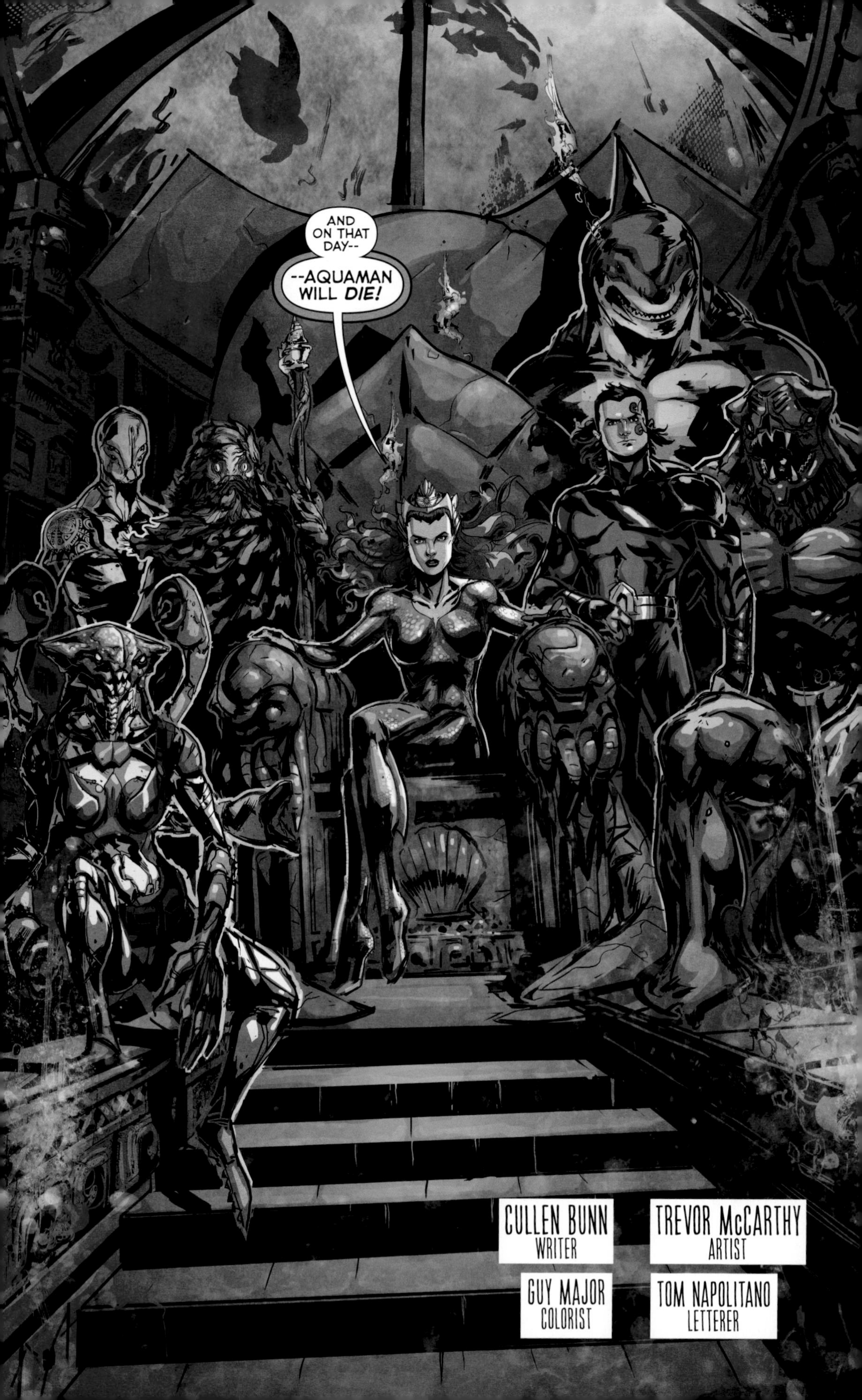

AND ON THAT DAY--
--AQUAMAN WILL DIE!
CULLEN BUNN WRITER
TREVOR McCARTHY ARTIST
GUY MAJOR COLORIST
TOM NAPOLITANO LETTERER

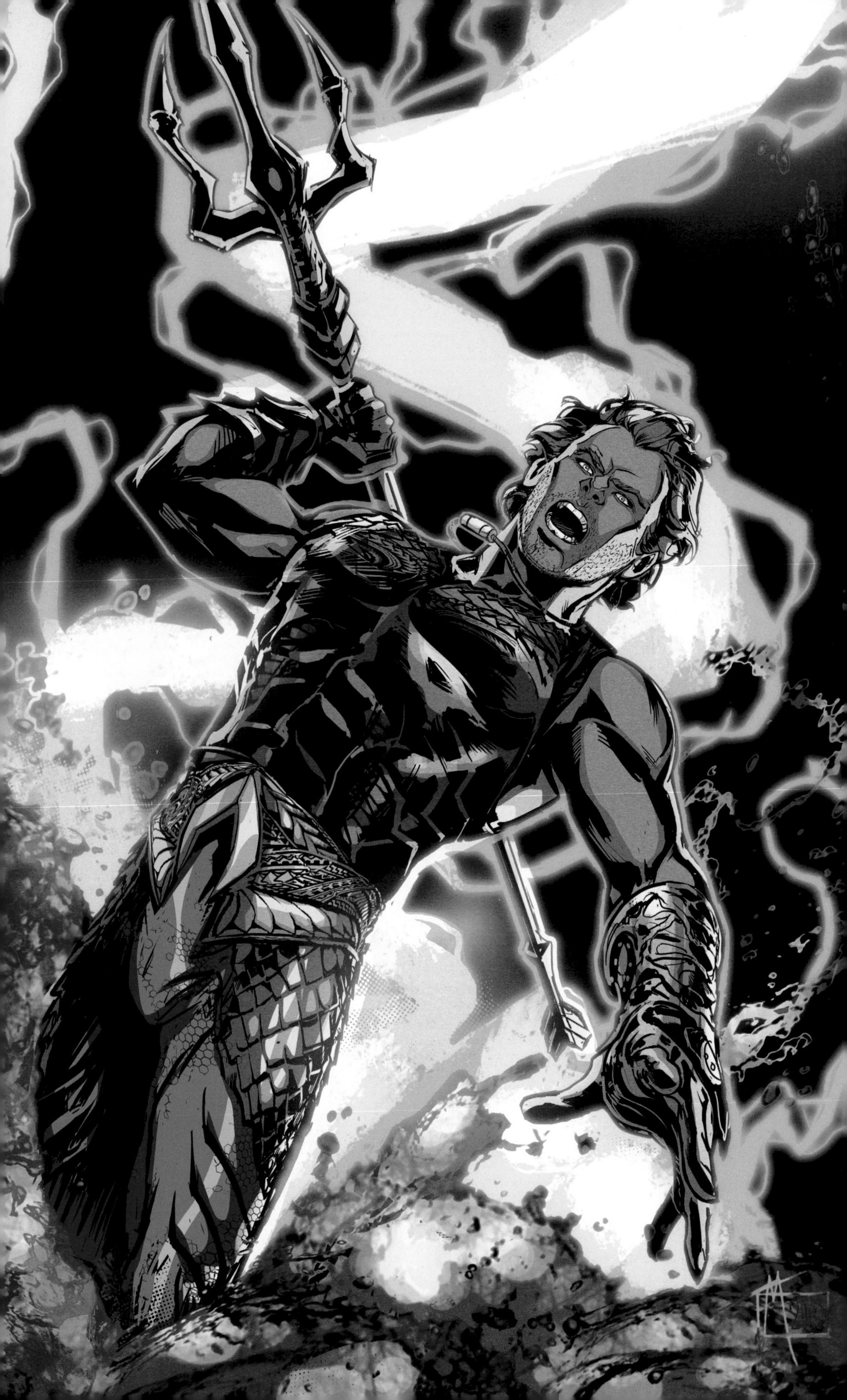

TERRA INCOGNITA

CULLEN BUNN writer **TREVOR MCCARTHY** artist **GUY MAJOR** colorist **TOM NAPOLITANO** letterer
TREVOR MCCARTHY and **GUY MAJOR** cover art

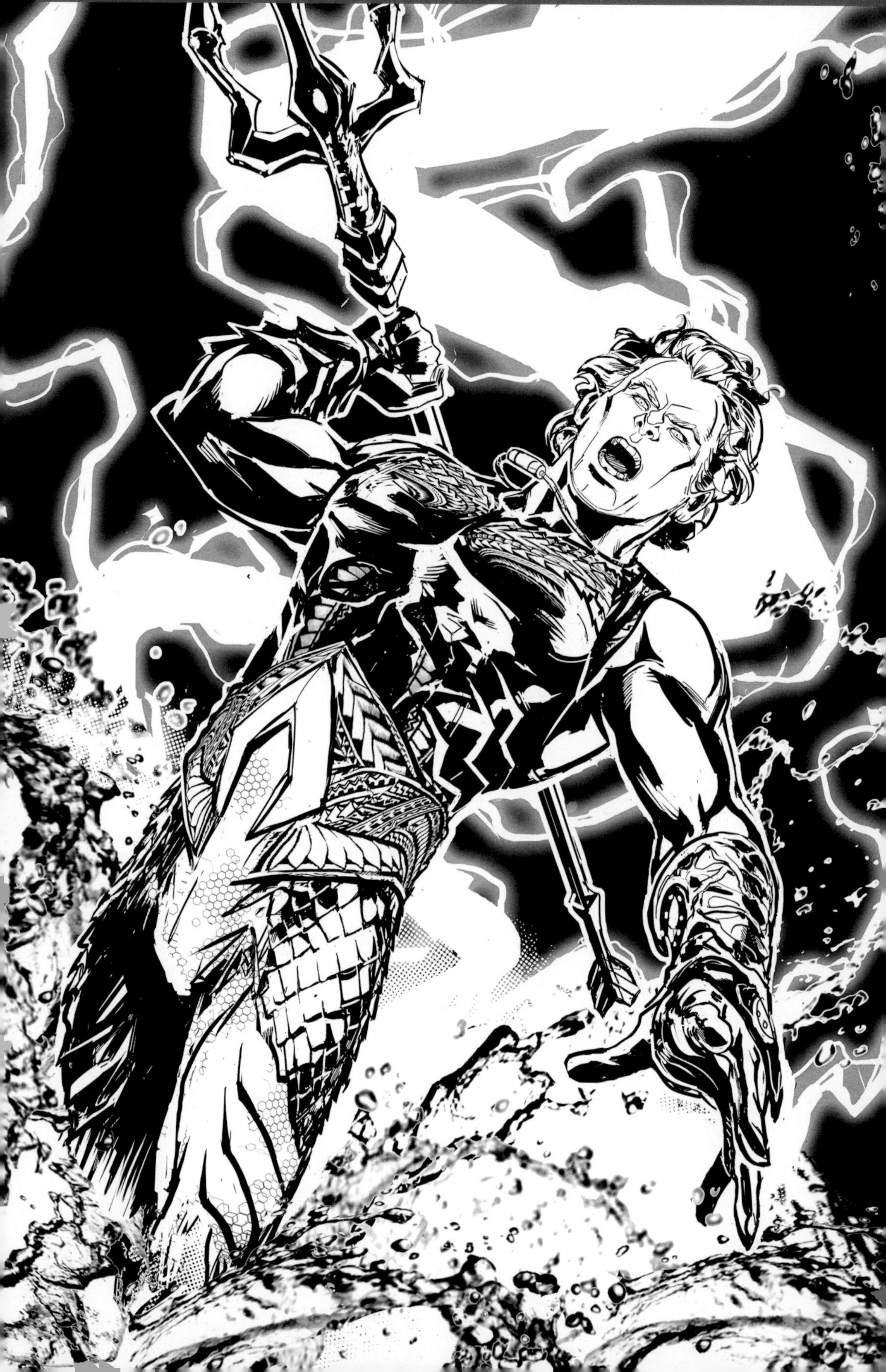

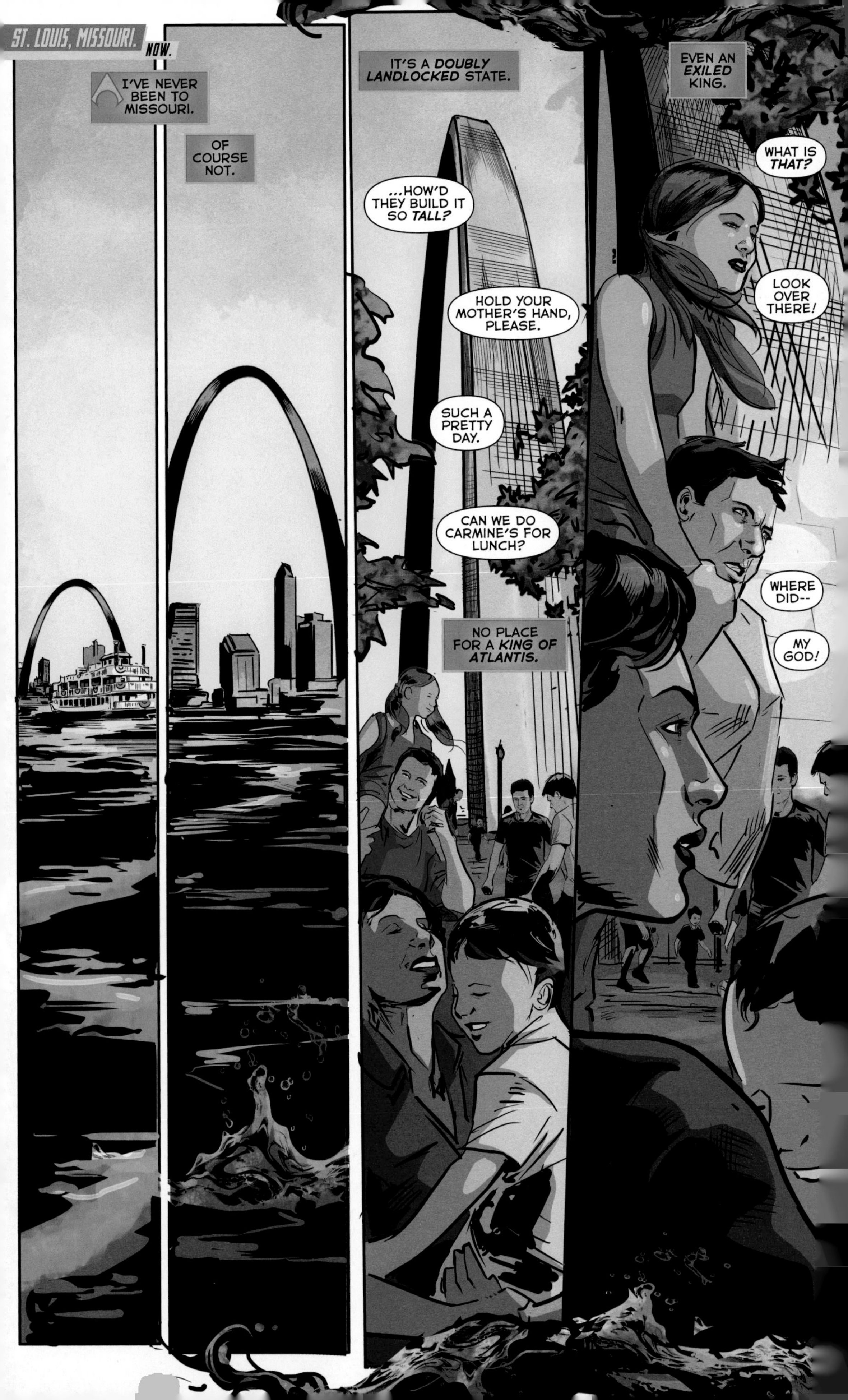
ST. LOUIS, MISSOURI.
NOW.
I'VE NEVER BEEN TO MISSOURI.
OF COURSE NOT.
IT'S A DOUBLY LANDLOCKED STATE.
...HOW'D THEY BUILD IT SO TALL?
HOLD YOUR MOTHER'S HAND, PLEASE.
SUCH A PRETTY DAY.
CAN WE DO CARMINE'S FOR LUNCH?
NO PLACE FOR A KING OF ATLANTIS.
EVEN AN EXILED KING.
WHAT IS THAT?
LOOK OVER THERE!
WHERE DID--
MY GOD!

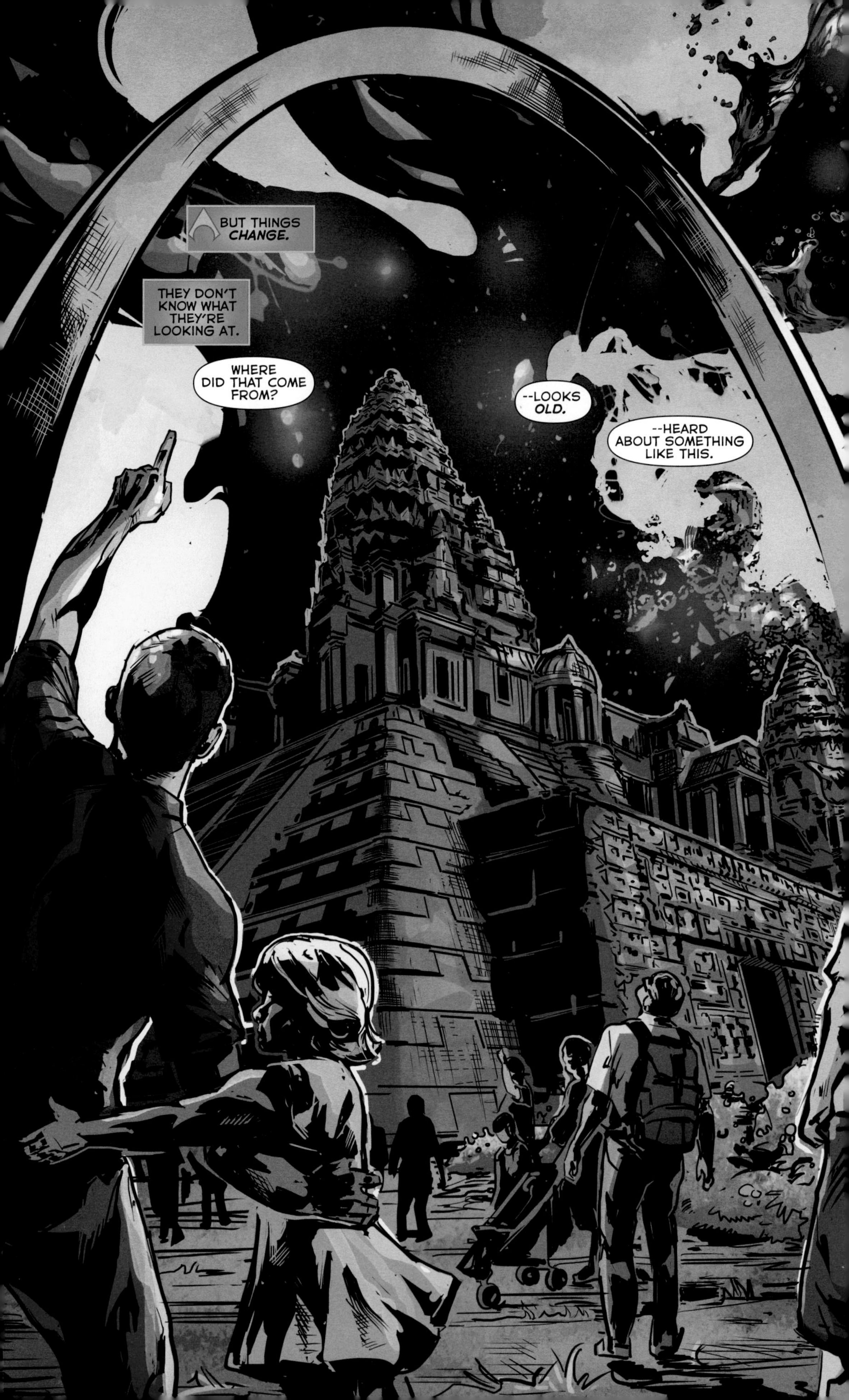
BUT THINGS CHANGE.
THEY DON'T KNOW WHAT THEY'RE LOOKING AT.
WHERE DID THAT COME FROM?
--LOOKS OLD.
--HEARD ABOUT SOMETHING LIKE THIS.

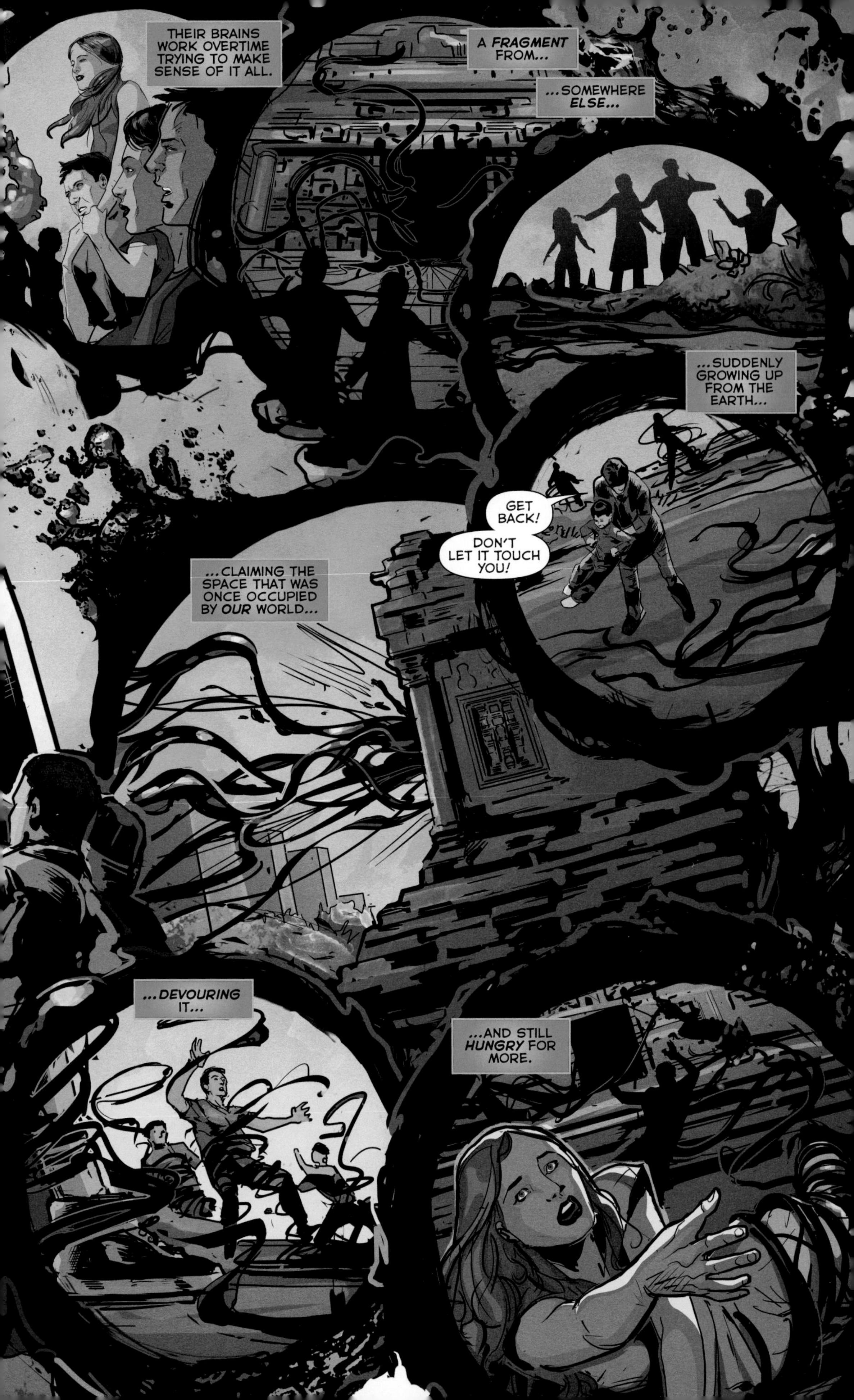

THEIR BRAINS WORK OVERTIME TRYING TO MAKE SENSE OF IT ALL.
A *FRAGMENT* FROM...
...SOMEWHERE *ELSE*...
...SUDDENLY GROWING UP FROM THE EARTH...
GET BACK!
DON'T LET IT TOUCH YOU!
...CLAIMING THE SPACE THAT WAS ONCE OCCUPIED BY *OUR* WORLD...
...*DEVOURING* IT...
...AND STILL *HUNGRY* FOR MORE.

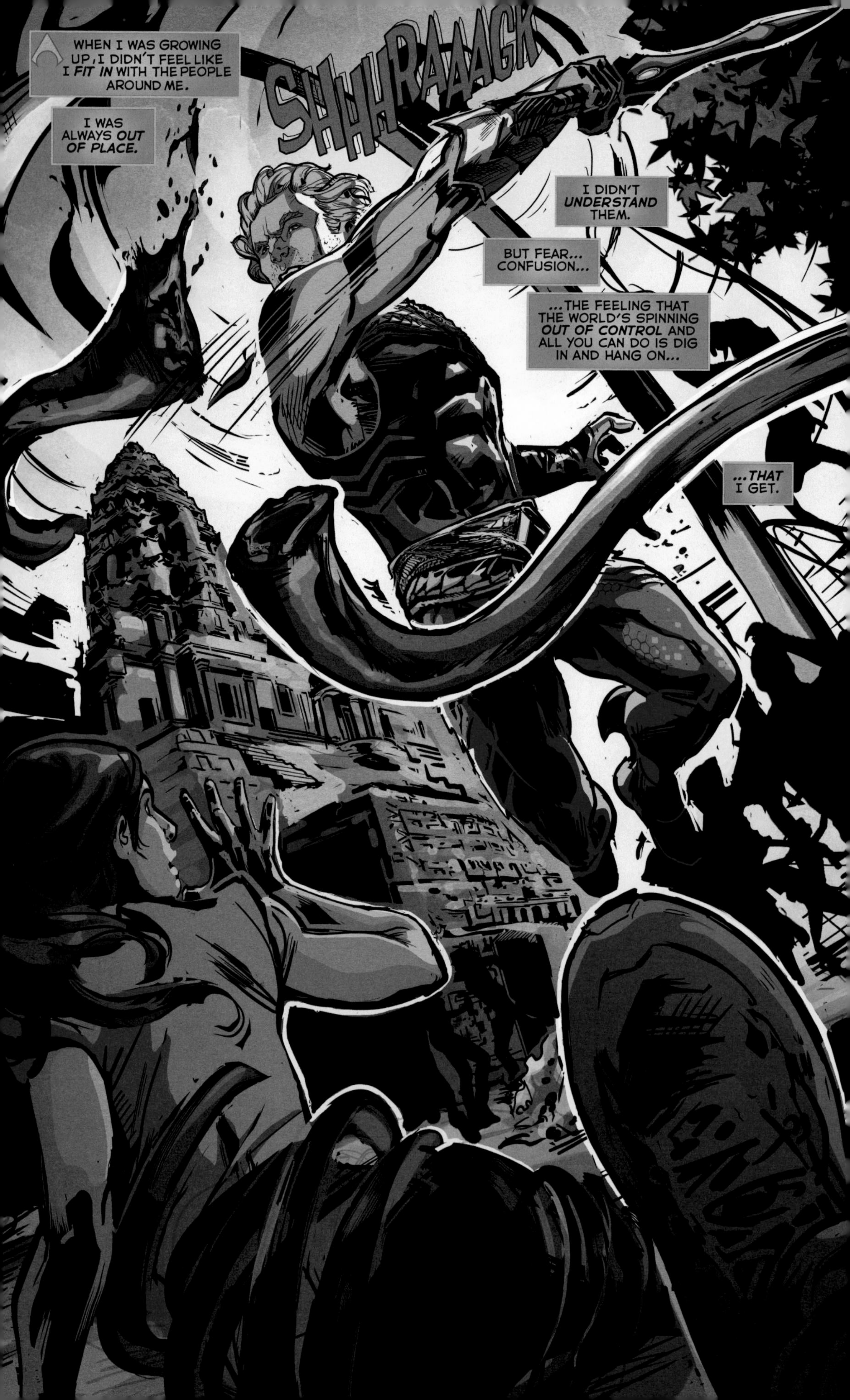
WHEN I WAS GROWING UP, I DIDN'T FEEL LIKE I FIT IN WITH THE PEOPLE AROUND ME.
SHHHRAAAGK
I WAS ALWAYS OUT OF PLACE.
I DIDN'T UNDERSTAND THEM.
BUT FEAR... CONFUSION...
...THE FEELING THAT THE WORLD'S SPINNING OUT OF CONTROL AND ALL YOU CAN DO IS DIG IN AND HANG ON...
...THAT I GET.

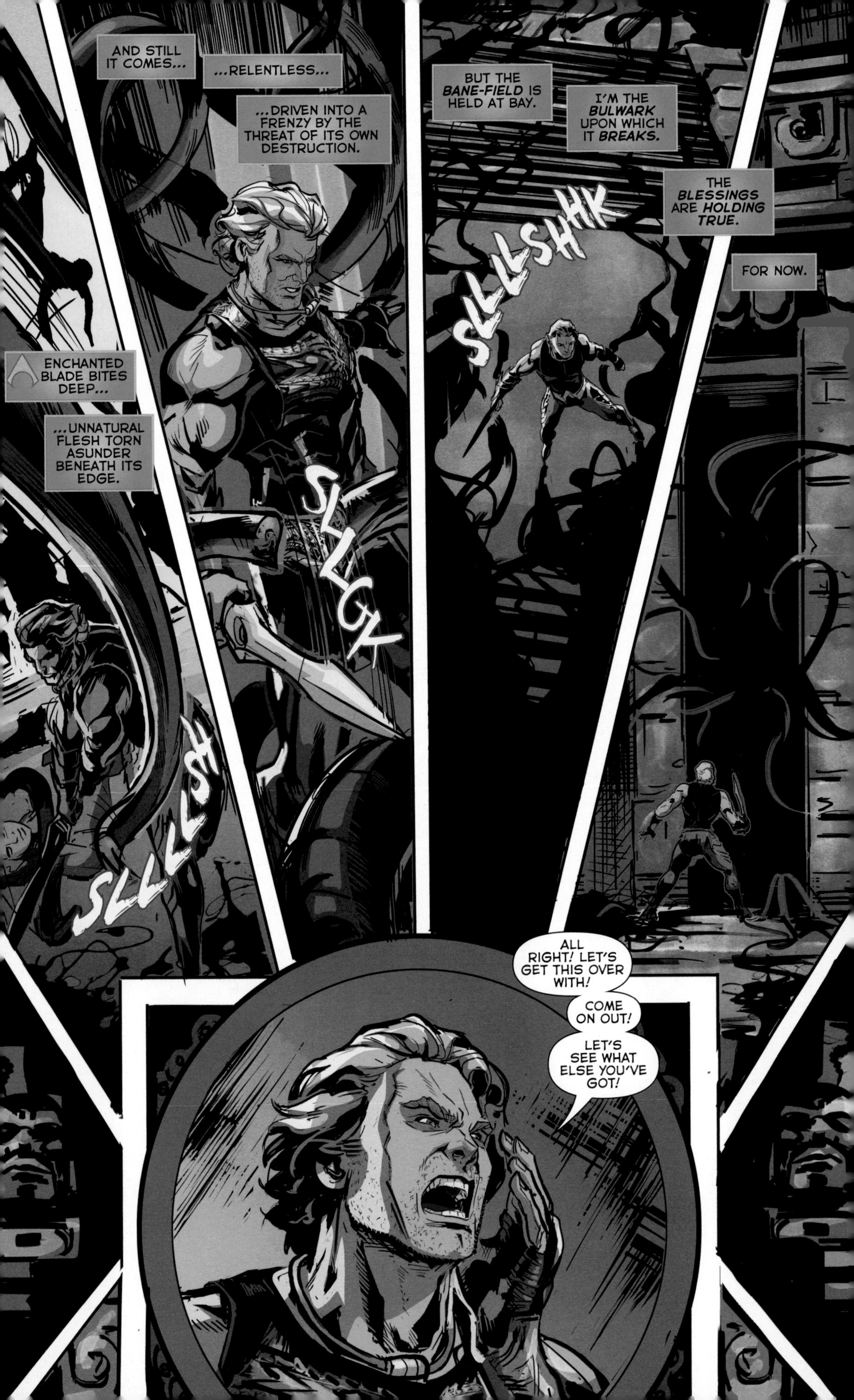
AND STILL IT COMES...
...RELENTLESS...
...DRIVEN INTO A FRENZY BY THE THREAT OF ITS OWN DESTRUCTION.
ENCHANTED BLADE BITES DEEP...
...UNNATURAL FLESH TORN ASUNDER BENEATH ITS EDGE.
SLLLLSH
SLLLSH
SLLLGK
BUT THE *BANE-FIELD* IS HELD AT BAY.
I'M THE *BULWARK* UPON WHICH IT *BREAKS.*
SLLLSHHK
THE *BLESSINGS* ARE *HOLDING TRUE.*
FOR NOW.
ALL RIGHT! LET'S GET THIS OVER WITH!
COME ON OUT!
LET'S SEE WHAT ELSE YOU'VE GOT!

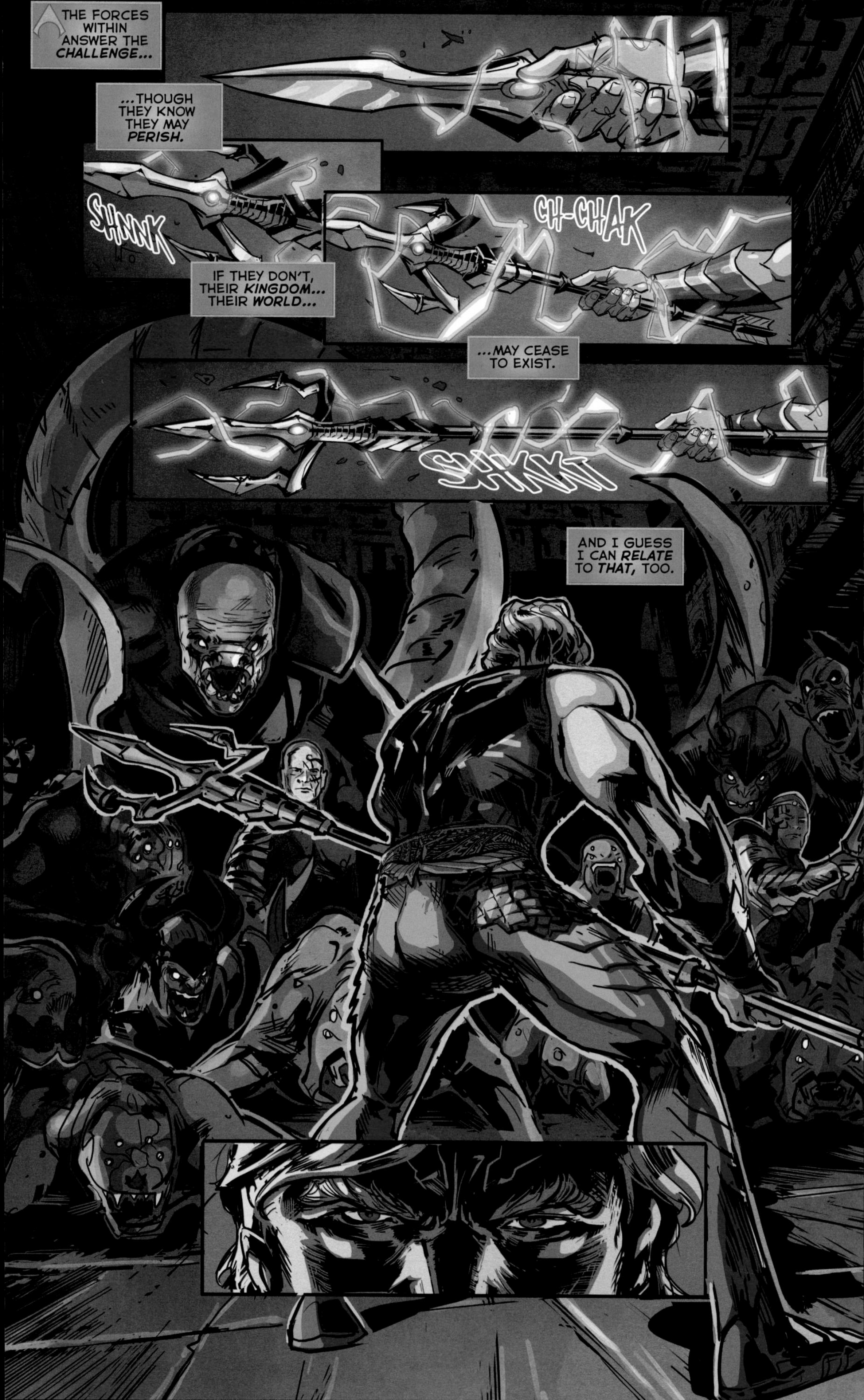
THE FORCES WITHIN ANSWER THE CHALLENGE...
...THOUGH THEY KNOW THEY MAY PERISH.
SHNNK
CH-CHAK
IF THEY DON'T, THEIR KINGDOM... THEIR WORLD...
...MAY CEASE TO EXIST.
SHKKT
AND I GUESS I CAN RELATE TO THAT, TOO.

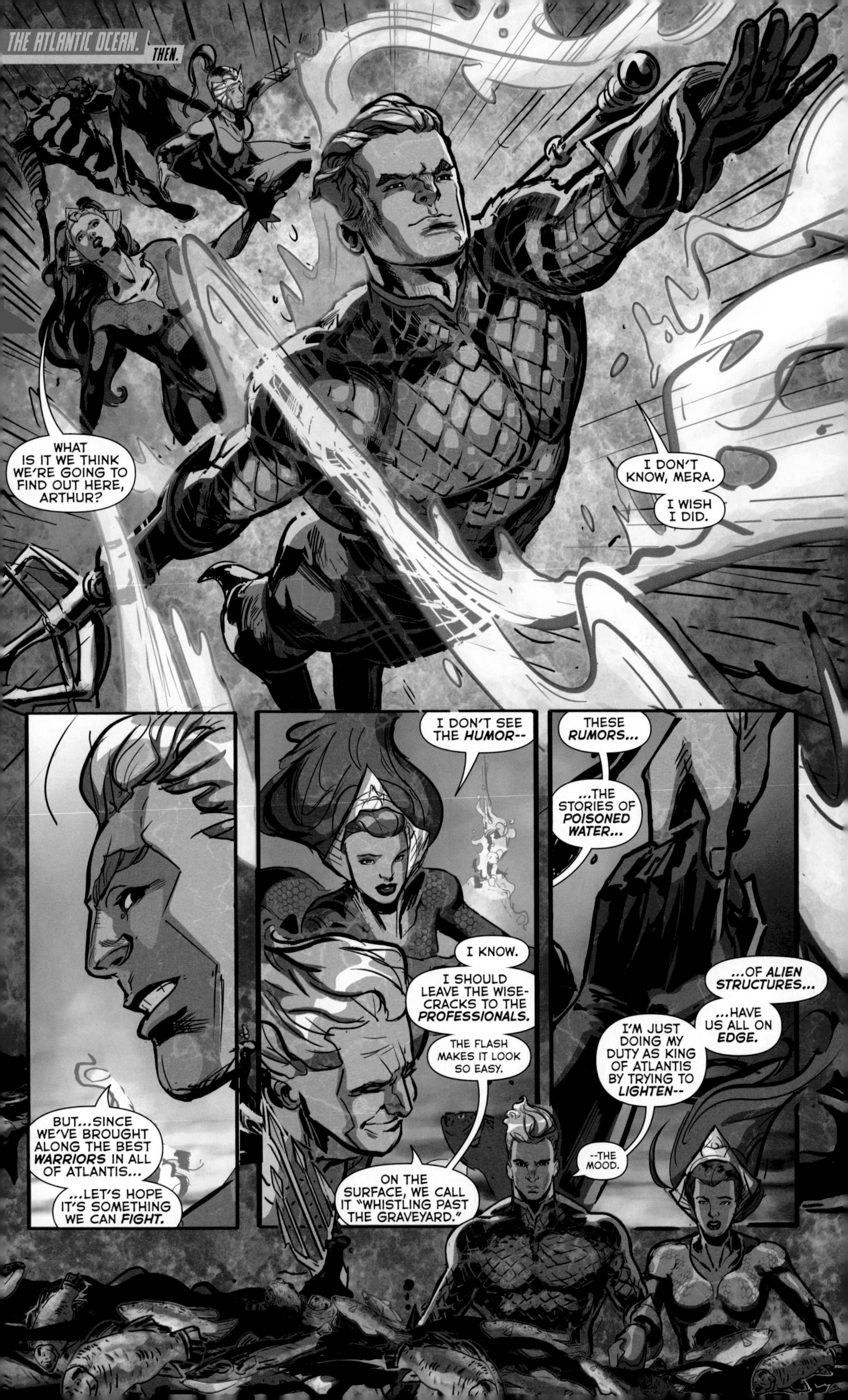
THE ATLANTIC OCEAN.
THEN.
WHAT IS IT WE THINK WE'RE GOING TO FIND OUT HERE, ARTHUR?
I DON'T KNOW, MERA.
I WISH I DID.
BUT...SINCE WE'VE BROUGHT ALONG THE BEST WARRIORS IN ALL OF ATLANTIS...
...LET'S HOPE IT'S SOMETHING WE CAN FIGHT.
I DON'T SEE THE HUMOR--
I KNOW.
I SHOULD LEAVE THE WISE-CRACKS TO THE PROFESSIONALS.
THE FLASH MAKES IT LOOK SO EASY.
ON THE SURFACE, WE CALL IT "WHISTLING PAST THE GRAVEYARD."
THESE RUMORS...
...THE STORIES OF POISONED WATER...
...OF ALIEN STRUCTURES...
...HAVE US ALL ON EDGE.
I'M JUST DOING MY DUTY AS KING OF ATLANTIS BY TRYING TO LIGHTEN--
--THE MOOD.

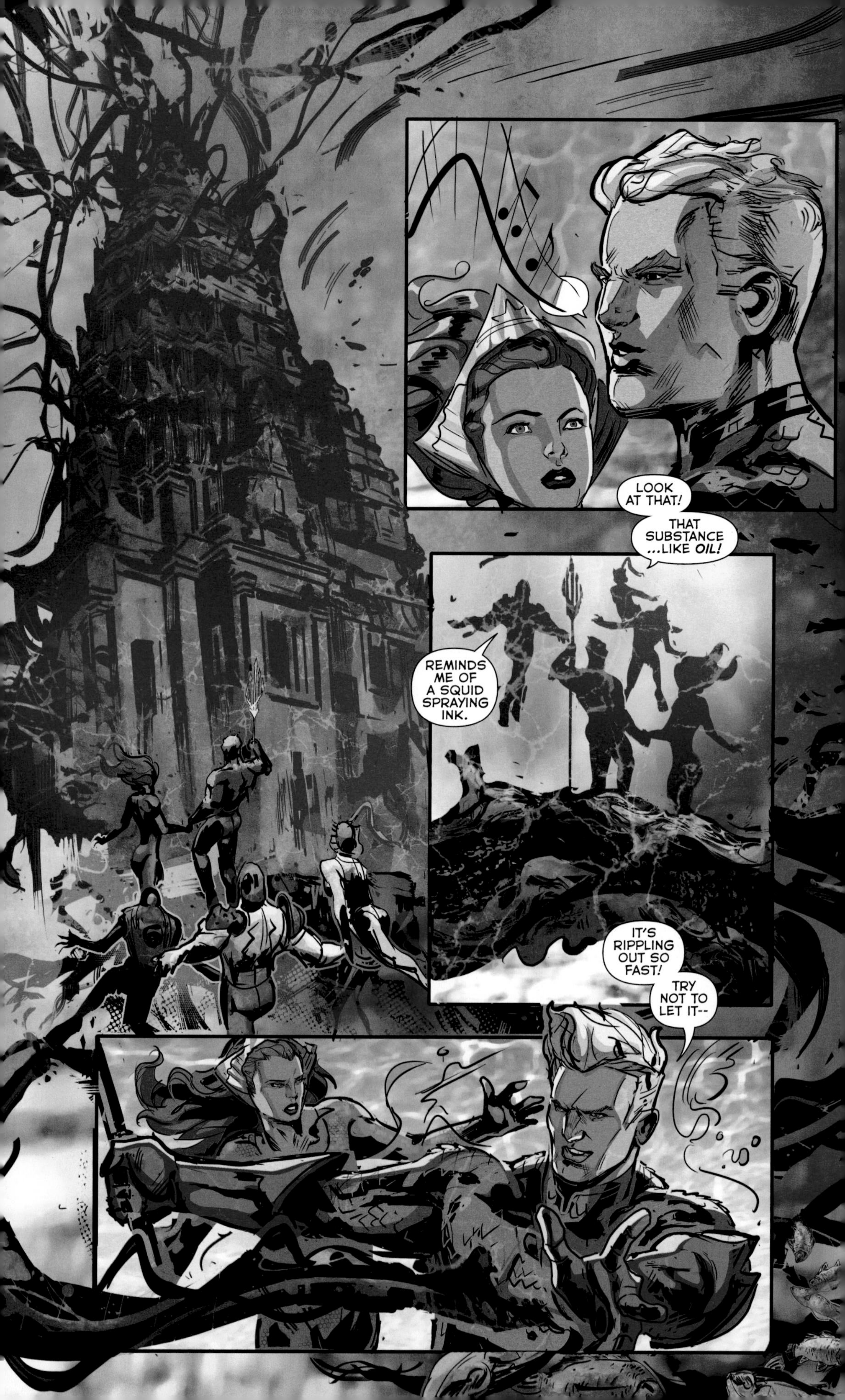
LOOK AT THAT!
THAT SUBSTANCE ...LIKE OIL!
REMINDS ME OF A SQUID SPRAYING INK.
IT'S RIPPLING OUT SO FAST!
TRY NOT TO LET IT--

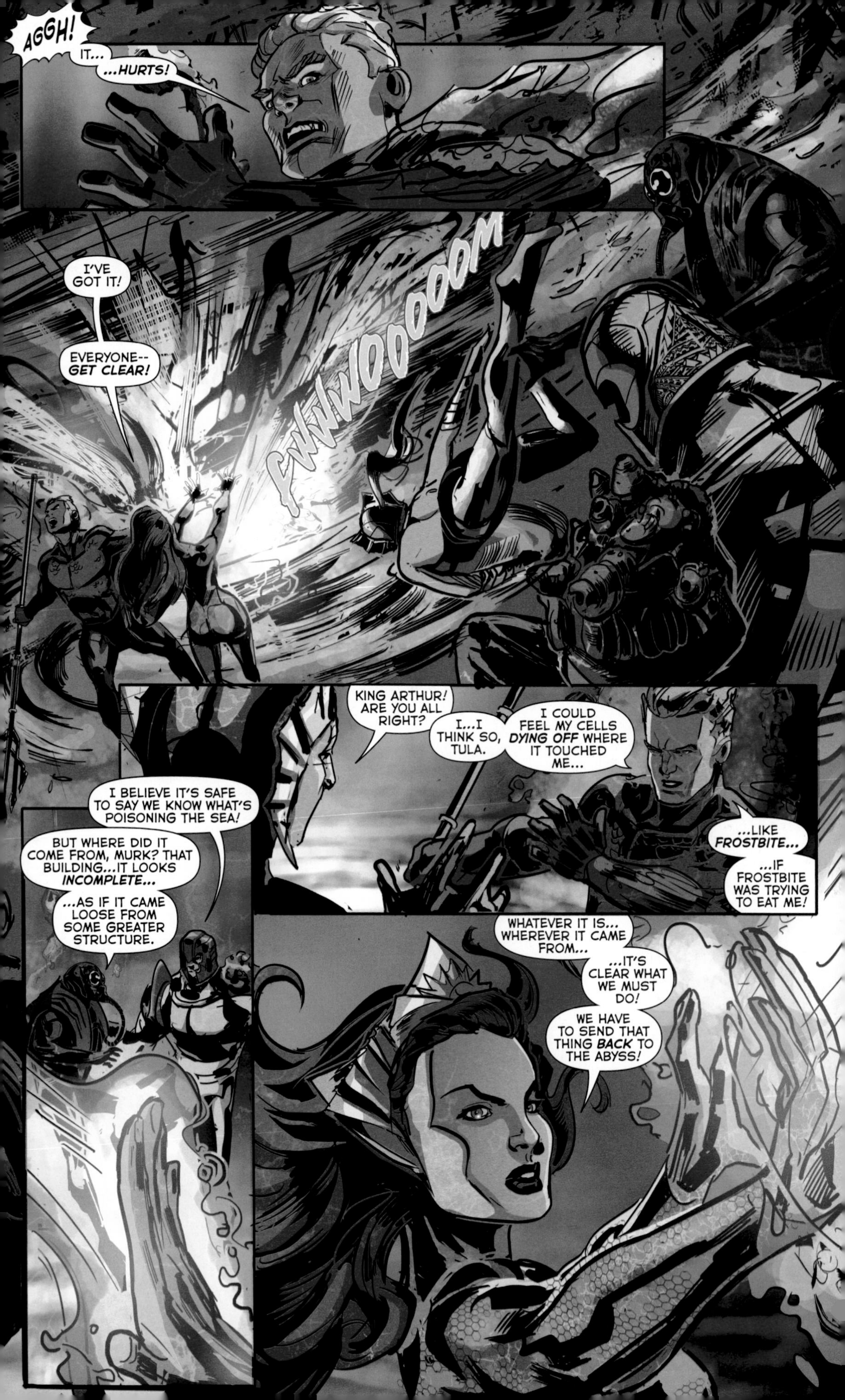
AGGH!
IT...
...HURTS!
I'VE GOT IT!
EVERYONE-- GET CLEAR!
FWWWOOOOOOM
KING ARTHUR! ARE YOU ALL RIGHT?
I...I THINK SO, TULA.
I COULD FEEL MY CELLS DYING OFF WHERE IT TOUCHED ME...
...LIKE FROSTBITE...
...IF FROSTBITE WAS TRYING TO EAT ME!
I BELIEVE IT'S SAFE TO SAY WE KNOW WHAT'S POISONING THE SEA!
BUT WHERE DID IT COME FROM, MURK? THAT BUILDING...IT LOOKS INCOMPLETE...
...AS IF IT CAME LOOSE FROM SOME GREATER STRUCTURE.
WHATEVER IT IS... WHEREVER IT CAME FROM...
...IT'S CLEAR WHAT WE MUST DO!
WE HAVE TO SEND THAT THING BACK TO THE ABYSS!

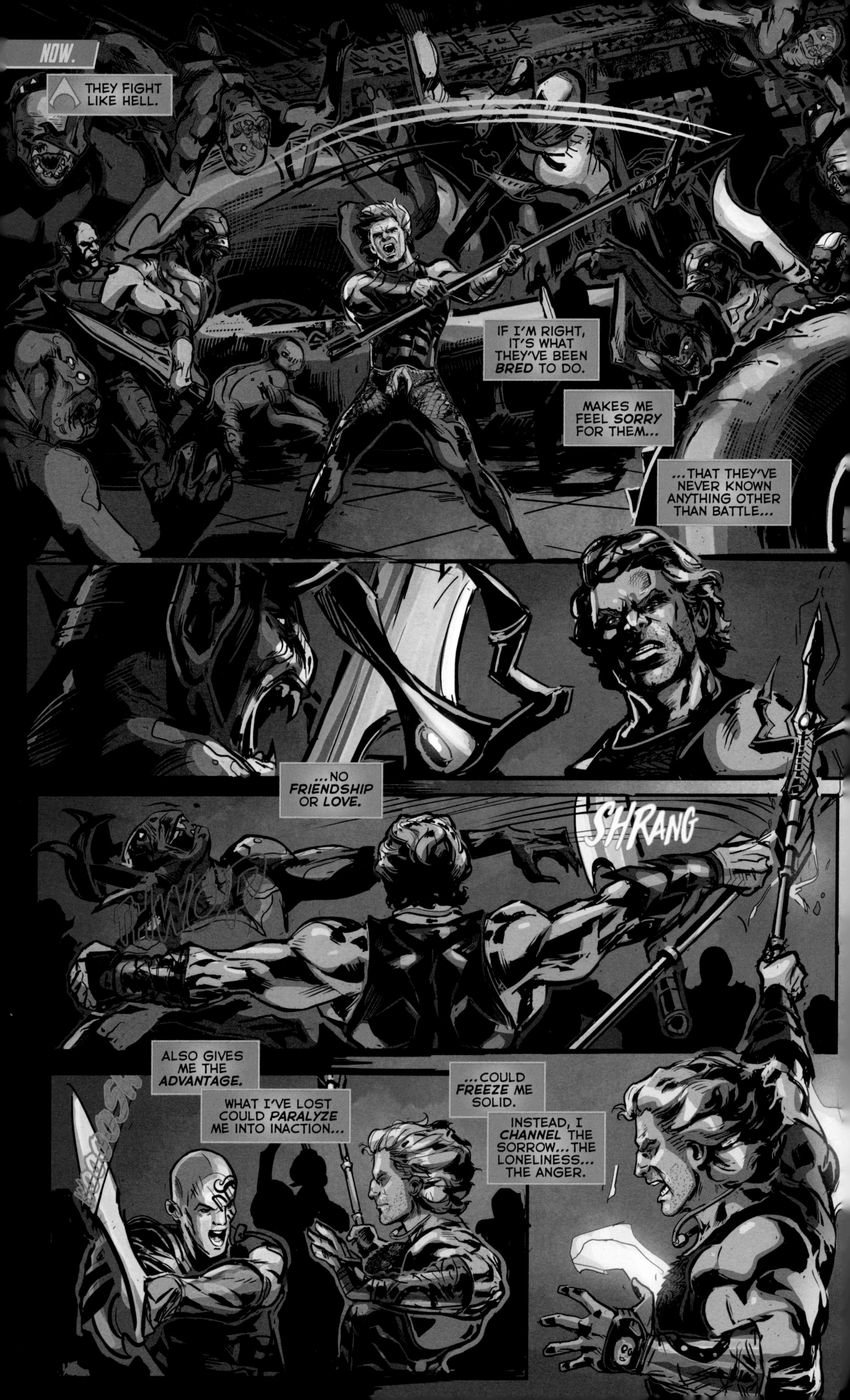
NOW.
THEY FIGHT LIKE HELL.
IF I'M RIGHT, IT'S WHAT THEY'VE BEEN BRED TO DO.
MAKES ME FEEL SORRY FOR THEM...
...THAT THEY'VE NEVER KNOWN ANYTHING OTHER THAN BATTLE...
...NO FRIENDSHIP OR LOVE.
SHRANG
ALSO GIVES ME THE ADVANTAGE.
WHAT I'VE LOST COULD PARALYZE ME INTO INACTION...
...COULD FREEZE ME SOLID.
INSTEAD, I CHANNEL THE SORROW...THE LONELINESS... THE ANGER.

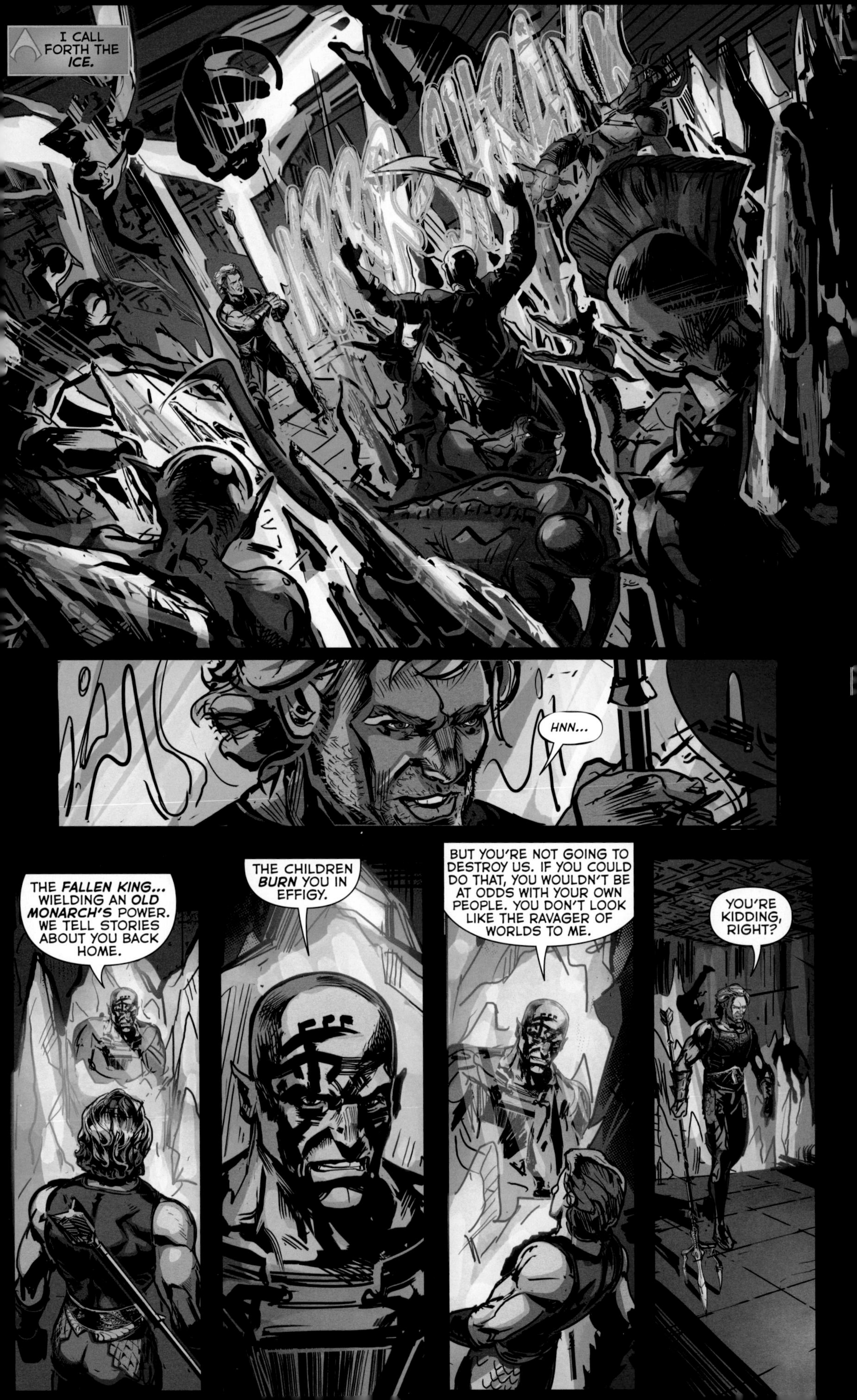
I CALL FORTH THE *ICE.*
HNN...
THE ***FALLEN KING...*** WIELDING AN ***OLD MONARCH'S*** POWER. WE TELL STORIES ABOUT YOU BACK HOME.
THE CHILDREN ***BURN*** YOU IN EFFIGY.
BUT YOU'RE NOT GOING TO DESTROY US. IF YOU COULD DO THAT, YOU WOULDN'T BE AT ODDS WITH YOUR OWN PEOPLE. YOU DON'T LOOK LIKE THE RAVAGER OF WORLDS TO ME.
YOU'RE KIDDING, RIGHT?

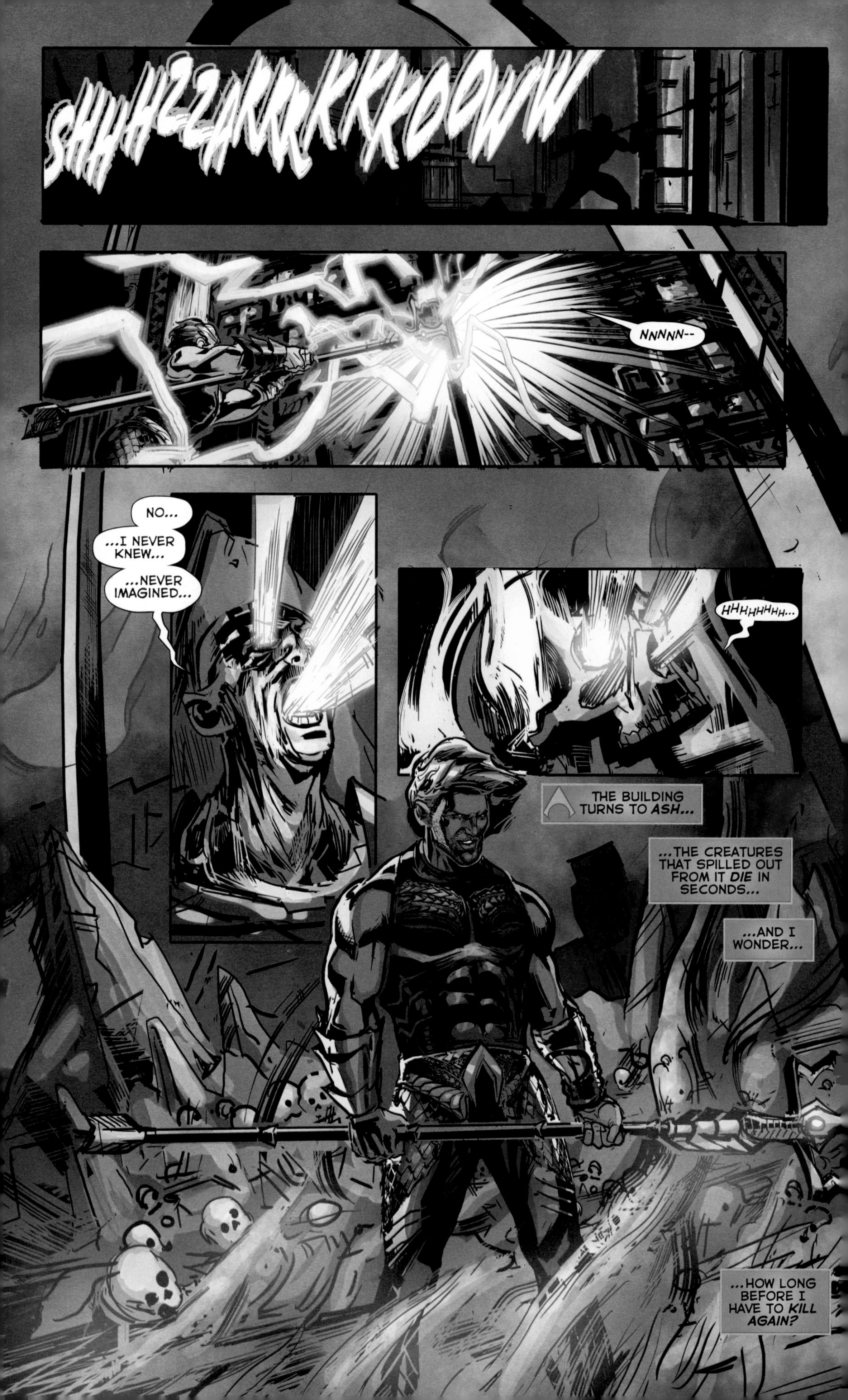
SHHHZZARRRRK KROOWW
NNNNN--
NO...
...I NEVER KNEW...
...NEVER IMAGINED...
HHHHHHHH...
THE BUILDING TURNS TO *ASH*...
...THE CREATURES THAT SPILLED OUT FROM IT *DIE* IN SECONDS...
...AND I WONDER...
...HOW LONG BEFORE I HAVE TO *KILL AGAIN?*

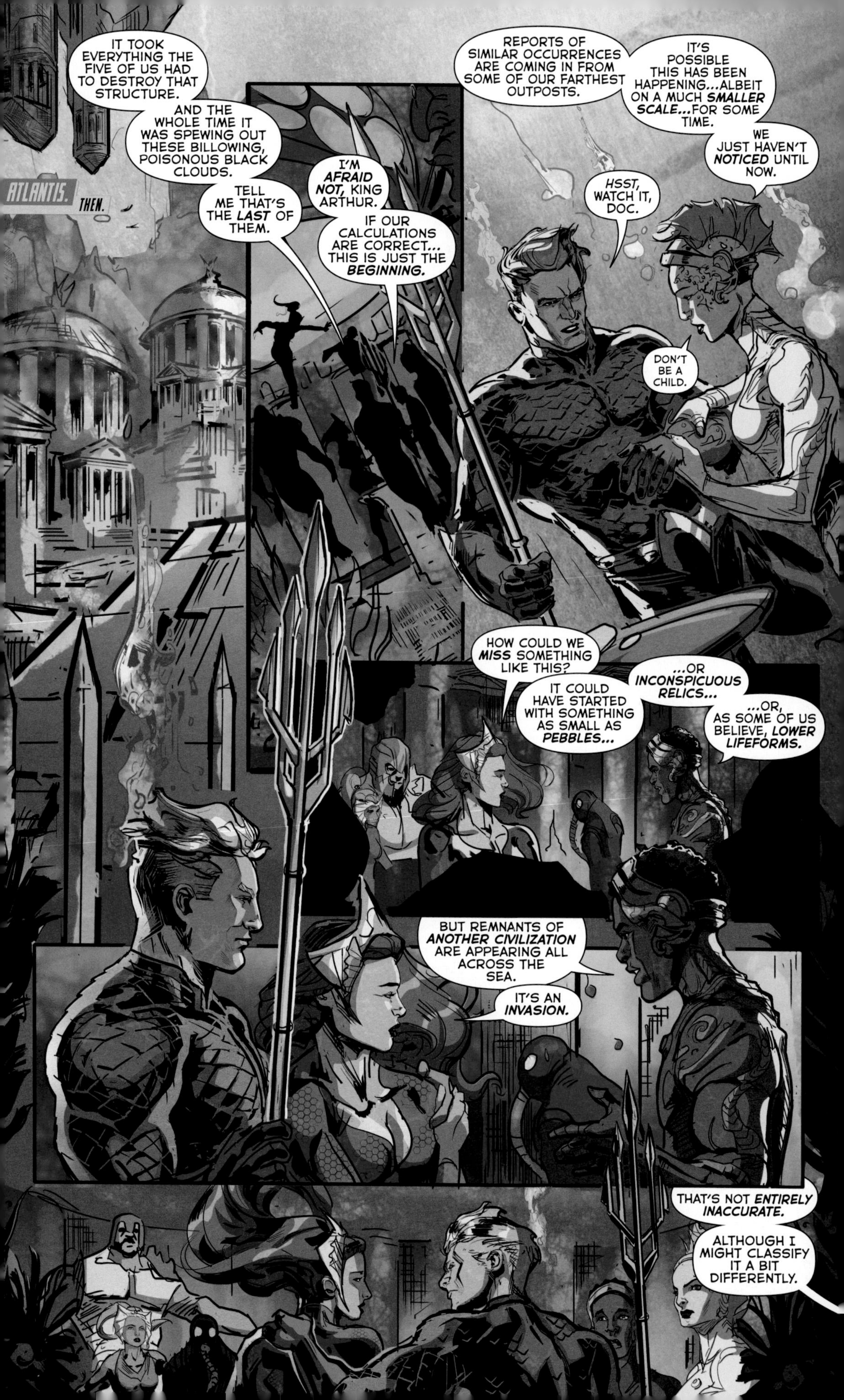
IT TOOK EVERYTHING THE FIVE OF US HAD TO DESTROY THAT STRUCTURE.
AND THE WHOLE TIME IT WAS SPEWING OUT THESE BILLOWING, POISONOUS BLACK CLOUDS.
ATLANTIS.
THEN.
TELL ME THAT'S THE LAST OF THEM.
I'M AFRAID NOT, KING ARTHUR.
IF OUR CALCULATIONS ARE CORRECT... THIS IS JUST THE BEGINNING.
REPORTS OF SIMILAR OCCURRENCES ARE COMING IN FROM SOME OF OUR FARTHEST OUTPOSTS.
IT'S POSSIBLE THIS HAS BEEN HAPPENING...ALBEIT ON A MUCH SMALLER SCALE...FOR SOME TIME.
WE JUST HAVEN'T NOTICED UNTIL NOW.
HSST, WATCH IT, DOC.
DON'T BE A CHILD.
HOW COULD WE MISS SOMETHING LIKE THIS?
IT COULD HAVE STARTED WITH SOMETHING AS SMALL AS PEBBLES...
...OR INCONSPICUOUS RELICS...
...OR, AS SOME OF US BELIEVE, LOWER LIFEFORMS.
BUT REMNANTS OF ANOTHER CIVILIZATION ARE APPEARING ALL ACROSS THE SEA.
IT'S AN INVASION.
THAT'S NOT ENTIRELY INACCURATE.
ALTHOUGH I MIGHT CLASSIFY IT A BIT DIFFERENTLY.

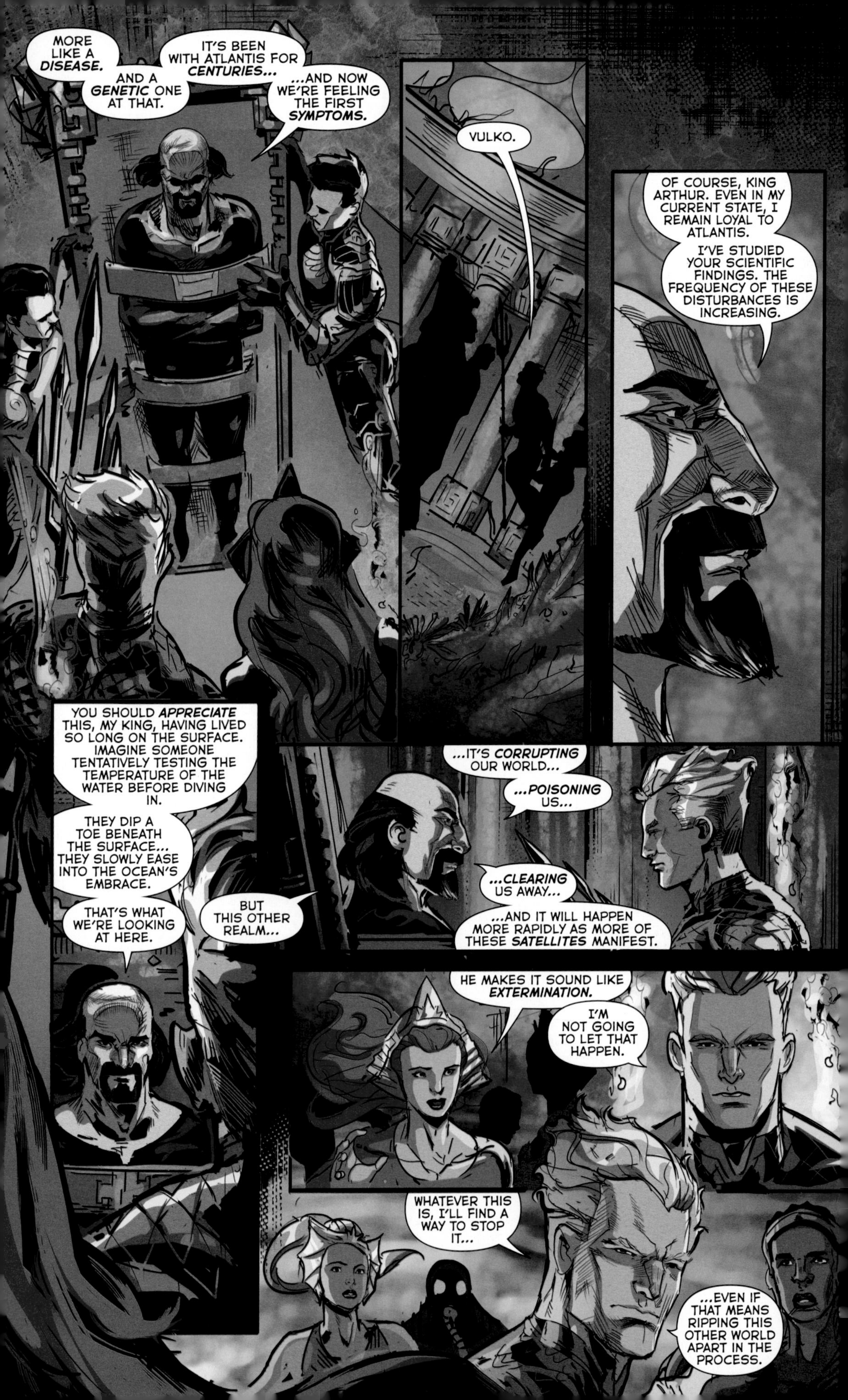

MORE LIKE A *DISEASE.*
IT'S BEEN WITH ATLANTIS FOR *CENTURIES...*
AND A *GENETIC* ONE AT THAT.
...AND NOW WE'RE FEELING THE FIRST *SYMPTOMS.*
VULKO.
OF COURSE, KING ARTHUR. EVEN IN MY CURRENT STATE, I REMAIN LOYAL TO ATLANTIS.
I'VE STUDIED YOUR SCIENTIFIC FINDINGS. THE FREQUENCY OF THESE DISTURBANCES IS INCREASING.
YOU SHOULD *APPRECIATE* THIS, MY KING, HAVING LIVED SO LONG ON THE SURFACE. IMAGINE SOMEONE TENTATIVELY TESTING THE TEMPERATURE OF THE WATER BEFORE DIVING IN.
THEY DIP A TOE BENEATH THE SURFACE... THEY SLOWLY EASE INTO THE OCEAN'S EMBRACE.
THAT'S WHAT WE'RE LOOKING AT HERE.
BUT THIS OTHER REALM...
...IT'S *CORRUPTING* OUR WORLD...
...*POISONING* US...
...*CLEARING* US AWAY...
...AND IT WILL HAPPEN MORE RAPIDLY AS MORE OF THESE *SATELLITES* MANIFEST.
HE MAKES IT SOUND LIKE *EXTERMINATION.*
I'M NOT GOING TO LET THAT HAPPEN.
WHATEVER THIS IS, I'LL FIND A WAY TO STOP IT...
...EVEN IF THAT MEANS RIPPING THIS OTHER WORLD APART IN THE PROCESS.

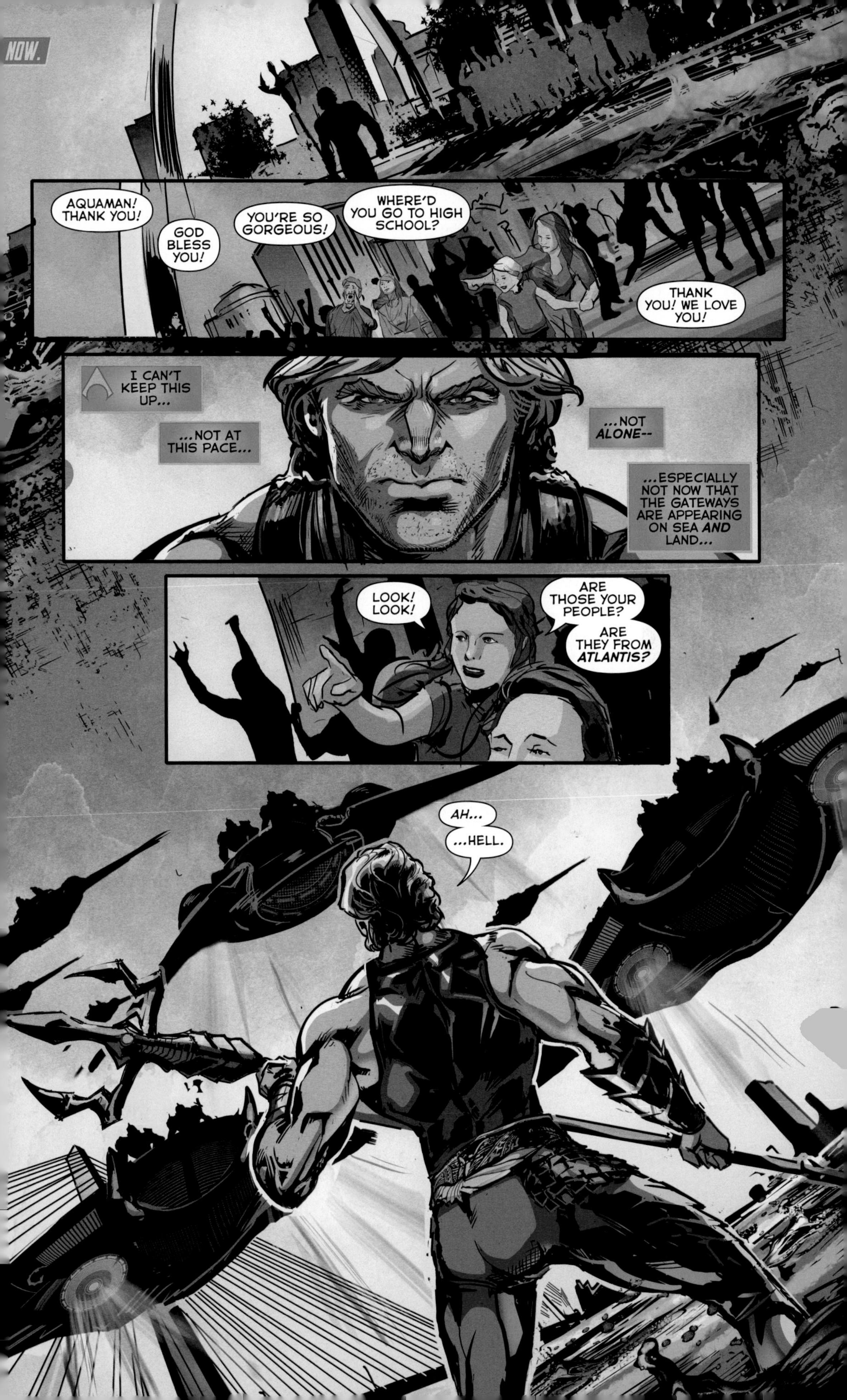
NOW.
AQUAMAN! THANK YOU!
GOD BLESS YOU!
YOU'RE SO GORGEOUS!
WHERE'D YOU GO TO HIGH SCHOOL?
THANK YOU! WE LOVE YOU!
I CAN'T KEEP THIS UP...
...NOT AT THIS PACE...
...NOT ALONE--
...ESPECIALLY NOT NOW THAT THE GATEWAYS ARE APPEARING ON SEA AND LAND...
LOOK! LOOK!
ARE THOSE YOUR PEOPLE?
ARE THEY FROM ATLANTIS?
AH...
...HELL.

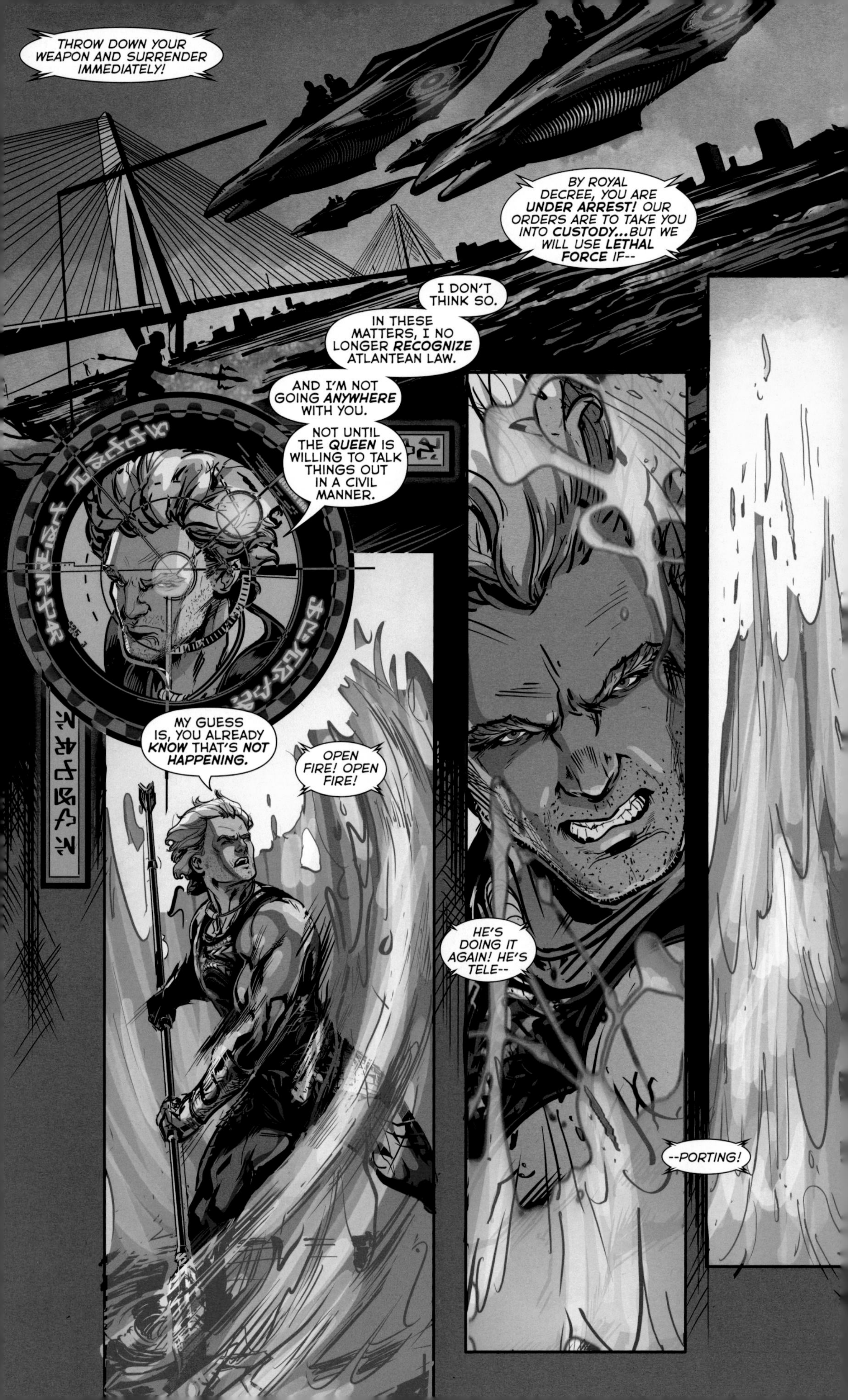
THROW DOWN YOUR WEAPON AND SURRENDER IMMEDIATELY!
BY ROYAL DECREE, YOU ARE **UNDER ARREST!** OUR ORDERS ARE TO TAKE YOU INTO **CUSTODY**...BUT WE WILL USE **LETHAL FORCE** IF--
I DON'T THINK SO.
IN THESE MATTERS, I NO LONGER ***RECOGNIZE*** ATLANTEAN LAW.
AND I'M NOT GOING ***ANYWHERE*** WITH YOU.
NOT UNTIL THE ***QUEEN*** IS WILLING TO TALK THINGS OUT IN A CIVIL MANNER.
MY GUESS IS, YOU ALREADY ***KNOW*** THAT'S ***NOT HAPPENING.***
OPEN FIRE! OPEN FIRE!
HE'S DOING IT AGAIN! HE'S TELE--
--PORTING!

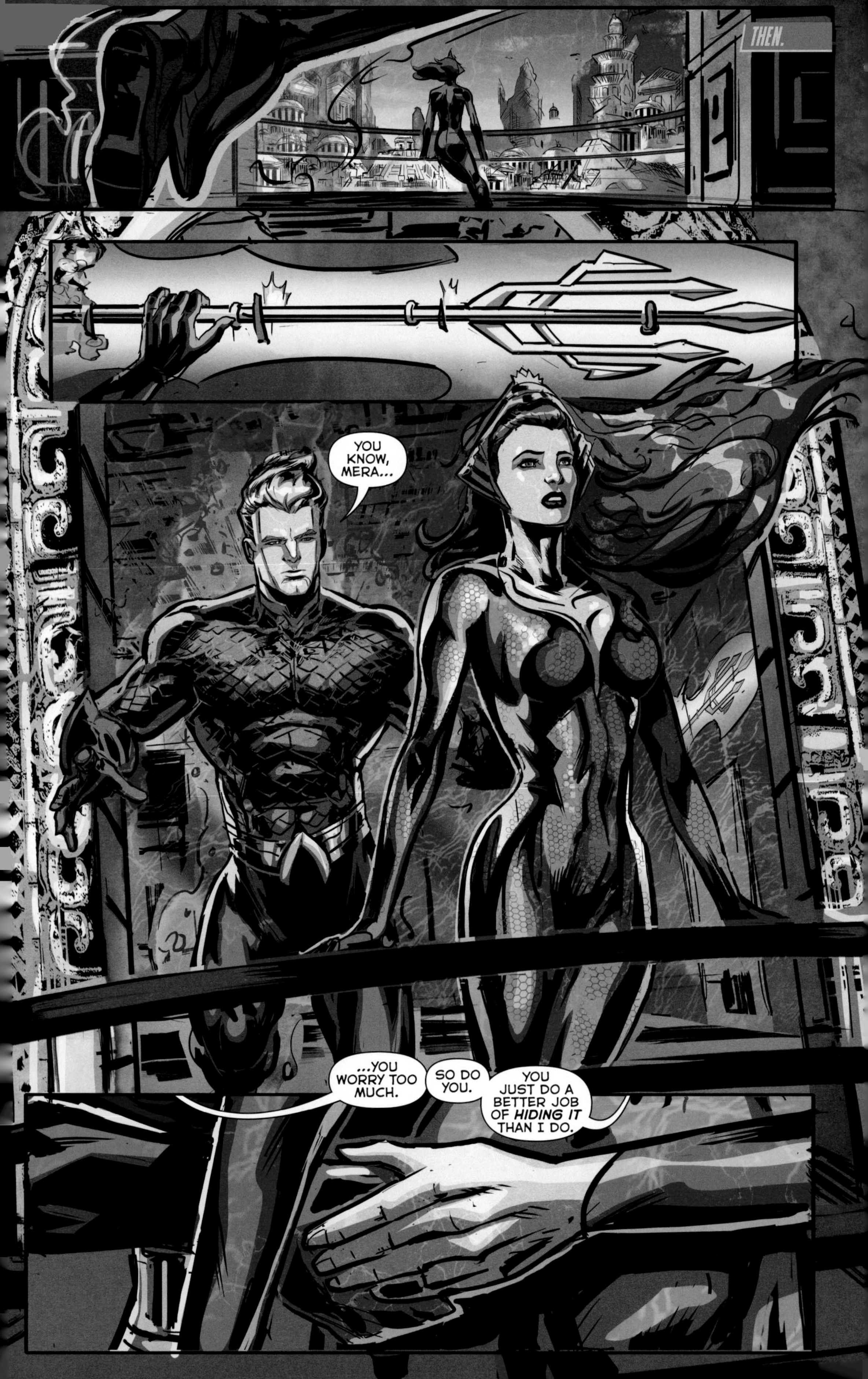
THEN.
YOU KNOW, MERA...
...YOU WORRY TOO MUCH.
SO DO YOU.
YOU JUST DO A BETTER JOB OF HIDING IT THAN I DO.

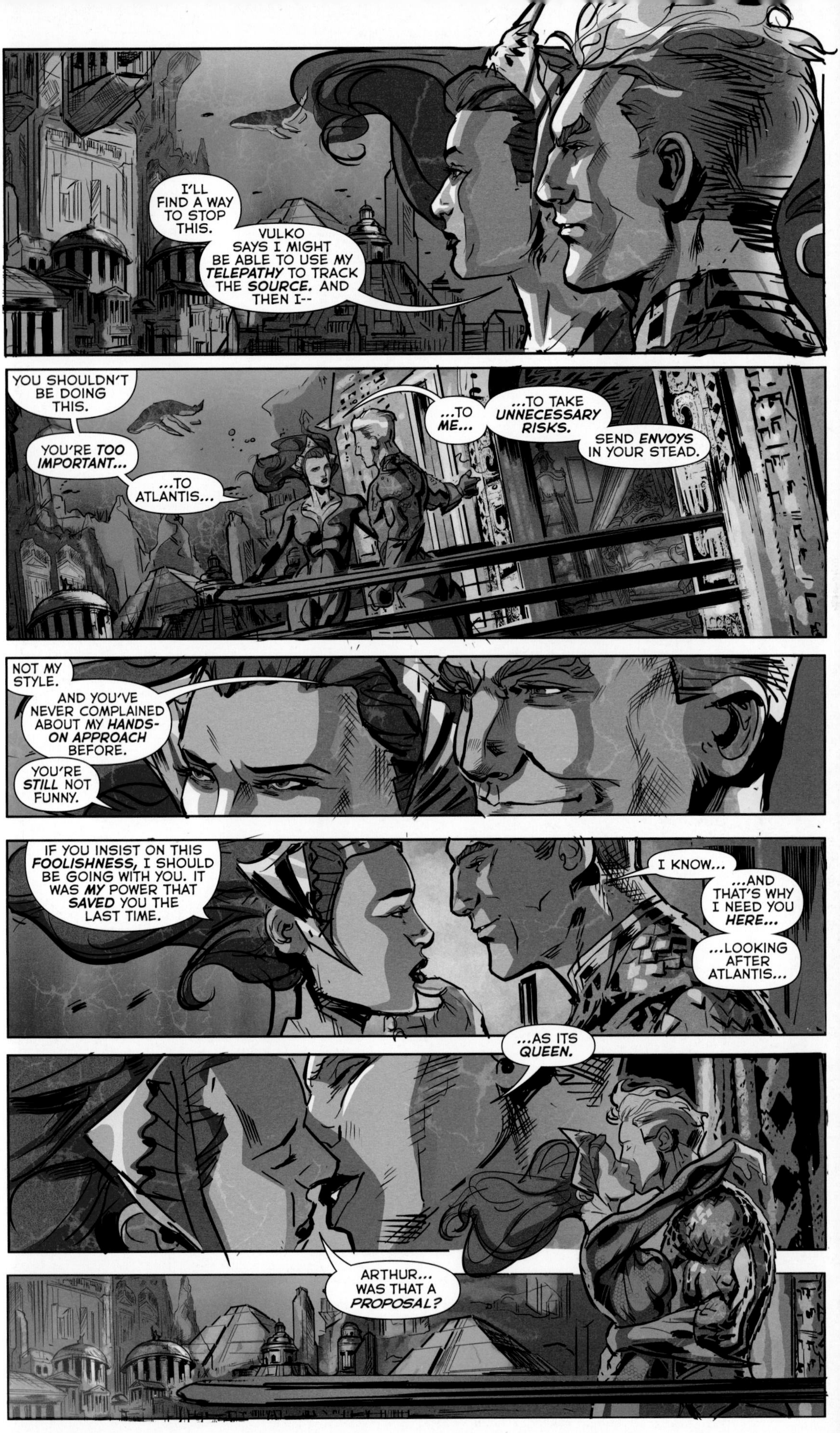
I'LL FIND A WAY TO STOP THIS.
VULKO SAYS I MIGHT BE ABLE TO USE MY TELEPATHY TO TRACK THE SOURCE. AND THEN I--
YOU SHOULDN'T BE DOING THIS.
YOU'RE TOO IMPORTANT...
...TO ATLANTIS...
...TO ME...
...TO TAKE UNNECESSARY RISKS.
SEND ENVOYS IN YOUR STEAD.
NOT MY STYLE.
AND YOU'VE NEVER COMPLAINED ABOUT MY HANDS-ON APPROACH BEFORE.
YOU'RE STILL NOT FUNNY.
IF YOU INSIST ON THIS FOOLISHNESS, I SHOULD BE GOING WITH YOU. IT WAS MY POWER THAT SAVED YOU THE LAST TIME.
I KNOW...
...AND THAT'S WHY I NEED YOU HERE...
...LOOKING AFTER ATLANTIS...
...AS ITS QUEEN.
ARTHUR... WAS THAT A PROPOSAL?

SPLOOOSH

HOW LONG HAS IT BEEN?

THREE MONTHS SINCE I'VE BEEN TO *ATLANTIS*...

...OR *AMNESTY BAY*...

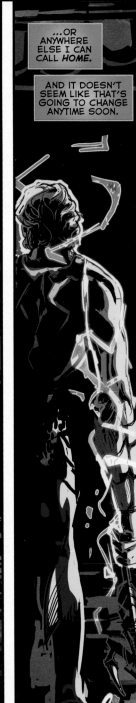

...OR *ANYWHERE ELSE I CAN CALL HOME.*

AND IT DOESN'T SEEM LIKE THAT'S GOING TO CHANGE ANYTIME SOON.

SHHNK

I PROMISED *MERA* I WOULD DO WHATEVER IT TOOK TO SAVE OUR PEOPLE...

...EVEN IF THAT MEANT DESTROYING THE OTHER WORLD.

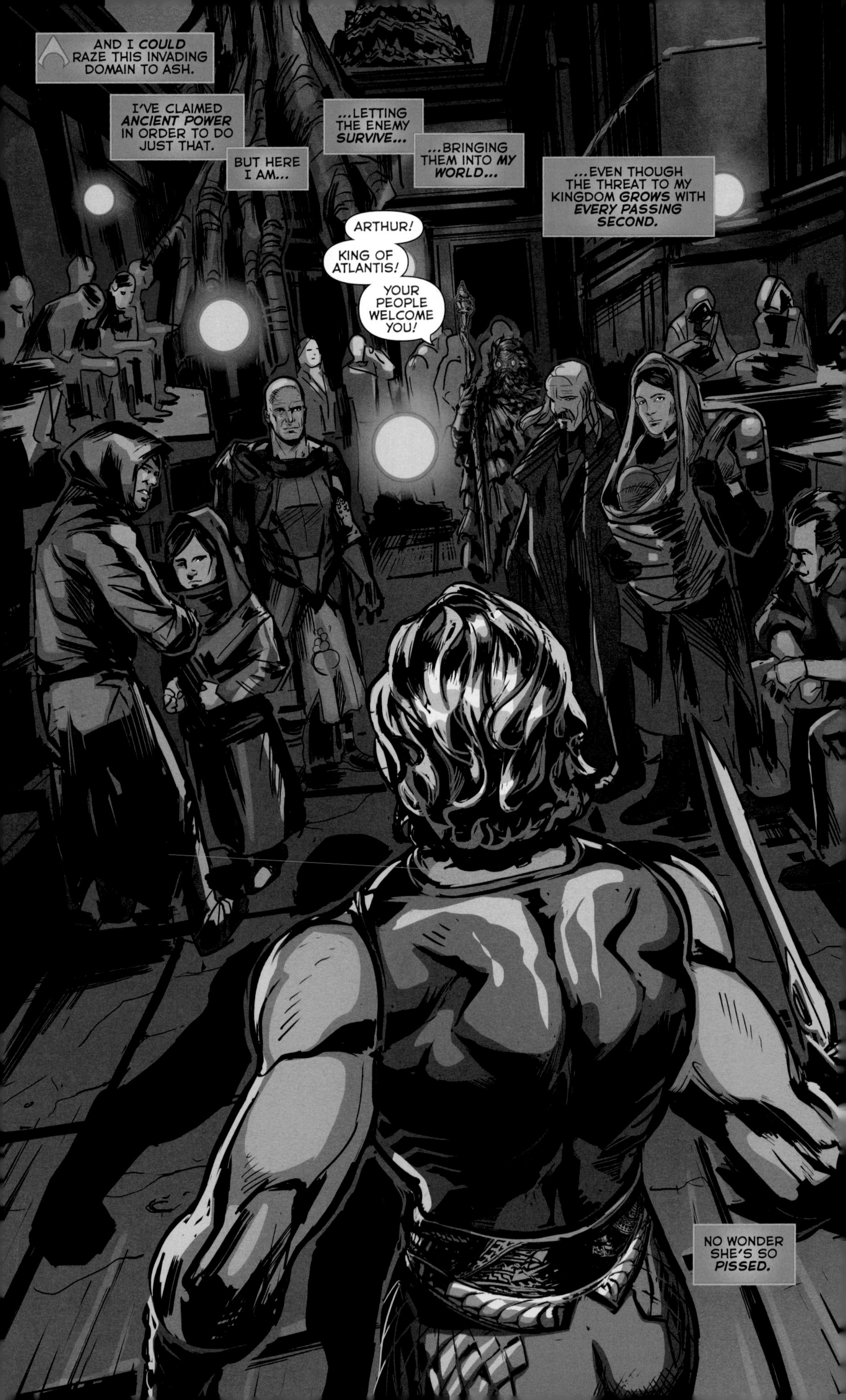
AND I COULD RAZE THIS INVADING DOMAIN TO ASH.
I'VE CLAIMED ANCIENT POWER IN ORDER TO DO JUST THAT.
BUT HERE I AM...
...LETTING THE ENEMY SURVIVE...
...BRINGING THEM INTO MY WORLD...
...EVEN THOUGH THE THREAT TO MY KINGDOM GROWS WITH EVERY PASSING SECOND.
ARTHUR!
KING OF ATLANTIS!
YOUR PEOPLE WELCOME YOU!
NO WONDER SHE'S SO PISSED.

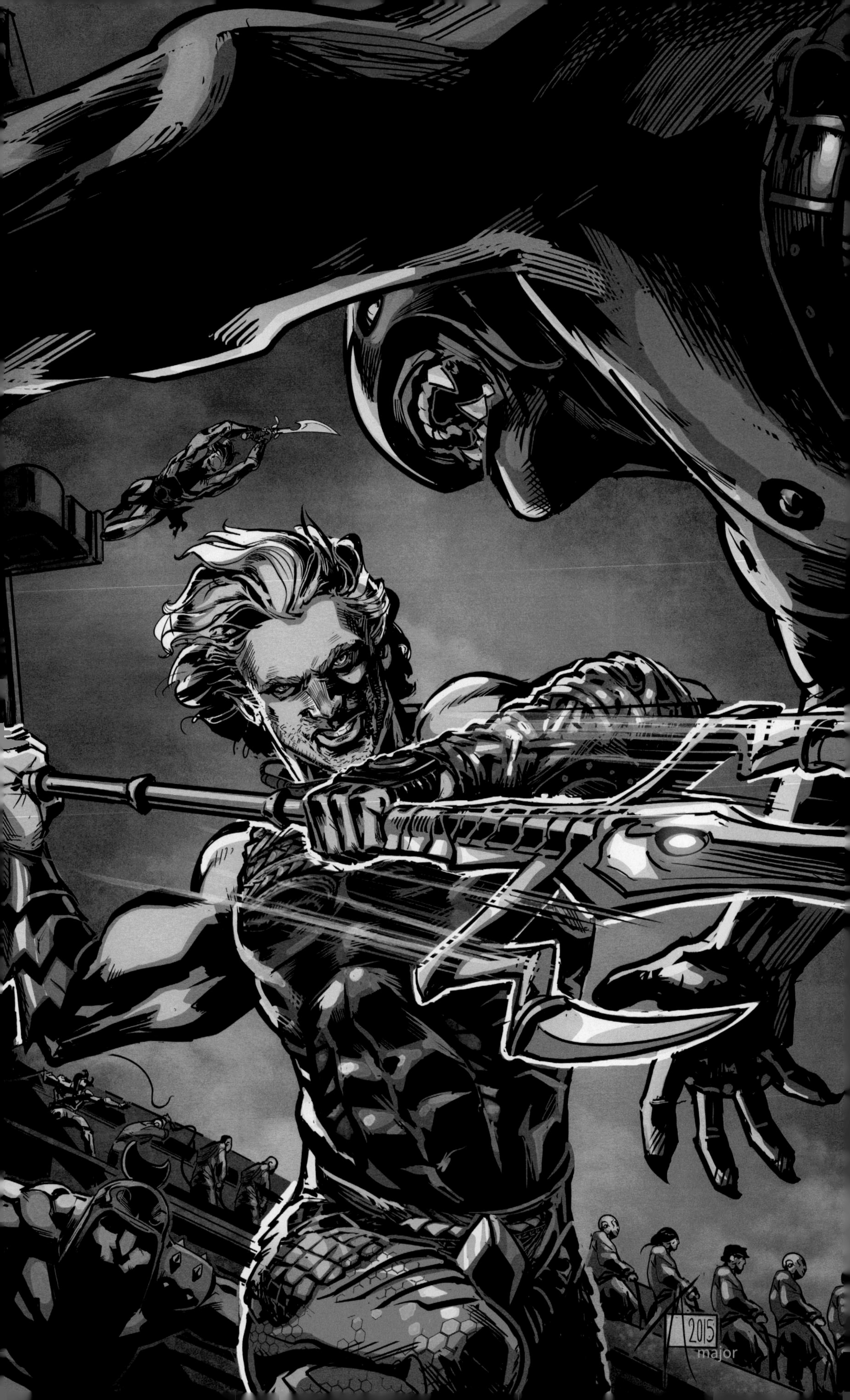
2015
major

THE OTHER ATLANTIS

CULLEN BUNN writer **TREVOR MCCARTHY** layouts **TREVOR MCCARTHY, JESUS MERINO, WALDEN WONG** finishes **GUY MAJOR** colorist **TOM NAPOLITANO** letterer
TREVOR MCCARTHY and **GUY MAJOR** cover art

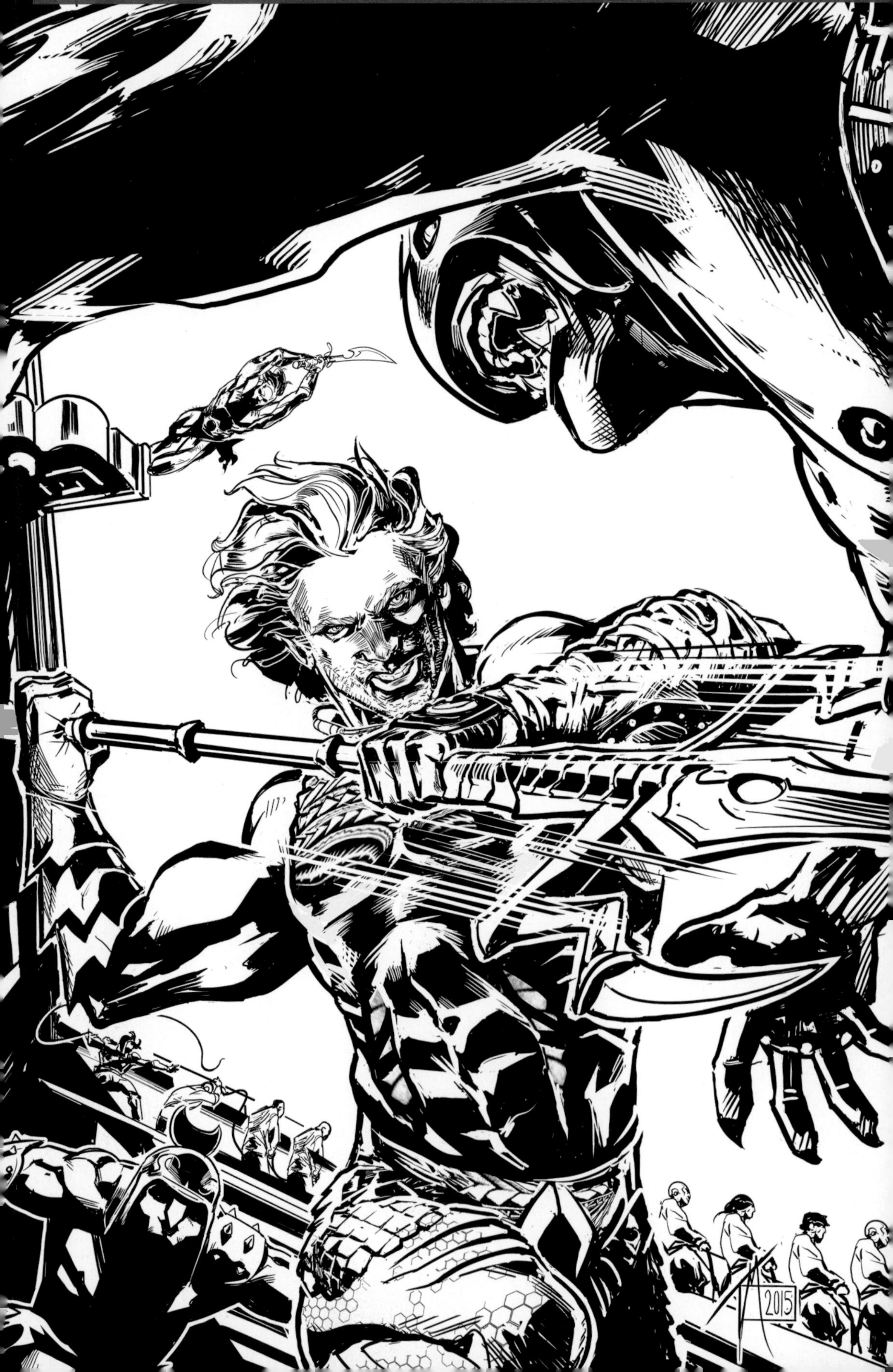

2015

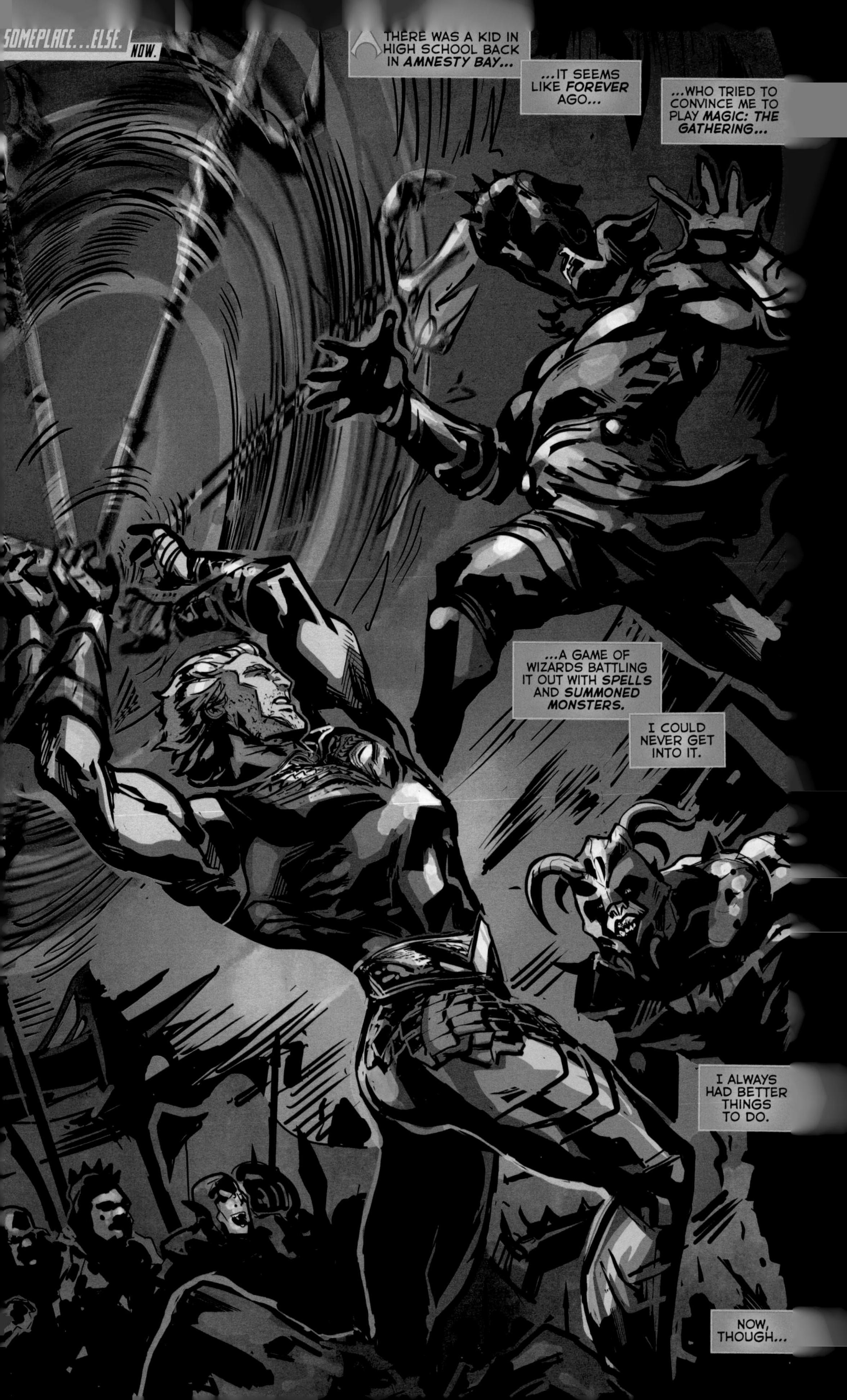
SOMEPLACE...ELSE.
NOW.
THERE WAS A KID IN HIGH SCHOOL BACK IN AMNESTY BAY...
...IT SEEMS LIKE FOREVER AGO...
...WHO TRIED TO CONVINCE ME TO PLAY MAGIC: THE GATHERING...
...A GAME OF WIZARDS BATTLING IT OUT WITH SPELLS AND SUMMONED MONSTERS.
I COULD NEVER GET INTO IT.
I ALWAYS HAD BETTER THINGS TO DO.
NOW, THOUGH...

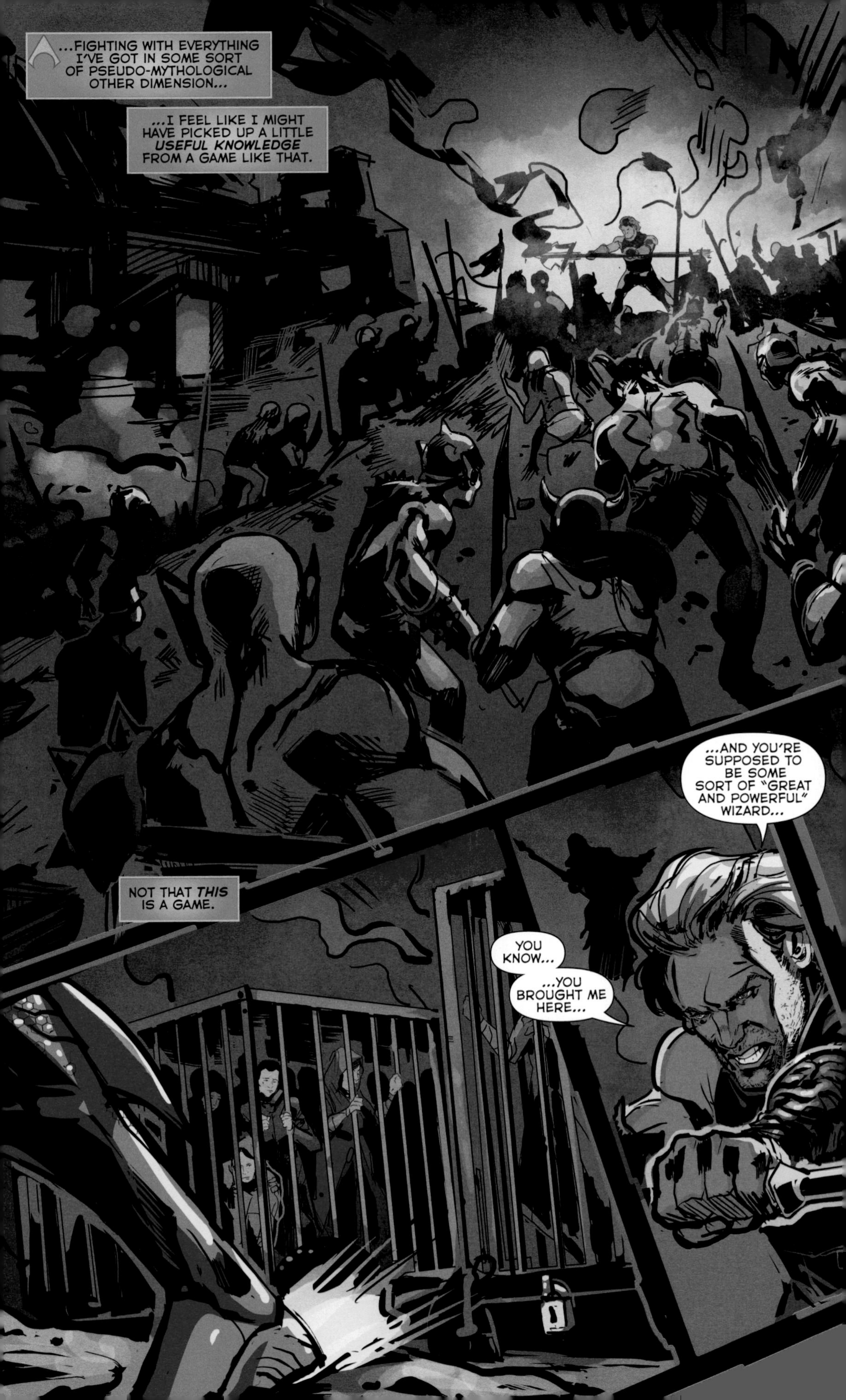
...FIGHTING WITH EVERYTHING I'VE GOT IN SOME SORT OF PSEUDO-MYTHOLOGICAL OTHER DIMENSION...
...I FEEL LIKE I MIGHT HAVE PICKED UP A LITTLE USEFUL KNOWLEDGE FROM A GAME LIKE THAT.
NOT THAT THIS IS A GAME.
...AND YOU'RE SUPPOSED TO BE SOME SORT OF "GREAT AND POWERFUL" WIZARD...
YOU KNOW...
...YOU BROUGHT ME HERE...

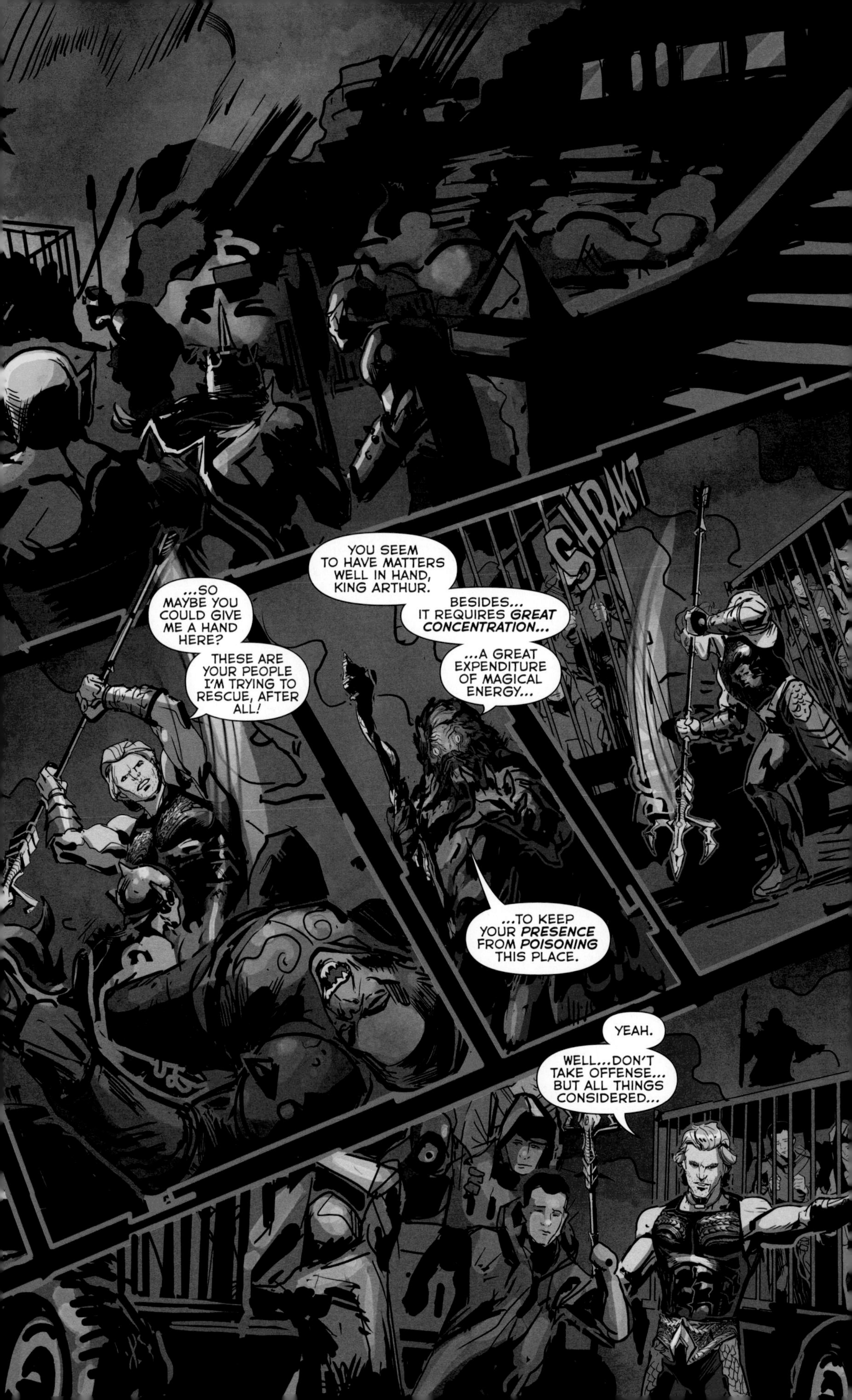
...SO MAYBE YOU COULD GIVE ME A HAND HERE?
THESE ARE YOUR PEOPLE I'M TRYING TO RESCUE, AFTER ALL!
YOU SEEM TO HAVE MATTERS WELL IN HAND, KING ARTHUR.
BESIDES... IT REQUIRES GREAT CONCENTRATION...
...A GREAT EXPENDITURE OF MAGICAL ENERGY...
SHRAKT
...TO KEEP YOUR PRESENCE FROM POISONING THIS PLACE.
YEAH.
WELL...DON'T TAKE OFFENSE... BUT ALL THINGS CONSIDERED...

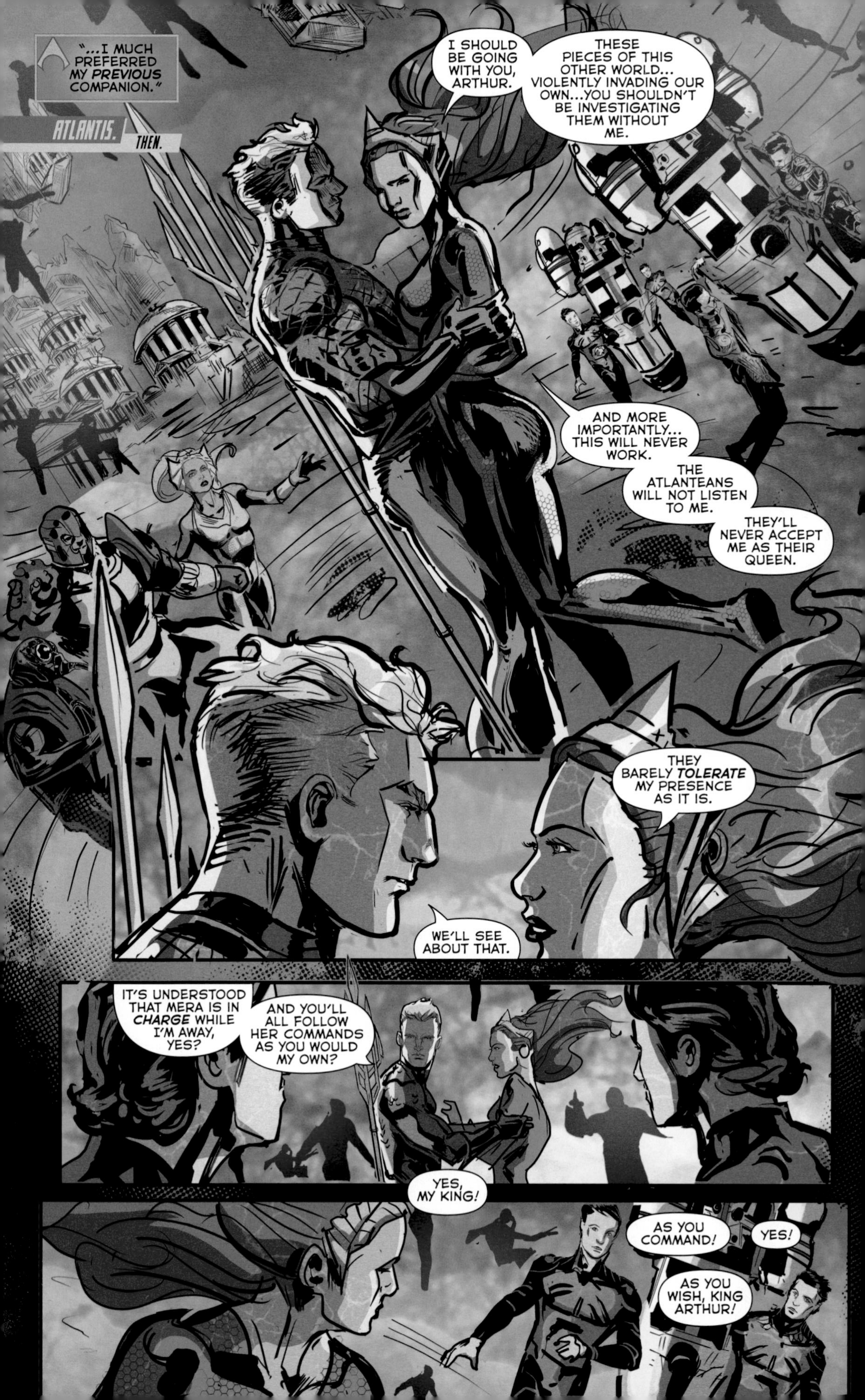
"...I MUCH PREFERRED MY PREVIOUS COMPANION."
ATLANTIS. THEN.
I SHOULD BE GOING WITH YOU, ARTHUR.
THESE PIECES OF THIS OTHER WORLD... VIOLENTLY INVADING OUR OWN...YOU SHOULDN'T BE INVESTIGATING THEM WITHOUT ME.
AND MORE IMPORTANTLY... THIS WILL NEVER WORK.
THE ATLANTEANS WILL NOT LISTEN TO ME.
THEY'LL NEVER ACCEPT ME AS THEIR QUEEN.
THEY BARELY TOLERATE MY PRESENCE AS IT IS.
WE'LL SEE ABOUT THAT.
IT'S UNDERSTOOD THAT MERA IS IN CHARGE WHILE I'M AWAY, YES?
AND YOU'LL ALL FOLLOW HER COMMANDS AS YOU WOULD MY OWN?
YES, MY KING!
AS YOU COMMAND!
YES!
AS YOU WISH, KING ARTHUR!

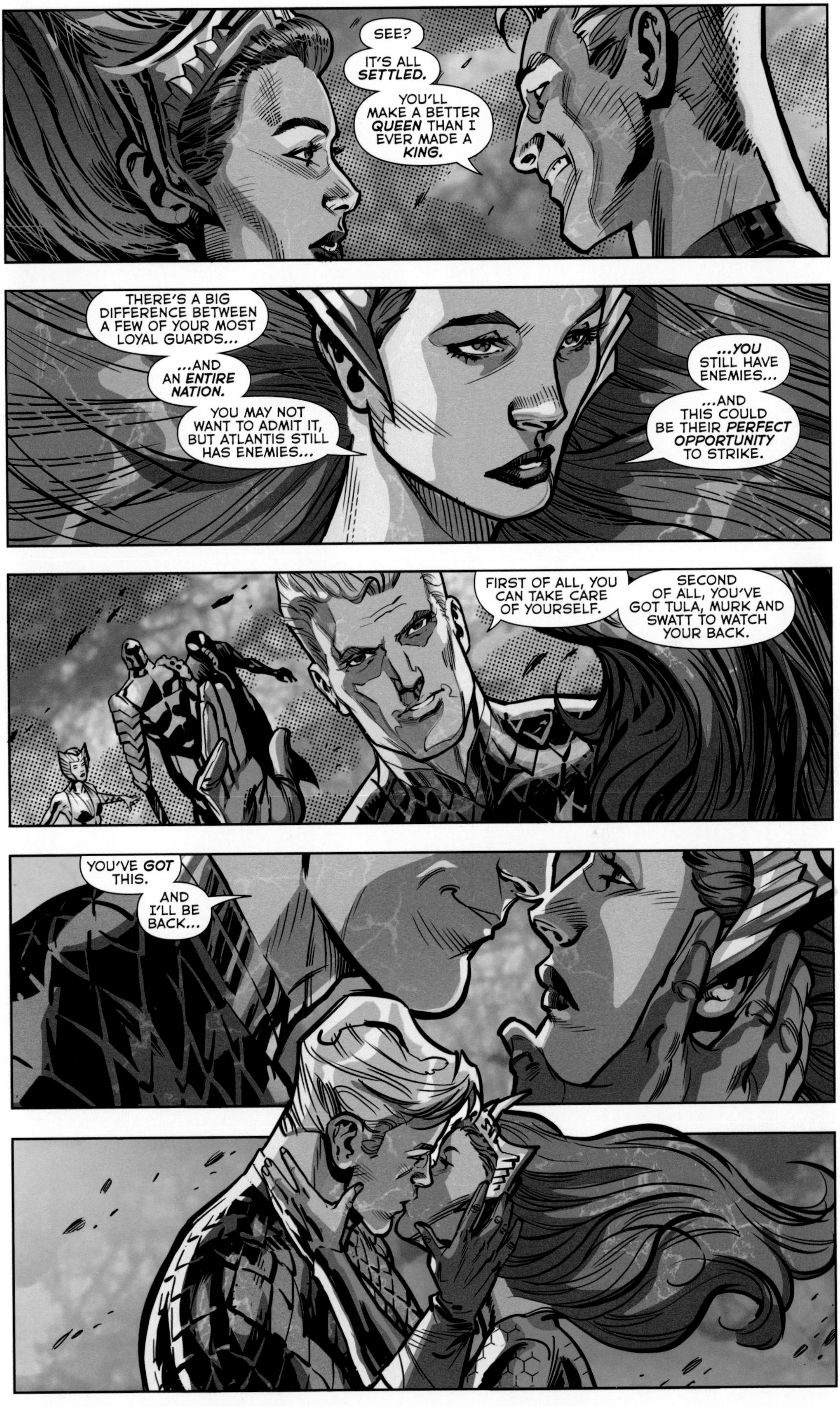
SEE?
IT'S ALL SETTLED.
YOU'LL MAKE A BETTER QUEEN THAN I EVER MADE A KING.
THERE'S A BIG DIFFERENCE BETWEEN A FEW OF YOUR MOST LOYAL GUARDS...
...AND AN ENTIRE NATION.
YOU MAY NOT WANT TO ADMIT IT, BUT ATLANTIS STILL HAS ENEMIES...
...YOU STILL HAVE ENEMIES...
...AND THIS COULD BE THEIR PERFECT OPPORTUNITY TO STRIKE.
FIRST OF ALL, YOU CAN TAKE CARE OF YOURSELF.
SECOND OF ALL, YOU'VE GOT TULA, MURK AND SWATT TO WATCH YOUR BACK.
YOU'VE GOT THIS.
AND I'LL BE BACK...

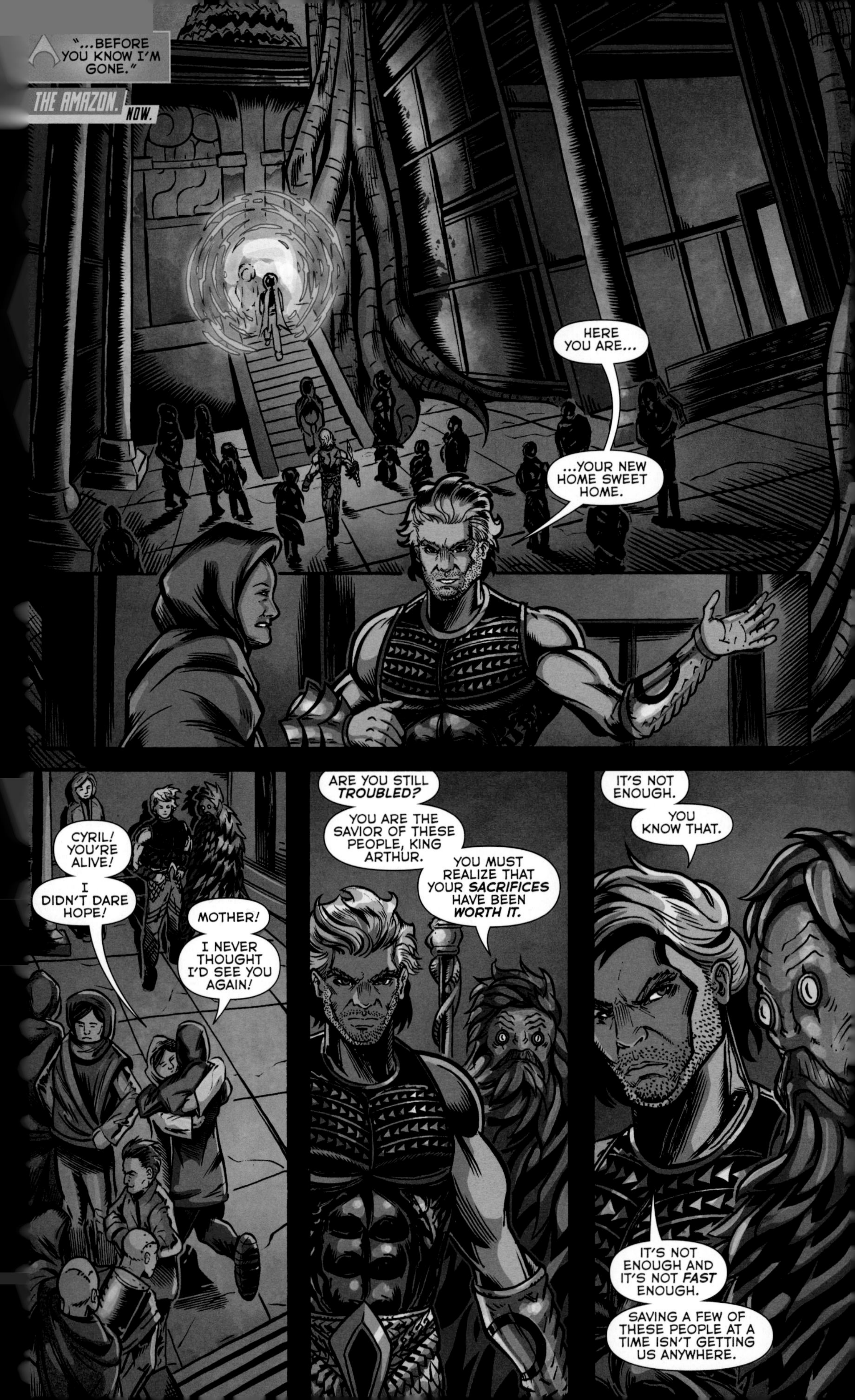
"...BEFORE YOU KNOW I'M GONE."
THE AMAZON. NOW.
HERE YOU ARE...
...YOUR NEW HOME SWEET HOME.
CYRIL! YOU'RE ALIVE!
I DIDN'T DARE HOPE!
MOTHER!
I NEVER THOUGHT I'D SEE YOU AGAIN!
ARE YOU STILL TROUBLED?
YOU ARE THE SAVIOR OF THESE PEOPLE, KING ARTHUR.
YOU MUST REALIZE THAT YOUR SACRIFICES HAVE BEEN WORTH IT.
IT'S NOT ENOUGH.
YOU KNOW THAT.
IT'S NOT ENOUGH AND IT'S NOT FAST ENOUGH.
SAVING A FEW OF THESE PEOPLE AT A TIME ISN'T GETTING US ANYWHERE.

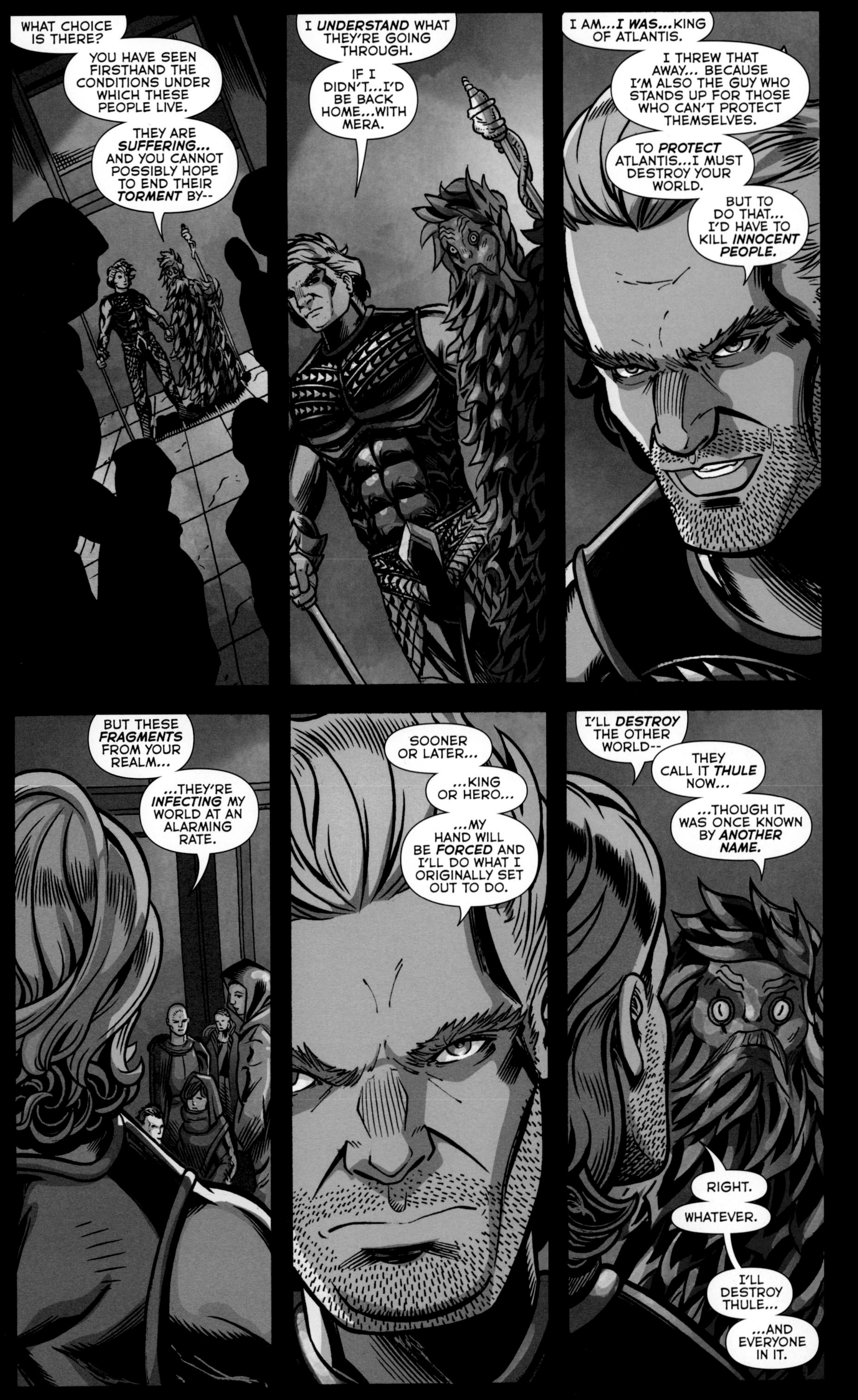
WHAT CHOICE IS THERE?
YOU HAVE SEEN FIRSTHAND THE CONDITIONS UNDER WHICH THESE PEOPLE LIVE.
THEY ARE *SUFFERING...* AND YOU CANNOT POSSIBLY HOPE TO END THEIR *TORMENT* BY--
I *UNDERSTAND* WHAT THEY'RE GOING THROUGH.
IF I DIDN'T...I'D BE BACK HOME...WITH MERA.
I AM...*I WAS...*KING OF ATLANTIS.
I THREW THAT AWAY... BECAUSE I'M ALSO THE GUY WHO STANDS UP FOR THOSE WHO CAN'T PROTECT THEMSELVES.
TO *PROTECT* ATLANTIS...I MUST DESTROY YOUR WORLD.
BUT TO DO THAT... I'D HAVE TO KILL *INNOCENT PEOPLE.*
BUT THESE *FRAGMENTS* FROM YOUR REALM...
...THEY'RE *INFECTING* MY WORLD AT AN ALARMING RATE.
SOONER OR LATER...
...KING OR HERO...
...MY HAND WILL BE *FORCED* AND I'LL DO WHAT I ORIGINALLY SET OUT TO DO.
I'LL *DESTROY* THE OTHER WORLD--
THEY CALL IT *THULE* NOW...
...THOUGH IT WAS ONCE KNOWN BY *ANOTHER NAME.*
RIGHT.
WHATEVER.
I'LL DESTROY THULE...
...AND EVERYONE IN IT.

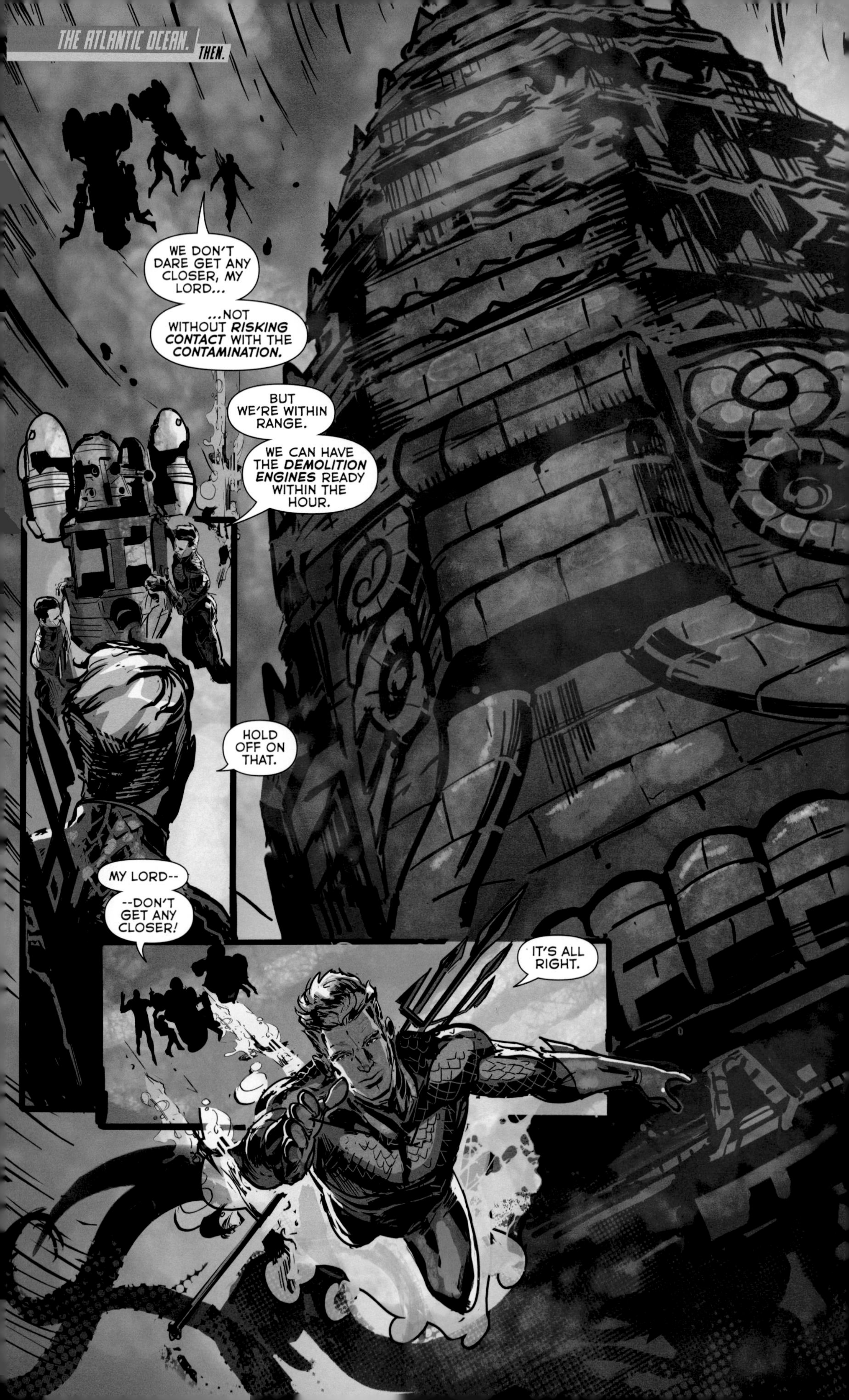
THE ATLANTIC OCEAN. THEN.
WE DON'T DARE GET ANY CLOSER, MY LORD...
...NOT WITHOUT RISKING CONTACT WITH THE CONTAMINATION.
BUT WE'RE WITHIN RANGE.
WE CAN HAVE THE DEMOLITION ENGINES READY WITHIN THE HOUR.
HOLD OFF ON THAT.
MY LORD--
--DON'T GET ANY CLOSER!
IT'S ALL RIGHT.

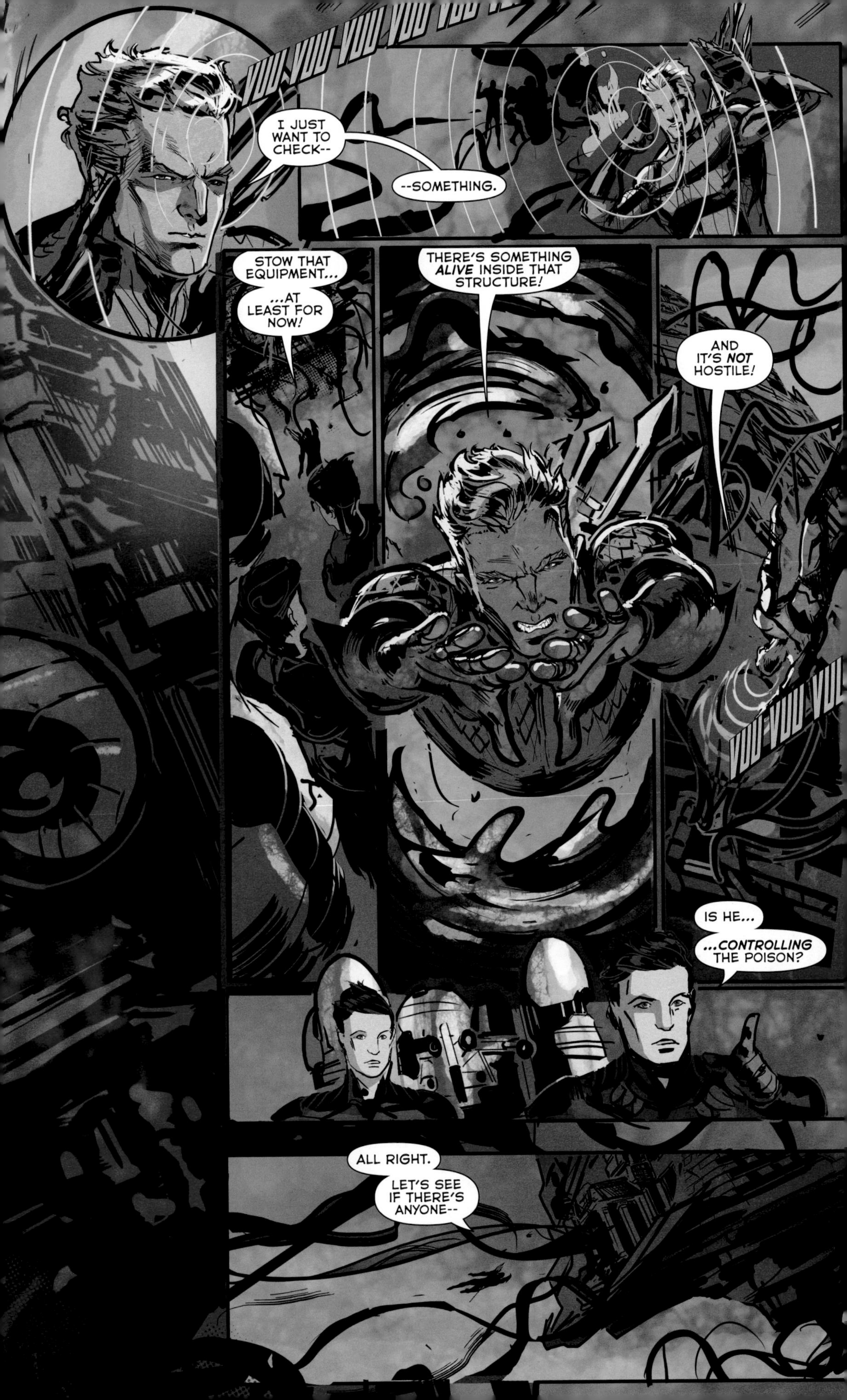
VUU VUU VUU VUU VUU
I JUST WANT TO CHECK--
--SOMETHING.
STOW THAT EQUIPMENT...
...AT LEAST FOR NOW!
THERE'S SOMETHING ALIVE INSIDE THAT STRUCTURE!
AND IT'S NOT HOSTILE!
VUU VUU VUU
IS HE...
...CONTROLLING THE POISON?
ALL RIGHT.
LET'S SEE IF THERE'S ANYONE--

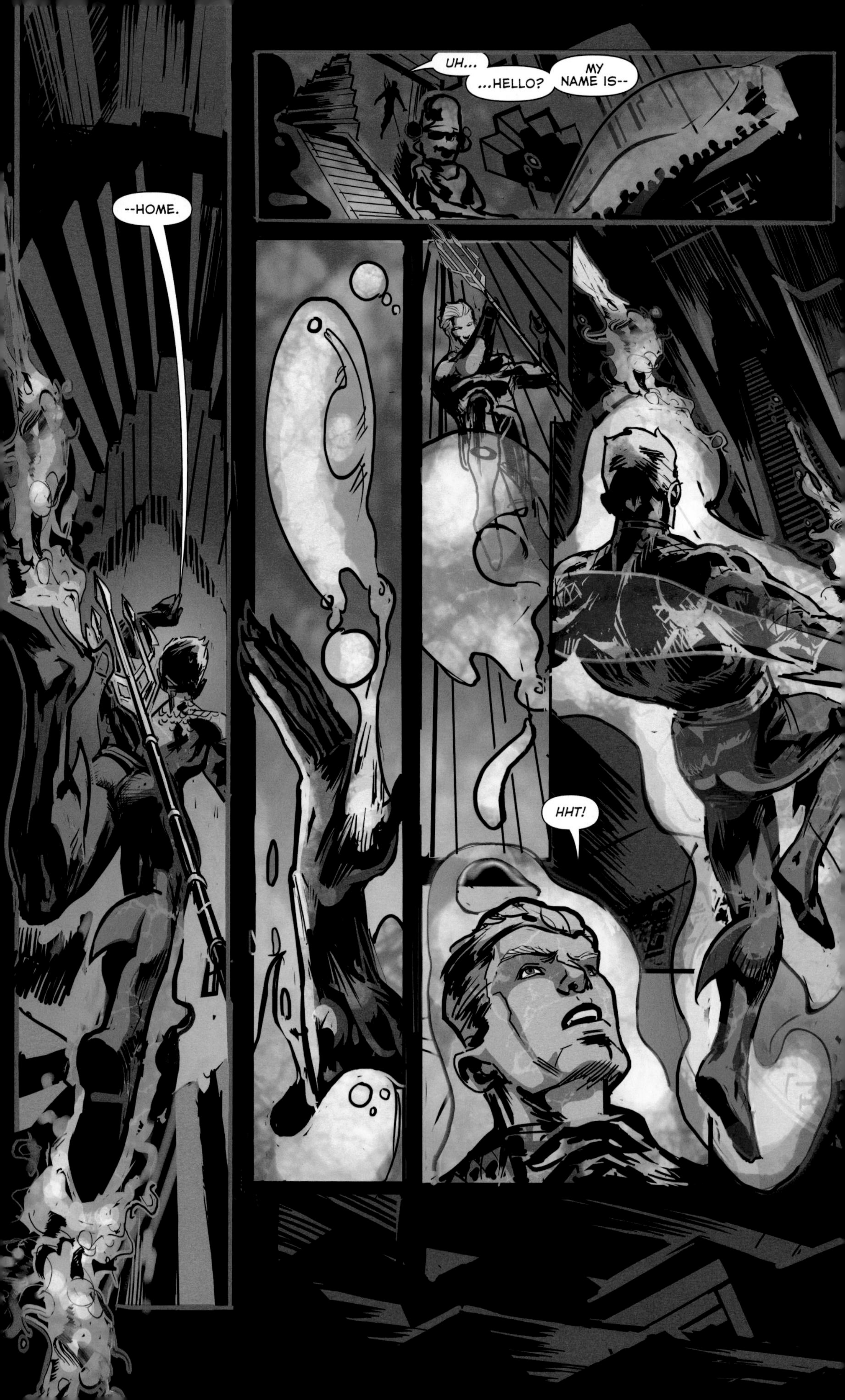
--HOME.
UH...
...HELLO?
MY NAME IS--
HHT!

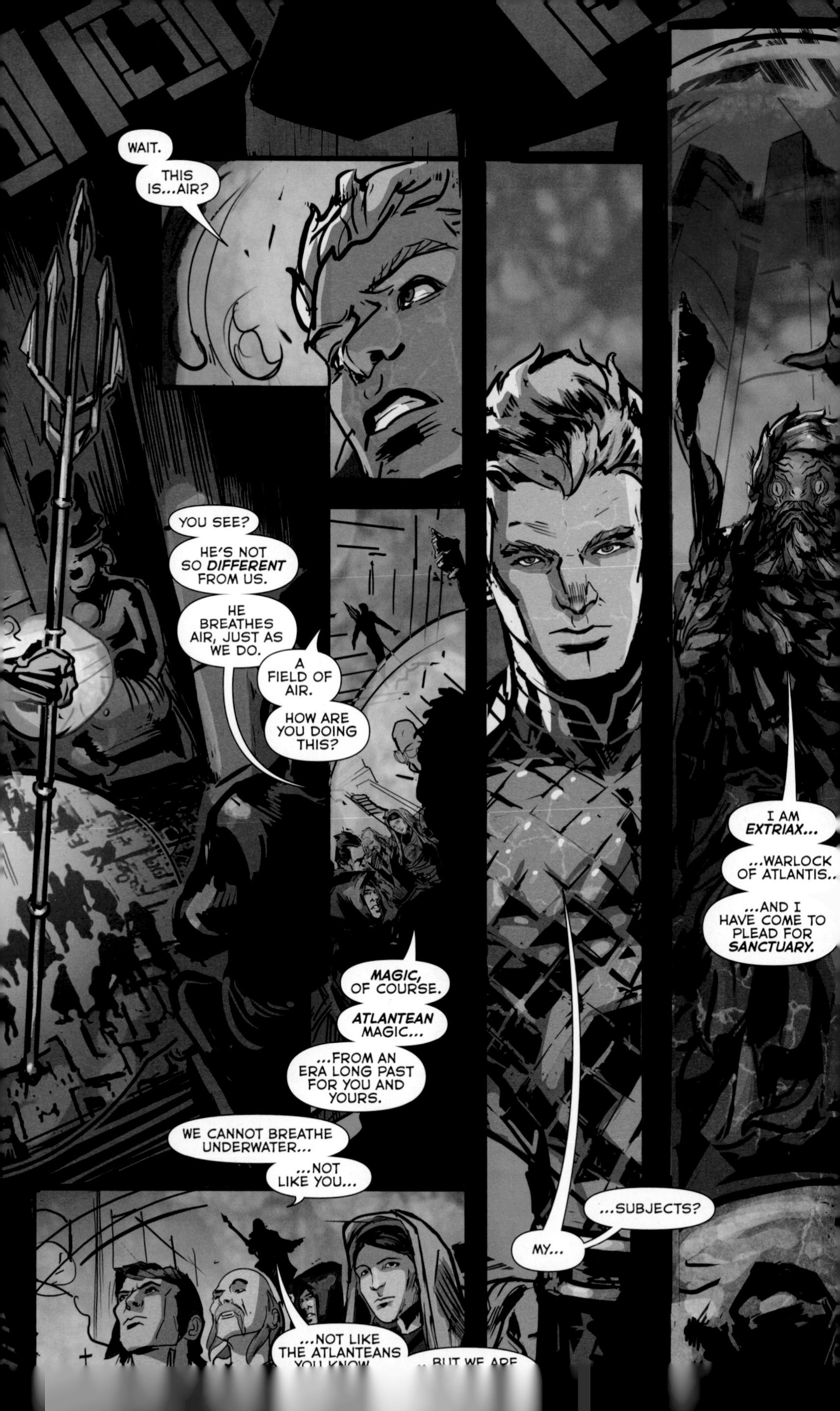
WAIT.
THIS IS...AIR?
YOU SEE?
HE'S NOT SO DIFFERENT FROM US.
HE BREATHES AIR, JUST AS WE DO.
A FIELD OF AIR.
HOW ARE YOU DOING THIS?
MAGIC, OF COURSE.
ATLANTEAN MAGIC...
...FROM AN ERA LONG PAST FOR YOU AND YOURS.
WE CANNOT BREATHE UNDERWATER...
...NOT LIKE YOU...
...NOT LIKE THE ATLANTEANS
I AM EXTRIAX...
...WARLOCK OF ATLANTIS...
...AND I HAVE COME TO PLEAD FOR SANCTUARY.
MY...
...SUBJECTS?

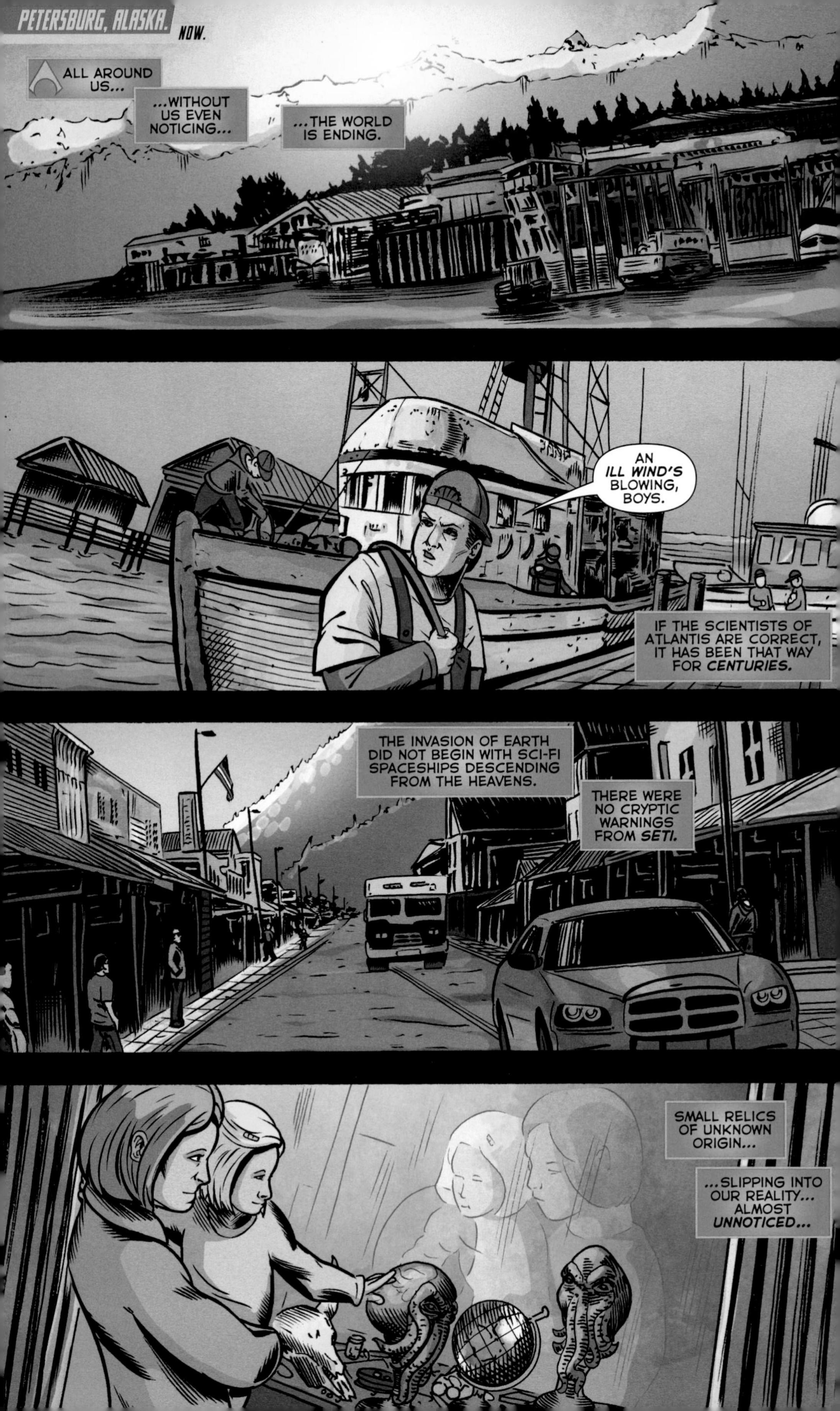

PETERSBURG, ALASKA.
NOW.
ALL AROUND US...
...WITHOUT US EVEN NOTICING...
...THE WORLD IS ENDING.
AN ILL WIND'S BLOWING, BOYS.
IF THE SCIENTISTS OF ATLANTIS ARE CORRECT, IT HAS BEEN THAT WAY FOR CENTURIES.
THE INVASION OF EARTH DID NOT BEGIN WITH SCI-FI SPACESHIPS DESCENDING FROM THE HEAVENS.
THERE WERE NO CRYPTIC WARNINGS FROM SETI.
SMALL RELICS OF UNKNOWN ORIGIN...
...SLIPPING INTO OUR REALITY... ALMOST UNNOTICED...

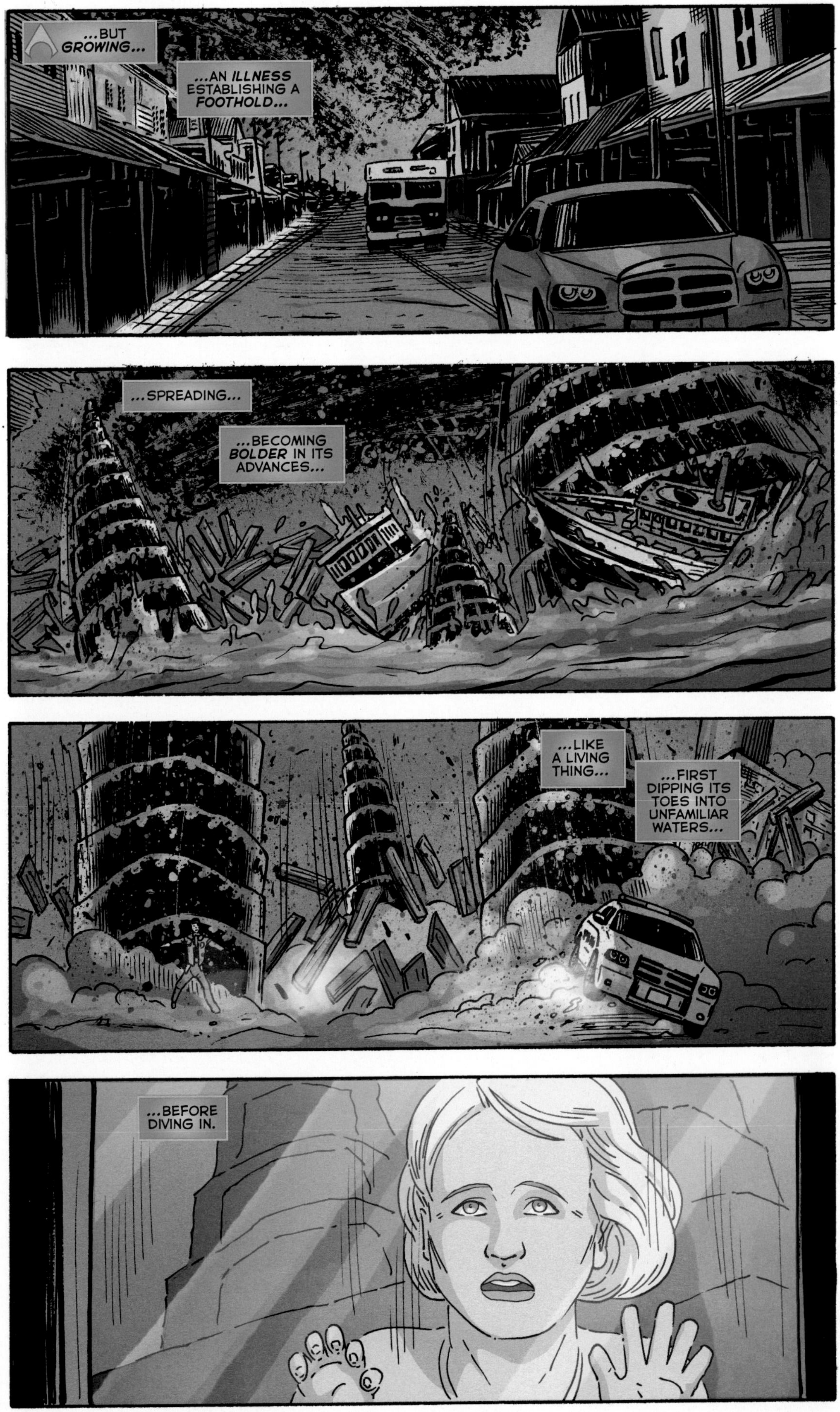
...BUT GROWING...
...AN ILLNESS ESTABLISHING A FOOTHOLD...
...SPREADING...
...BECOMING BOLDER IN ITS ADVANCES...
...LIKE A LIVING THING...
...FIRST DIPPING ITS TOES INTO UNFAMILIAR WATERS...
...BEFORE DIVING IN.

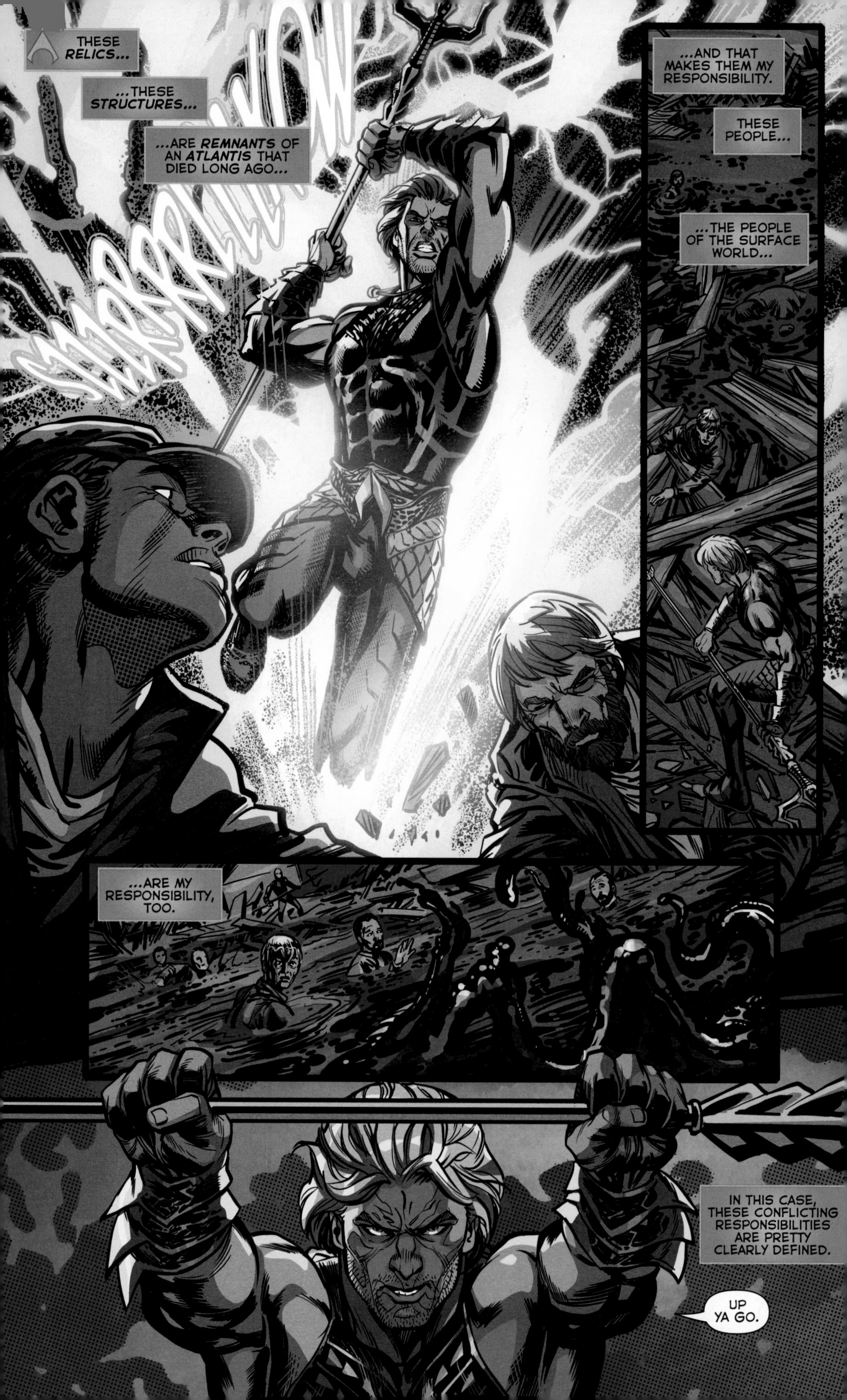
THESE RELICS...
...THESE STRUCTURES...
...ARE REMNANTS OF AN ATLANTIS THAT DIED LONG AGO...
...AND THAT MAKES THEM MY RESPONSIBILITY.
THESE PEOPLE...
...THE PEOPLE OF THE SURFACE WORLD...
...ARE MY RESPONSIBILITY, TOO.
IN THIS CASE, THESE CONFLICTING RESPONSIBILITIES ARE PRETTY CLEARLY DEFINED.
UP YA GO.

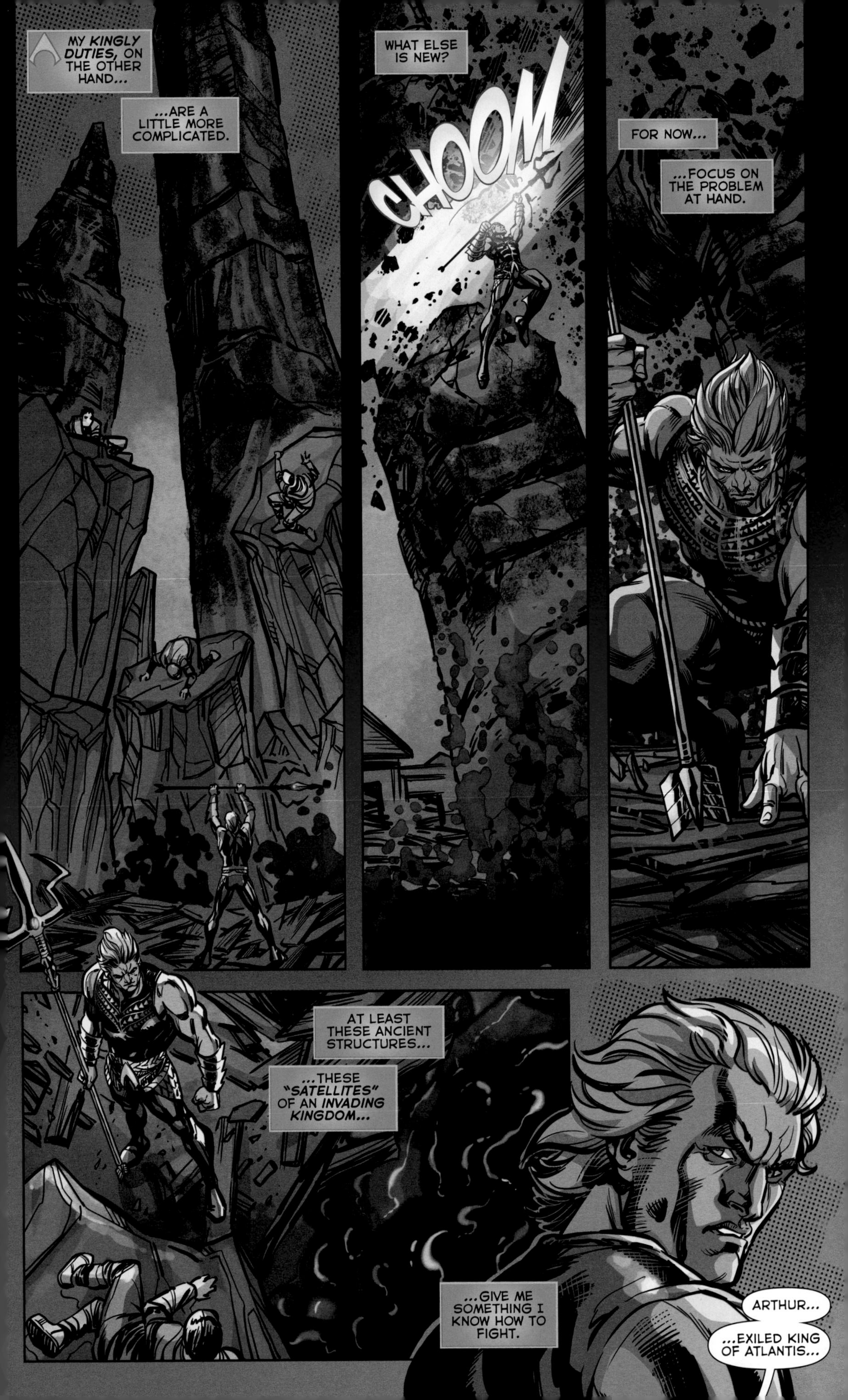
MY KINGLY DUTIES, ON THE OTHER HAND...
...ARE A LITTLE MORE COMPLICATED.
WHAT ELSE IS NEW?
CHOOM!
FOR NOW...
...FOCUS ON THE PROBLEM AT HAND.
AT LEAST THESE ANCIENT STRUCTURES...
...THESE "SATELLITES" OF AN INVADING KINGDOM...
...GIVE ME SOMETHING I KNOW HOW TO FIGHT.
ARTHUR...
...EXILED KING OF ATLANTIS...

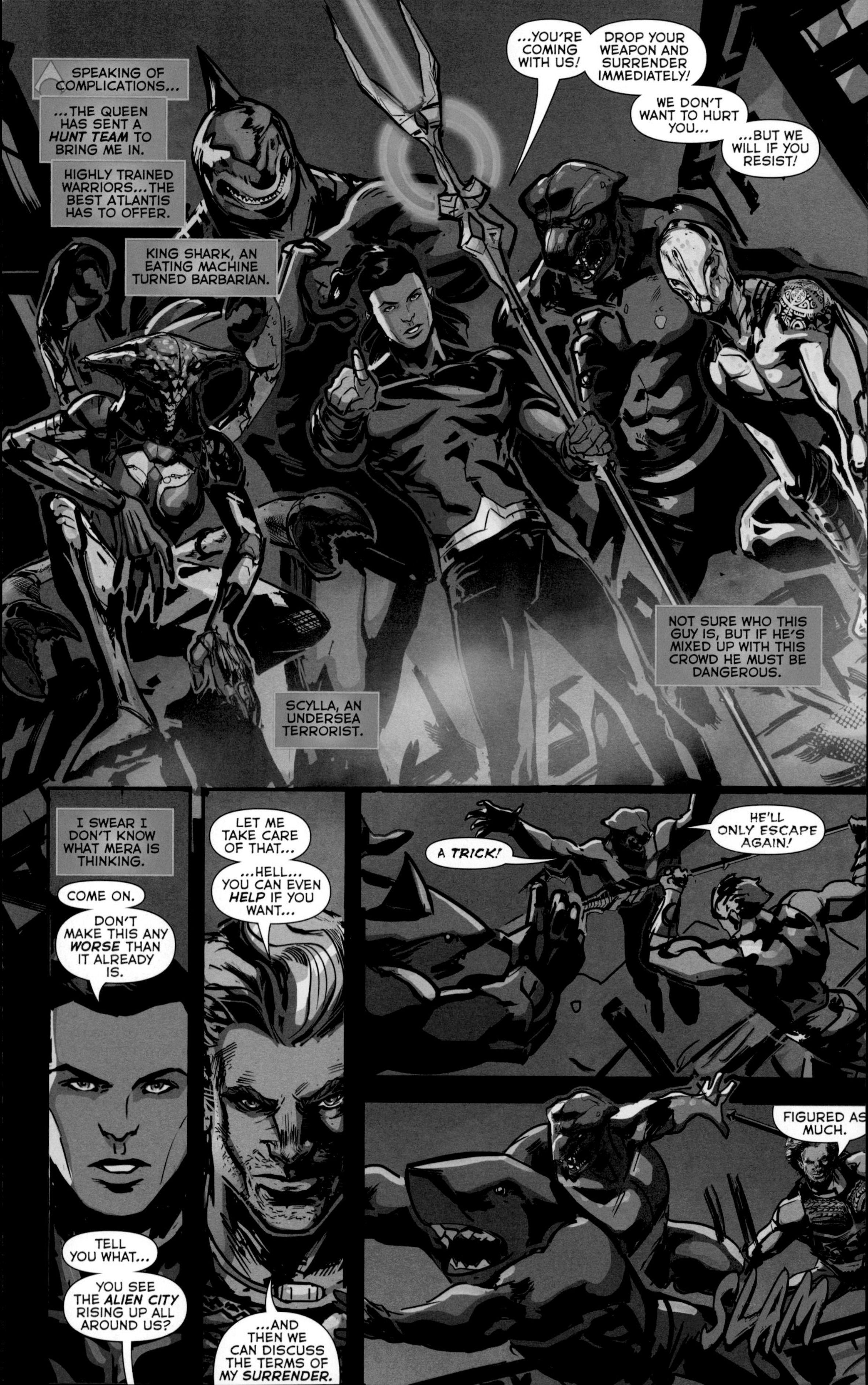
SPEAKING OF COMPLICATIONS...
...THE QUEEN HAS SENT A HUNT TEAM TO BRING ME IN.
HIGHLY TRAINED WARRIORS...THE BEST ATLANTIS HAS TO OFFER.
KING SHARK, AN EATING MACHINE TURNED BARBARIAN.
...YOU'RE COMING WITH US!
DROP YOUR WEAPON AND SURRENDER IMMEDIATELY!
WE DON'T WANT TO HURT YOU...
...BUT WE WILL IF YOU RESIST!
NOT SURE WHO THIS GUY IS, BUT IF HE'S MIXED UP WITH THIS CROWD HE MUST BE DANGEROUS.
SCYLLA, AN UNDERSEA TERRORIST.
I SWEAR I DON'T KNOW WHAT MERA IS THINKING.
COME ON.
DON'T MAKE THIS ANY WORSE THAN IT ALREADY IS.
TELL YOU WHAT...
YOU SEE THE ALIEN CITY RISING UP ALL AROUND US?
LET ME TAKE CARE OF THAT...
...HELL... YOU CAN EVEN HELP IF YOU WANT...
...AND THEN WE CAN DISCUSS THE TERMS OF MY SURRENDER.
A TRICK!
HE'LL ONLY ESCAPE AGAIN!
FIGURED AS MUCH.
SLAM

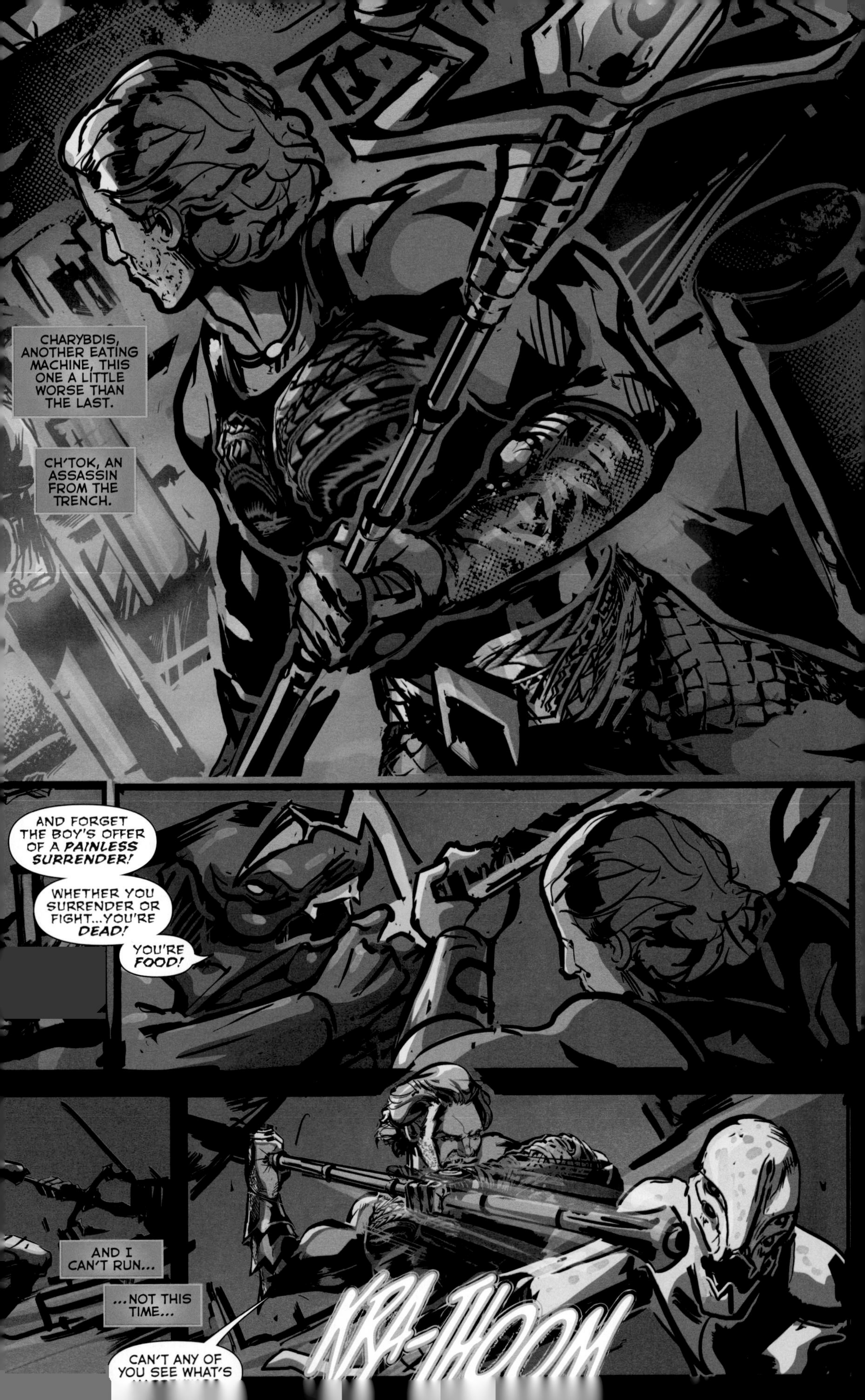
CHARYBDIS, ANOTHER EATING MACHINE, THIS ONE A LITTLE WORSE THAN THE LAST.
CH'TOK, AN ASSASSIN FROM THE TRENCH.
AND FORGET THE BOY'S OFFER OF A *PAINLESS SURRENDER!*
WHETHER YOU SURRENDER OR FIGHT...YOU'RE *DEAD!*
YOU'RE *FOOD!*
AND I CAN'T RUN...
...NOT THIS TIME...
CAN'T ANY OF YOU SEE WHAT'S
KRA-THOOM

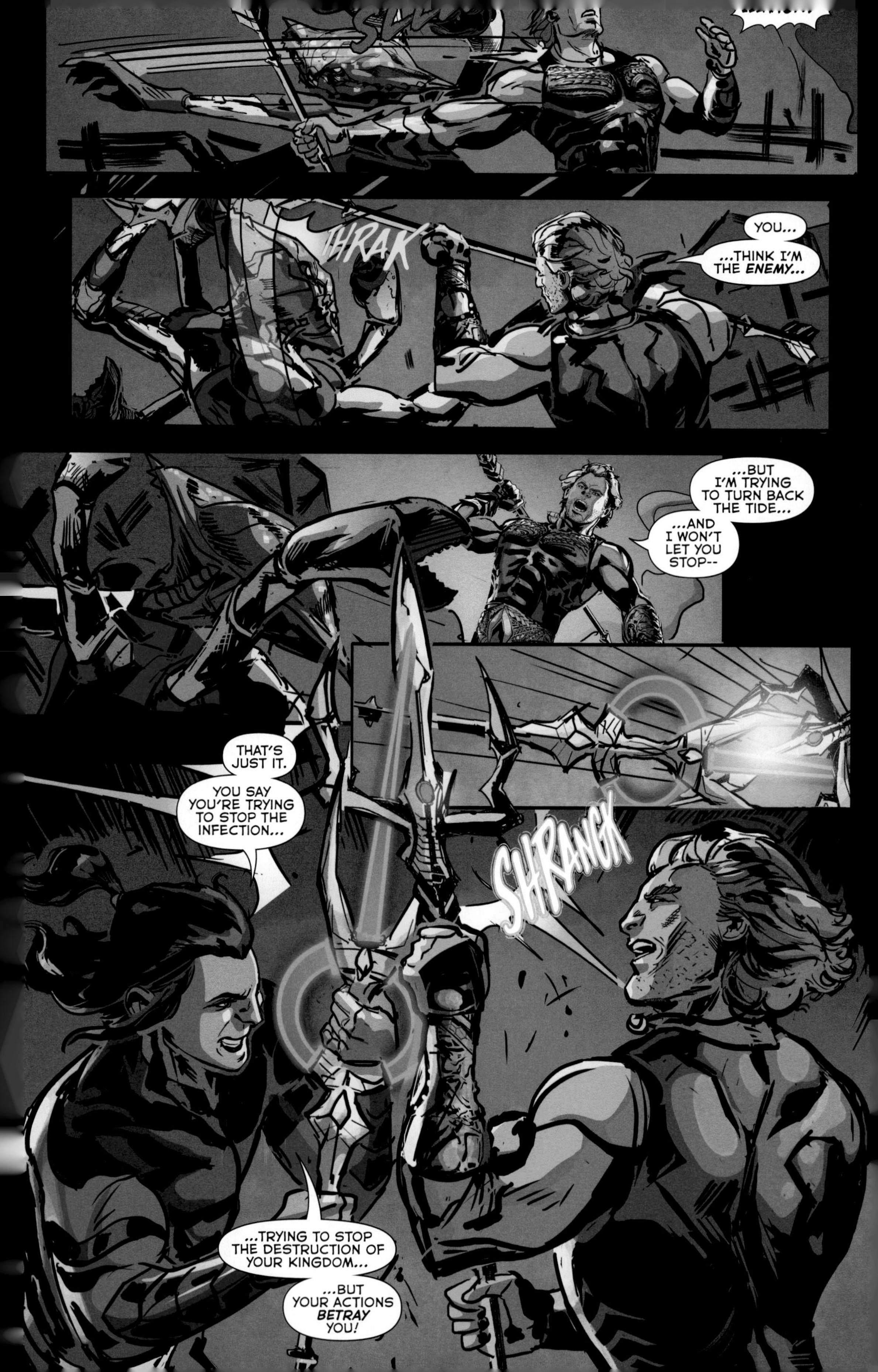
THRAK
YOU...
...THINK I'M THE ENEMY...
...BUT I'M TRYING TO TURN BACK THE TIDE...
...AND I WON'T LET YOU STOP--
THAT'S JUST IT.
YOU SAY YOU'RE TRYING TO STOP THE INFECTION...
SHRANGK
...TRYING TO STOP THE DESTRUCTION OF YOUR KINGDOM...
...BUT YOUR ACTIONS BETRAY YOU!

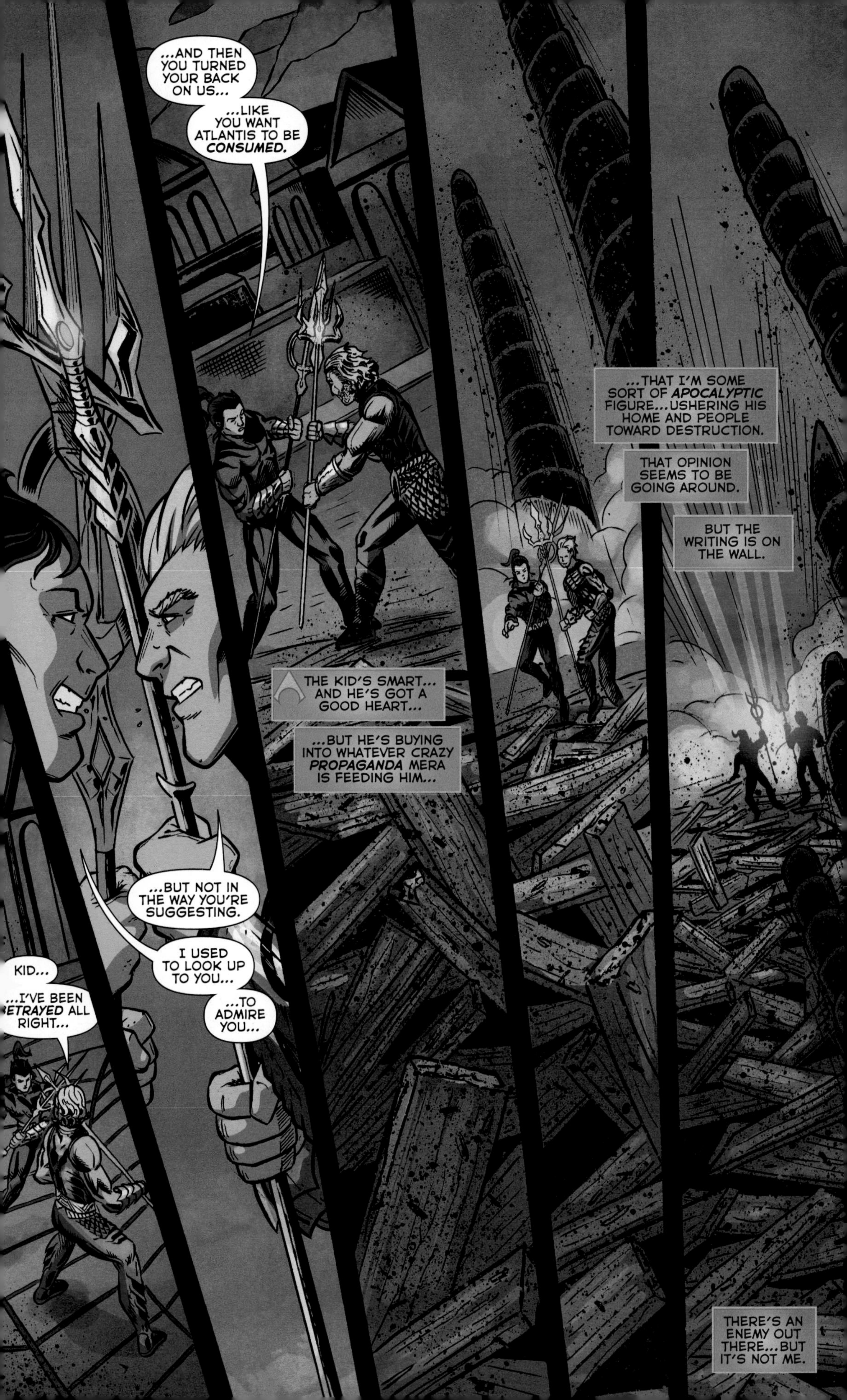
...AND THEN YOU TURNED YOUR BACK ON US...
...LIKE YOU WANT ATLANTIS TO BE CONSUMED.
...BUT NOT IN THE WAY YOU'RE SUGGESTING.
I USED TO LOOK UP TO YOU...
...TO ADMIRE YOU...
KID...
...I'VE BEEN BETRAYED ALL RIGHT...
THE KID'S SMART... AND HE'S GOT A GOOD HEART...
...BUT HE'S BUYING INTO WHATEVER CRAZY PROPAGANDA MERA IS FEEDING HIM...
...THAT I'M SOME SORT OF APOCALYPTIC FIGURE...USHERING HIS HOME AND PEOPLE TOWARD DESTRUCTION.
THAT OPINION SEEMS TO BE GOING AROUND.
BUT THE WRITING IS ON THE WALL.
THERE'S AN ENEMY OUT THERE...BUT IT'S NOT ME.

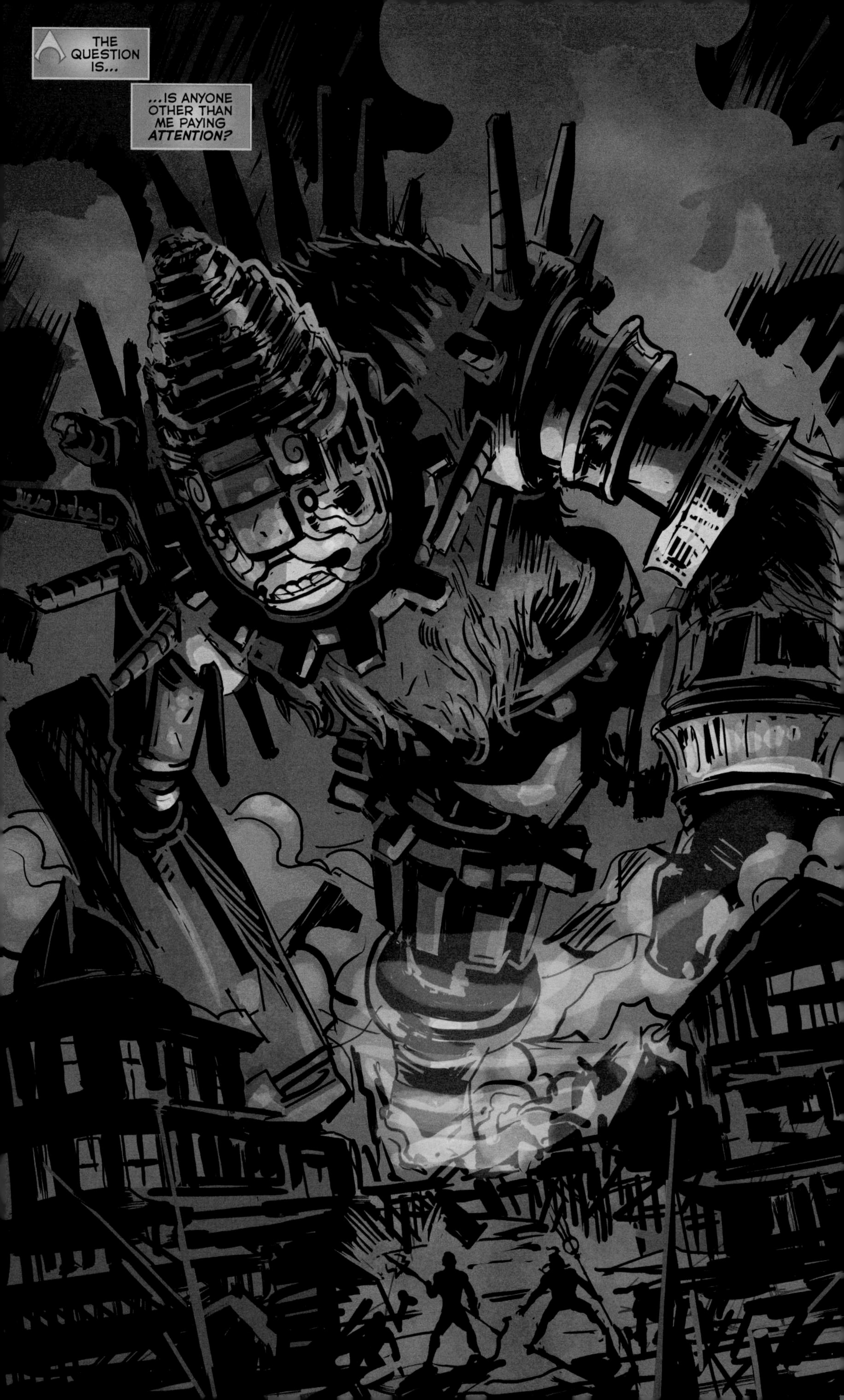
THE QUESTION IS...
...IS ANYONE OTHER THAN ME PAYING *ATTENTION?*

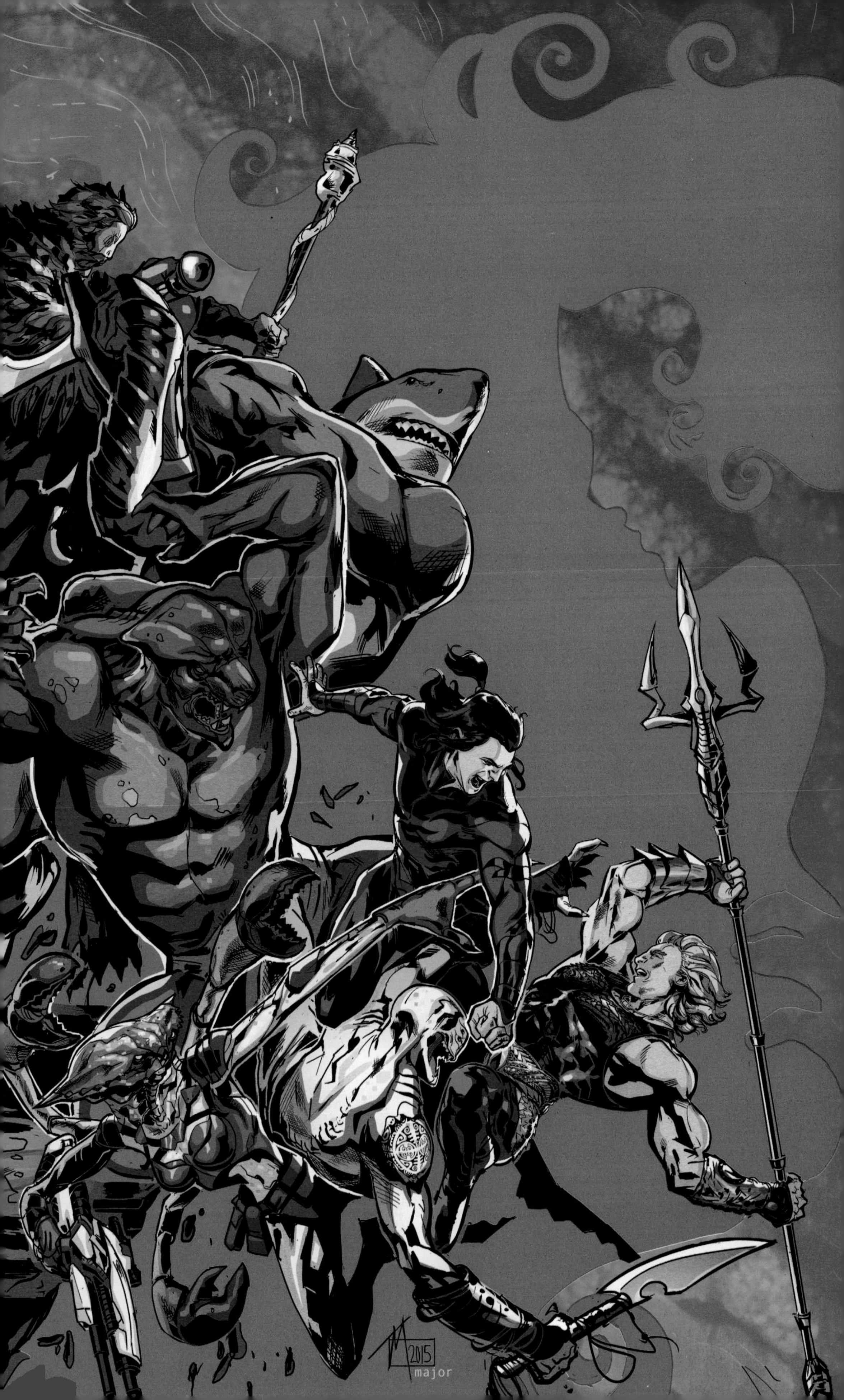
2015
major

GOSPEL OF DESTRUCTION

CULLEN BUNN writer **TREVOR MCCARTHY, JESUS MERINO** artists **GUY MAJOR** colorist **TOM NAPOLITANO** letterer
TREVOR MCCARTHY and **GUY MAJOR** cover art

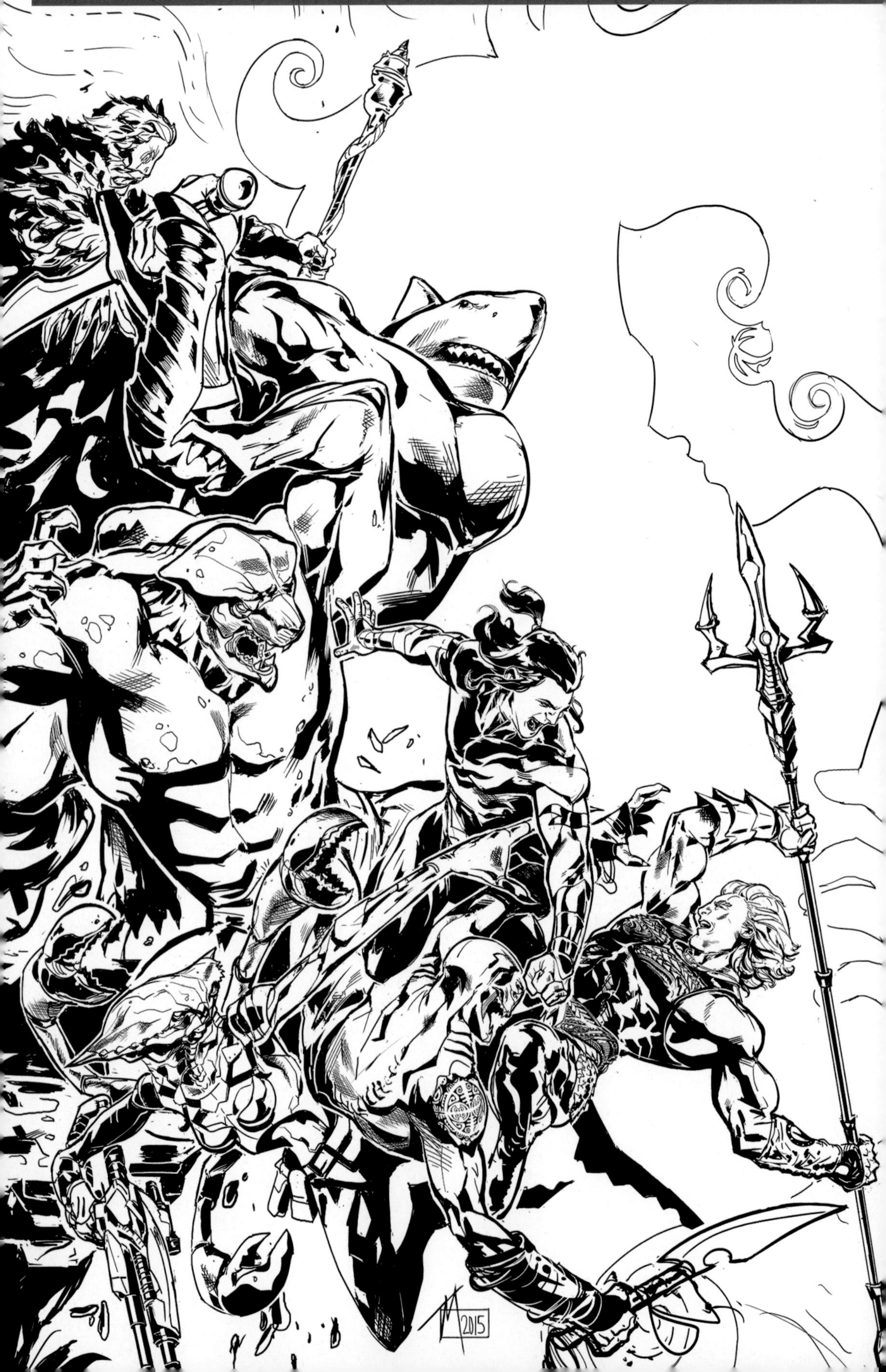

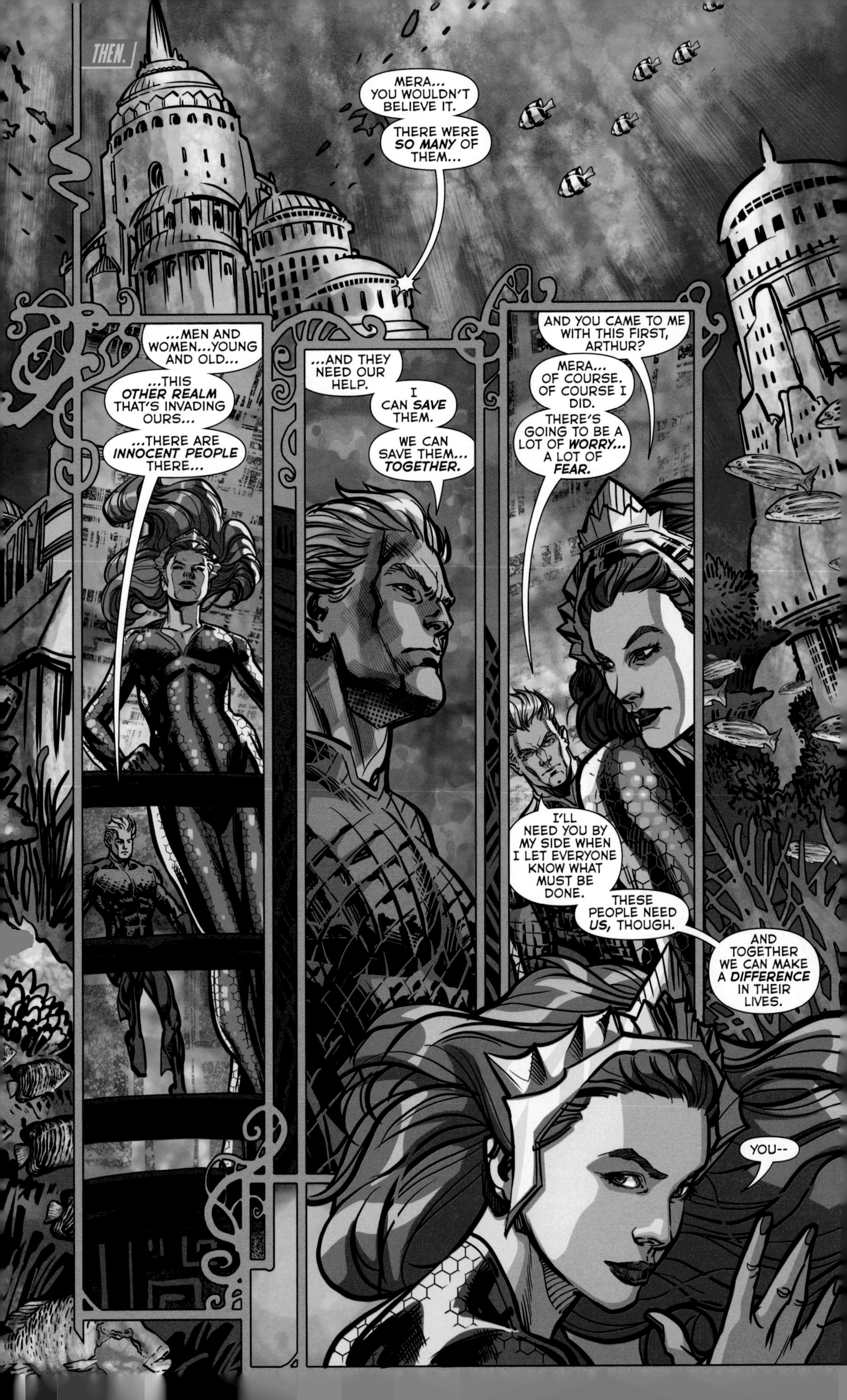

THEN.
MERA... YOU WOULDN'T BELIEVE IT.
THERE WERE SO MANY OF THEM...
...MEN AND WOMEN...YOUNG AND OLD...
...THIS OTHER REALM THAT'S INVADING OURS...
...THERE ARE INNOCENT PEOPLE THERE...
...AND THEY NEED OUR HELP.
I CAN SAVE THEM.
WE CAN SAVE THEM... TOGETHER.
AND YOU CAME TO ME WITH THIS FIRST, ARTHUR?
MERA... OF COURSE. OF COURSE I DID.
THERE'S GOING TO BE A LOT OF WORRY... A LOT OF FEAR.
I'LL NEED YOU BY MY SIDE WHEN I LET EVERYONE KNOW WHAT MUST BE DONE.
THESE PEOPLE NEED US, THOUGH.
AND TOGETHER WE CAN MAKE A DIFFERENCE IN THEIR LIVES.
YOU--

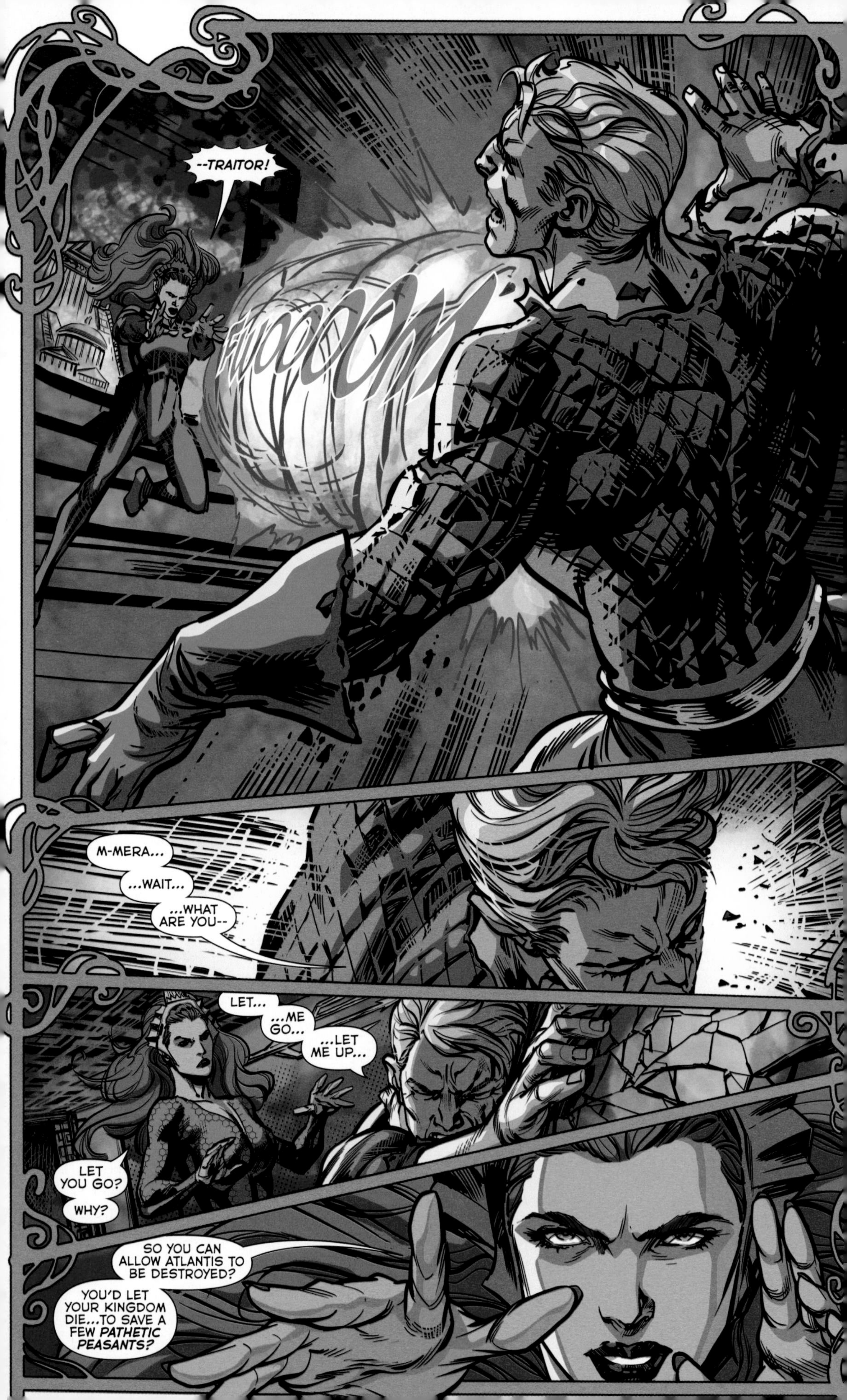
--TRAITOR!
FWOOOOM
M-MERA...
...WAIT...
...WHAT ARE YOU--
LET...
...ME GO...
...LET ME UP...
LET YOU GO?
WHY?
SO YOU CAN ALLOW ATLANTIS TO BE DESTROYED?
YOU'D LET YOUR KINGDOM DIE...TO SAVE A FEW *PATHETIC PEASANTS?*

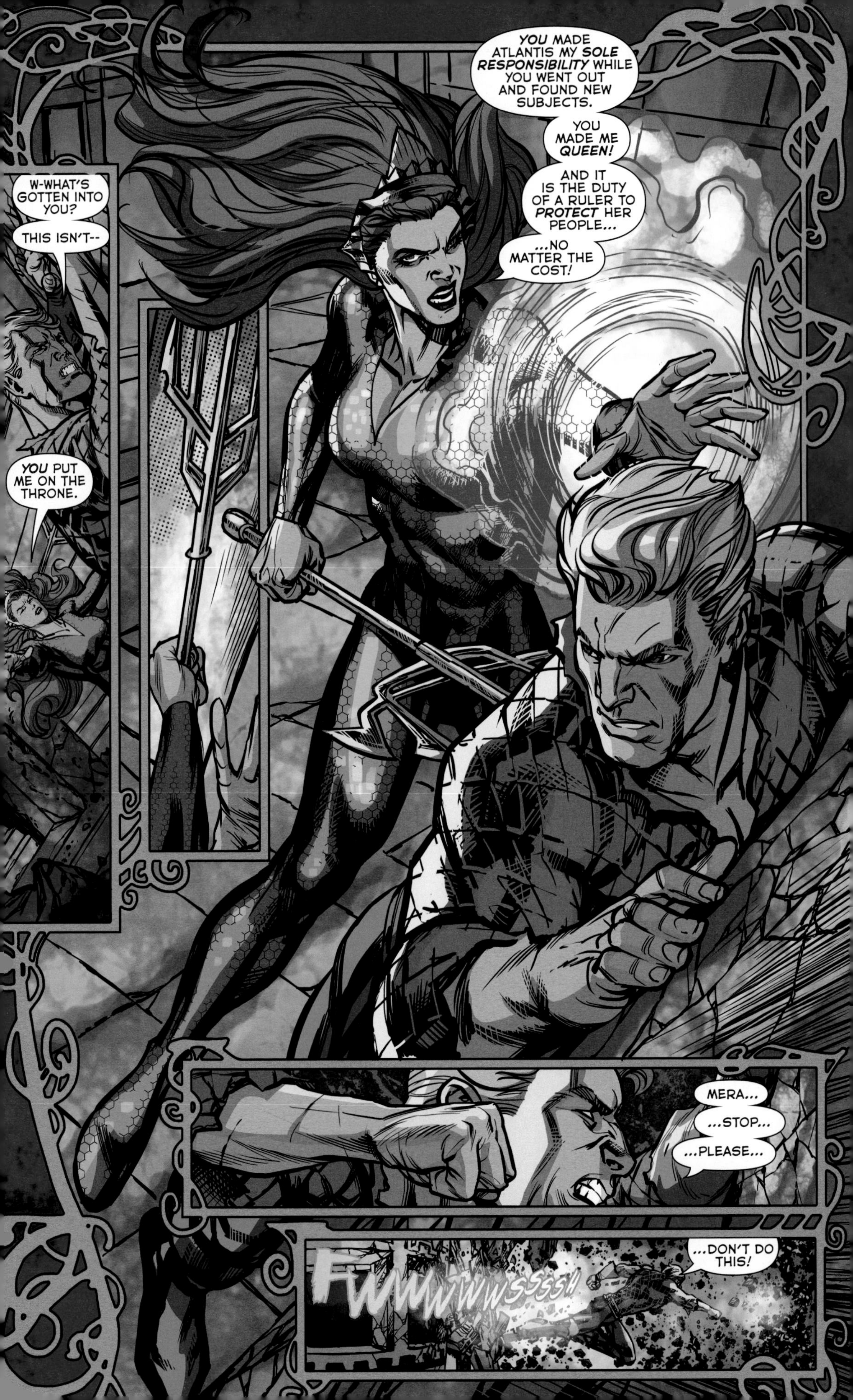
YOU MADE ATLANTIS MY SOLE RESPONSIBILITY WHILE YOU WENT OUT AND FOUND NEW SUBJECTS.
YOU MADE ME QUEEN!
AND IT IS THE DUTY OF A RULER TO PROTECT HER PEOPLE...
...NO MATTER THE COST!
W-WHAT'S GOTTEN INTO YOU?
THIS ISN'T--
YOU PUT ME ON THE THRONE.
MERA...
...STOP...
...PLEASE...
...DON'T DO THIS!
FWWWWWSSSSH

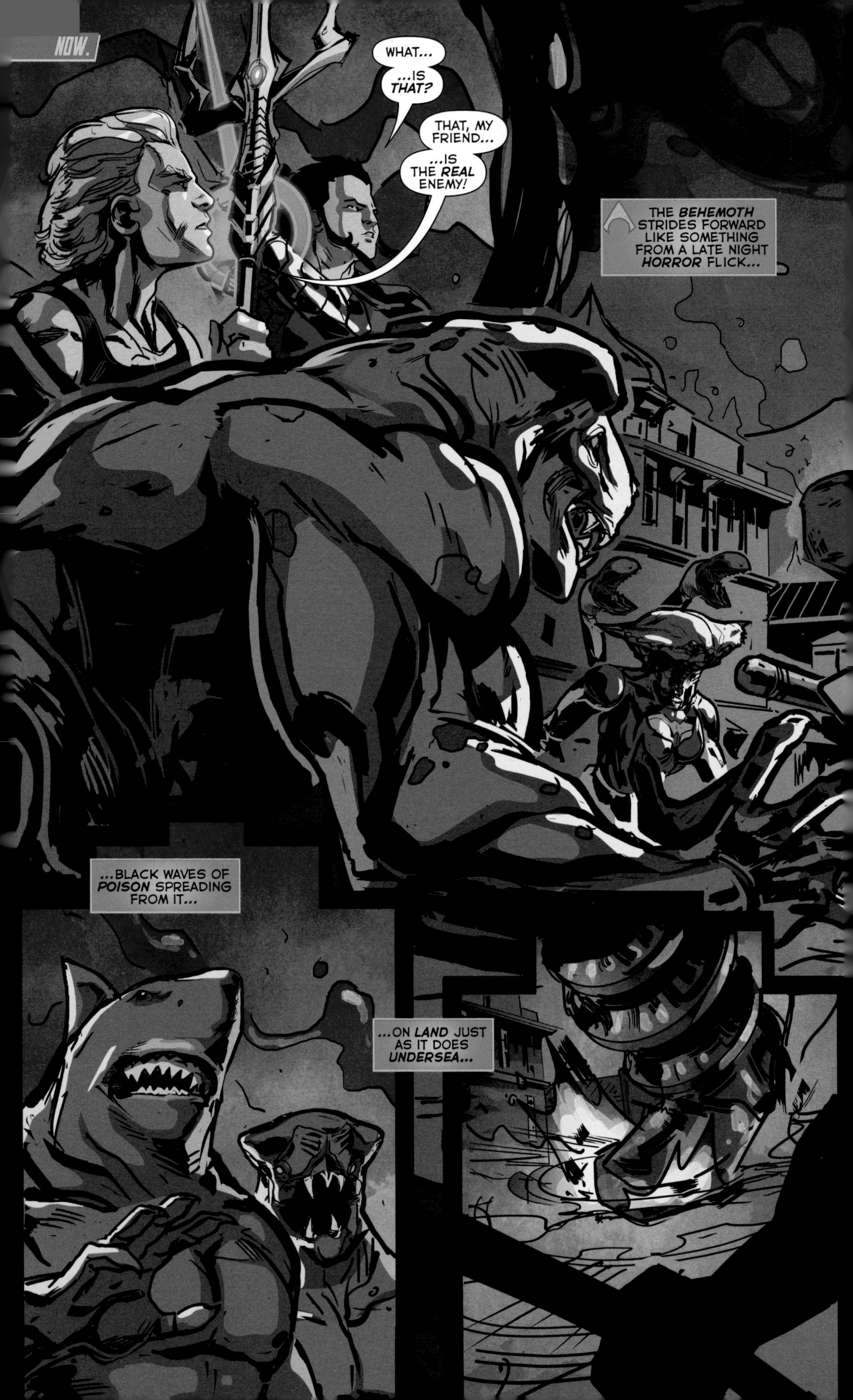
NOW.
WHAT...
...IS THAT?
THAT, MY FRIEND...
...IS THE REAL ENEMY!
THE BEHEMOTH STRIDES FORWARD LIKE SOMETHING FROM A LATE NIGHT HORROR FLICK...
...BLACK WAVES OF POISON SPREADING FROM IT...
...ON LAND JUST AS IT DOES UNDERSEA...

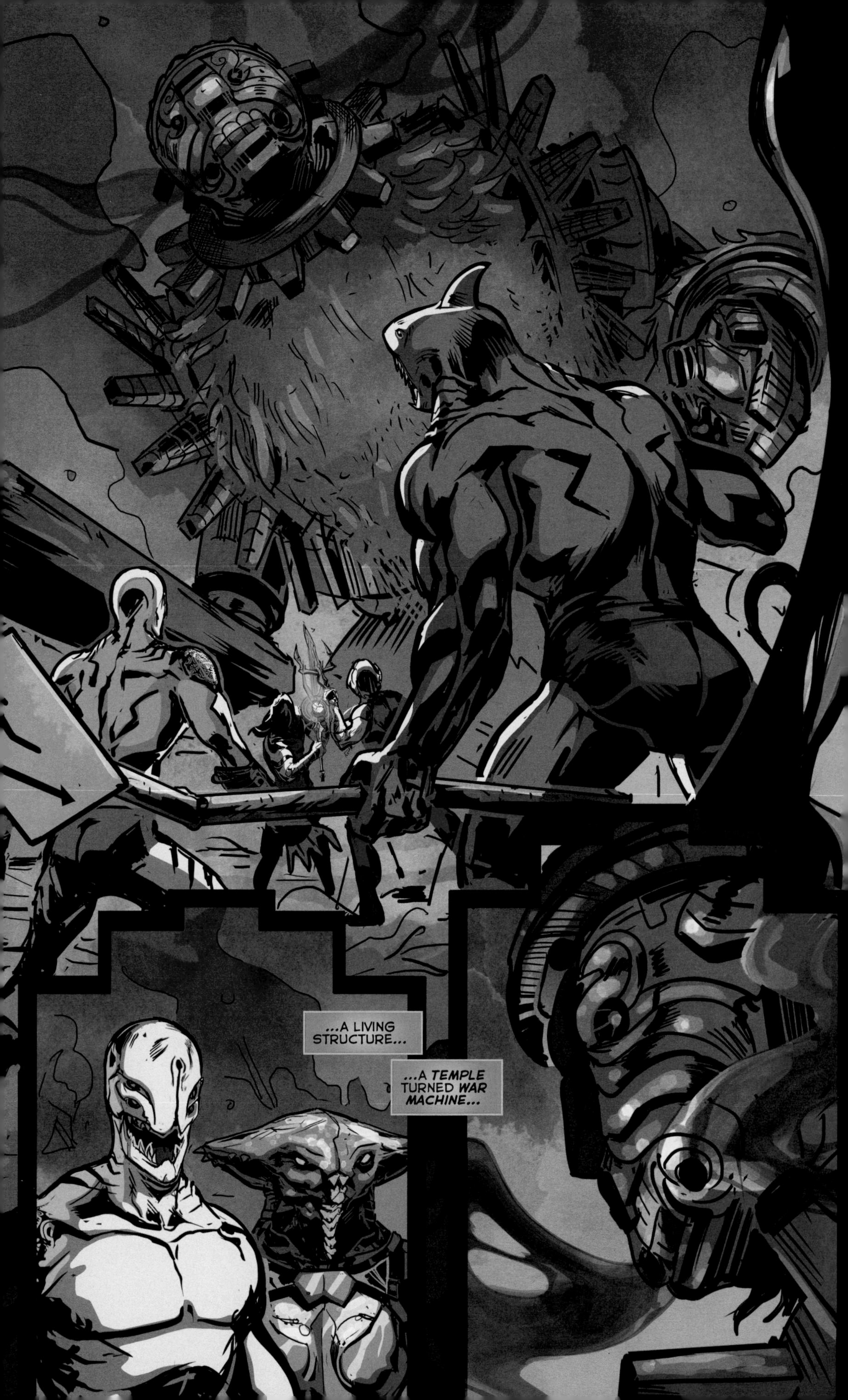
...A LIVING STRUCTURE...
...A TEMPLE TURNED WAR MACHINE...

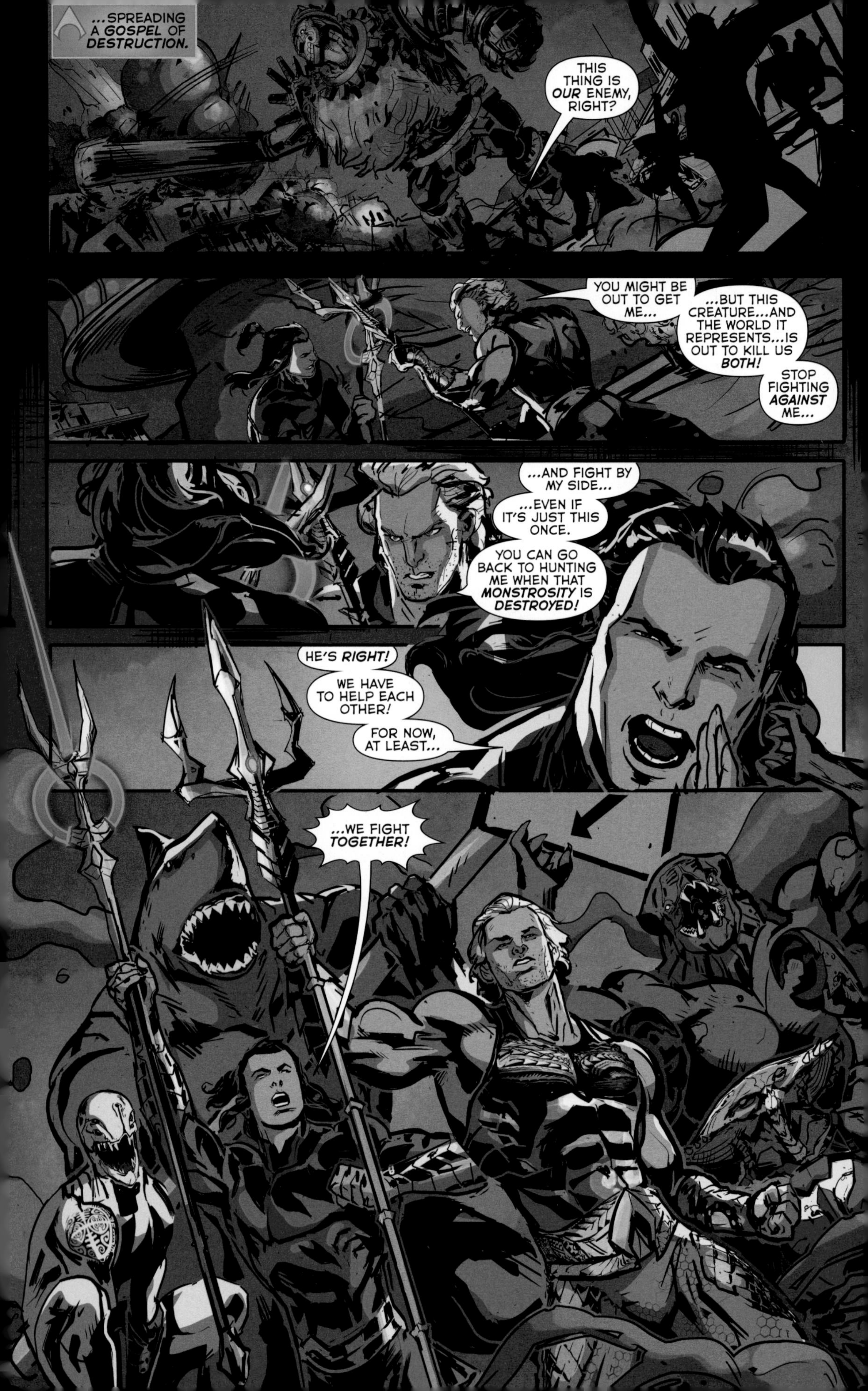

...SPREADING A GOSPEL OF DESTRUCTION.
THIS THING IS OUR ENEMY, RIGHT?
YOU MIGHT BE OUT TO GET ME...
...BUT THIS CREATURE...AND THE WORLD IT REPRESENTS...IS OUT TO KILL US BOTH!
STOP FIGHTING AGAINST ME...
...AND FIGHT BY MY SIDE...
...EVEN IF IT'S JUST THIS ONCE.
YOU CAN GO BACK TO HUNTING ME WHEN THAT MONSTROSITY IS DESTROYED!
HE'S RIGHT!
WE HAVE TO HELP EACH OTHER!
FOR NOW, AT LEAST...
...WE FIGHT TOGETHER!

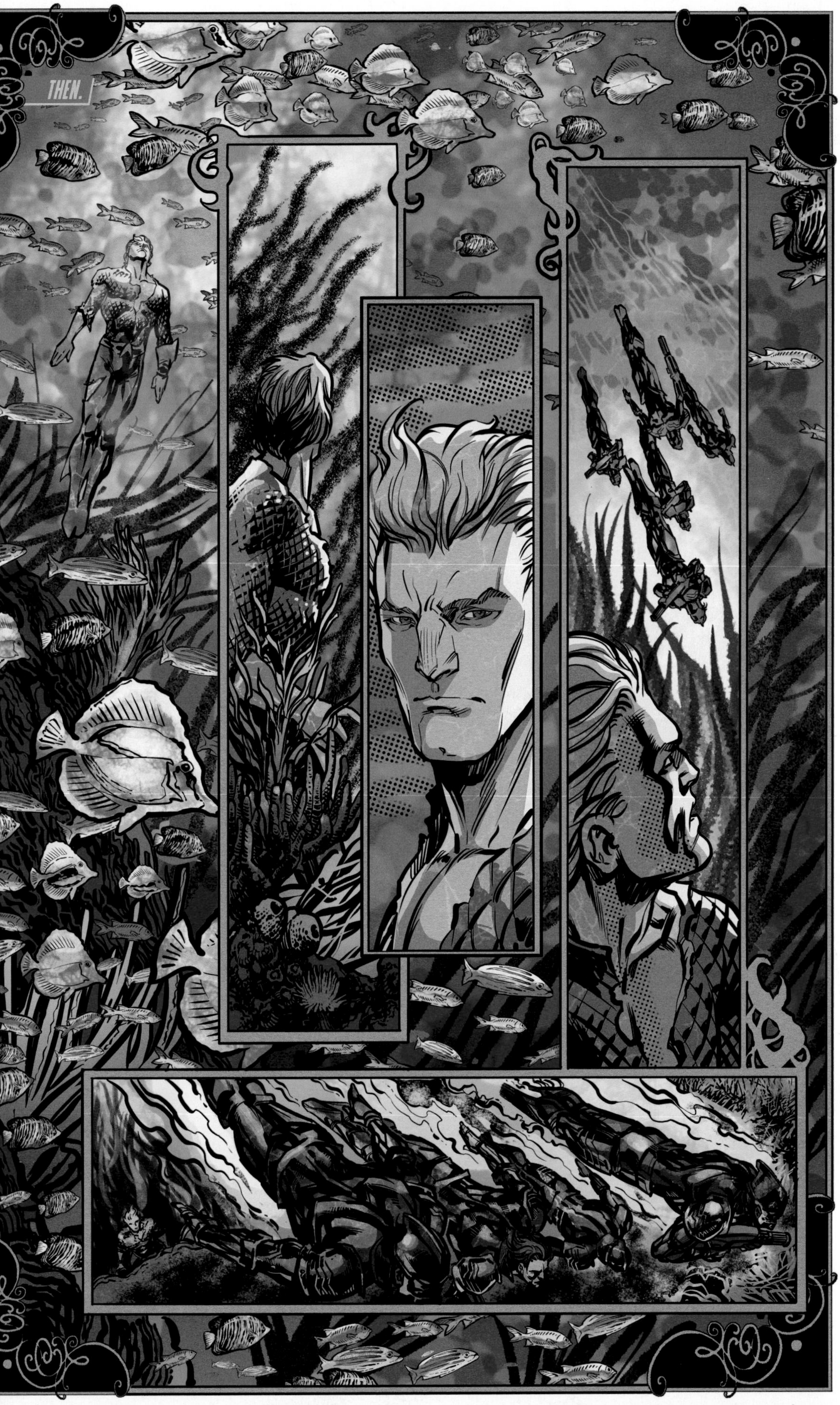
THEN.

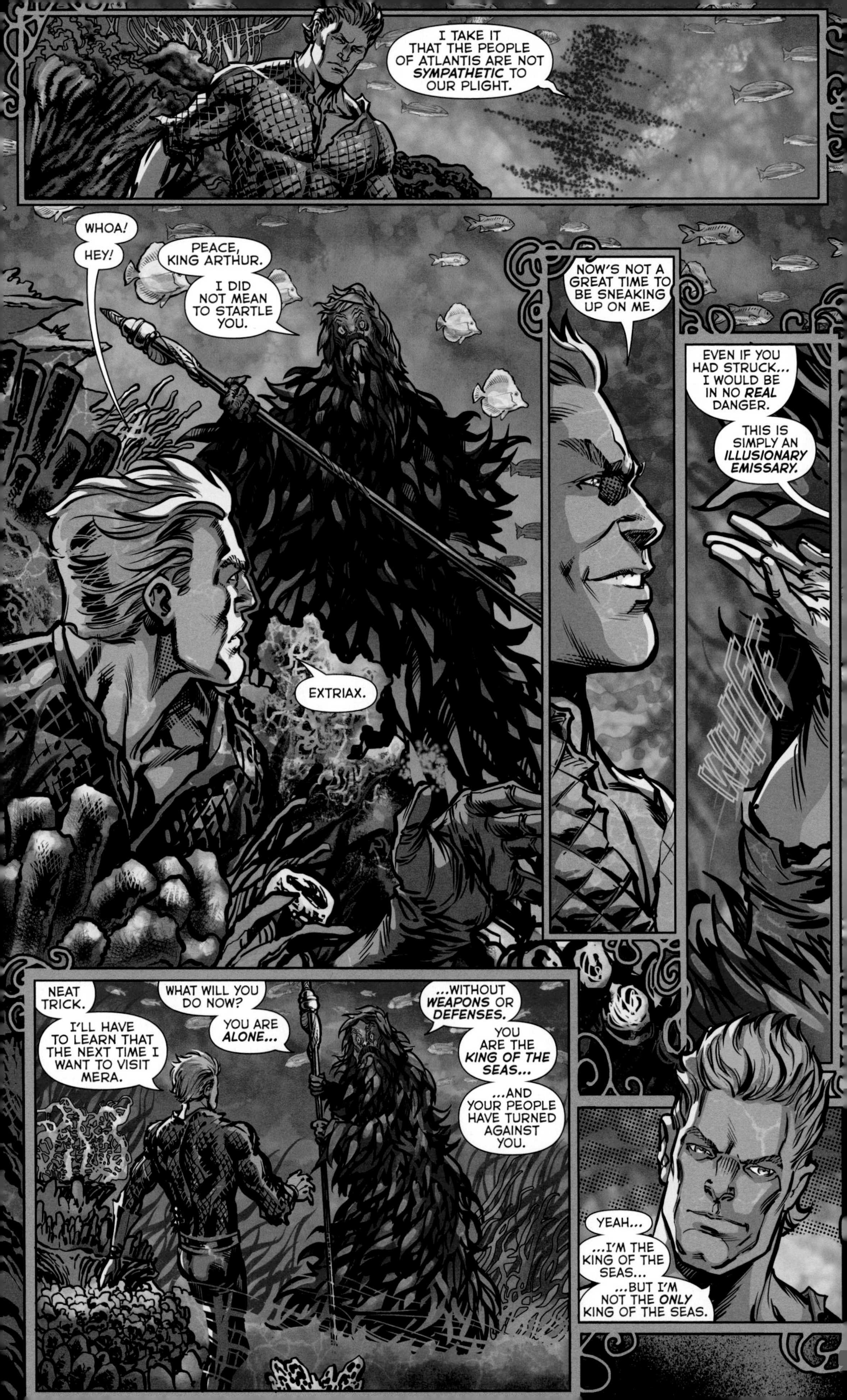

I TAKE IT THAT THE PEOPLE OF ATLANTIS ARE NOT *SYMPATHETIC* TO OUR PLIGHT.
WHOA!
HEY!
PEACE, KING ARTHUR.
I DID NOT MEAN TO STARTLE YOU.
EXTRIAX.
NOW'S NOT A GREAT TIME TO BE SNEAKING UP ON ME.
EVEN IF YOU HAD STRUCK... I WOULD BE IN NO *REAL* DANGER.
THIS IS SIMPLY AN *ILLUSIONARY EMISSARY.*
WHFF
NEAT TRICK.
I'LL HAVE TO LEARN THAT THE NEXT TIME I WANT TO VISIT MERA.
WHAT WILL YOU DO NOW?
YOU ARE *ALONE...*
...WITHOUT *WEAPONS* OR *DEFENSES.*
YOU ARE THE *KING OF THE SEAS...*
...AND YOUR PEOPLE HAVE TURNED AGAINST YOU.
YEAH...
...I'M THE KING OF THE SEAS...
...BUT I'M NOT THE *ONLY* KING OF THE SEAS.

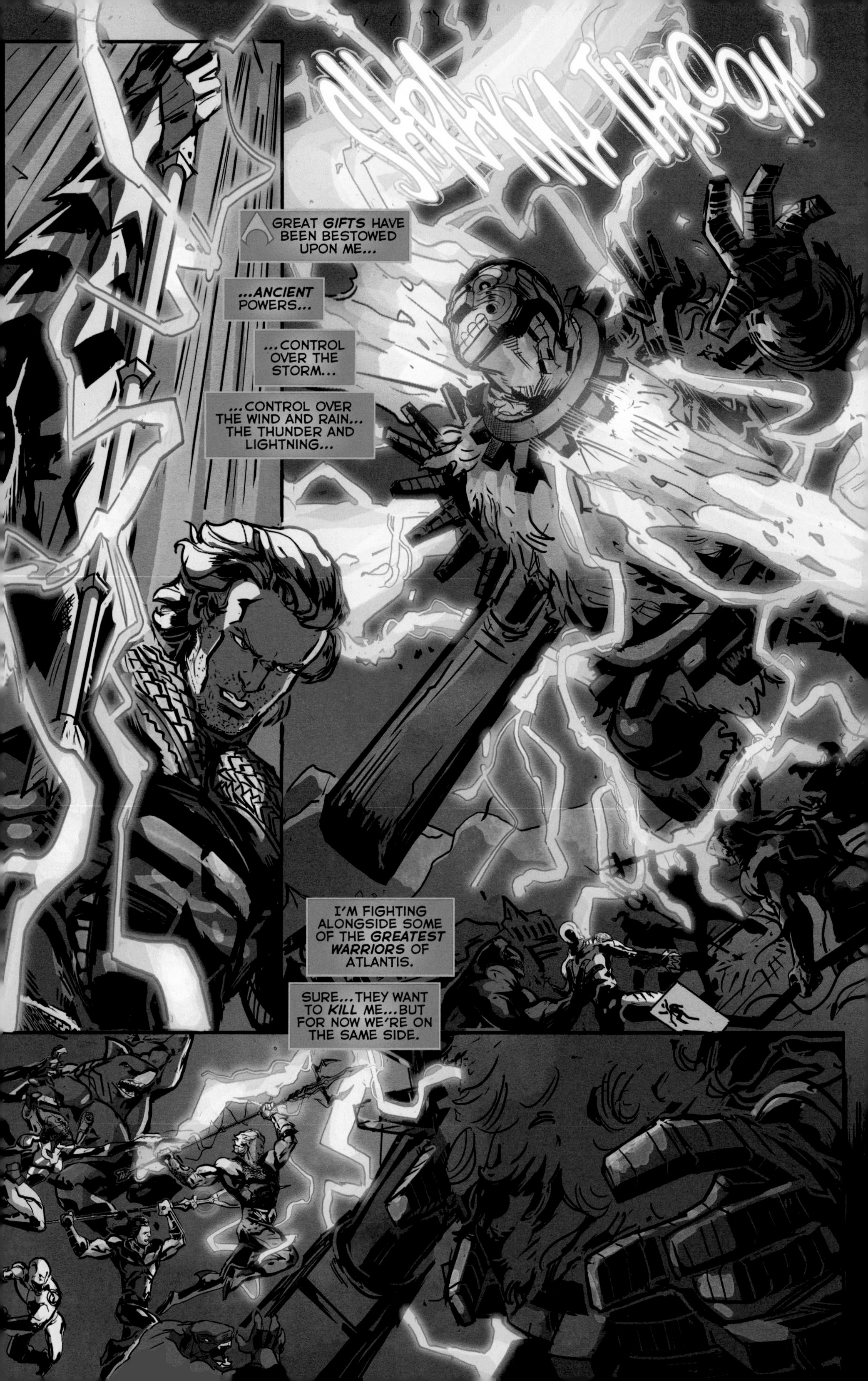
GREAT *GIFTS* HAVE BEEN BESTOWED UPON ME...
...*ANCIENT* POWERS...
...CONTROL OVER THE STORM...
...CONTROL OVER THE WIND AND RAIN... THE THUNDER AND LIGHTNING...
I'M FIGHTING ALONGSIDE SOME OF THE *GREATEST WARRIORS* OF ATLANTIS.
SURE...THEY WANT TO *KILL ME*...BUT FOR NOW WE'RE ON THE SAME SIDE.

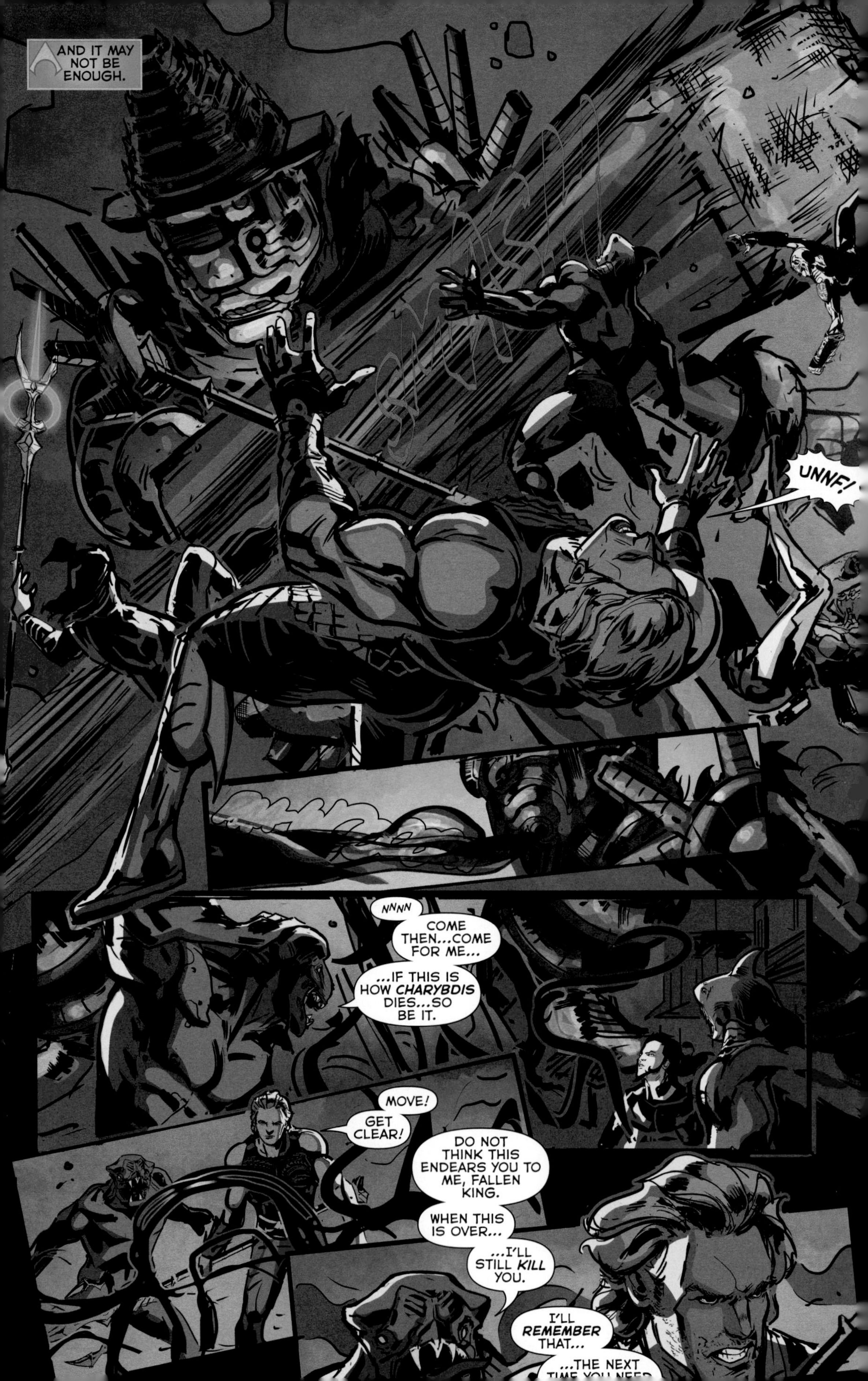
AND IT MAY NOT BE ENOUGH.
UNNF!
NNNN
COME THEN...COME FOR ME...
...IF THIS IS HOW CHARYBDIS DIES...SO BE IT.
MOVE!
GET CLEAR!
DO NOT THINK THIS ENDEARS YOU TO ME, FALLEN KING.
WHEN THIS IS OVER...
...I'LL STILL KILL YOU.
I'LL REMEMBER THAT...
...THE NEXT

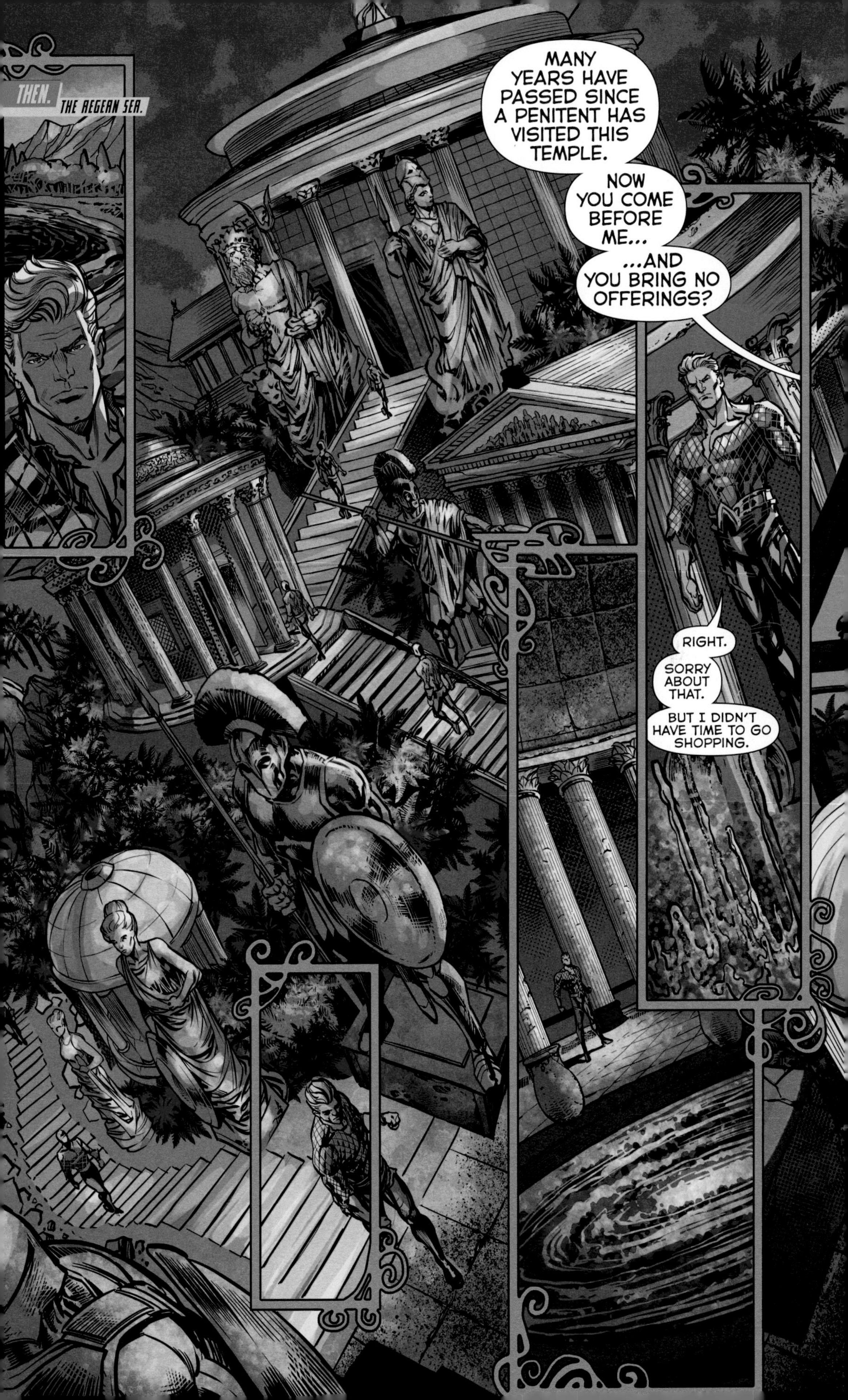
THEN. THE AEGEAN SEA.
MANY YEARS HAVE PASSED SINCE A PENITENT HAS VISITED THIS TEMPLE.
NOW YOU COME BEFORE ME...
...AND YOU BRING NO OFFERINGS?
RIGHT.
SORRY ABOUT THAT.
BUT I DIDN'T HAVE TIME TO GO SHOPPING.

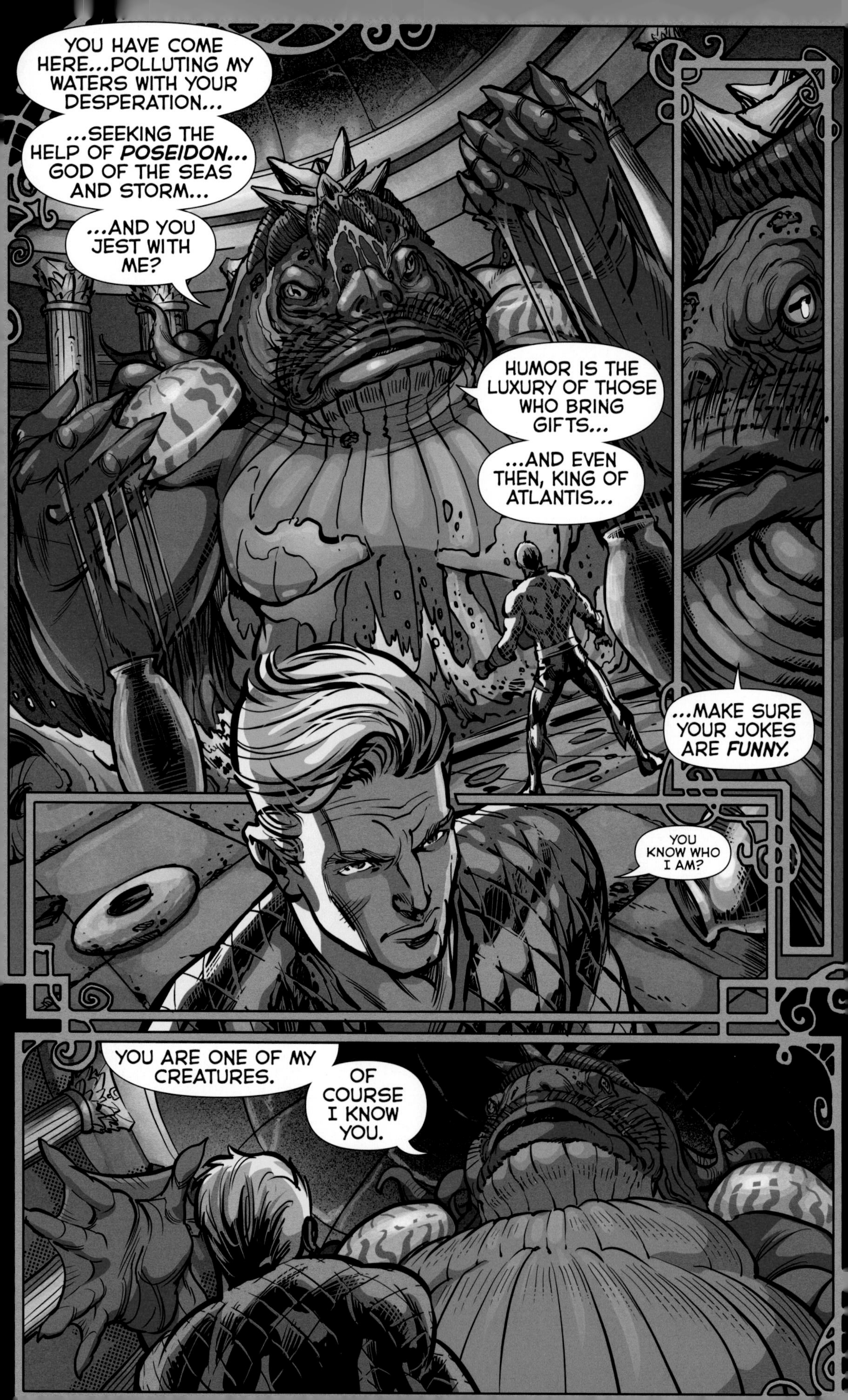
YOU HAVE COME HERE...POLLUTING MY WATERS WITH YOUR DESPERATION...
...SEEKING THE HELP OF POSEIDON... GOD OF THE SEAS AND STORM...
...AND YOU JEST WITH ME?
HUMOR IS THE LUXURY OF THOSE WHO BRING GIFTS...
...AND EVEN THEN, KING OF ATLANTIS...
...MAKE SURE YOUR JOKES ARE FUNNY.
YOU KNOW WHO I AM?
YOU ARE ONE OF MY CREATURES.
OF COURSE I KNOW YOU.

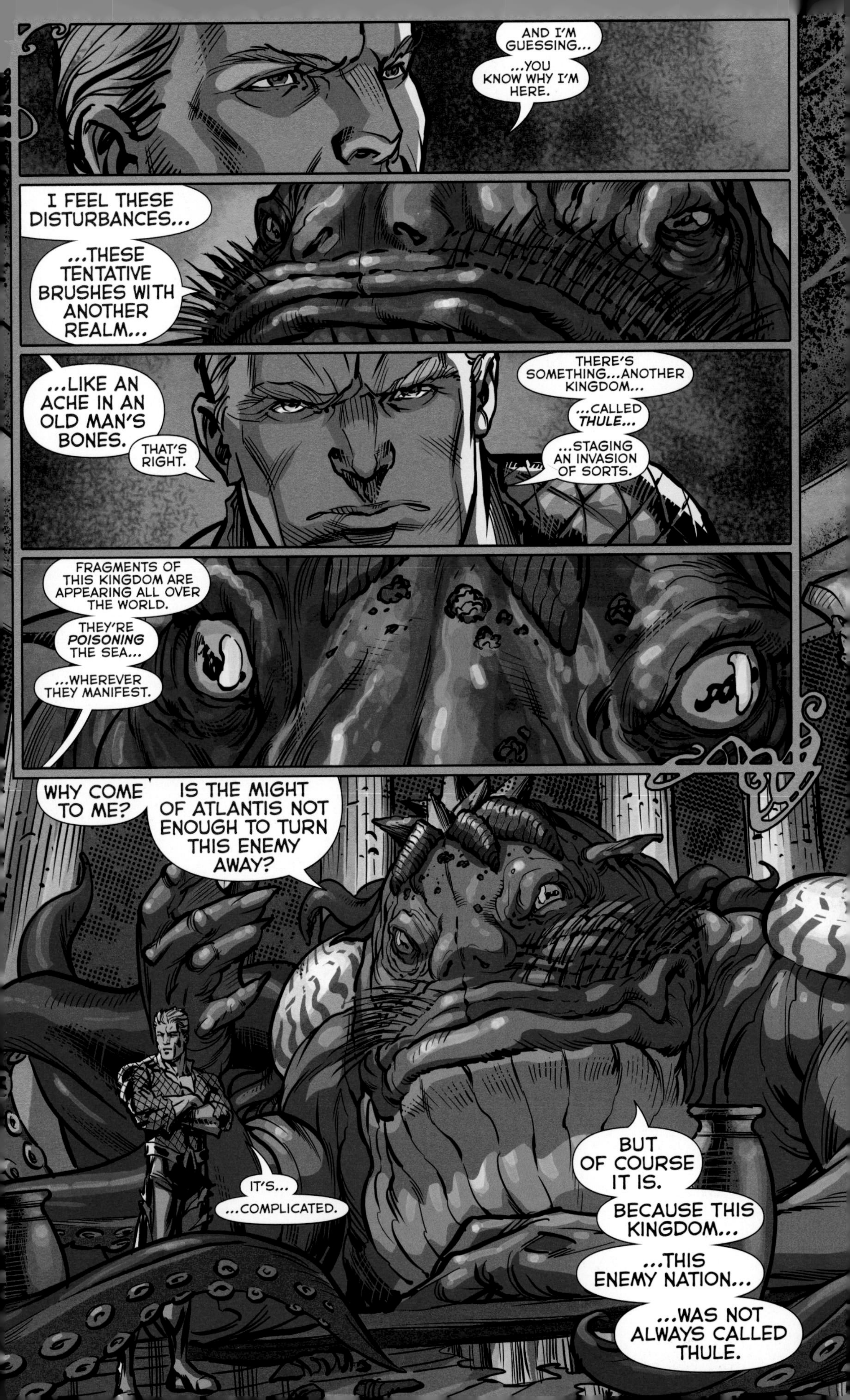
AND I'M GUESSING...
...YOU KNOW WHY I'M HERE.
I FEEL THESE DISTURBANCES...
...THESE TENTATIVE BRUSHES WITH ANOTHER REALM...
...LIKE AN ACHE IN AN OLD MAN'S BONES.
THAT'S RIGHT.
THERE'S SOMETHING...ANOTHER KINGDOM...
...CALLED *THULE*...
...STAGING AN INVASION OF SORTS.
FRAGMENTS OF THIS KINGDOM ARE APPEARING ALL OVER THE WORLD.
THEY'RE *POISONING* THE SEA...
...WHEREVER THEY MANIFEST.
WHY COME TO ME?
IS THE MIGHT OF ATLANTIS NOT ENOUGH TO TURN THIS ENEMY AWAY?
IT'S...
...COMPLICATED.
BUT OF COURSE IT IS.
BECAUSE THIS KINGDOM...
...THIS ENEMY NATION...
...WAS NOT ALWAYS CALLED THULE.

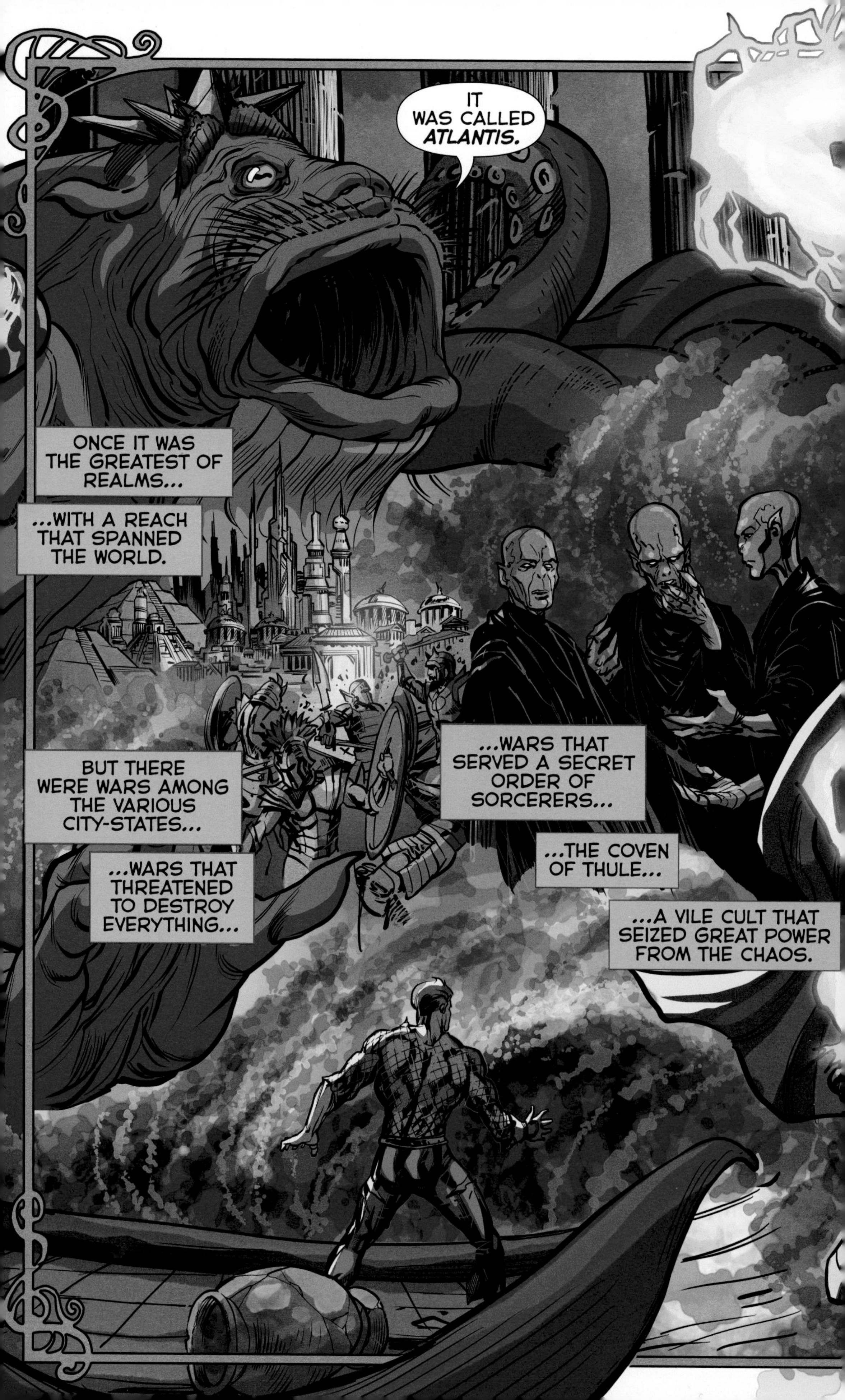
IT WAS CALLED *ATLANTIS.*
ONCE IT WAS THE GREATEST OF REALMS...
...WITH A REACH THAT SPANNED THE WORLD.
BUT THERE WERE WARS AMONG THE VARIOUS CITY-STATES...
...WARS THAT THREATENED TO DESTROY EVERYTHING...
...WARS THAT SERVED A SECRET ORDER OF SORCERERS...
...THE COVEN OF THULE...
...A VILE CULT THAT SEIZED GREAT POWER FROM THE CHAOS.

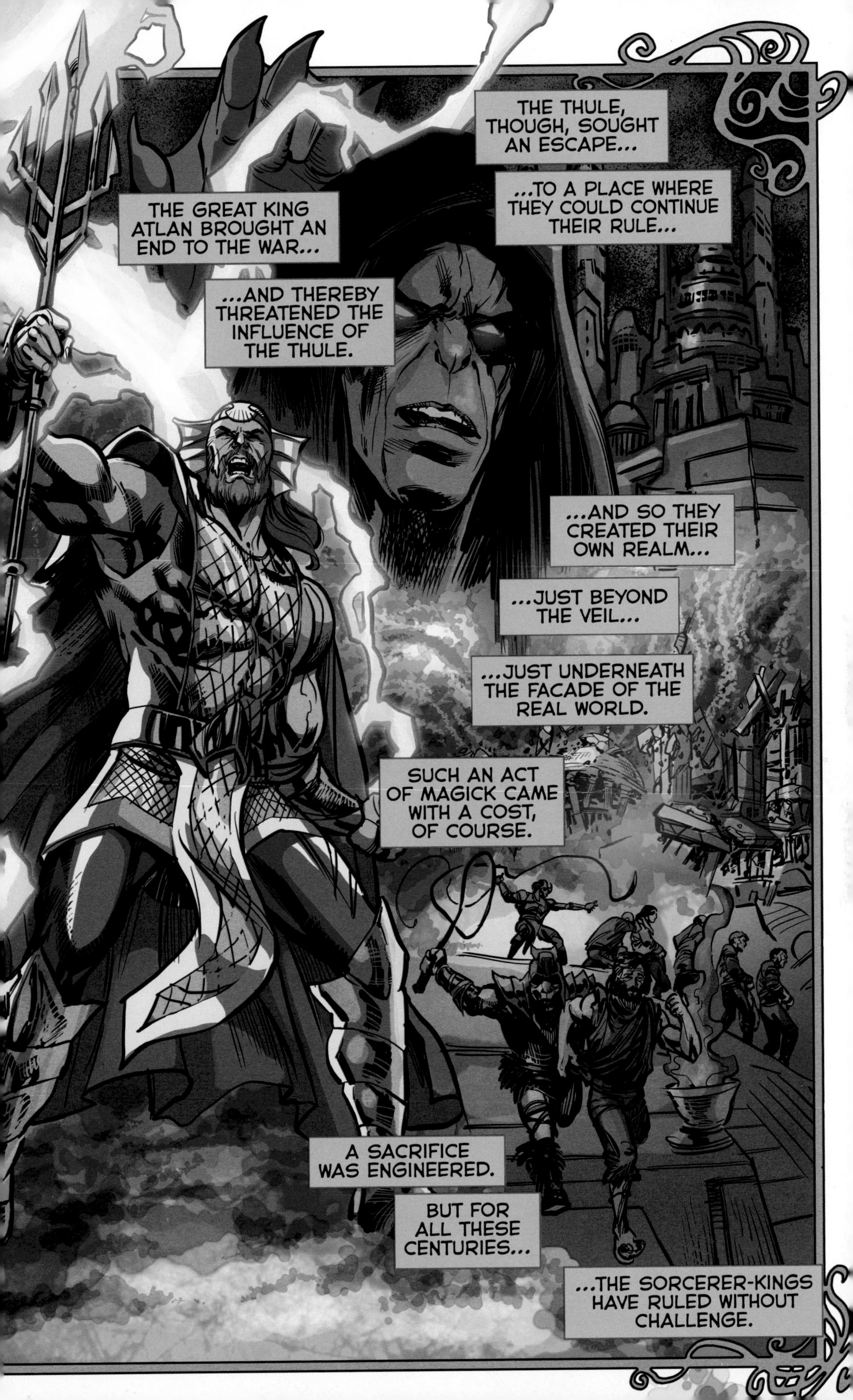
THE GREAT KING ATLAN BROUGHT AN END TO THE WAR...
...AND THEREBY THREATENED THE INFLUENCE OF THE THULE.
THE THULE, THOUGH, SOUGHT AN ESCAPE...
...TO A PLACE WHERE THEY COULD CONTINUE THEIR RULE...
...AND SO THEY CREATED THEIR OWN REALM...
...JUST BEYOND THE VEIL...
...JUST UNDERNEATH THE FACADE OF THE REAL WORLD.
SUCH AN ACT OF MAGICK CAME WITH A COST, OF COURSE.
A SACRIFICE WAS ENGINEERED.
BUT FOR ALL THESE CENTURIES...
...THE SORCERER-KINGS HAVE RULED WITHOUT CHALLENGE.

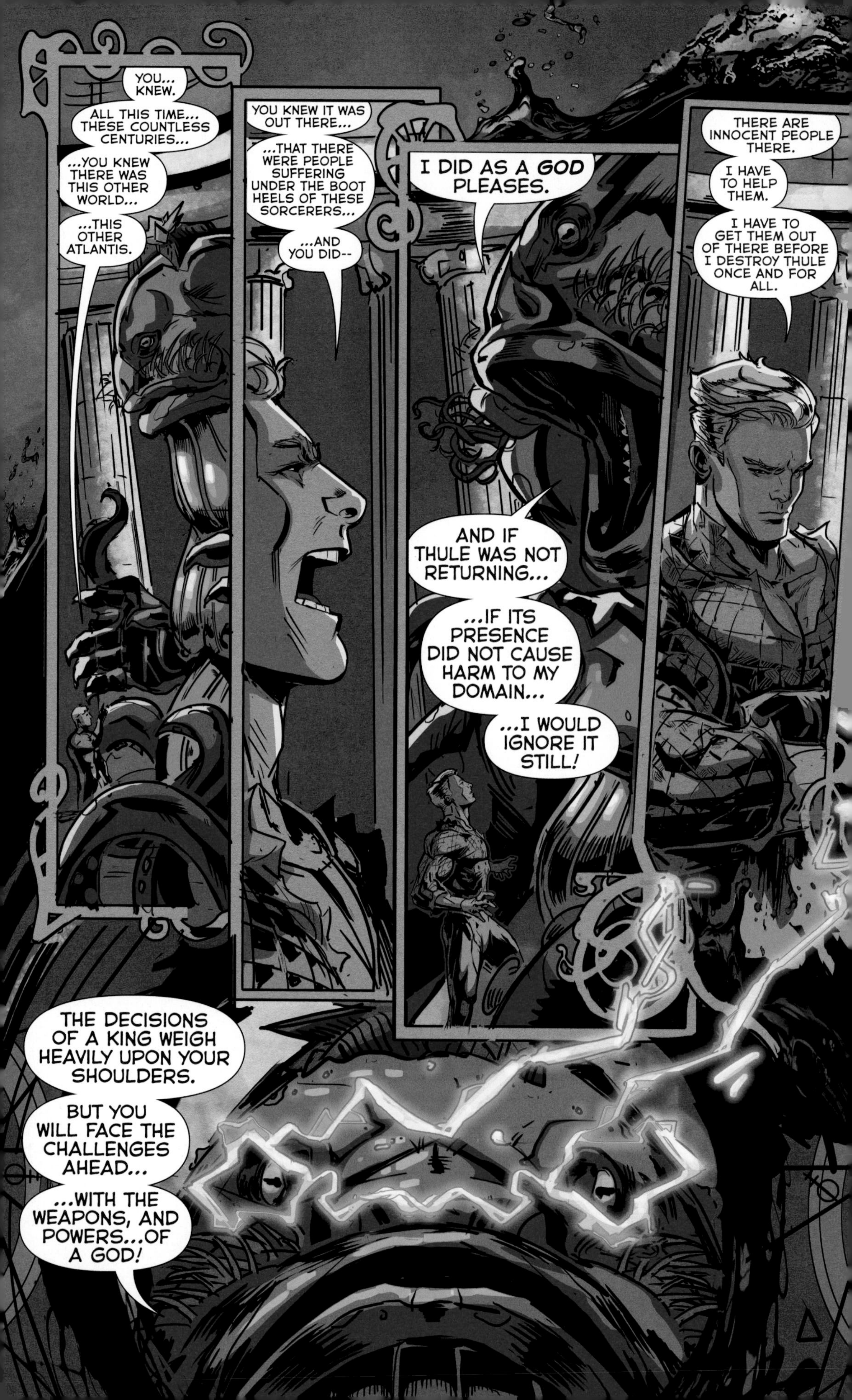

YOU... KNEW.
ALL THIS TIME... THESE COUNTLESS CENTURIES...
...YOU KNEW THERE WAS THIS OTHER WORLD...
...THIS OTHER ATLANTIS.
YOU KNEW IT WAS OUT THERE...
...THAT THERE WERE PEOPLE SUFFERING UNDER THE BOOT HEELS OF THESE SORCERERS...
...AND YOU DID--
I DID AS A GOD PLEASES.
AND IF THULE WAS NOT RETURNING...
...IF ITS PRESENCE DID NOT CAUSE HARM TO MY DOMAIN...
...I WOULD IGNORE IT STILL!
THERE ARE INNOCENT PEOPLE THERE.
I HAVE TO HELP THEM.
I HAVE TO GET THEM OUT OF THERE BEFORE I DESTROY THULE ONCE AND FOR ALL.
THE DECISIONS OF A KING WEIGH HEAVILY UPON YOUR SHOULDERS.
BUT YOU WILL FACE THE CHALLENGES AHEAD...
...WITH THE WEAPONS, AND POWERS...OF A GOD!

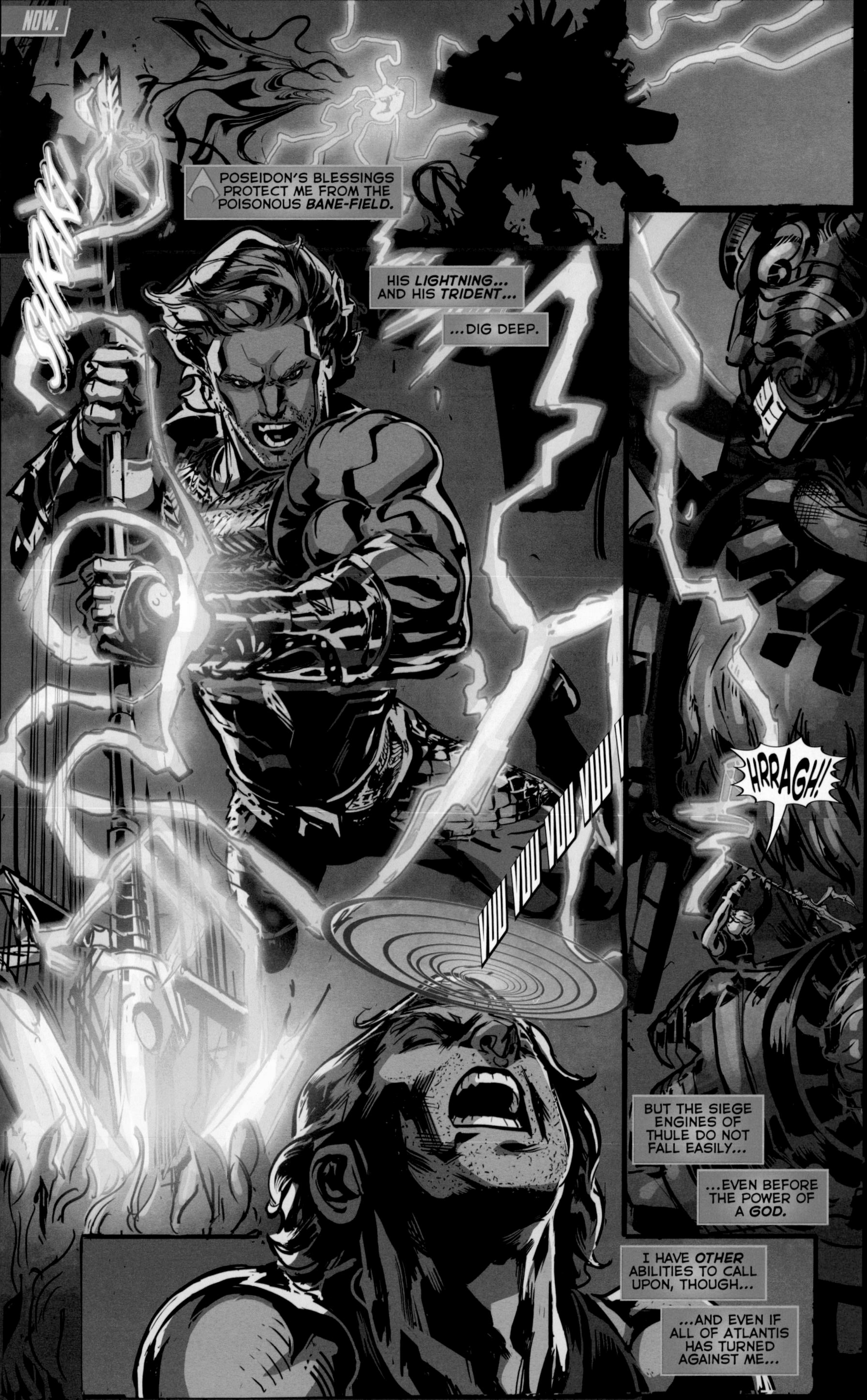
NOW.
POSEIDON'S BLESSINGS PROTECT ME FROM THE POISONOUS BANE-FIELD.
HIS LIGHTNING... AND HIS TRIDENT...
...DIG DEEP.
VUU VUU VUU VUU V
HRRAGH!
BUT THE SIEGE ENGINES OF THULE DO NOT FALL EASILY...
...EVEN BEFORE THE POWER OF A GOD.
I HAVE OTHER ABILITIES TO CALL UPON, THOUGH...
...AND EVEN IF ALL OF ATLANTIS HAS TURNED AGAINST ME...

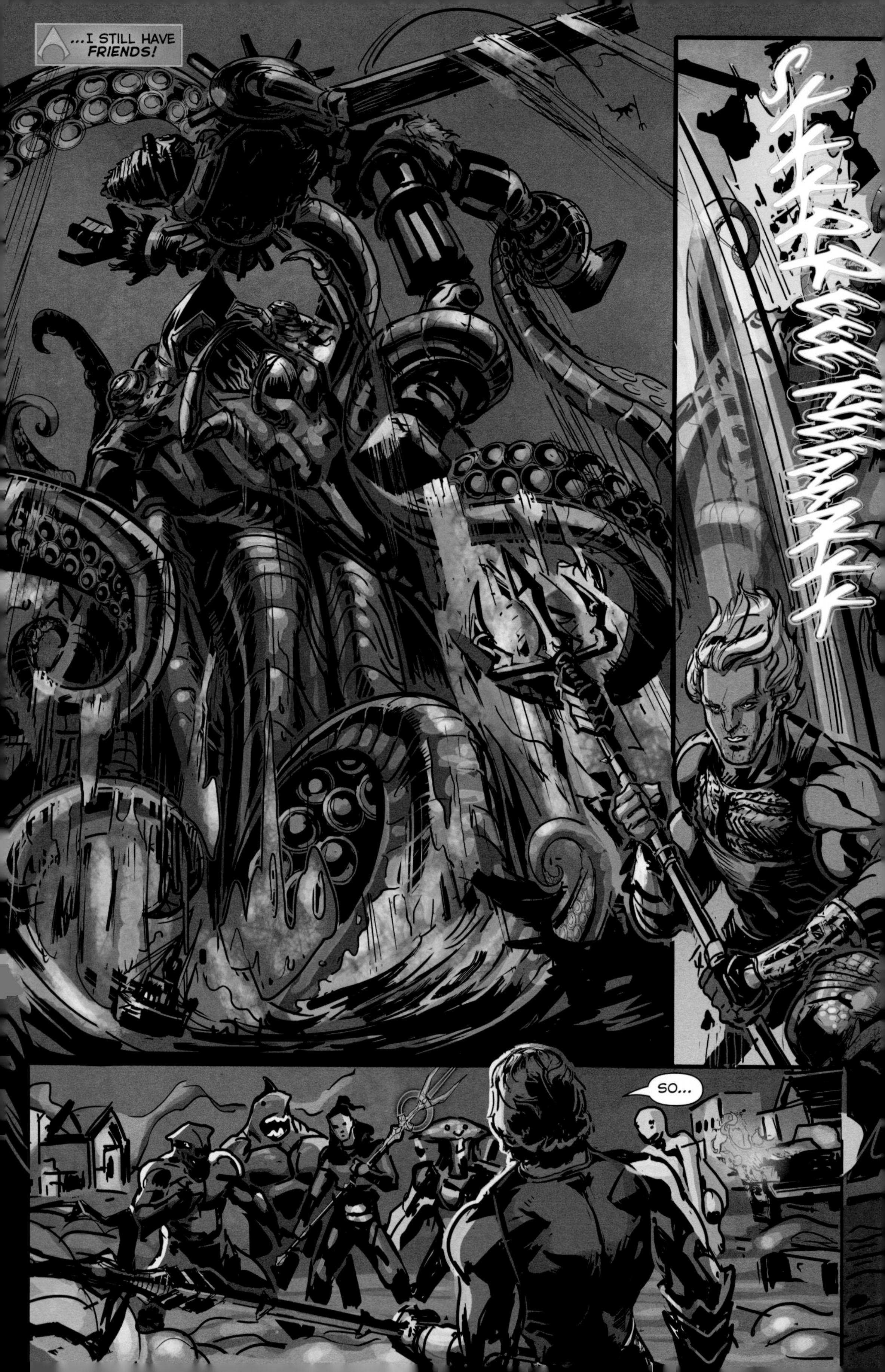
...I STILL HAVE FRIENDS!
SO...

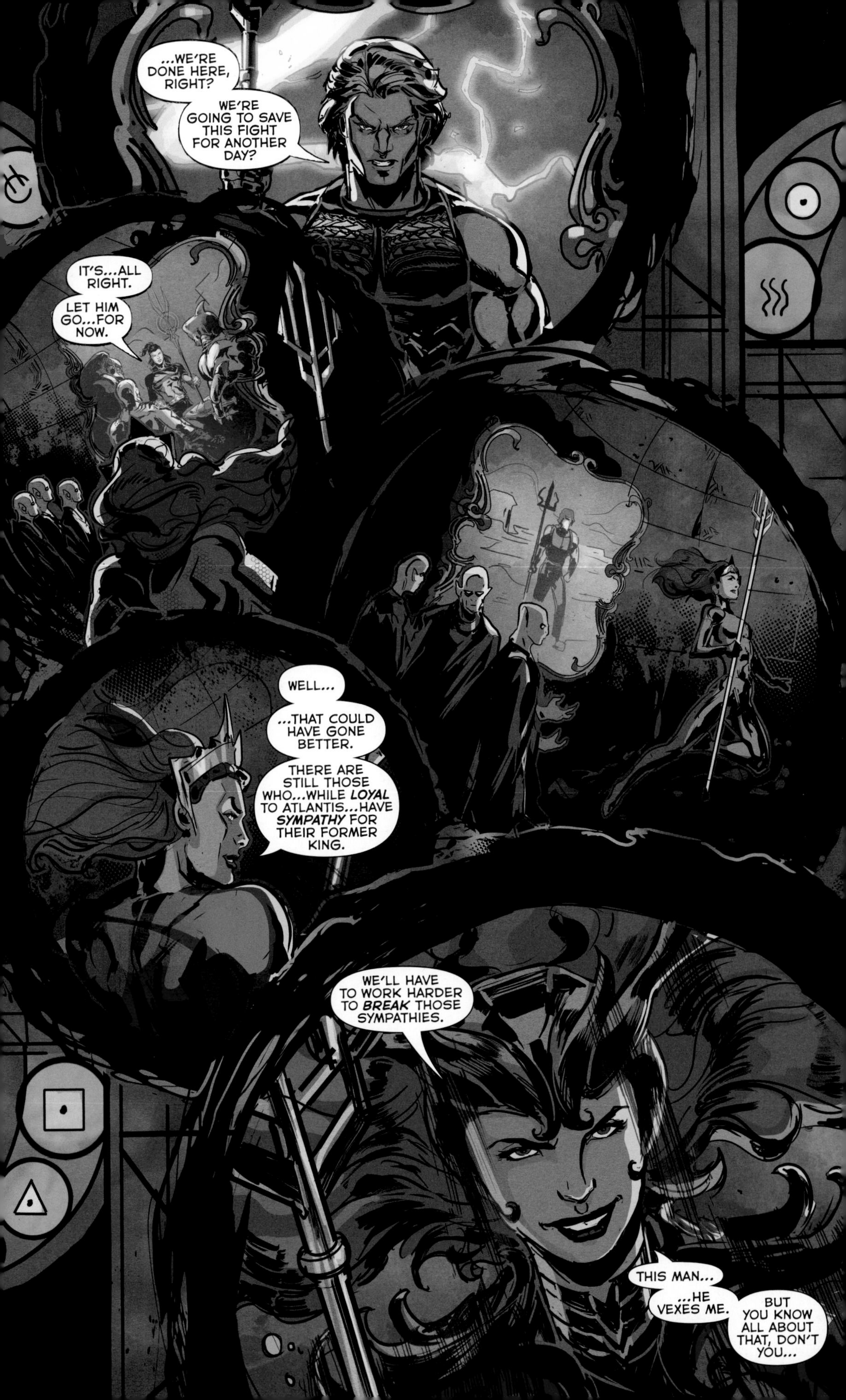
...WE'RE DONE HERE, RIGHT?
WE'RE GOING TO SAVE THIS FIGHT FOR ANOTHER DAY?
IT'S...ALL RIGHT.
LET HIM GO...FOR NOW.
WELL...
...THAT COULD HAVE GONE BETTER.
THERE ARE STILL THOSE WHO...WHILE *LOYAL* TO ATLANTIS...HAVE *SYMPATHY* FOR THEIR FORMER KING.
WE'LL HAVE TO WORK HARDER TO *BREAK* THOSE SYMPATHIES.
THIS MAN...
...HE VEXES ME.
BUT YOU KNOW ALL ABOUT THAT, DON'T YOU...

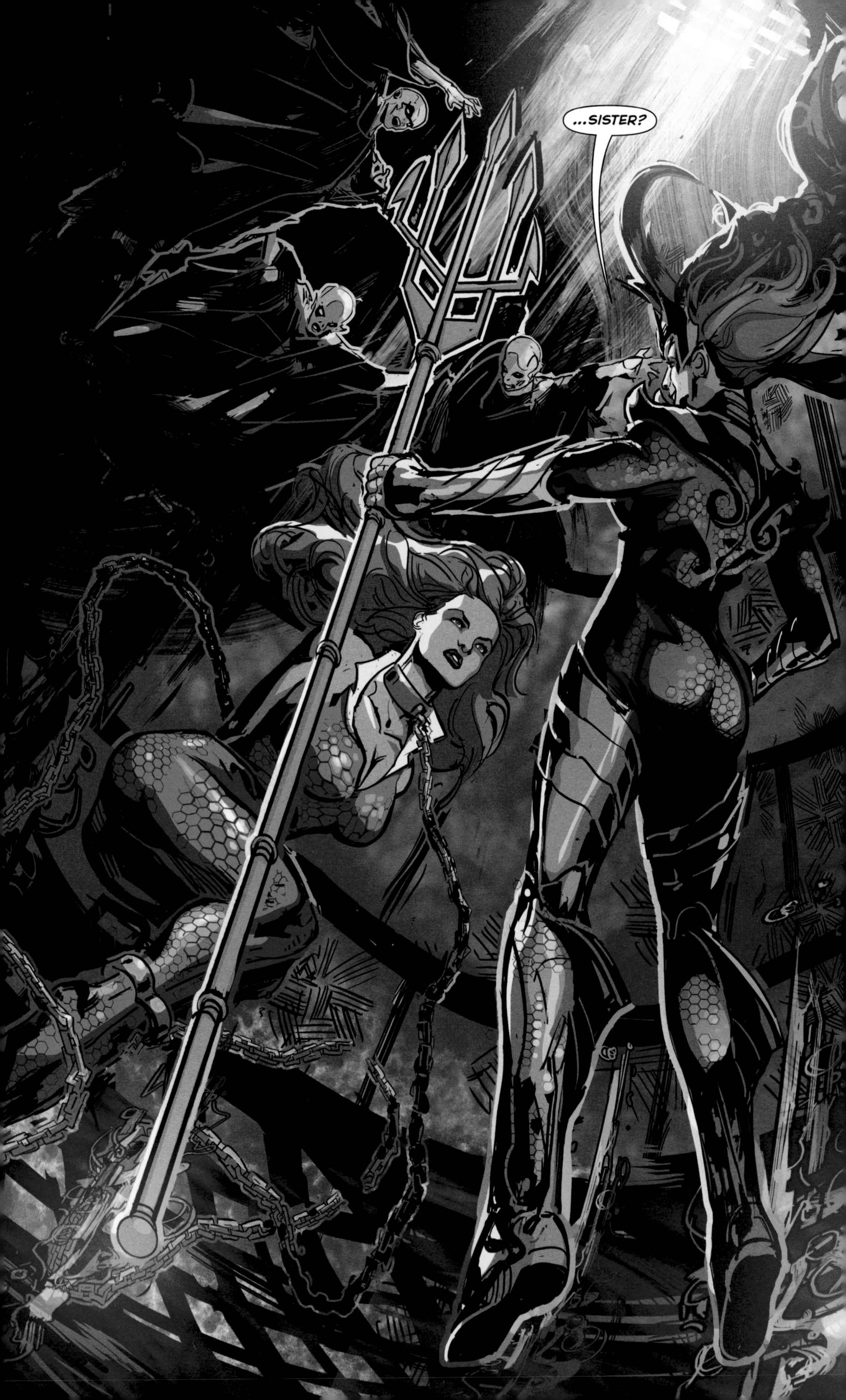
...SISTER?

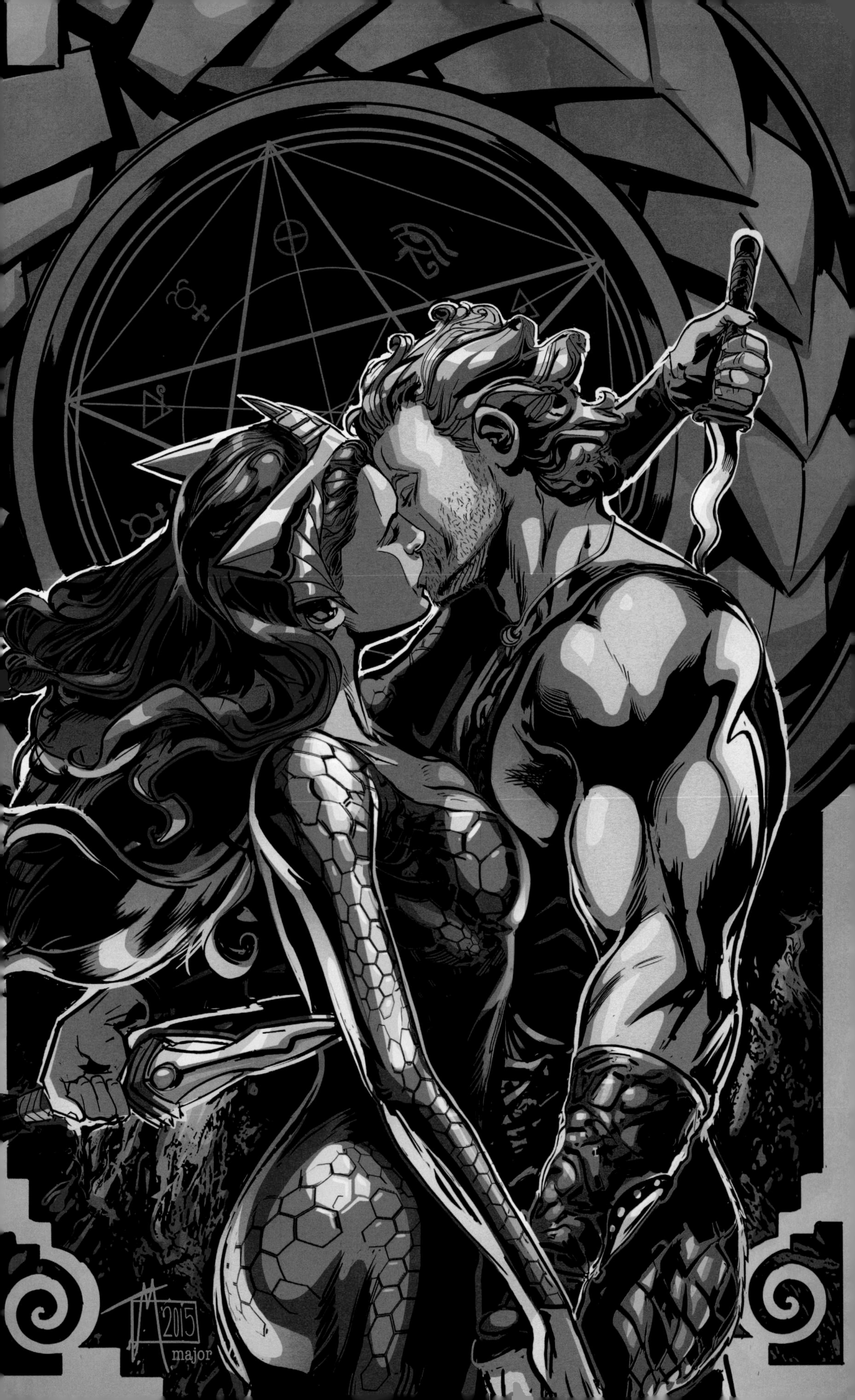
2015
major

SIREN'S CALL

CULLEN BUNN writer **ALEC MORGAN** layouts **ART THIBERT, JESUS MERINO** finishes **GUY MAJOR** colorist **TOM NAPOLITANO** letterer
TREVOR MCCARTHY and **GUY MAJOR** cover art

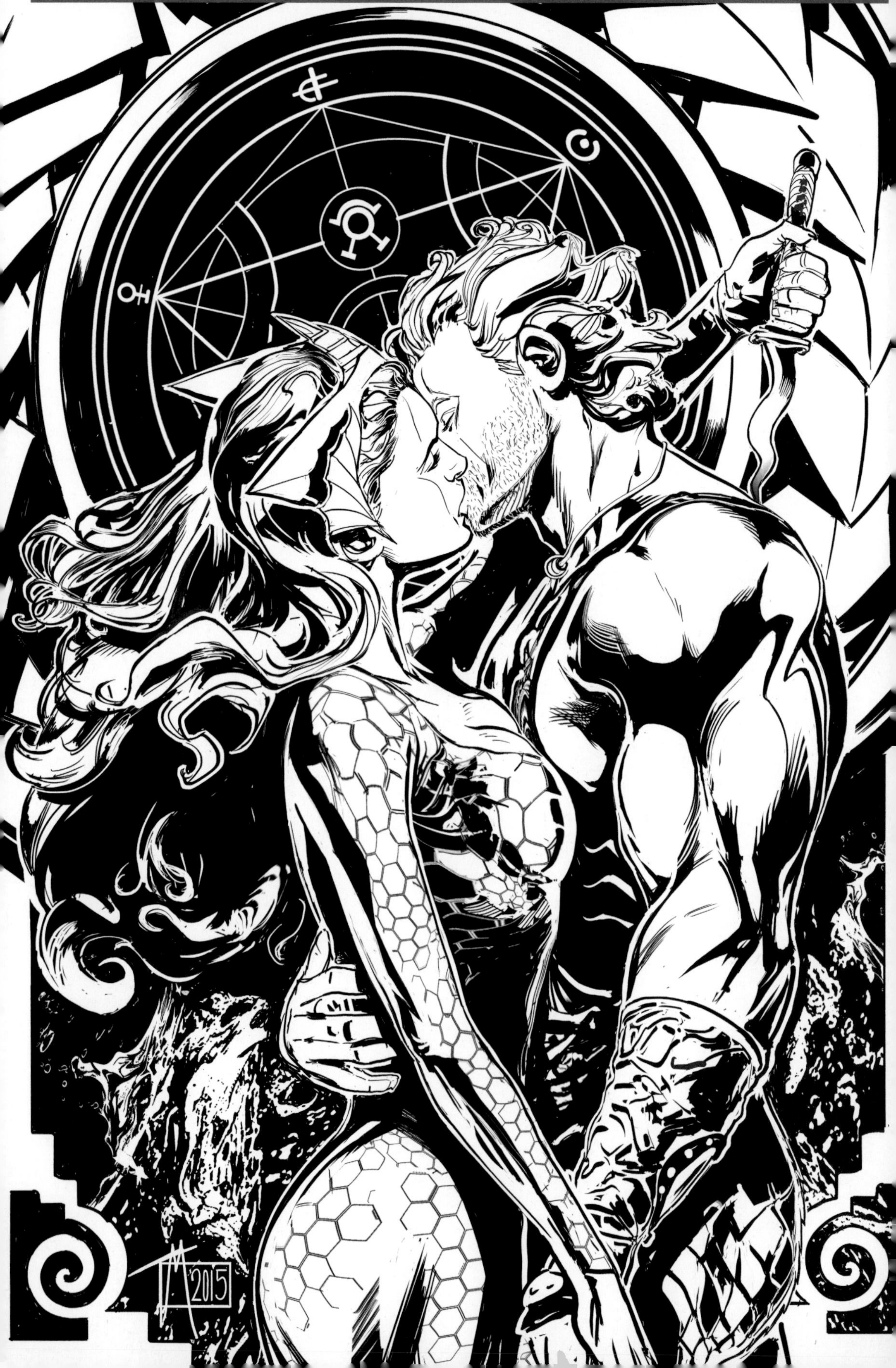
2015

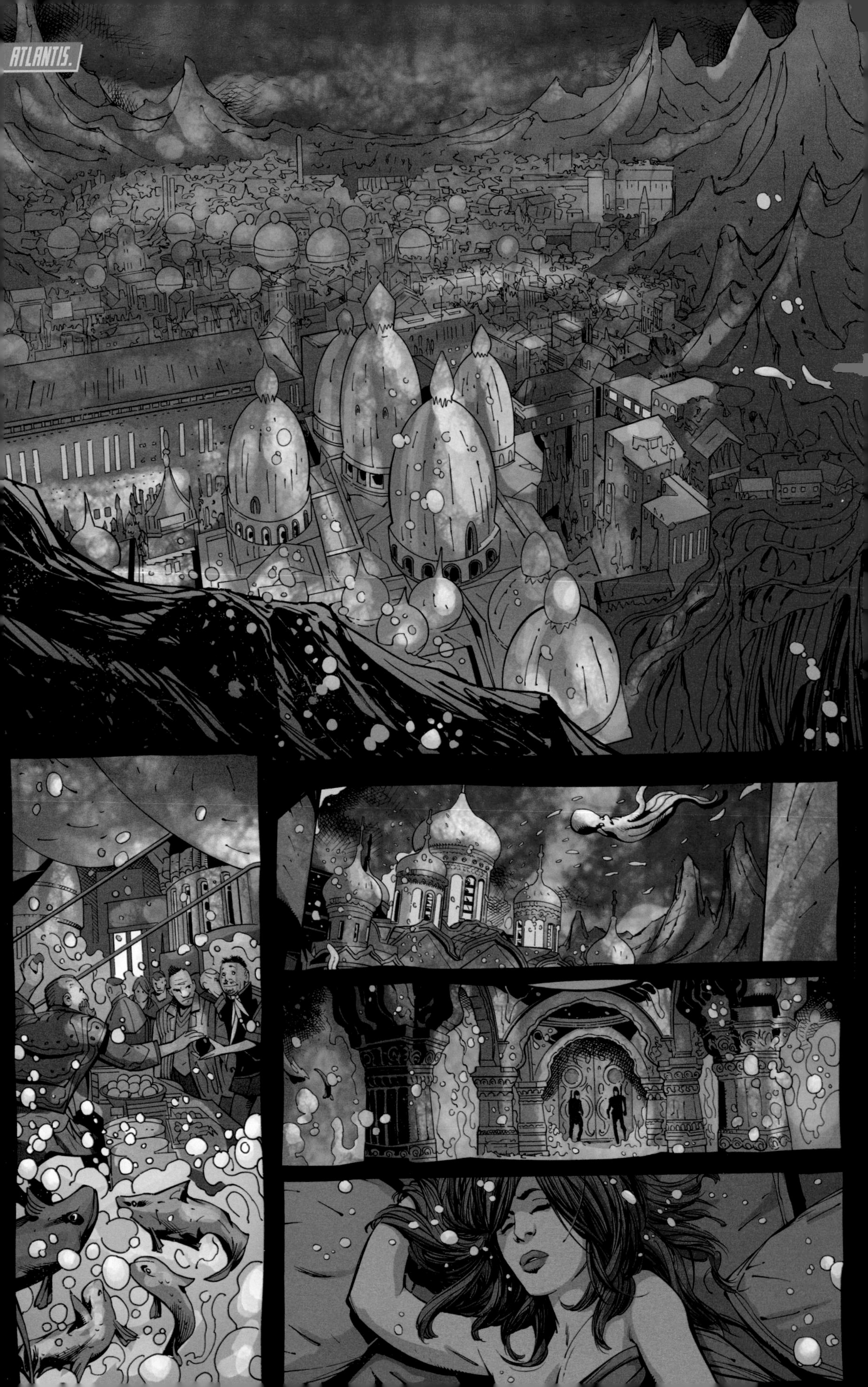
ATLANTIS.

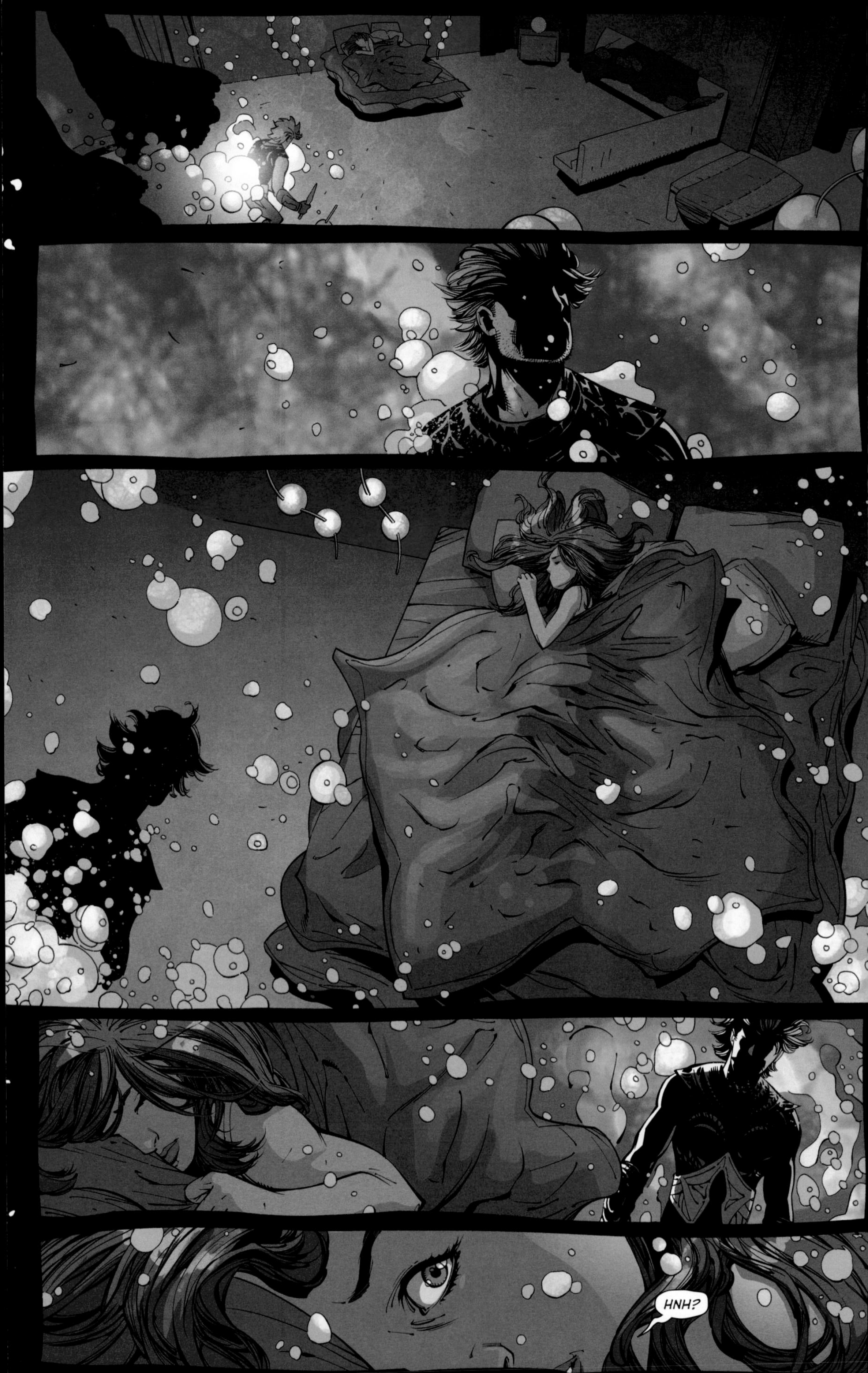
HNH?

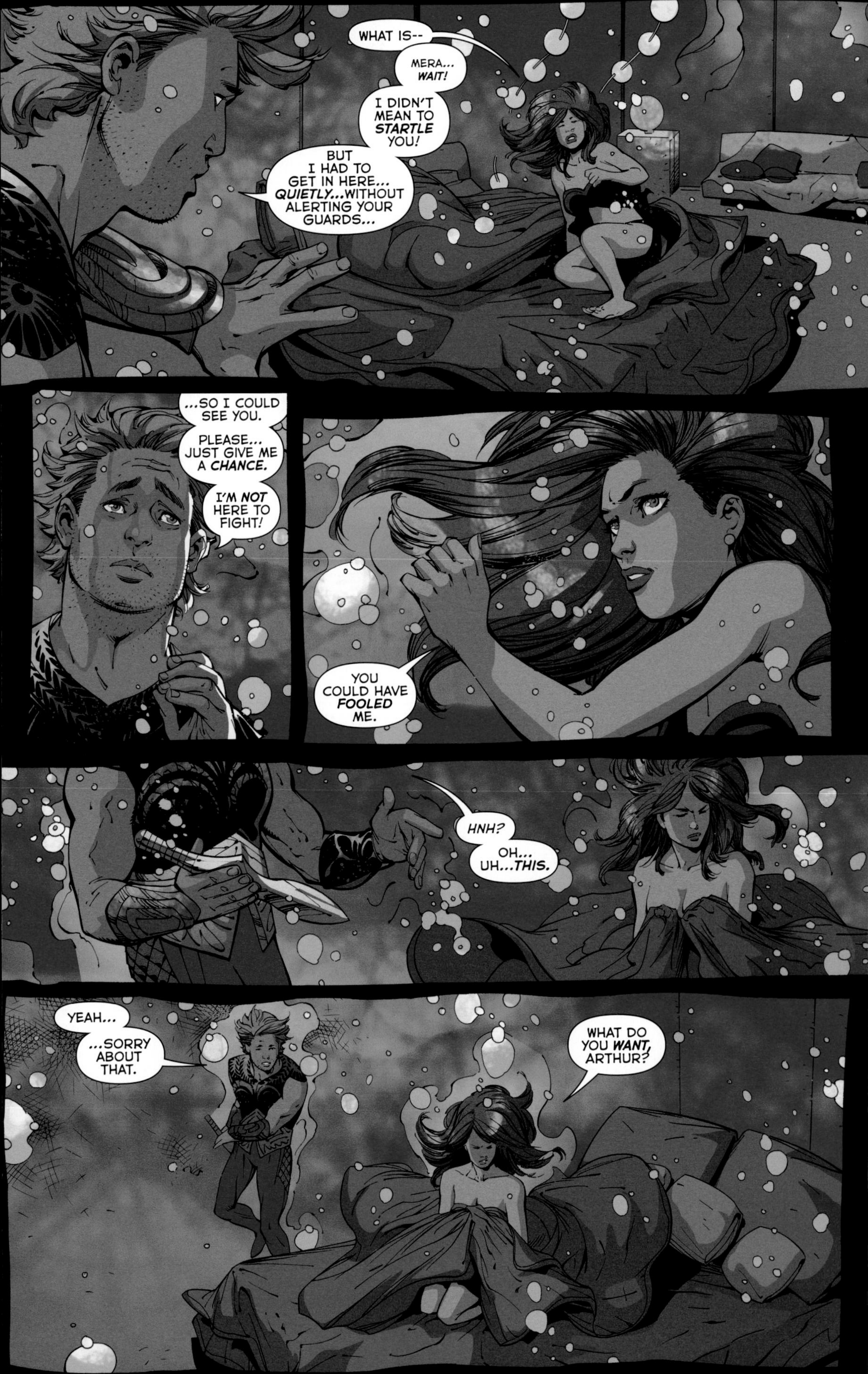

WHAT IS--
MERA... WAIT!
I DIDN'T MEAN TO STARTLE YOU!
BUT I HAD TO GET IN HERE... QUIETLY...WITHOUT ALERTING YOUR GUARDS...
...SO I COULD SEE YOU.
PLEASE... JUST GIVE ME A CHANCE.
I'M NOT HERE TO FIGHT!
YOU COULD HAVE FOOLED ME.
HNH?
OH... UH...THIS.
YEAH...
...SORRY ABOUT THAT.
WHAT DO YOU WANT, ARTHUR?

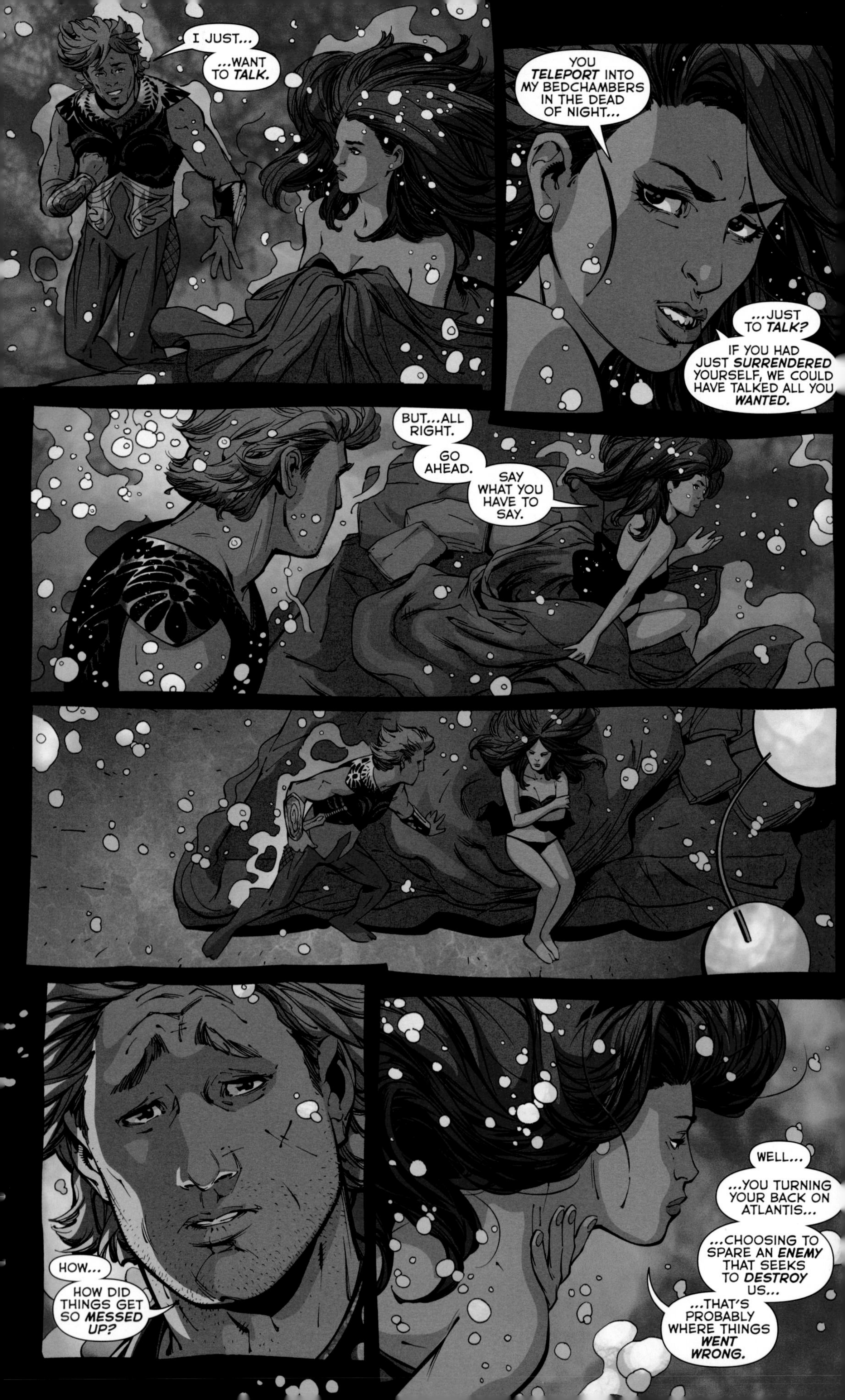
I JUST...
...WANT TO TALK.
YOU TELEPORT INTO MY BEDCHAMBERS IN THE DEAD OF NIGHT...
...JUST TO TALK?
IF YOU HAD JUST SURRENDERED YOURSELF, WE COULD HAVE TALKED ALL YOU WANTED.
BUT...ALL RIGHT.
GO AHEAD.
SAY WHAT YOU HAVE TO SAY.
HOW...
HOW DID THINGS GET SO MESSED UP?
WELL...
...YOU TURNING YOUR BACK ON ATLANTIS...
...CHOOSING TO SPARE AN ENEMY THAT SEEKS TO DESTROY US...
...THAT'S PROBABLY WHERE THINGS WENT WRONG.

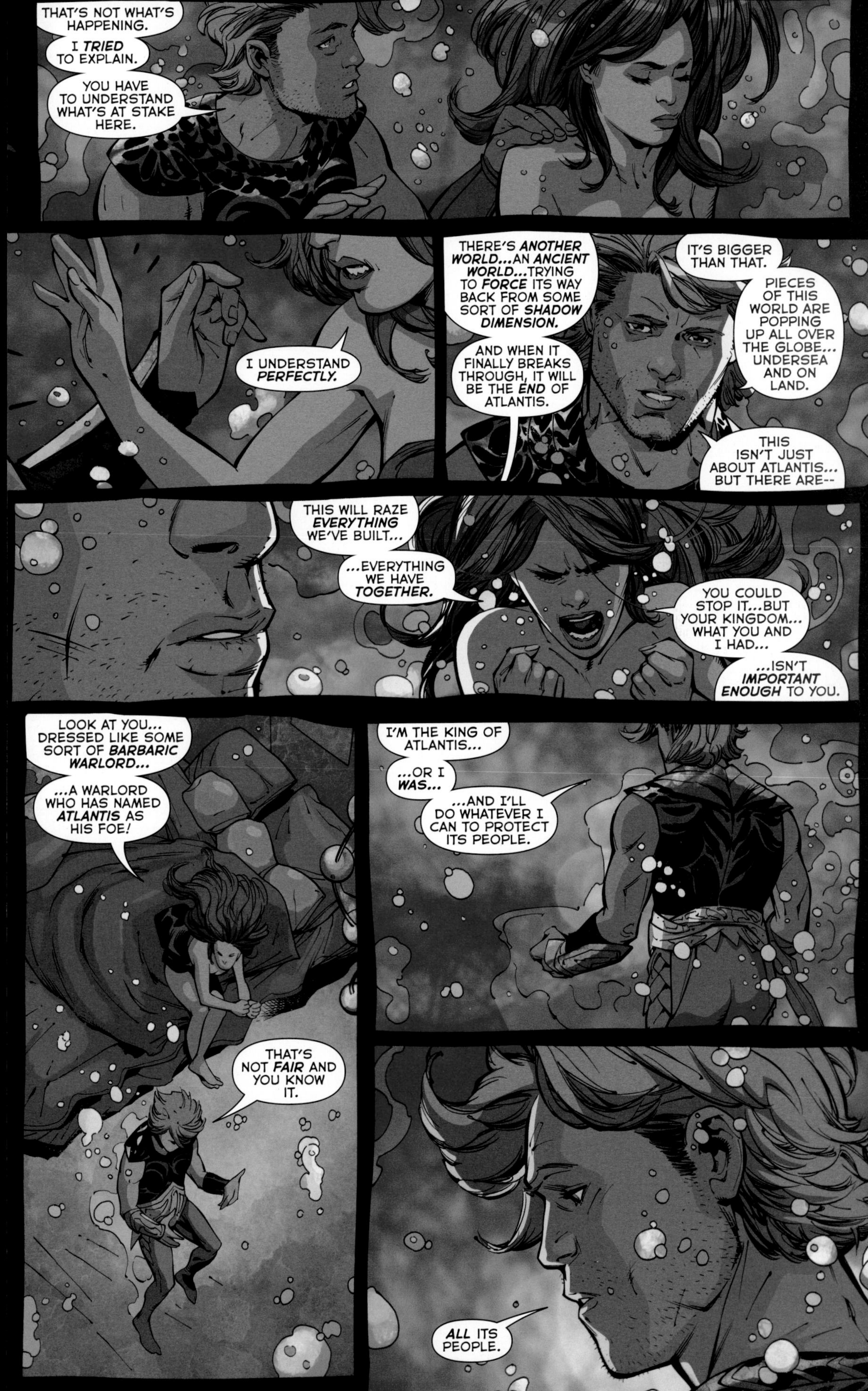
THAT'S NOT WHAT'S HAPPENING.
I TRIED TO EXPLAIN.
YOU HAVE TO UNDERSTAND WHAT'S AT STAKE HERE.
I UNDERSTAND PERFECTLY.
THERE'S ANOTHER WORLD...AN ANCIENT WORLD...TRYING TO FORCE ITS WAY BACK FROM SOME SORT OF SHADOW DIMENSION.
AND WHEN IT FINALLY BREAKS THROUGH, IT WILL BE THE END OF ATLANTIS.
IT'S BIGGER THAN THAT.
PIECES OF THIS WORLD ARE POPPING UP ALL OVER THE GLOBE... UNDERSEA AND ON LAND.
THIS ISN'T JUST ABOUT ATLANTIS... BUT THERE ARE--
THIS WILL RAZE EVERYTHING WE'VE BUILT...
...EVERYTHING WE HAVE TOGETHER.
YOU COULD STOP IT...BUT YOUR KINGDOM... WHAT YOU AND I HAD...
...ISN'T IMPORTANT ENOUGH TO YOU.
LOOK AT YOU... DRESSED LIKE SOME SORT OF BARBARIC WARLORD...
...A WARLORD WHO HAS NAMED ATLANTIS AS HIS FOE!
THAT'S NOT FAIR AND YOU KNOW IT.
I'M THE KING OF ATLANTIS...
...OR I WAS...
...AND I'LL DO WHATEVER I CAN TO PROTECT ITS PEOPLE.
ALL ITS PEOPLE.

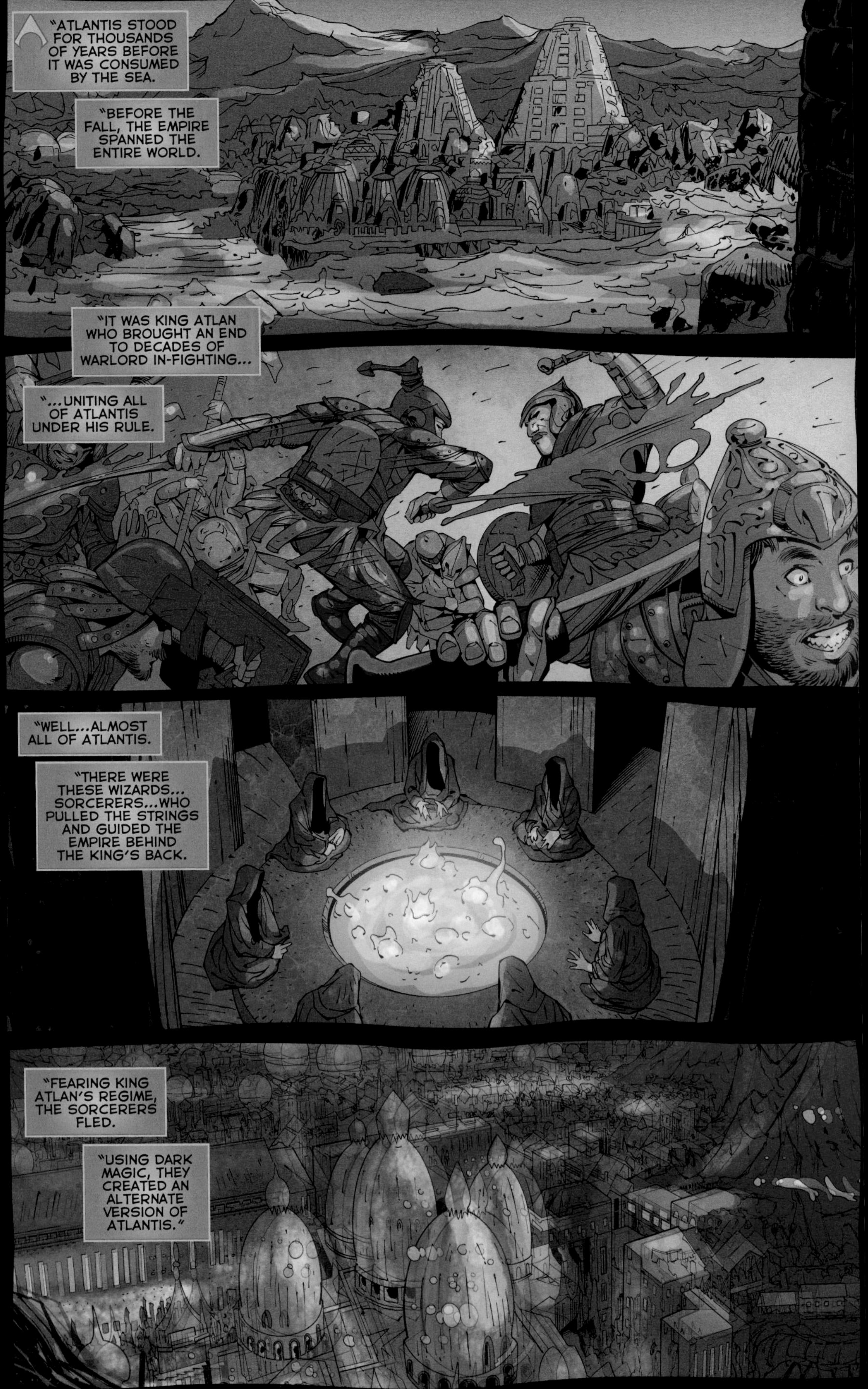
"ATLANTIS STOOD FOR THOUSANDS OF YEARS BEFORE IT WAS CONSUMED BY THE SEA.
"BEFORE THE FALL, THE EMPIRE SPANNED THE ENTIRE WORLD.
"IT WAS KING ATLAN WHO BROUGHT AN END TO DECADES OF WARLORD IN-FIGHTING...
"...UNITING ALL OF ATLANTIS UNDER HIS RULE.
"WELL...ALMOST ALL OF ATLANTIS.
"THERE WERE THESE WIZARDS... SORCERERS...WHO PULLED THE STRINGS AND GUIDED THE EMPIRE BEHIND THE KING'S BACK.
"FEARING KING ATLAN'S REGIME, THE SORCERERS FLED.
"USING DARK MAGIC, THEY CREATED AN ALTERNATE VERSION OF ATLANTIS."

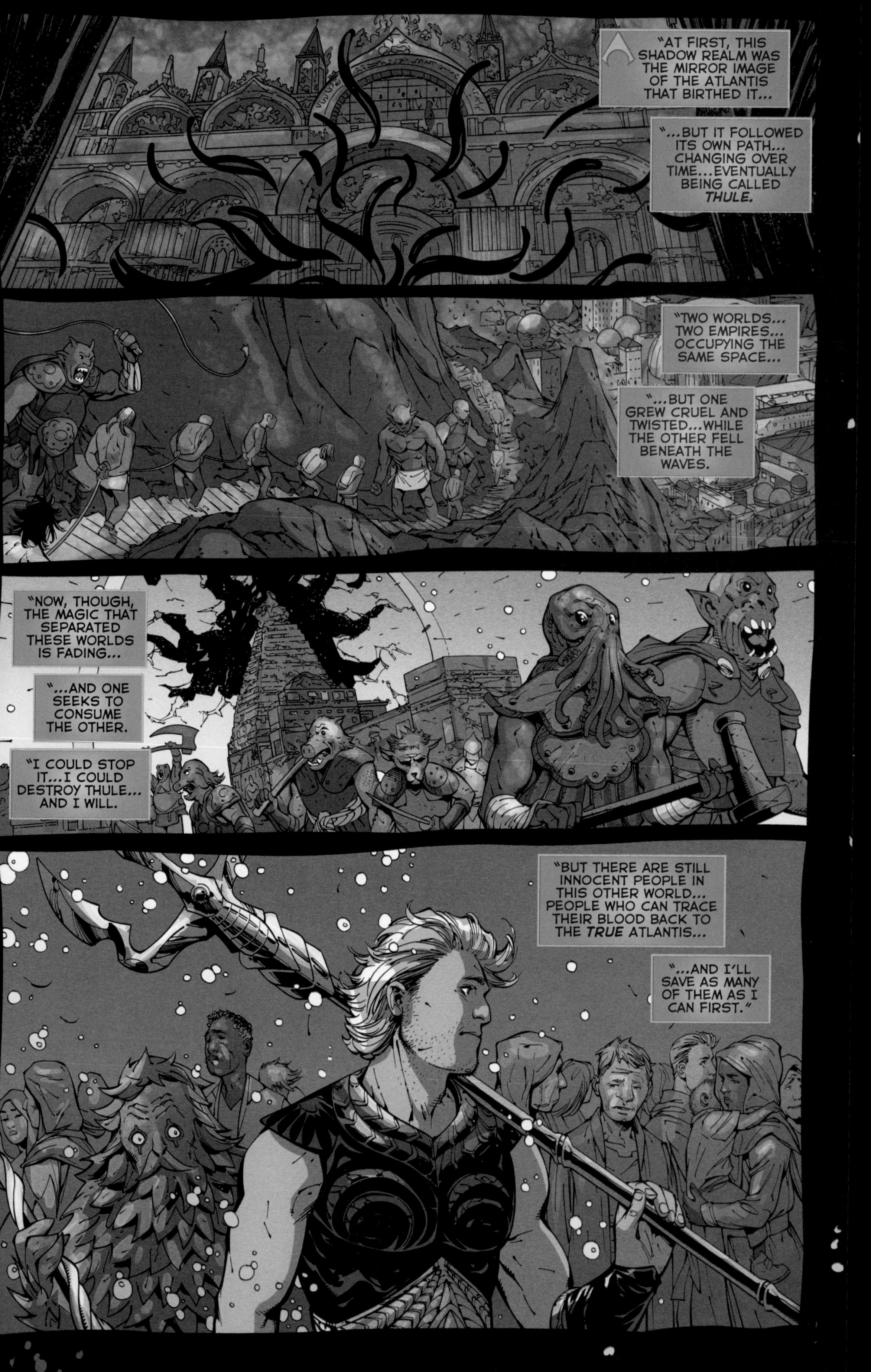
"AT FIRST, THIS SHADOW REALM WAS THE MIRROR IMAGE OF THE ATLANTIS THAT BIRTHED IT...
"...BUT IT FOLLOWED ITS OWN PATH... CHANGING OVER TIME...EVENTUALLY BEING CALLED *THULE.*
"TWO WORLDS... TWO EMPIRES... OCCUPYING THE SAME SPACE...
"...BUT ONE GREW CRUEL AND TWISTED...WHILE THE OTHER FELL BENEATH THE WAVES.
"NOW, THOUGH, THE MAGIC THAT SEPARATED THESE WORLDS IS FADING...
"...AND ONE SEEKS TO CONSUME THE OTHER.
"I COULD STOP IT...I COULD DESTROY THULE... AND I WILL.
"BUT THERE ARE STILL INNOCENT PEOPLE IN THIS OTHER WORLD... PEOPLE WHO CAN TRACE THEIR BLOOD BACK TO THE *TRUE* ATLANTIS...
"...AND I'LL SAVE AS MANY OF THEM AS I CAN FIRST."

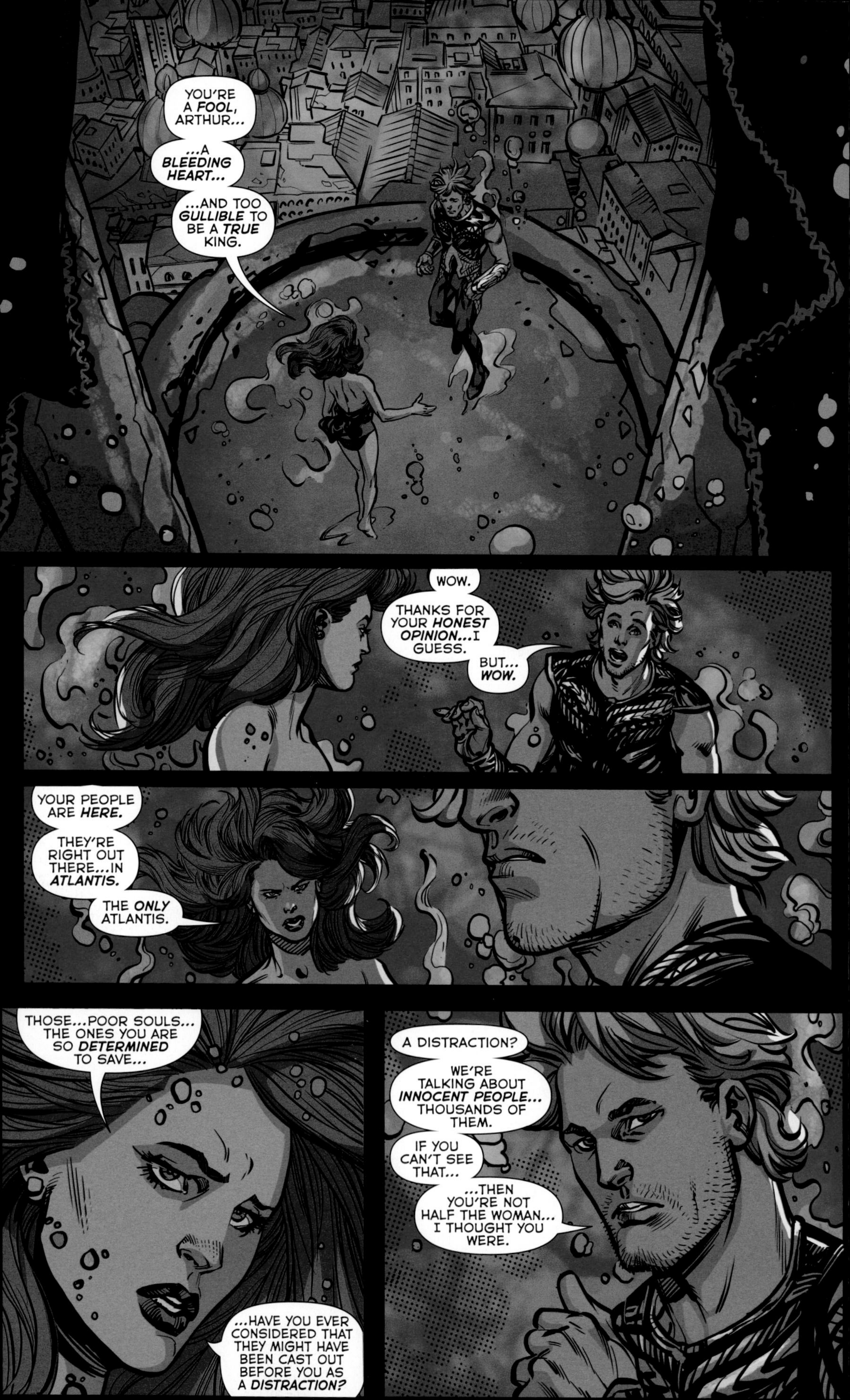
YOU'RE A FOOL, ARTHUR...
...A BLEEDING HEART...
...AND TOO GULLIBLE TO BE A TRUE KING.
WOW.
THANKS FOR YOUR HONEST OPINION...I GUESS.
BUT... WOW.
YOUR PEOPLE ARE HERE.
THEY'RE RIGHT OUT THERE...IN ATLANTIS.
THE ONLY ATLANTIS.
THOSE...POOR SOULS... THE ONES YOU ARE SO DETERMINED TO SAVE...
...HAVE YOU EVER CONSIDERED THAT THEY MIGHT HAVE BEEN CAST OUT BEFORE YOU AS A DISTRACTION?
A DISTRACTION?
WE'RE TALKING ABOUT INNOCENT PEOPLE... THOUSANDS OF THEM.
IF YOU CAN'T SEE THAT...
...THEN YOU'RE NOT HALF THE WOMAN... I THOUGHT YOU WERE.

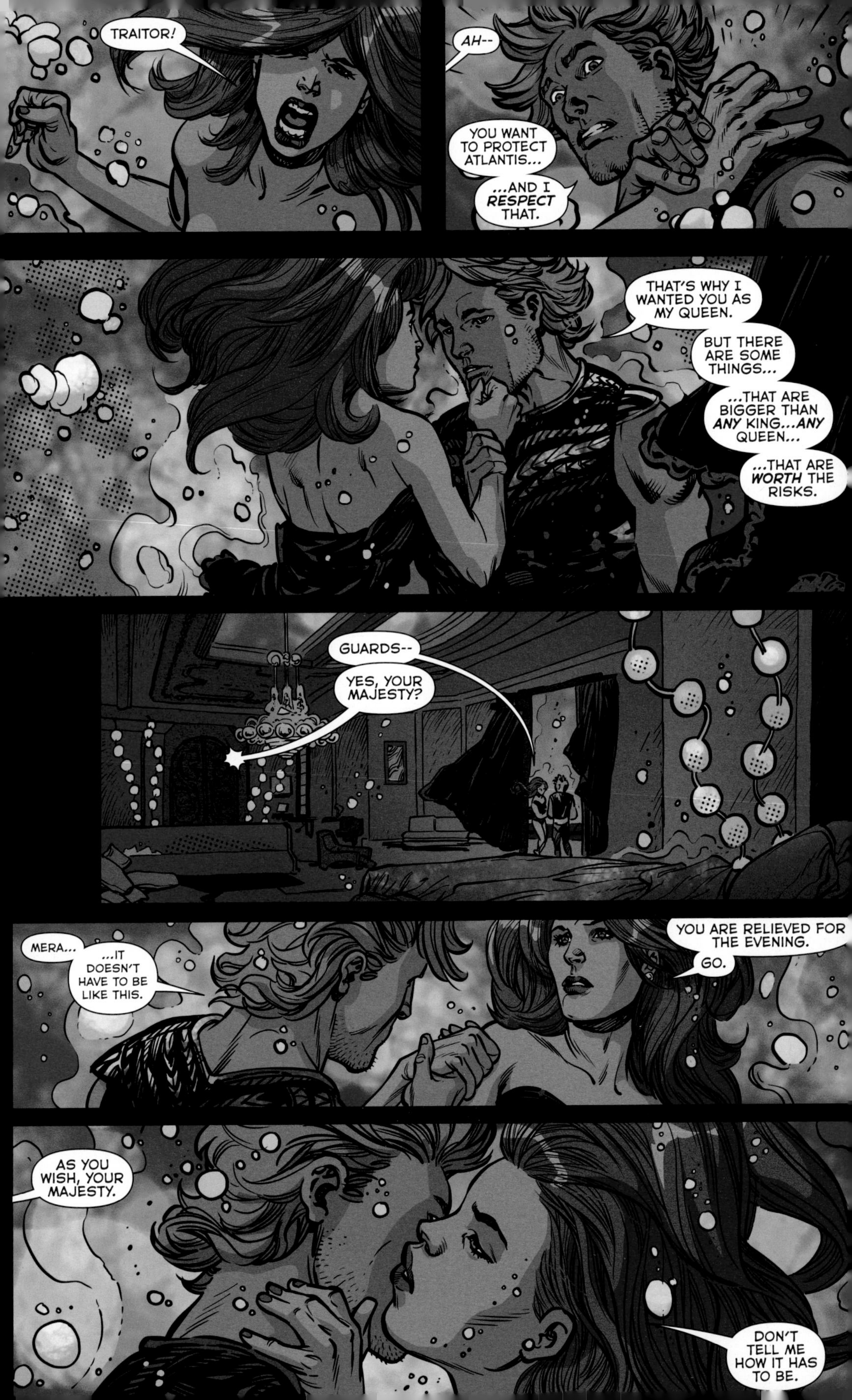
TRAITOR!
AH--
YOU WANT TO PROTECT ATLANTIS...
...AND I *RESPECT* THAT.
THAT'S WHY I WANTED YOU AS MY QUEEN.
BUT THERE ARE SOME THINGS...
...THAT ARE BIGGER THAN *ANY* KING...*ANY* QUEEN...
...THAT ARE *WORTH* THE RISKS.
GUARDS--
YES, YOUR MAJESTY?
MERA...
...IT DOESN'T HAVE TO BE LIKE THIS.
YOU ARE RELIEVED FOR THE EVENING.
GO.
AS YOU WISH, YOUR MAJESTY.
DON'T TELL ME HOW IT HAS TO BE.

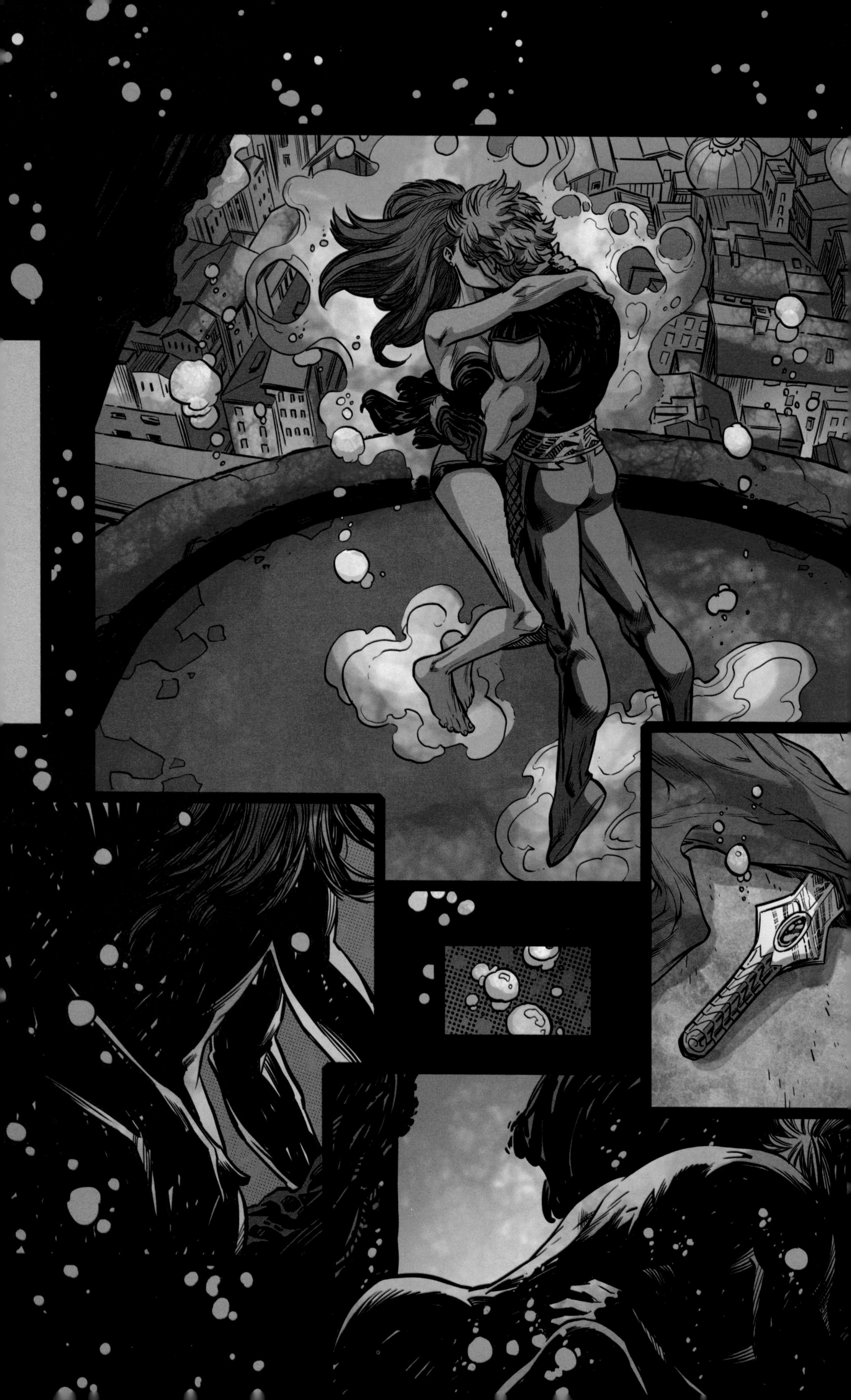

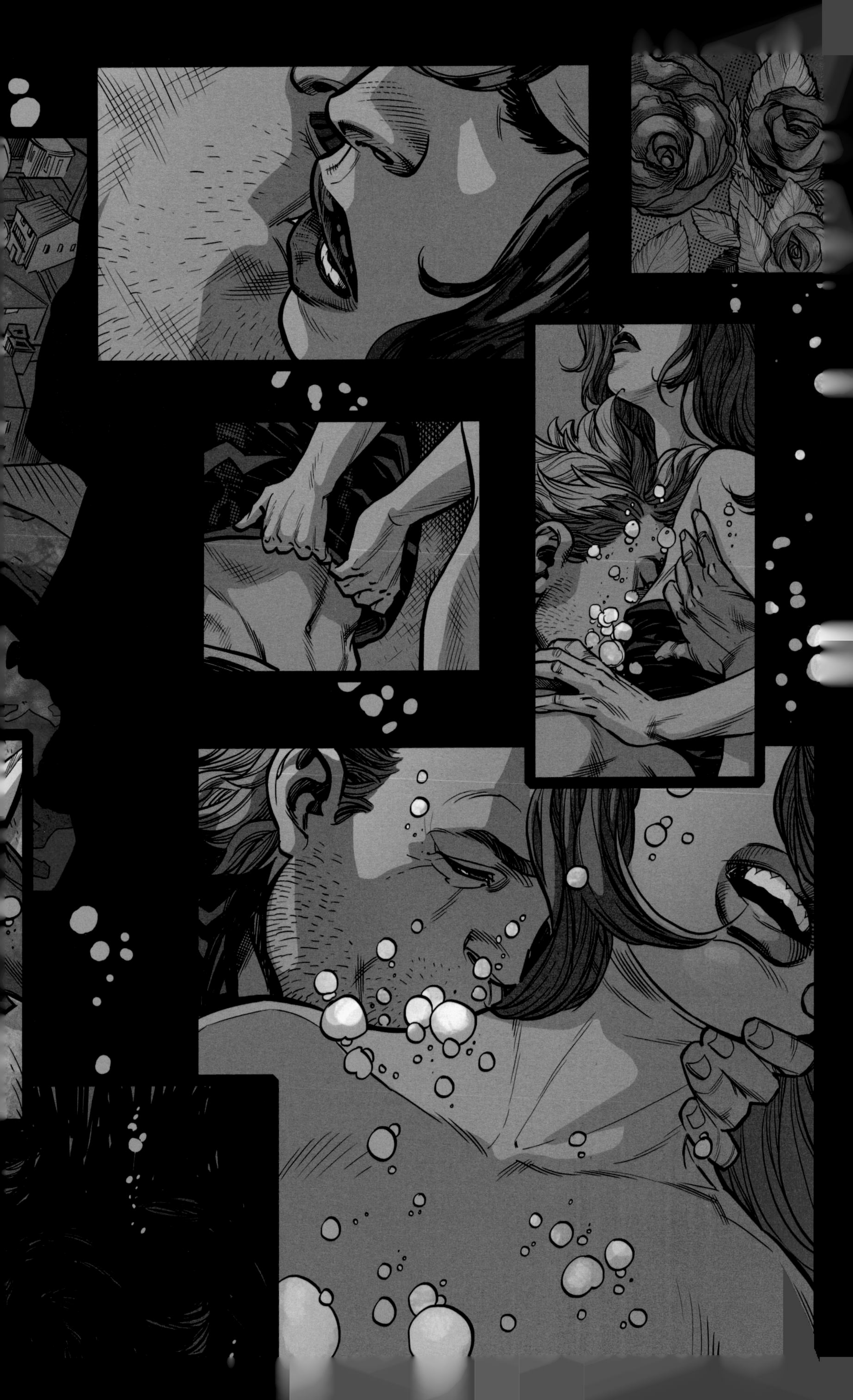

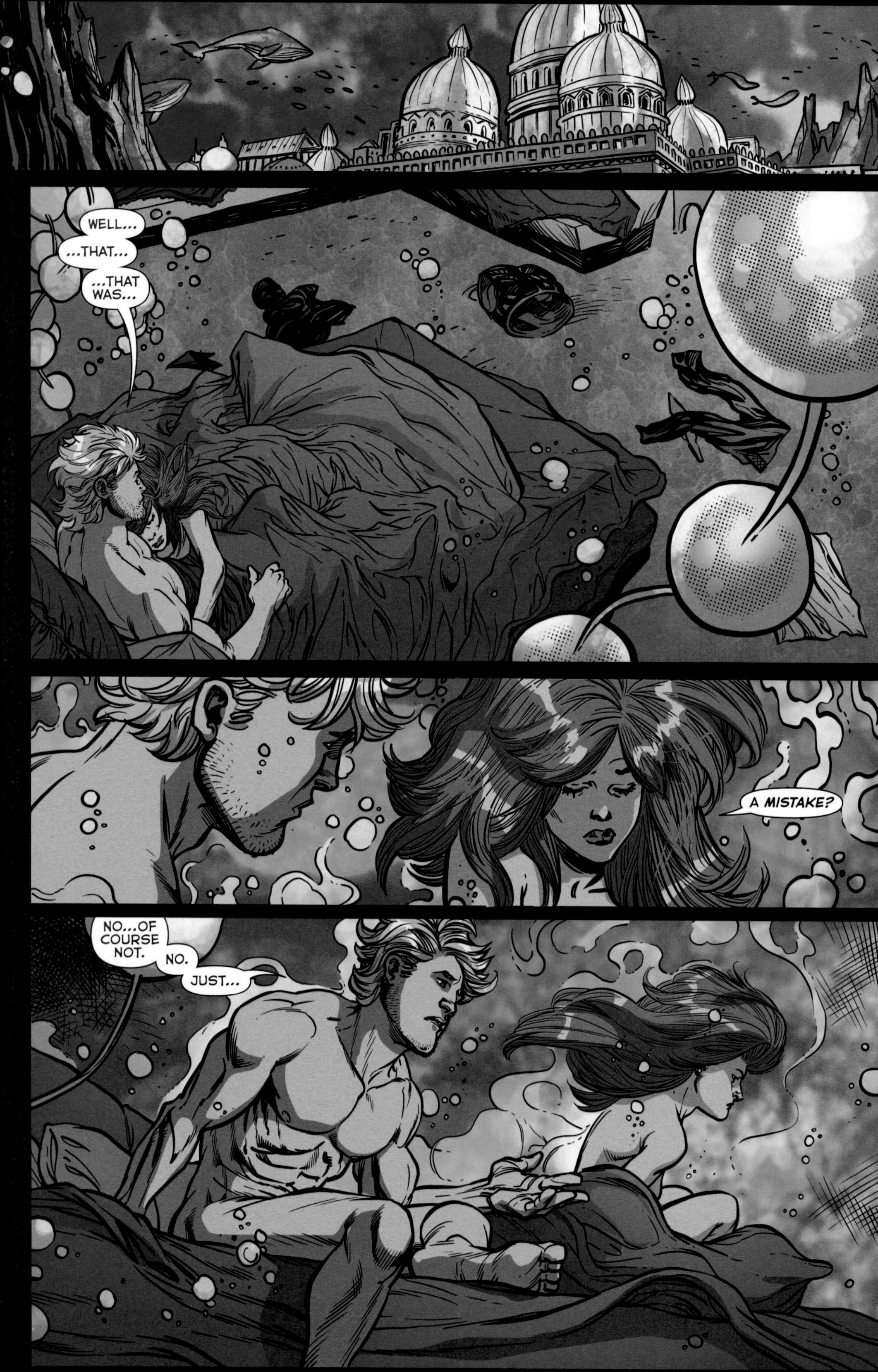
WELL...
...THAT...
...THAT WAS...
A MISTAKE?
NO...OF COURSE NOT.
NO.
JUST...

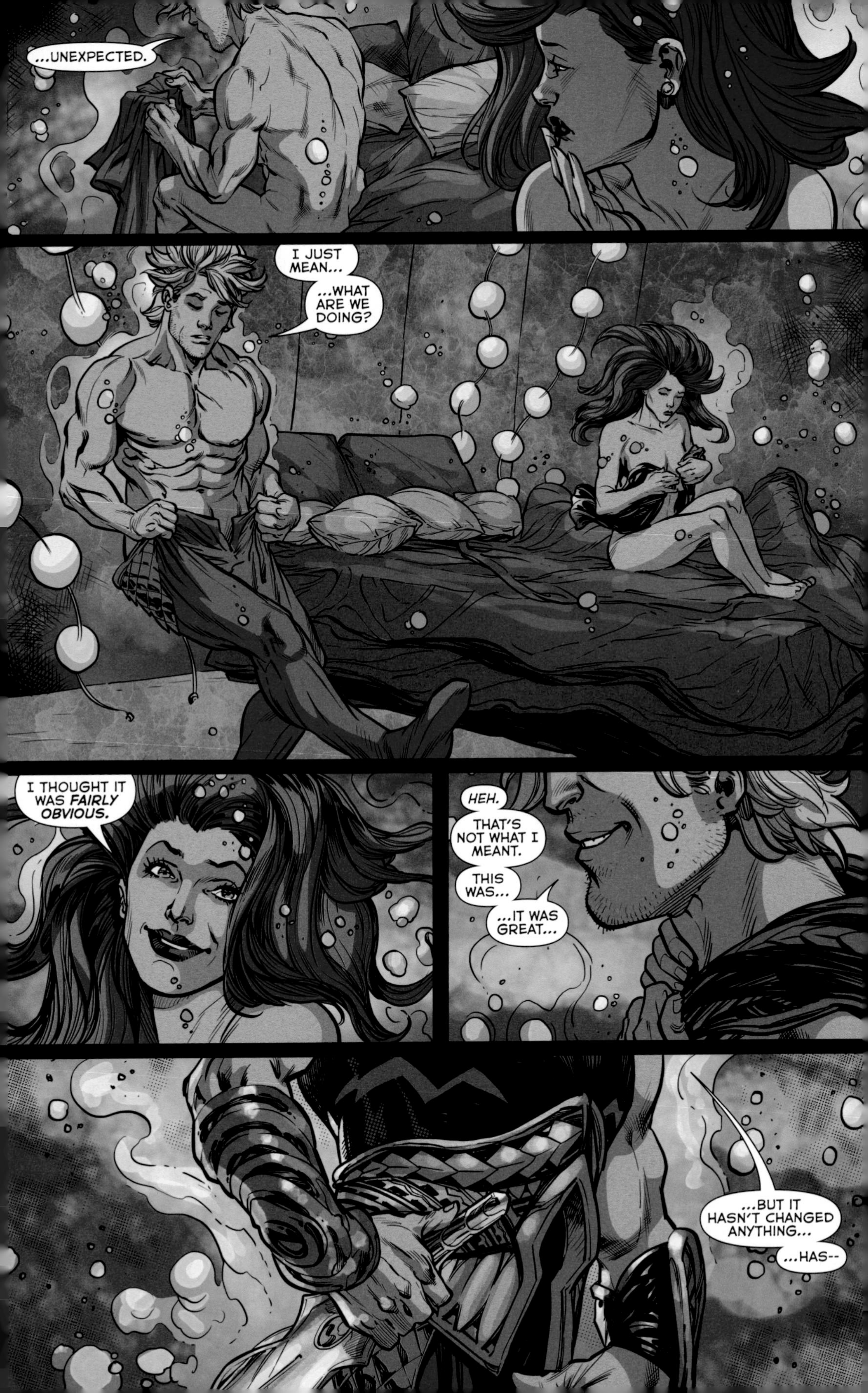
...UNEXPECTED.
I JUST MEAN...
...WHAT ARE WE DOING?
I THOUGHT IT WAS *FAIRLY OBVIOUS.*
HEH.
THAT'S NOT WHAT I MEANT.
THIS WAS...
...IT WAS GREAT...
...BUT IT HASN'T CHANGED ANYTHING...
...HAS--

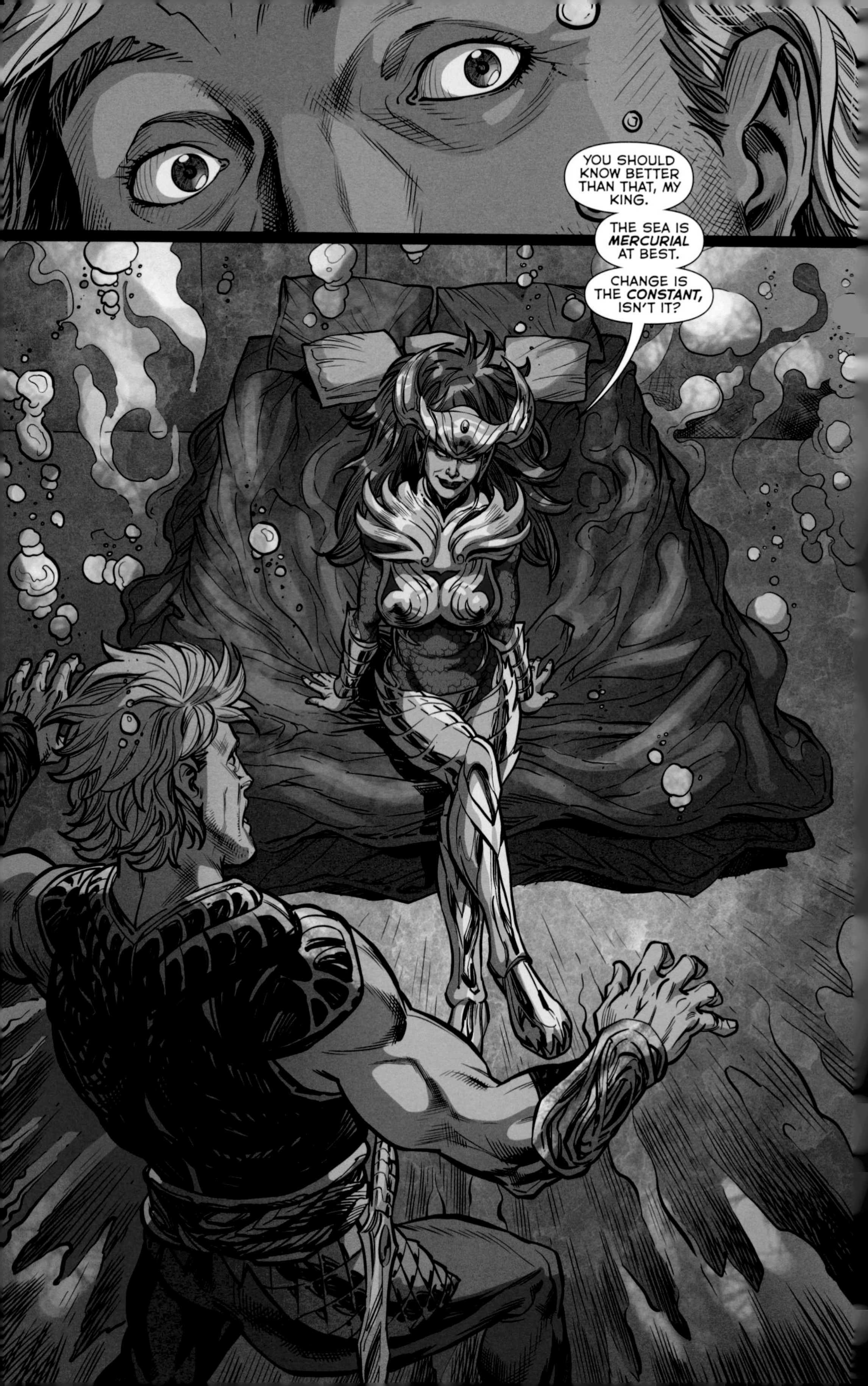
YOU SHOULD KNOW BETTER THAN THAT, MY KING.
THE SEA IS MERCURIAL AT BEST.
CHANGE IS THE CONSTANT, ISN'T IT?

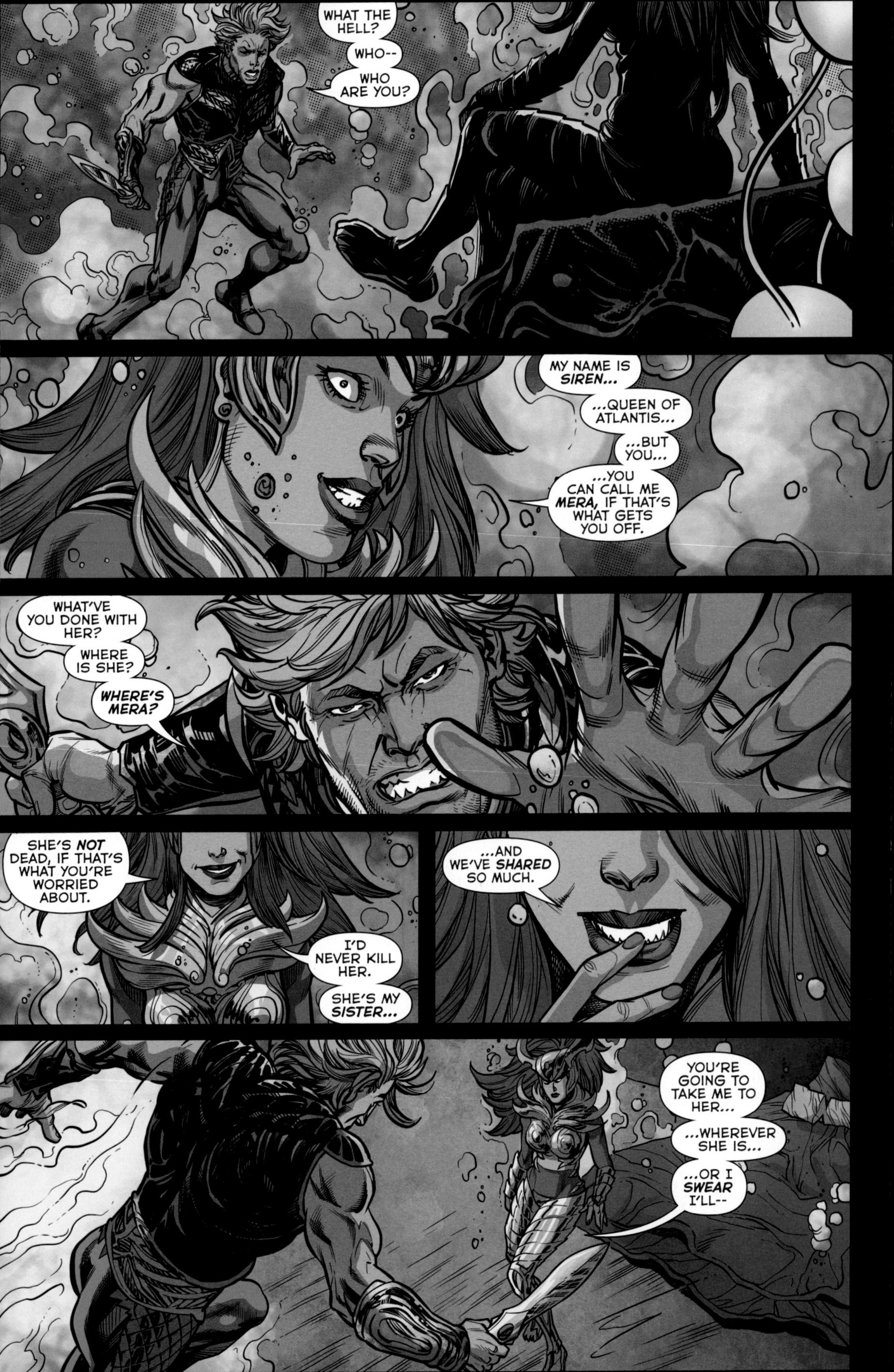
WHAT THE HELL?
WHO--
WHO ARE YOU?
MY NAME IS SIREN...
...QUEEN OF ATLANTIS...
...BUT YOU...
...YOU CAN CALL ME MERA, IF THAT'S WHAT GETS YOU OFF.
WHAT'VE YOU DONE WITH HER?
WHERE IS SHE?
WHERE'S MERA?
SHE'S NOT DEAD, IF THAT'S WHAT YOU'RE WORRIED ABOUT.
I'D NEVER KILL HER.
SHE'S MY SISTER...
...AND WE'VE SHARED SO MUCH.
YOU'RE GOING TO TAKE ME TO HER...
...WHEREVER SHE IS...
...OR I SWEAR I'LL--

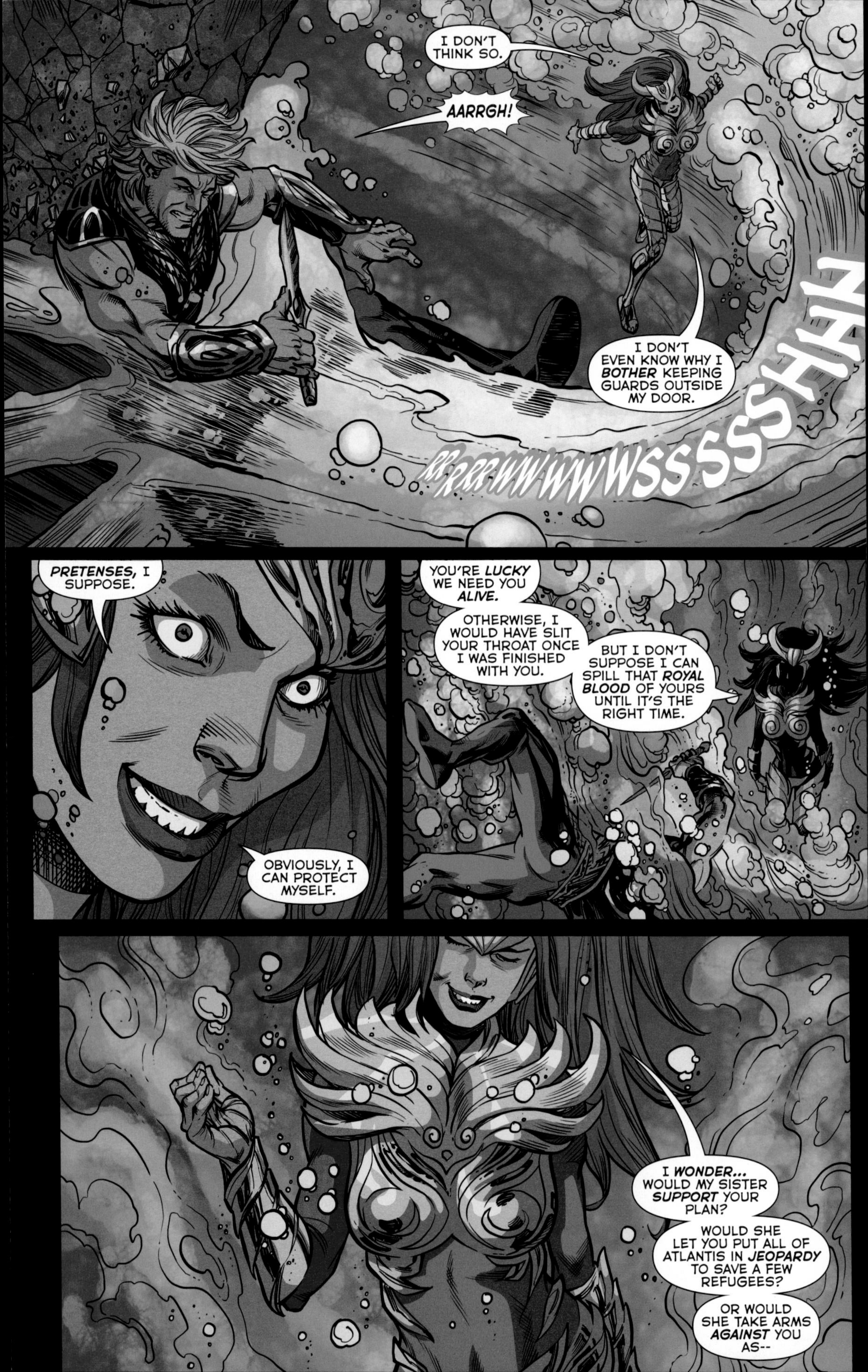
I DON'T THINK SO.
AARRGH!
I DON'T EVEN KNOW WHY I BOTHER KEEPING GUARDS OUTSIDE MY DOOR.
RRRRRRWWWWWWSSSSSSHHH
PRETENSES, I SUPPOSE.
OBVIOUSLY, I CAN PROTECT MYSELF.
YOU'RE LUCKY WE NEED YOU ALIVE.
OTHERWISE, I WOULD HAVE SLIT YOUR THROAT ONCE I WAS FINISHED WITH YOU.
BUT I DON'T SUPPOSE I CAN SPILL THAT ROYAL BLOOD OF YOURS UNTIL IT'S THE RIGHT TIME.
I WONDER... WOULD MY SISTER SUPPORT YOUR PLAN?
WOULD SHE LET YOU PUT ALL OF ATLANTIS IN JEOPARDY TO SAVE A FEW REFUGEES?
OR WOULD SHE TAKE ARMS AGAINST YOU AS--

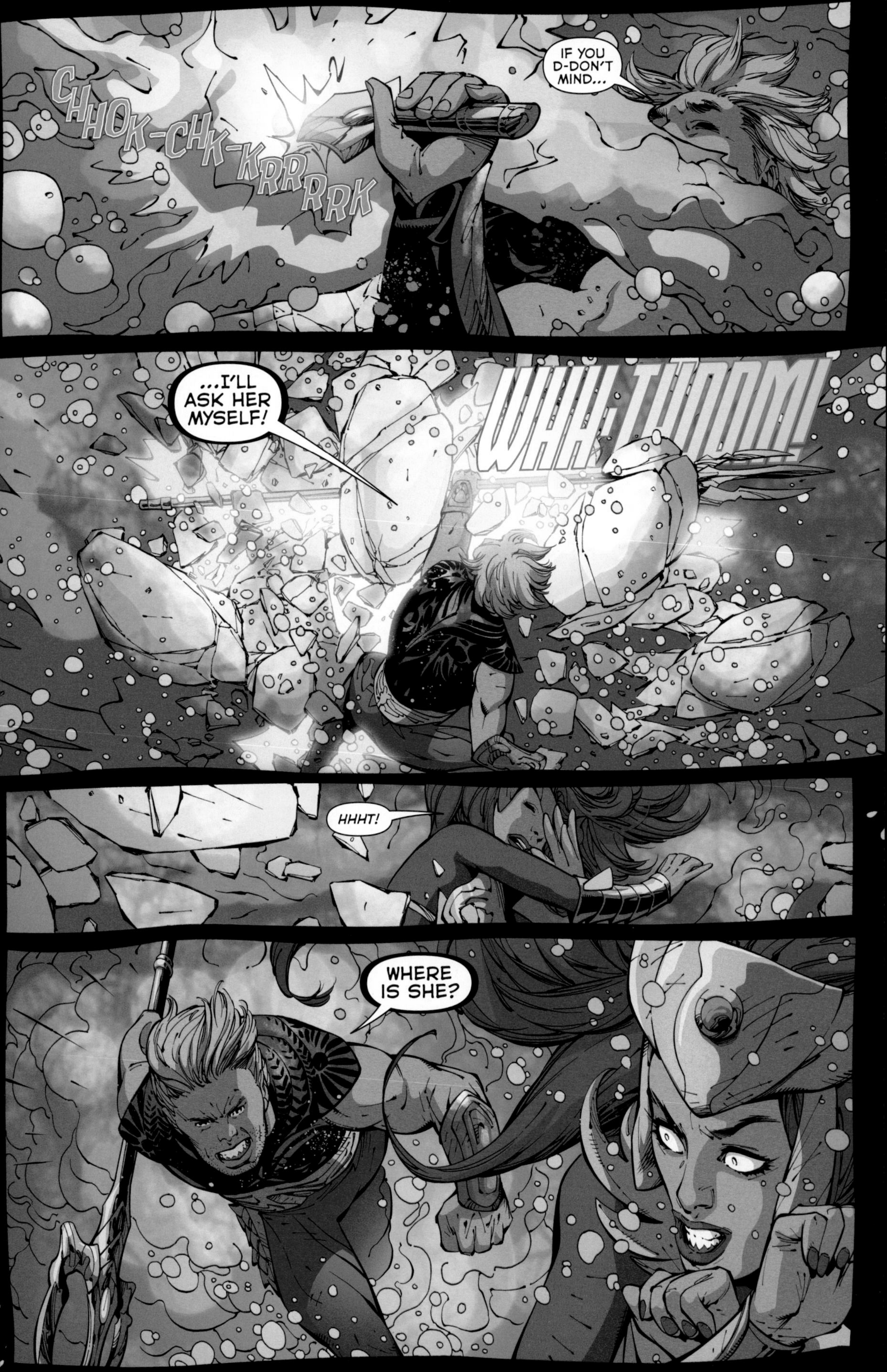
CHHOK-CHK-KRRRRRK
IF YOU D-DON'T MIND...
...I'LL ASK HER MYSELF!
HHHT!
WHERE IS SHE?

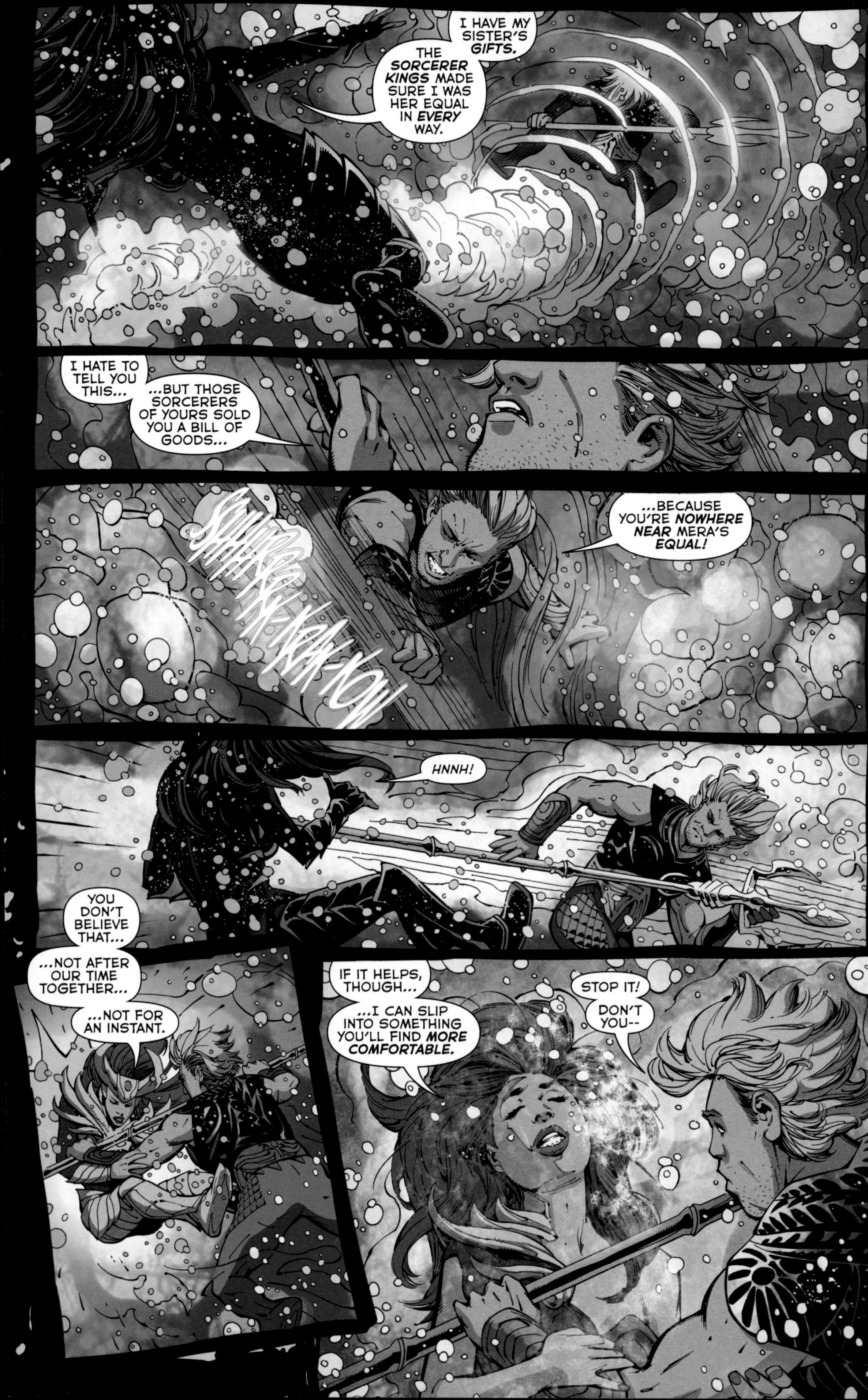
I HAVE MY SISTER'S GIFTS.
THE SORCERER KINGS MADE SURE I WAS HER EQUAL IN EVERY WAY.
I HATE TO TELL YOU THIS...
...BUT THOSE SORCERERS OF YOURS SOLD YOU A BILL OF GOODS...
...BECAUSE YOU'RE NOWHERE NEAR MERA'S EQUAL!
HNNH!
YOU DON'T BELIEVE THAT...
...NOT AFTER OUR TIME TOGETHER...
...NOT FOR AN INSTANT.
IF IT HELPS, THOUGH...
...I CAN SLIP INTO SOMETHING YOU'LL FIND MORE COMFORTABLE.
STOP IT!
DON'T YOU--

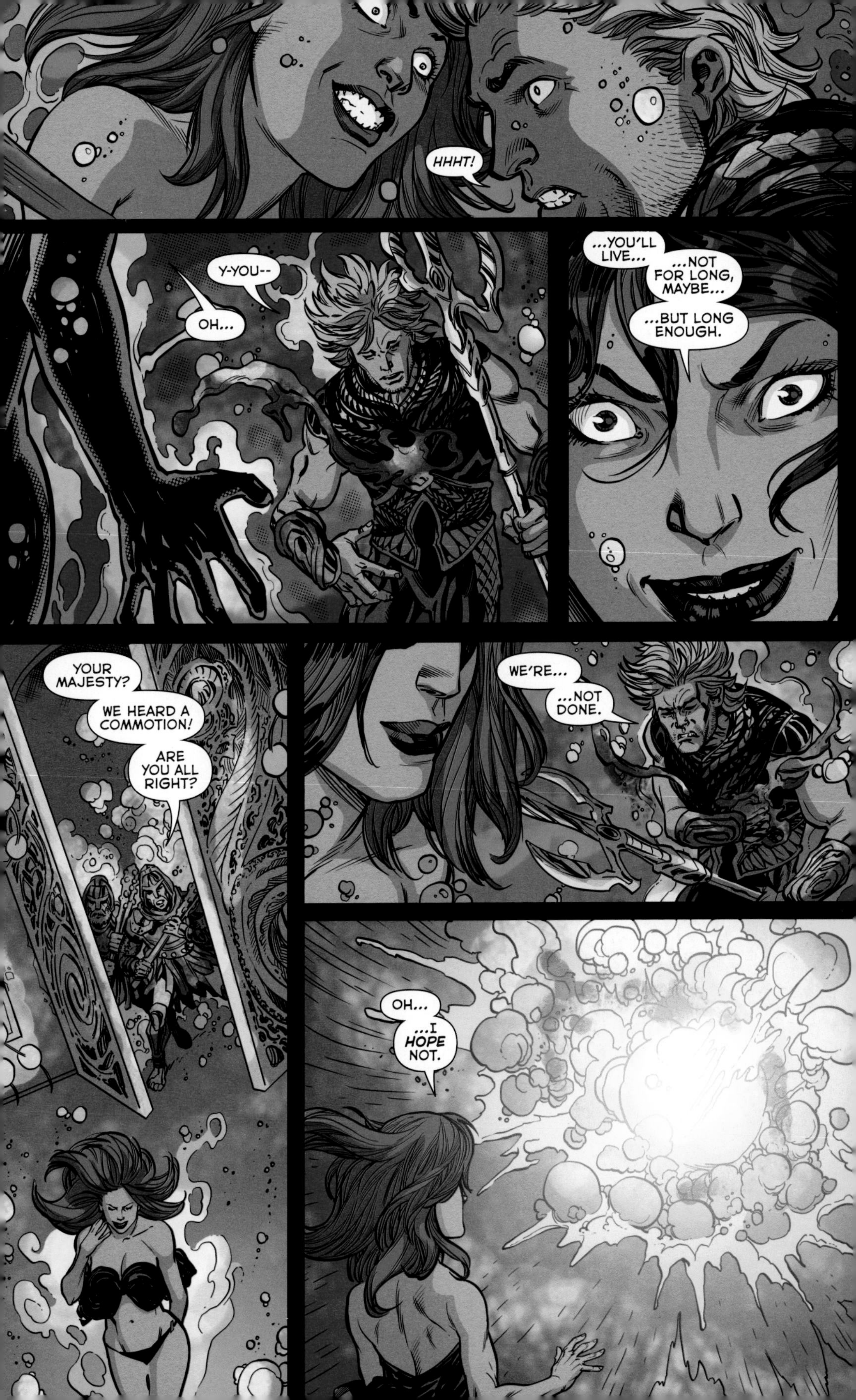
HHHT!
Y-YOU--
OH...
...YOU'LL LIVE...
...NOT FOR LONG, MAYBE...
...BUT LONG ENOUGH.
YOUR MAJESTY?
WE HEARD A COMMOTION!
ARE YOU ALL RIGHT?
WE'RE...
...NOT DONE.
OH...
...I *HOPE* NOT.

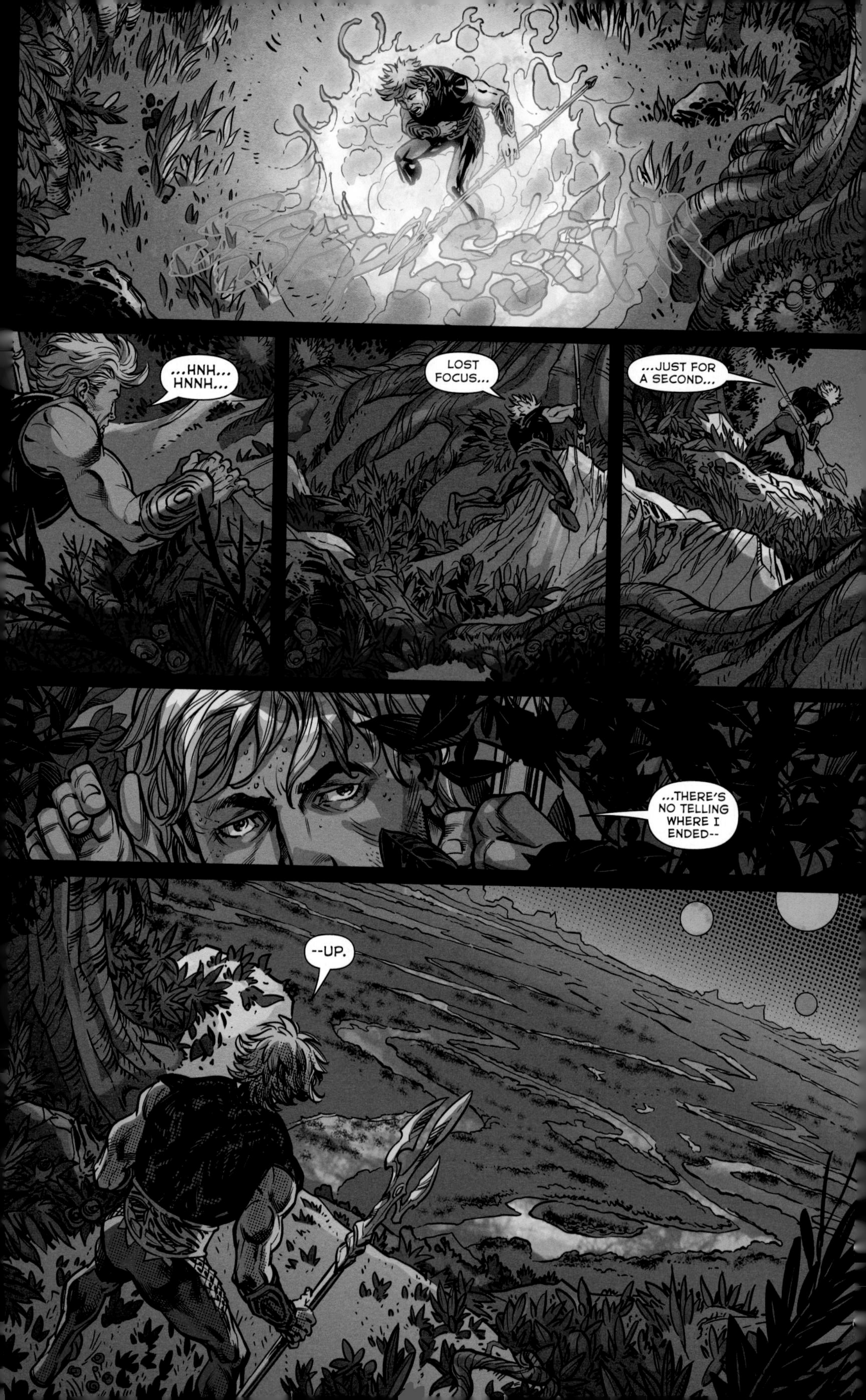
...HNH...
HNNH...
LOST
FOCUS...
...JUST FOR
A SECOND...
...THERE'S
NO TELLING
WHERE I
ENDED--
--UP.

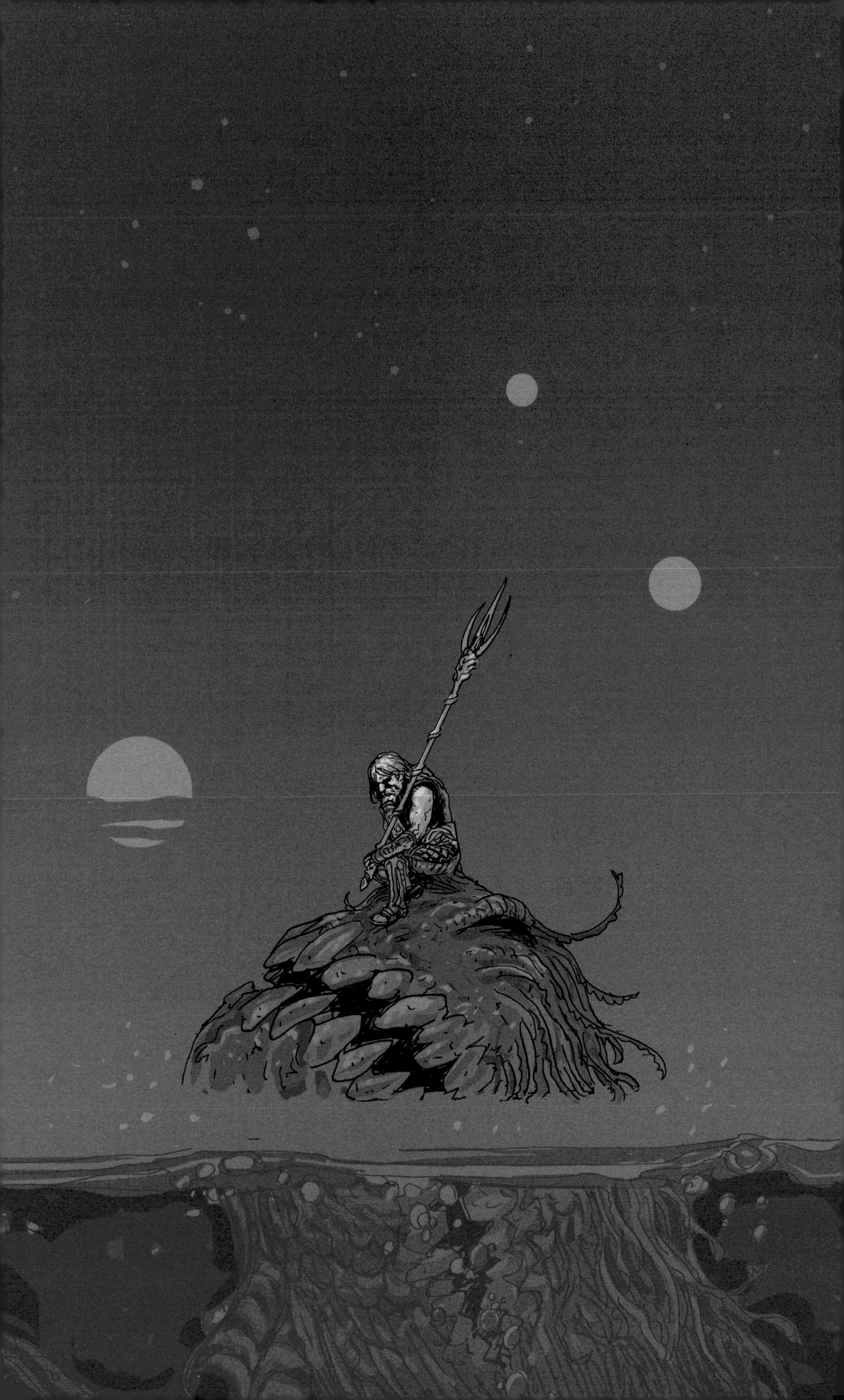

ALIEN DISCOVERY

CULLEN BUNN writer TREVOR MCCARTHY penciller JOHN DELL, ART THIBERT, VICENTE CIFUENTES inkers GUY MAJOR colorist TOM NAPOLITANO letterer
ALEC MORGAN cover art

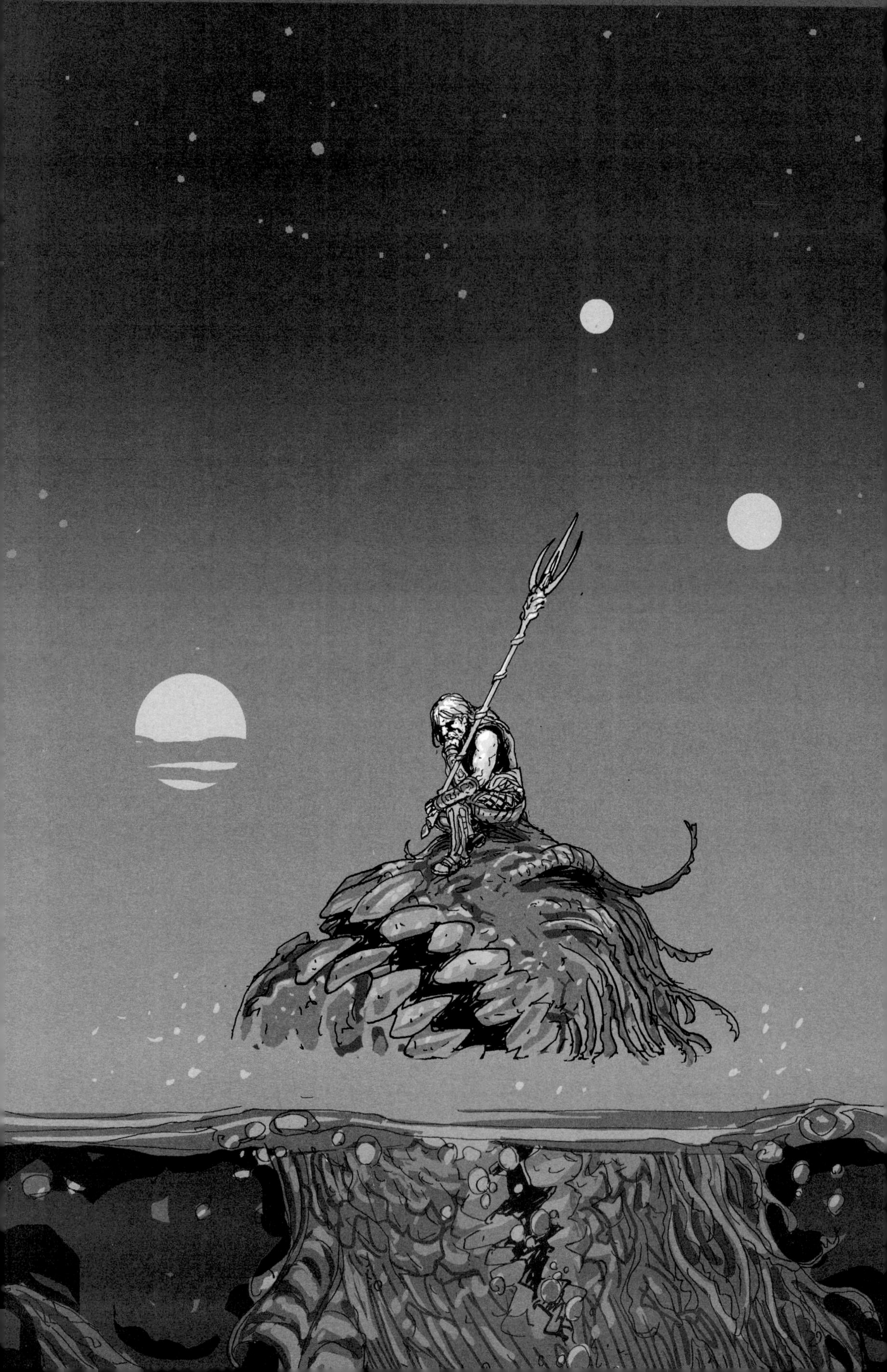

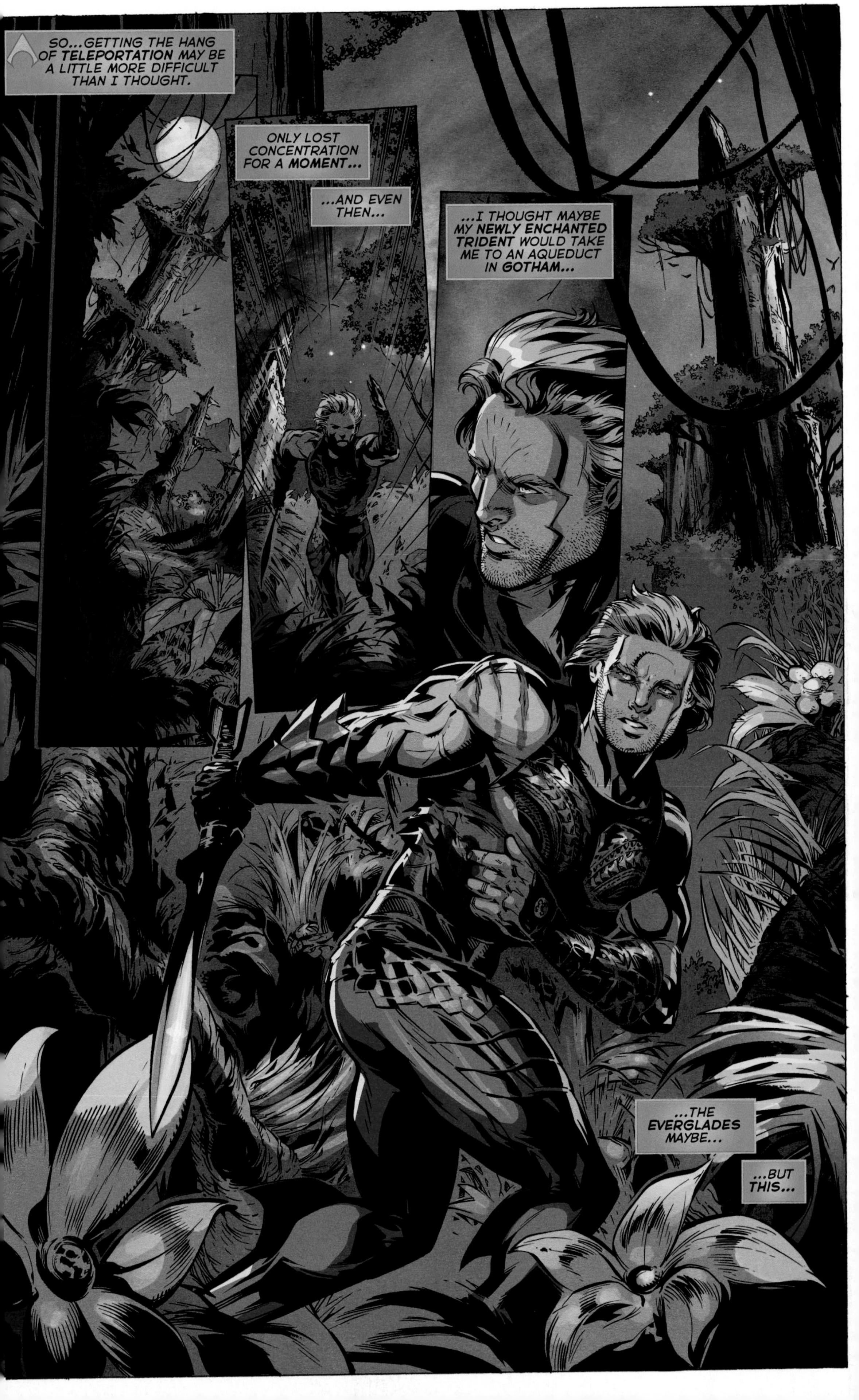
SO...GETTING THE HANG OF TELEPORTATION MAY BE A LITTLE MORE DIFFICULT THAN I THOUGHT.
ONLY LOST CONCENTRATION FOR A MOMENT...
...AND EVEN THEN...
...I THOUGHT MAYBE MY NEWLY ENCHANTED TRIDENT WOULD TAKE ME TO AN AQUEDUCT IN GOTHAM...
...THE EVERGLADES MAYBE...
...BUT THIS...

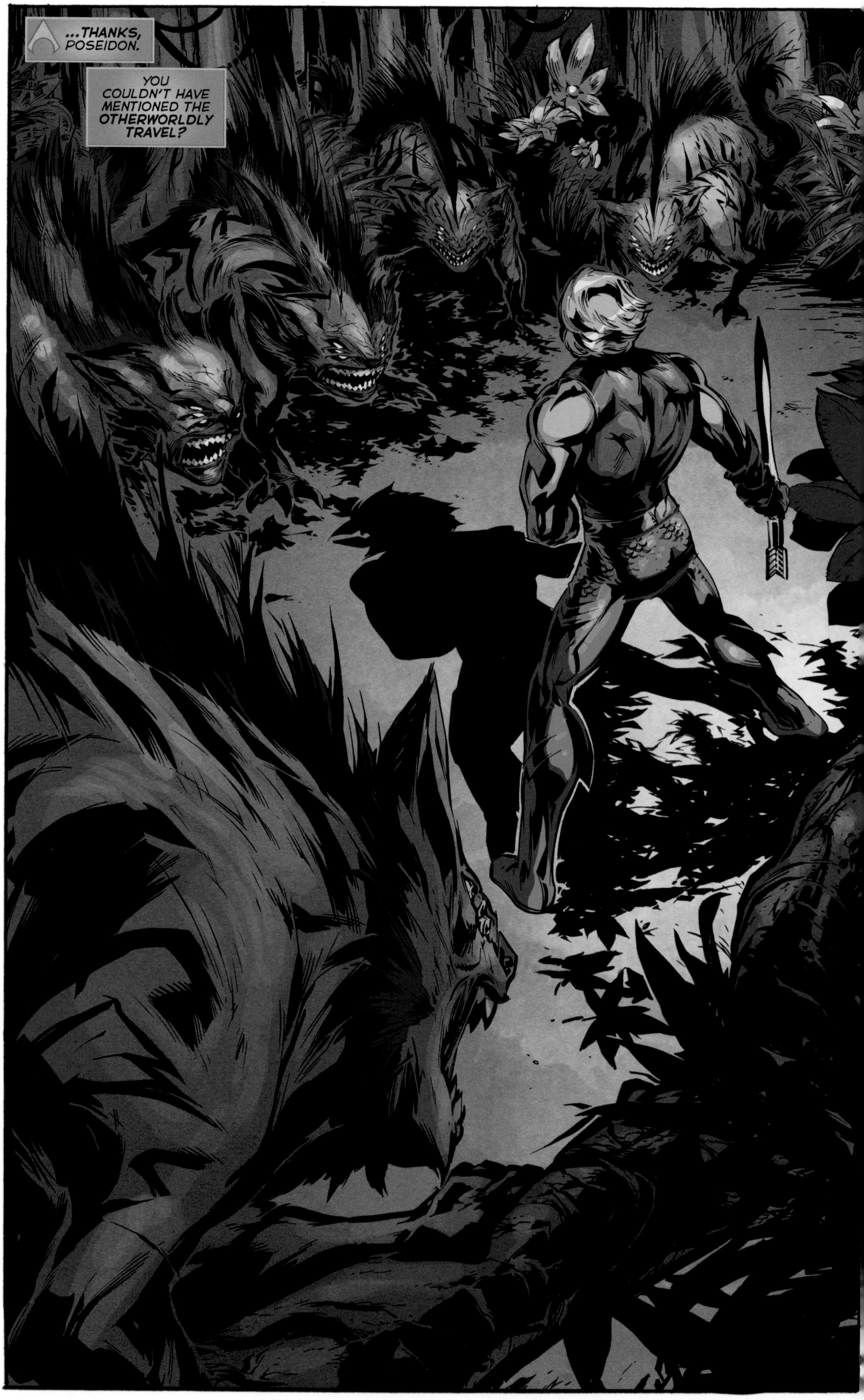
...THANKS, POSEIDON.
YOU COULDN'T HAVE MENTIONED THE OTHERWORLDLY TRAVEL?

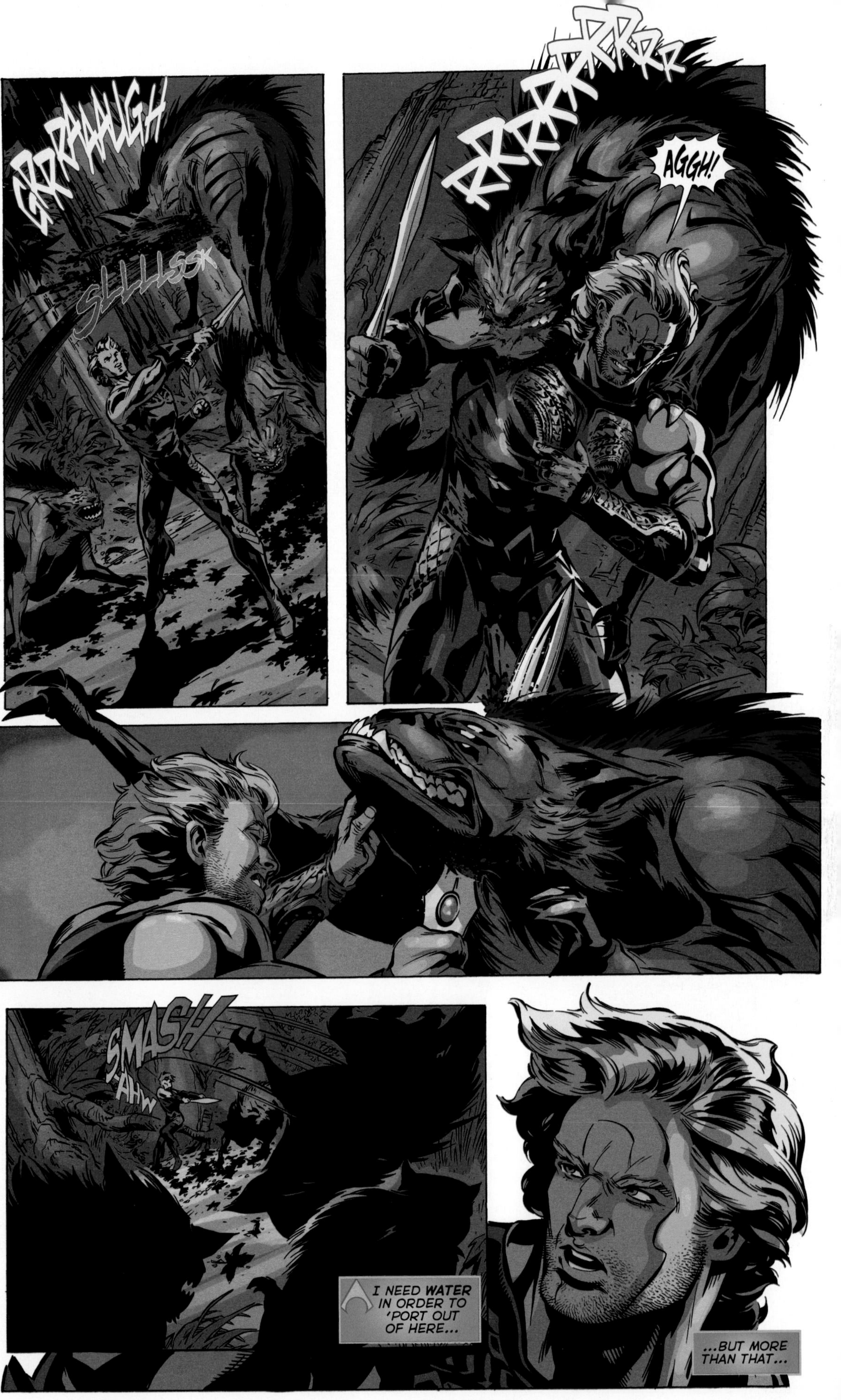
GRRRAAUGH
SLLLLSSK
RRRRRRRRRRR
AGGH!
SMASH
-AHW
I NEED WATER IN ORDER TO 'PORT OUT OF HERE...
...BUT MORE THAN THAT...

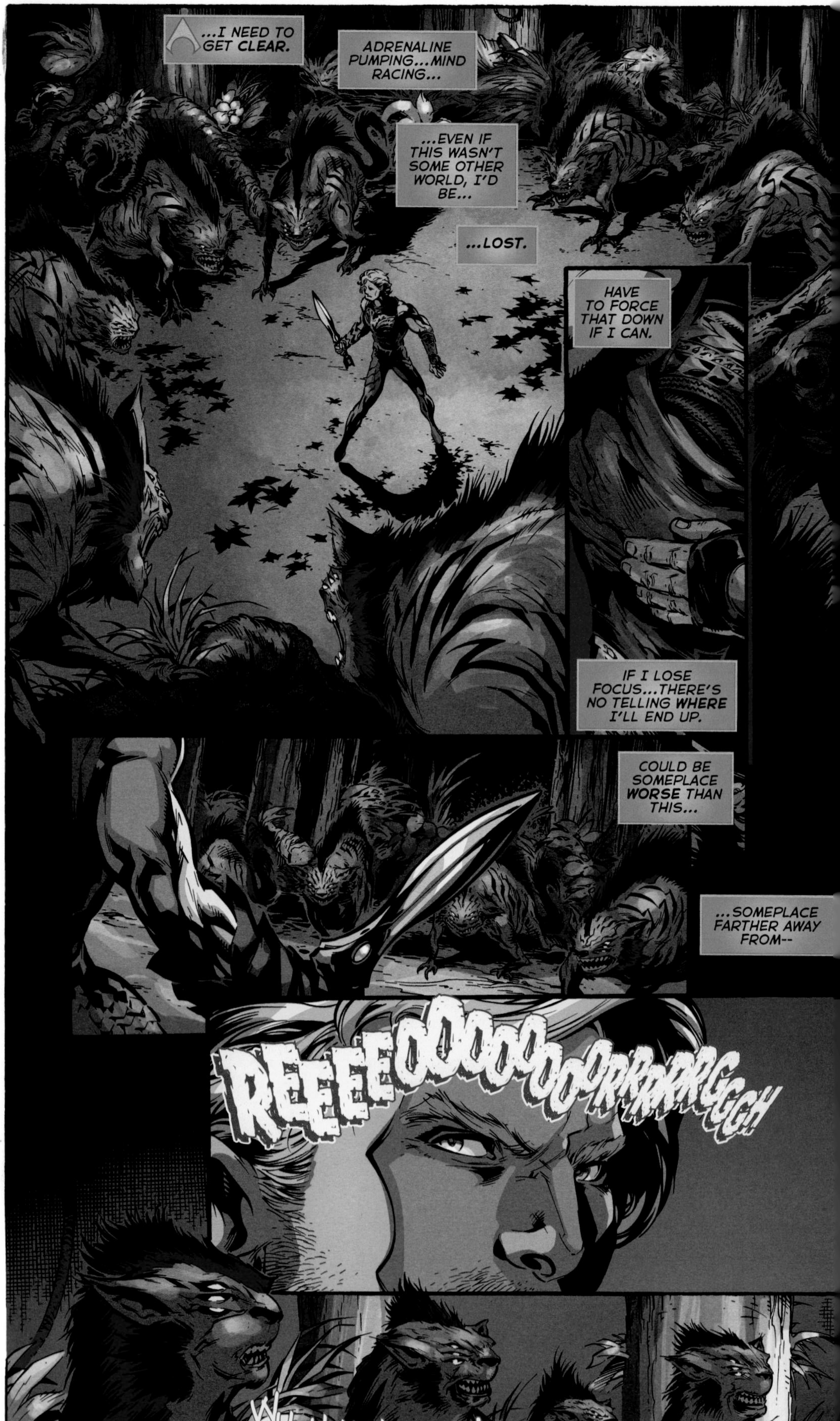

...I NEED TO GET CLEAR.
ADRENALINE PUMPING...MIND RACING...
...EVEN IF THIS WASN'T SOME OTHER WORLD, I'D BE...
...LOST.
HAVE TO FORCE THAT DOWN IF I CAN.
IF I LOSE FOCUS...THERE'S NO TELLING WHERE I'LL END UP.
COULD BE SOMEPLACE WORSE THAN THIS...
...SOMEPLACE FARTHER AWAY FROM--
REEEEOOOOOOOORRRRRGGGH
WHHHNWN
WHHHN

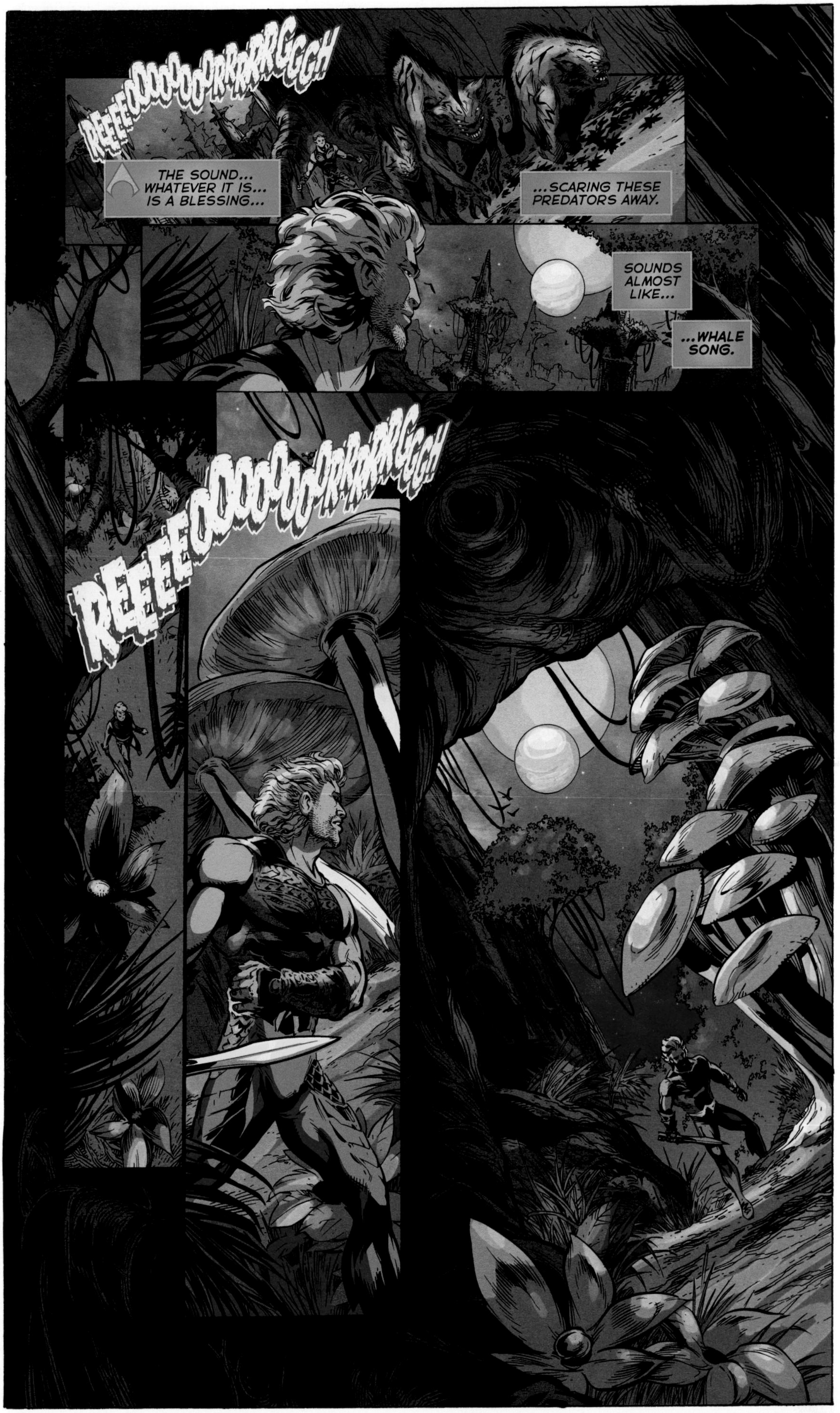
REEEOOOOOOORRRRRGGGH
THE SOUND... WHATEVER IT IS... IS A BLESSING...
...SCARING THESE PREDATORS AWAY.
SOUNDS ALMOST LIKE...
...WHALE SONG.
REEEEOOOOOOOORRRRRRGGGH

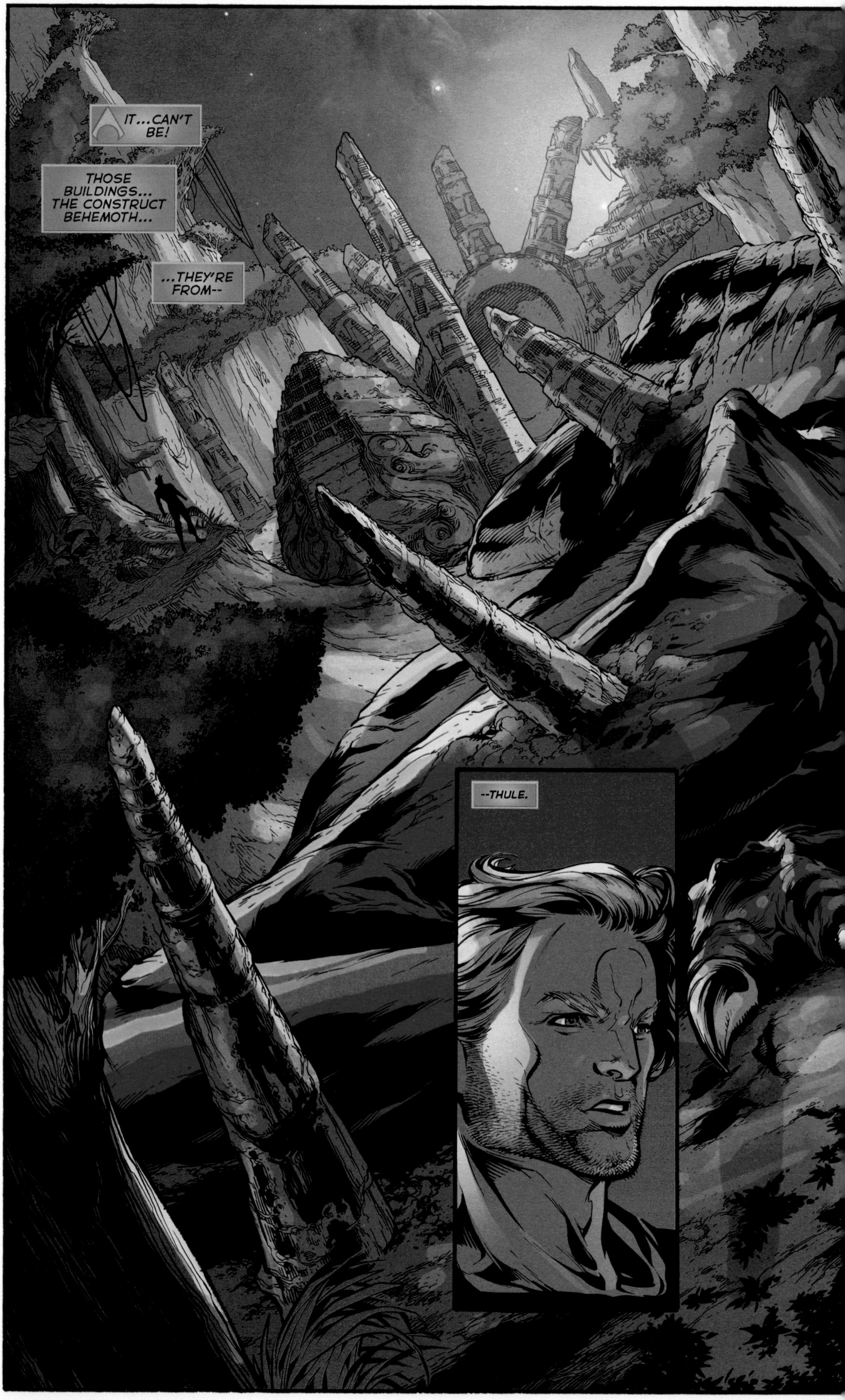
IT...CAN'T BE!
THOSE BUILDINGS... THE CONSTRUCT BEHEMOTH...
...THEY'RE FROM--
--THULE.

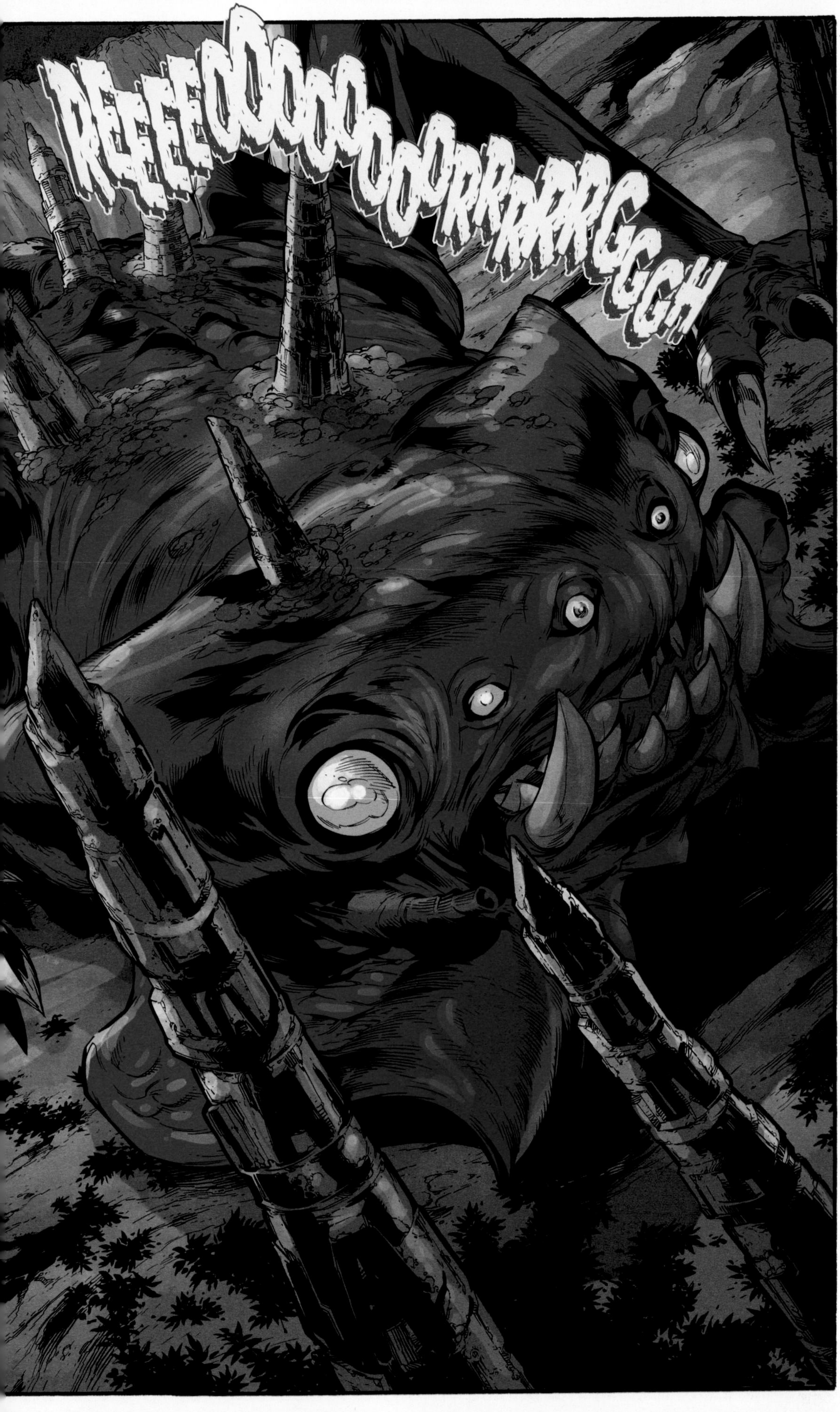
REEEEOOOOOOOOORRRRRRGGGH

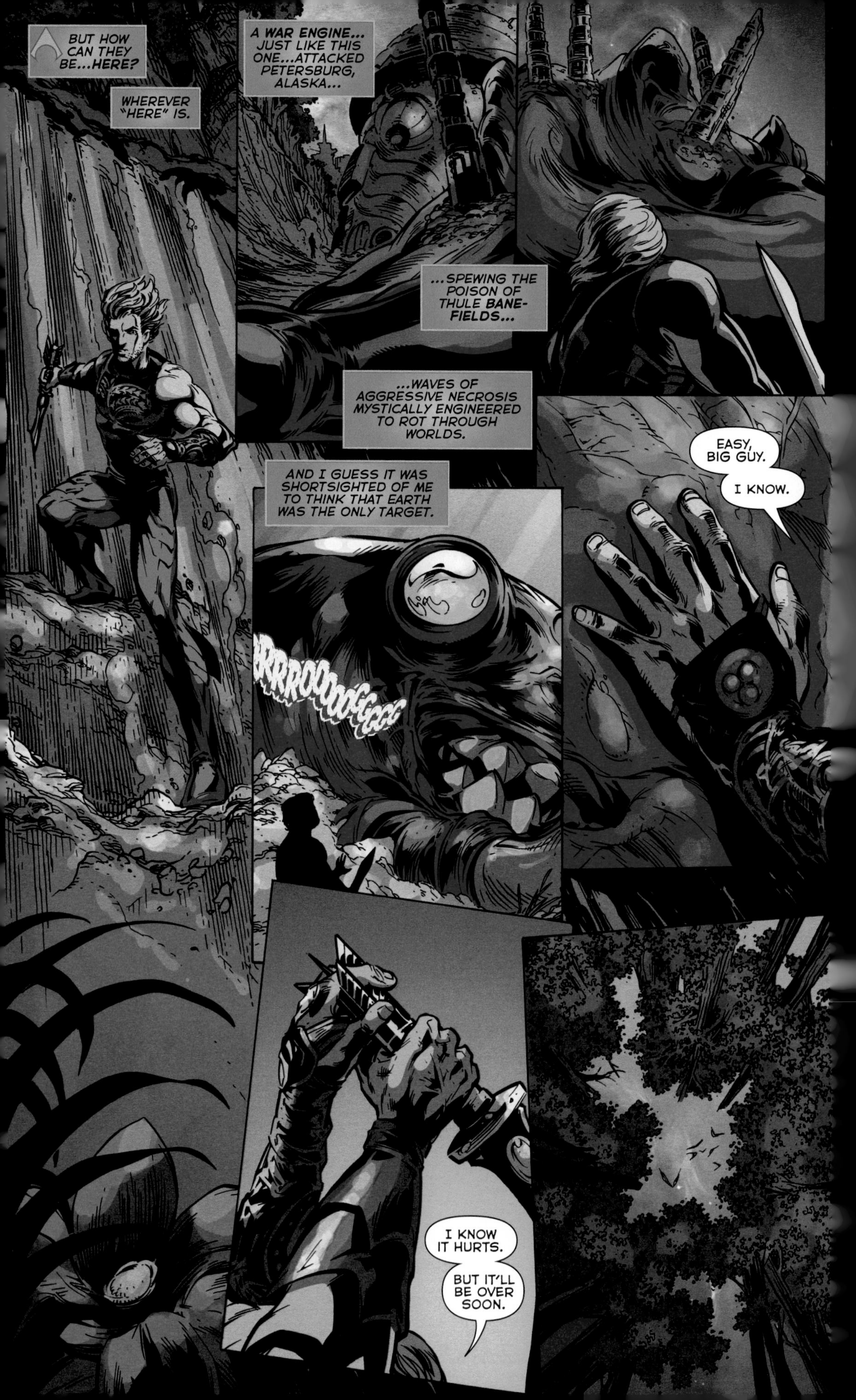
BUT HOW CAN THEY BE...HERE?
WHEREVER "HERE" IS.
A WAR ENGINE... JUST LIKE THIS ONE...ATTACKED PETERSBURG, ALASKA...
...SPEWING THE POISON OF THULE BANE-FIELDS...
...WAVES OF AGGRESSIVE NECROSIS MYSTICALLY ENGINEERED TO ROT THROUGH WORLDS.
AND I GUESS IT WAS SHORTSIGHTED OF ME TO THINK THAT EARTH WAS THE ONLY TARGET.
BRRROOOOOGGGG
EASY, BIG GUY.
I KNOW.
I KNOW IT HURTS.
BUT IT'LL BE OVER SOON.

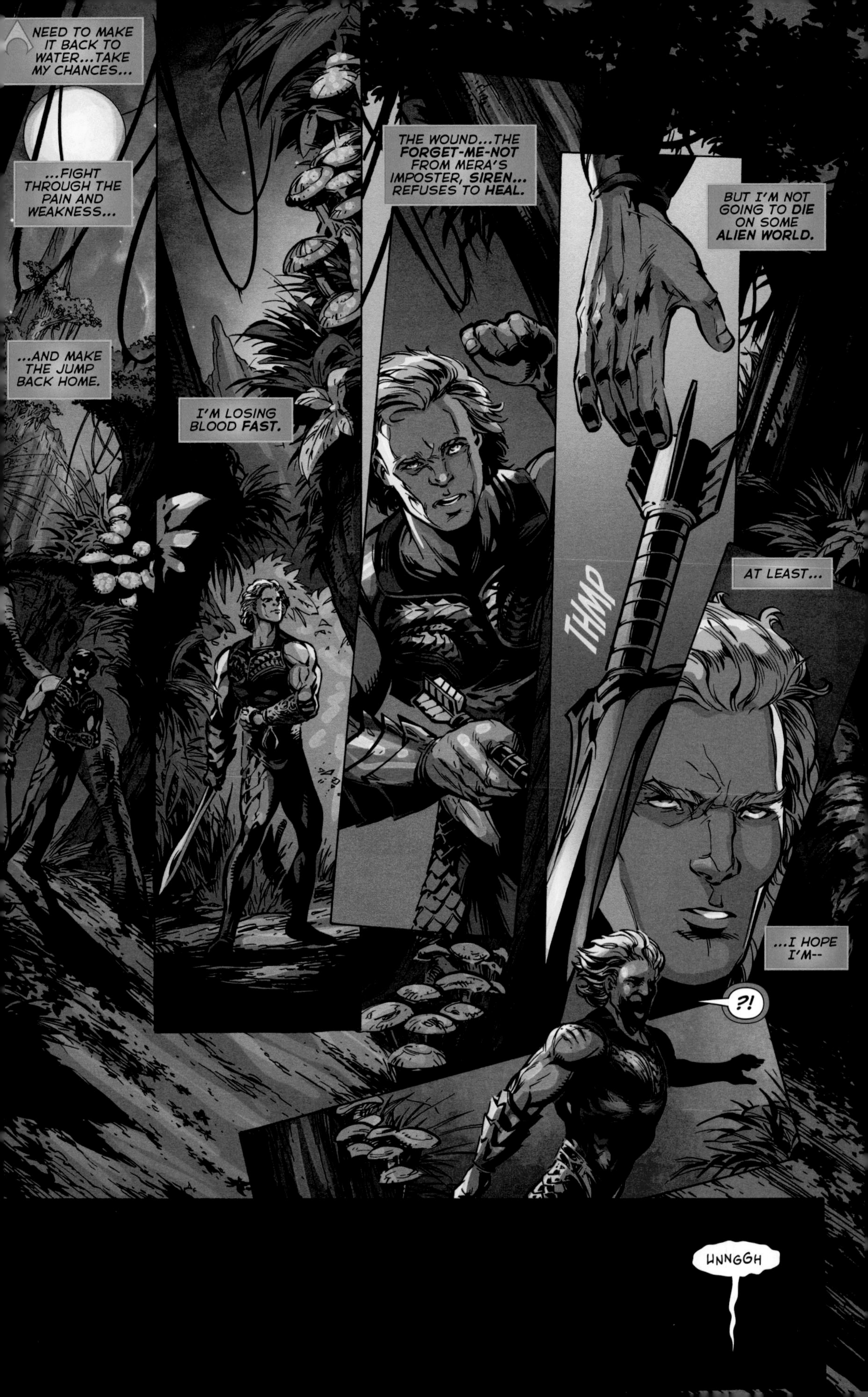
NEED TO MAKE IT BACK TO WATER...TAKE MY CHANCES...
...FIGHT THROUGH THE PAIN AND WEAKNESS...
...AND MAKE THE JUMP BACK HOME.
I'M LOSING BLOOD FAST.
THE WOUND...THE FORGET-ME-NOT FROM MERA'S IMPOSTER, SIREN... REFUSES TO HEAL.
BUT I'M NOT GOING TO DIE ON SOME ALIEN WORLD.
THMP
AT LEAST...
...I HOPE I'M--
?!
UNNGGH

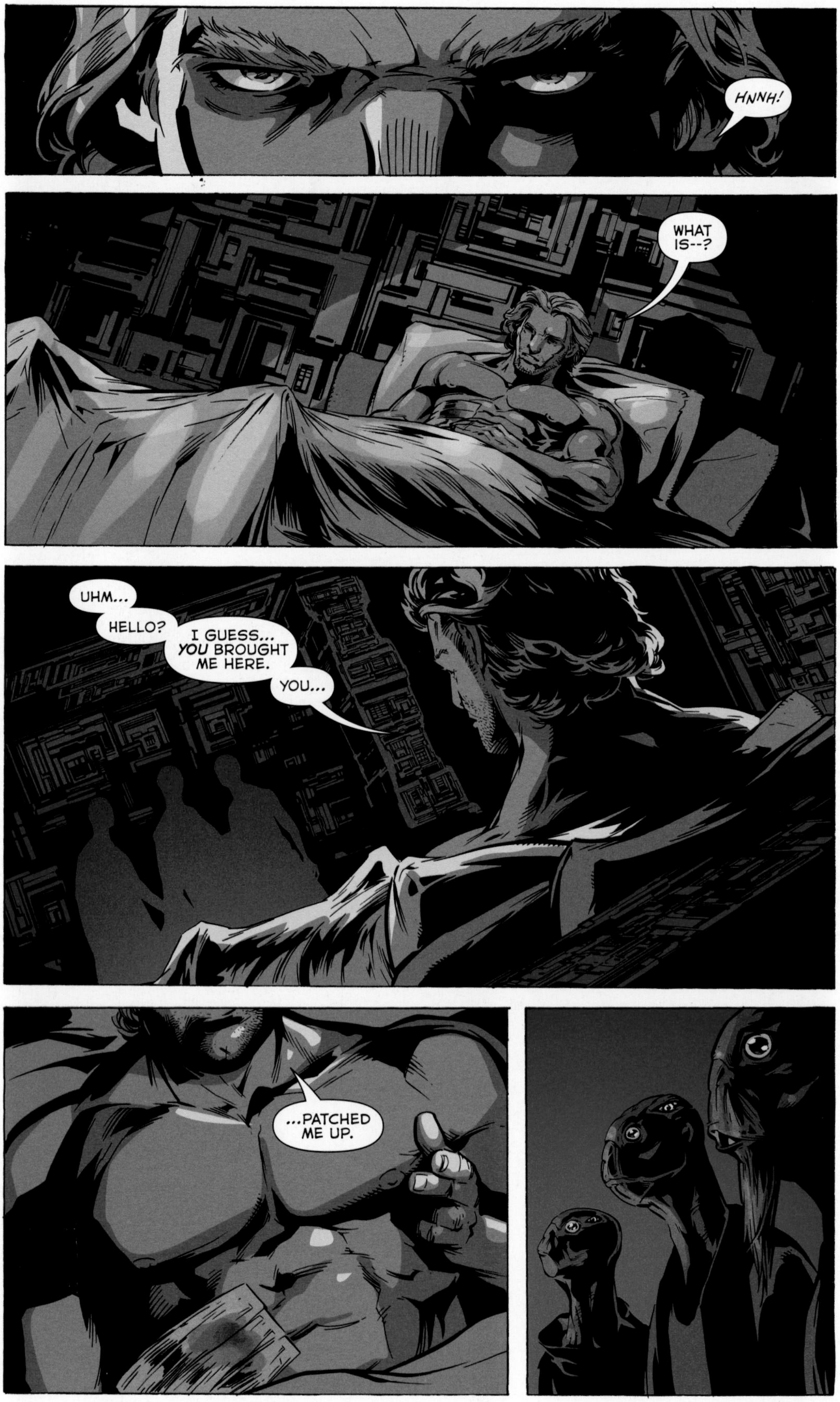
HNNH!
WHAT IS--?
UHM...
HELLO?
I GUESS... YOU BROUGHT ME HERE.
YOU...
...PATCHED ME UP.

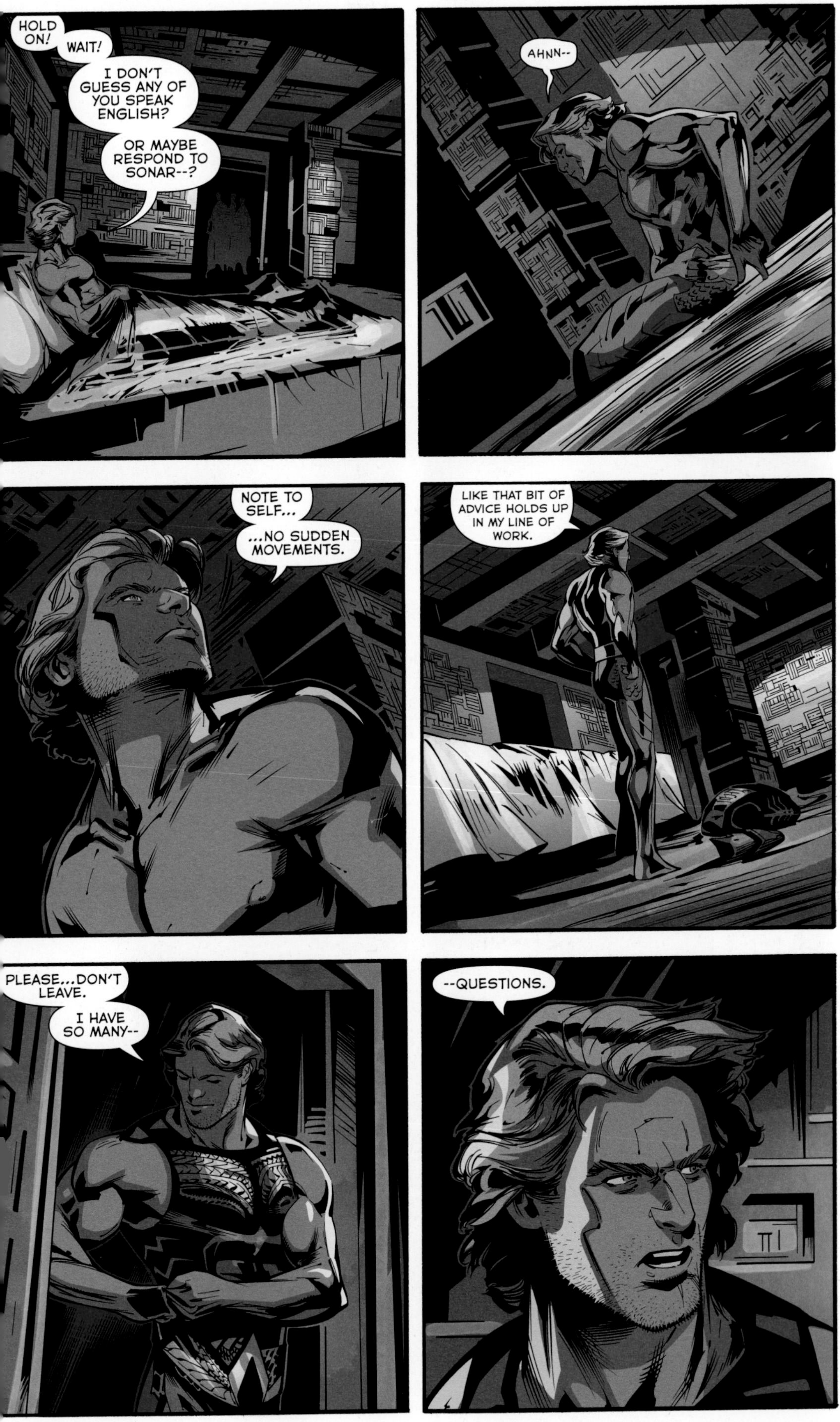

HOLD ON!
WAIT!
I DON'T GUESS ANY OF YOU SPEAK ENGLISH?
OR MAYBE RESPOND TO SONAR--?
AHNN--
NOTE TO SELF...
...NO SUDDEN MOVEMENTS.
LIKE THAT BIT OF ADVICE HOLDS UP IN MY LINE OF WORK.
PLEASE...DON'T LEAVE.
I HAVE SO MANY--
--QUESTIONS.

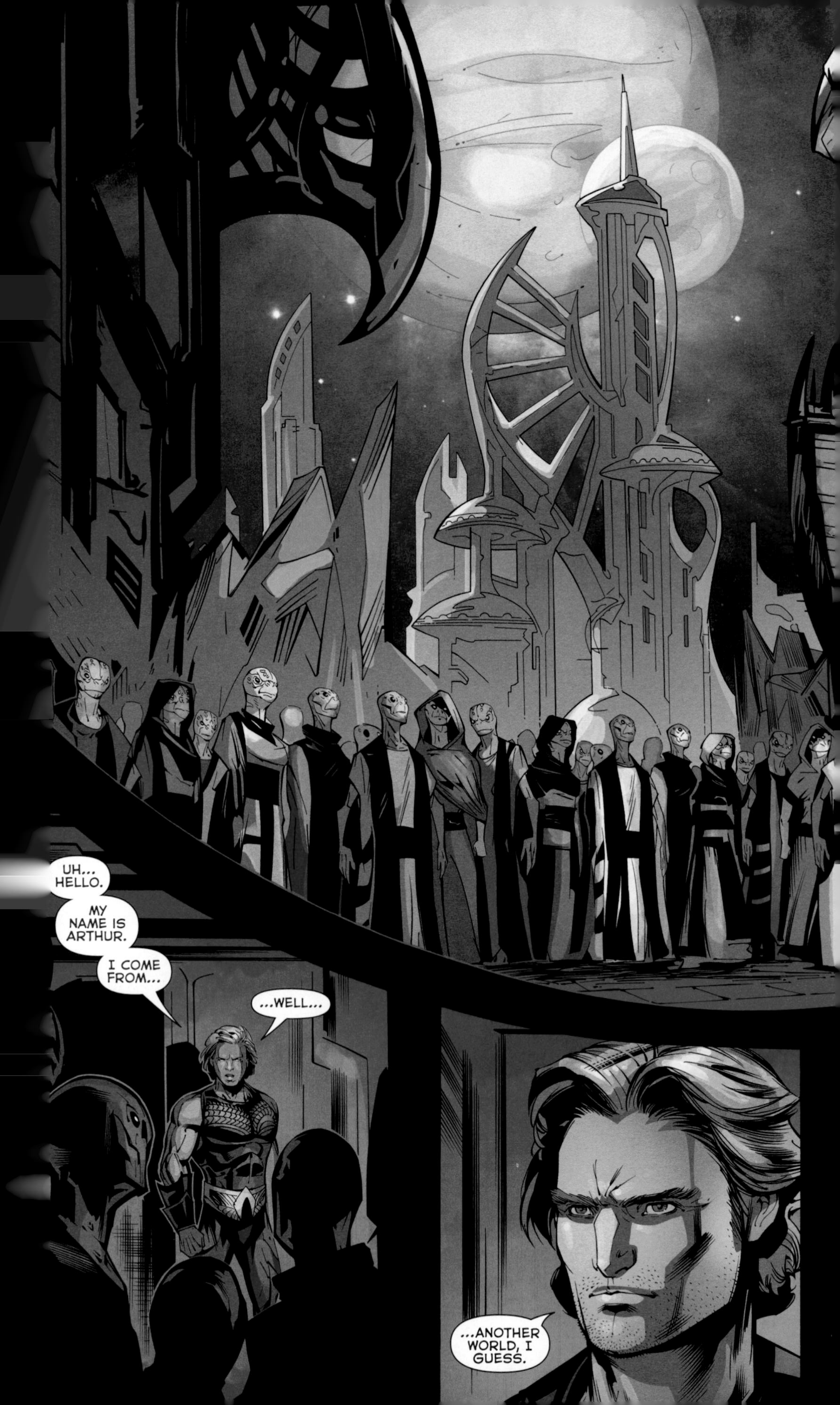
UH... HELLO.
MY NAME IS ARTHUR.
I COME FROM...
...WELL...
...ANOTHER WORLD, I GUESS.

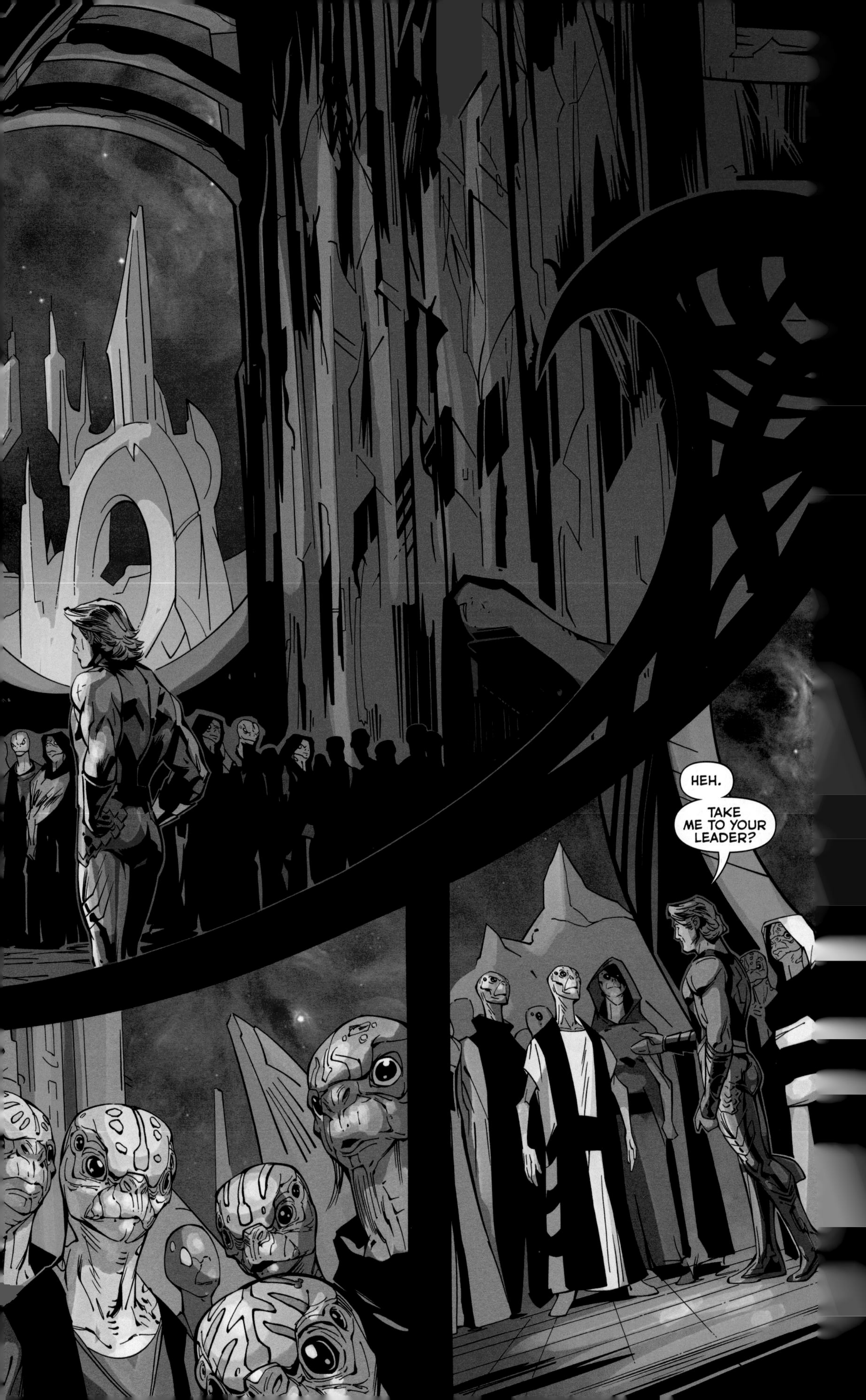
HEH.
TAKE ME TO YOUR LEADER?

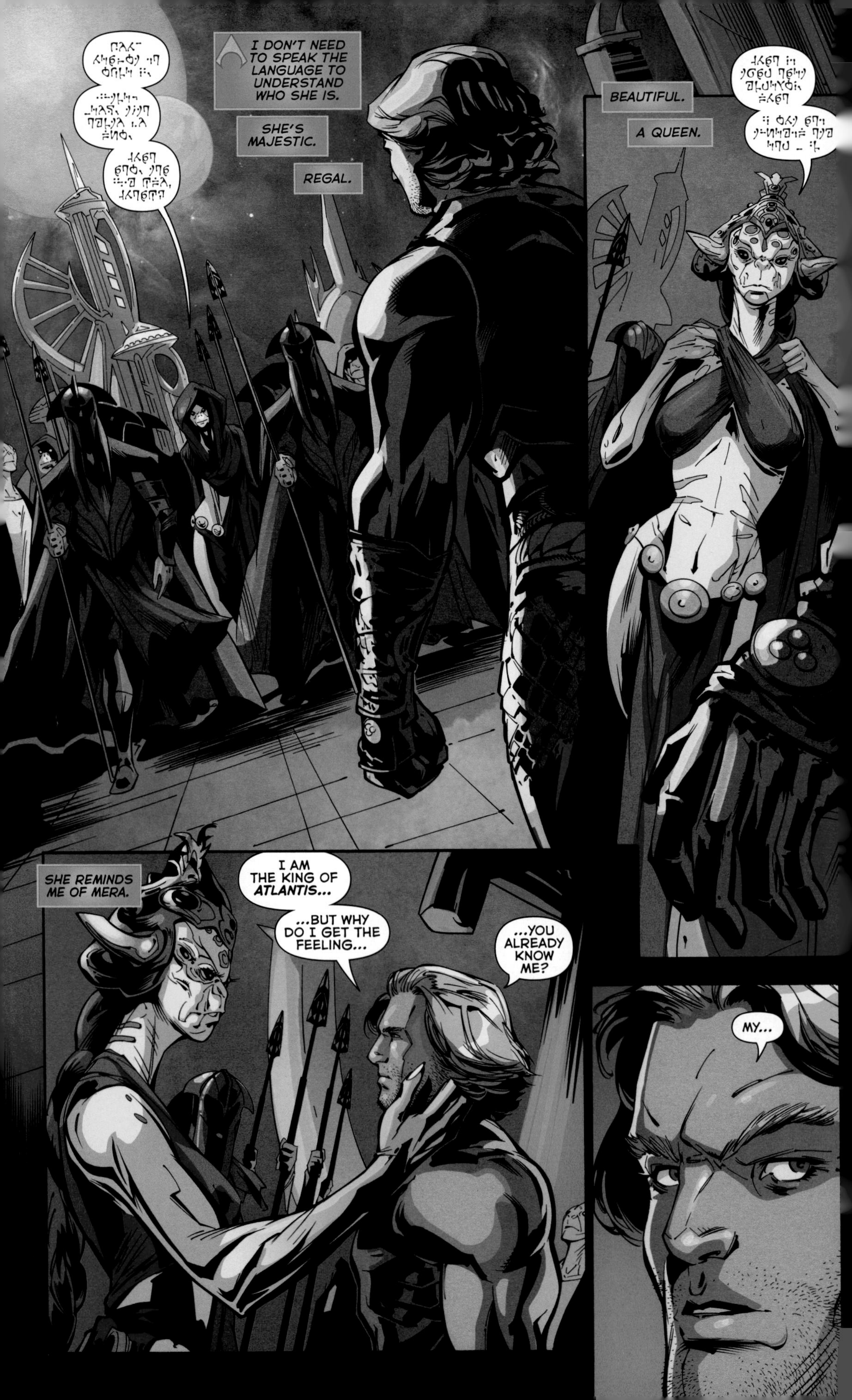
I DON'T NEED TO SPEAK THE LANGUAGE TO UNDERSTAND WHO SHE IS.
SHE'S MAJESTIC.
REGAL.
BEAUTIFUL.
A QUEEN.
SHE REMINDS ME OF MERA.
I AM THE KING OF *ATLANTIS*...
...BUT WHY DO I GET THE FEELING...
...YOU ALREADY KNOW ME?
MY...

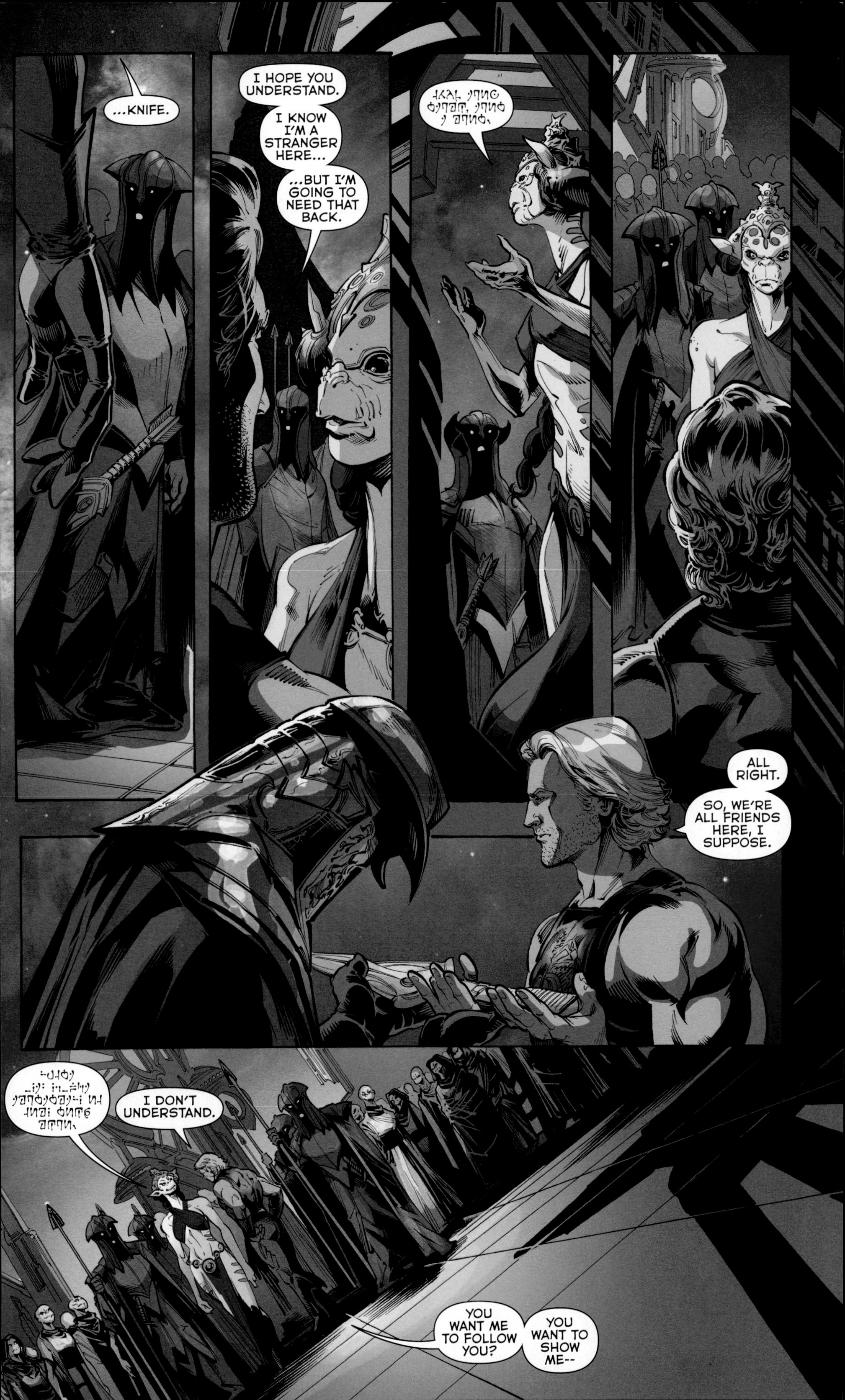
...KNIFE.
I HOPE YOU UNDERSTAND.
I KNOW I'M A STRANGER HERE...
...BUT I'M GOING TO NEED THAT BACK.
ALL RIGHT.
SO, WE'RE ALL FRIENDS HERE, I SUPPOSE.
I DON'T UNDERSTAND.
YOU WANT ME TO FOLLOW YOU?
YOU WANT TO SHOW ME--

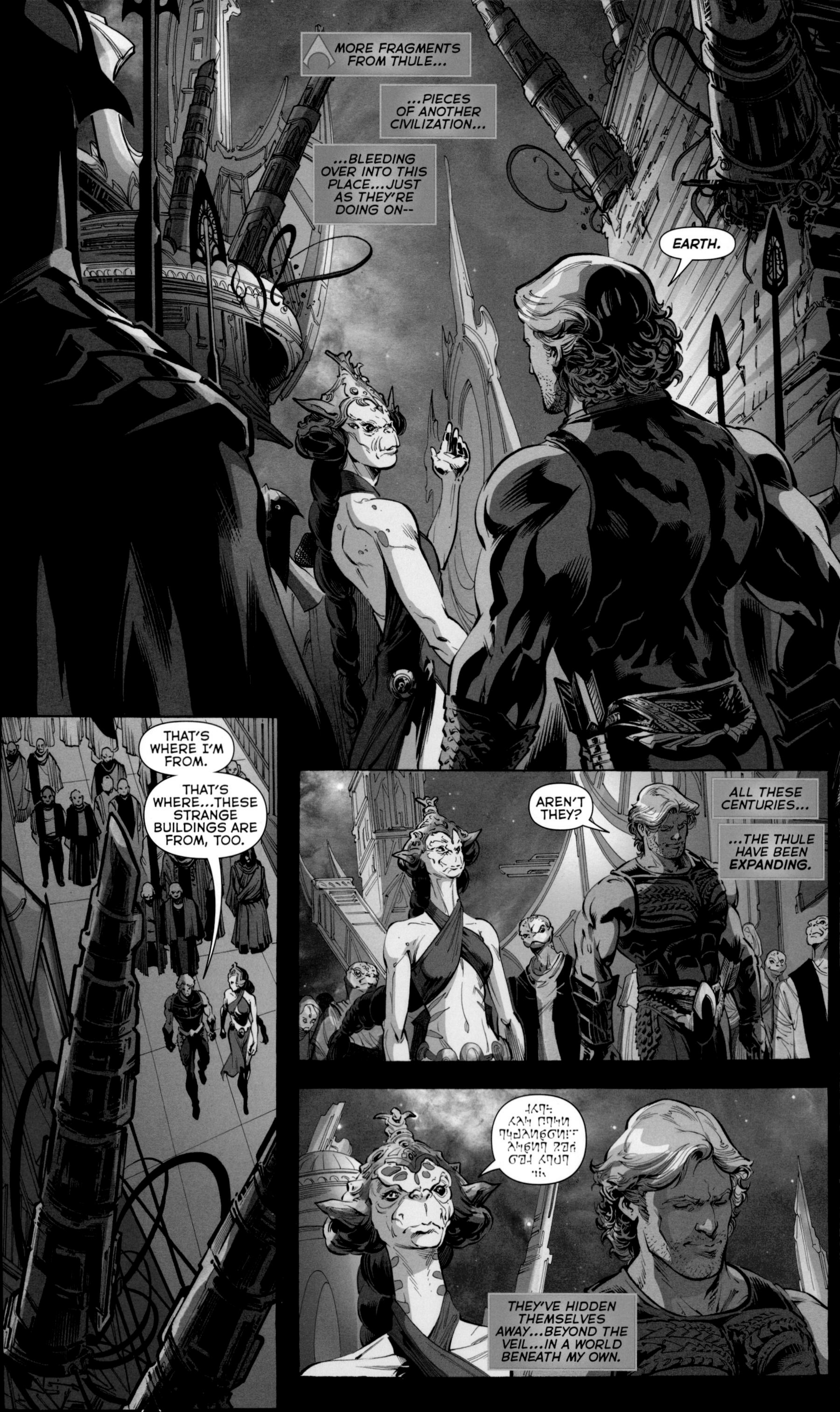
MORE FRAGMENTS FROM THULE...
...PIECES OF ANOTHER CIVILIZATION...
...BLEEDING OVER INTO THIS PLACE...JUST AS THEY'RE DOING ON--
EARTH.
THAT'S WHERE I'M FROM.
THAT'S WHERE...THESE STRANGE BUILDINGS ARE FROM, TOO.
AREN'T THEY?
ALL THESE CENTURIES...
...THE THULE HAVE BEEN EXPANDING.
THEY'VE HIDDEN THEMSELVES AWAY...BEYOND THE VEIL...IN A WORLD BENEATH MY OWN.

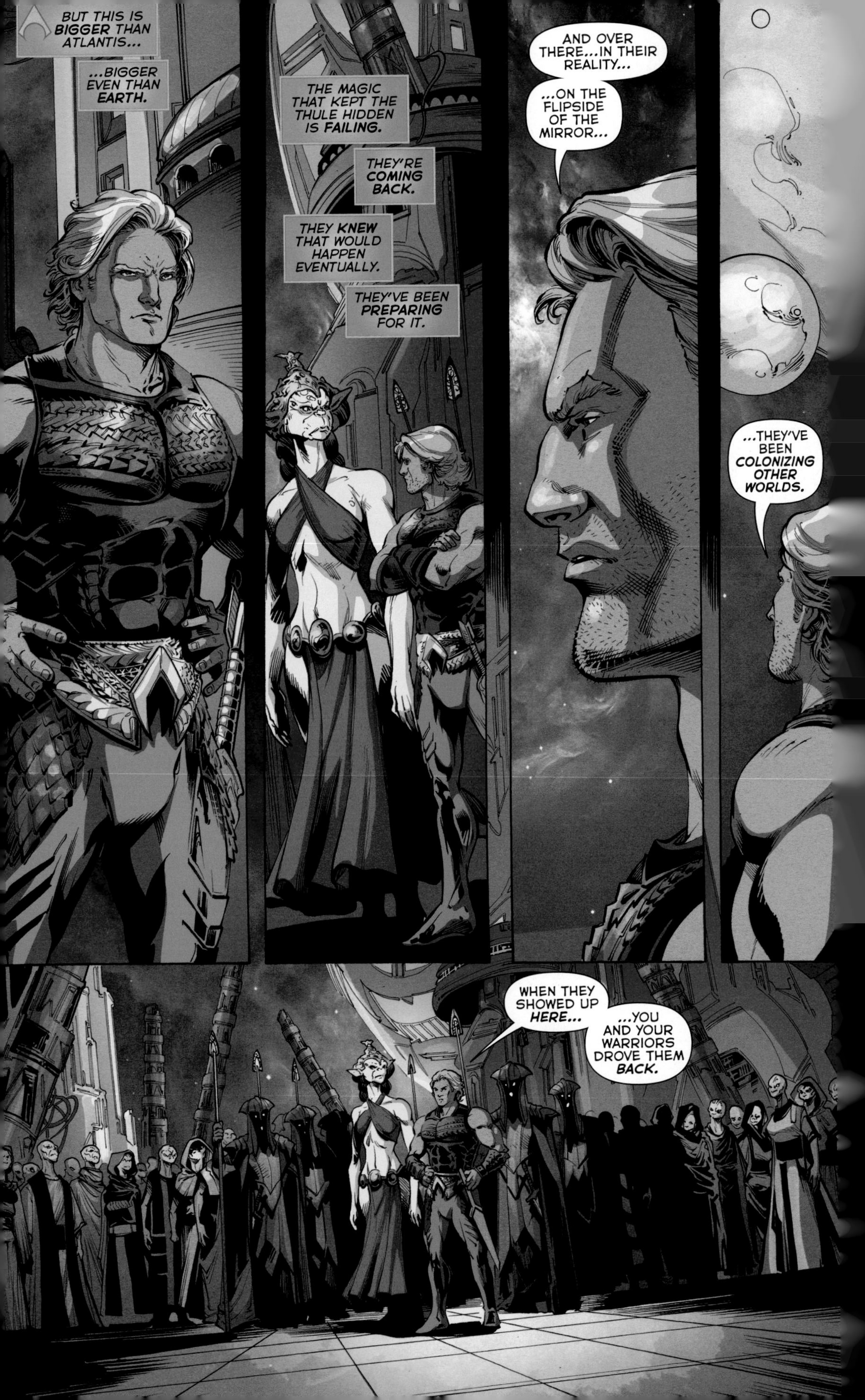
BUT THIS IS BIGGER THAN ATLANTIS...
...BIGGER EVEN THAN EARTH.
THE MAGIC THAT KEPT THE THULE HIDDEN IS FAILING.
THEY'RE COMING BACK.
THEY KNEW THAT WOULD HAPPEN EVENTUALLY.
THEY'VE BEEN PREPARING FOR IT.
AND OVER THERE...IN THEIR REALITY...
...ON THE FLIPSIDE OF THE MIRROR...
...THEY'VE BEEN COLONIZING OTHER WORLDS.
WHEN THEY SHOWED UP HERE...
...YOU AND YOUR WARRIORS DROVE THEM BACK.

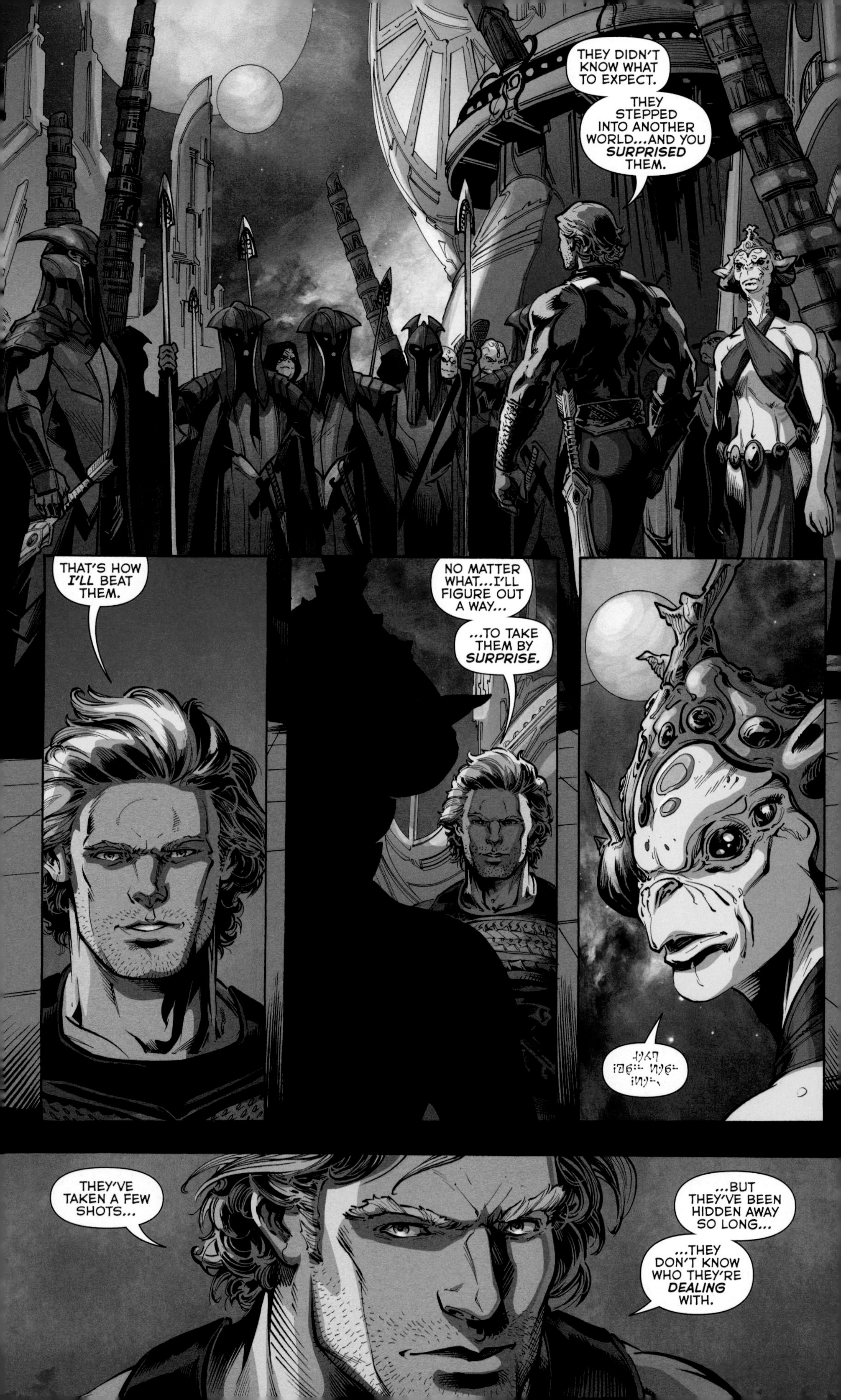
THEY DIDN'T KNOW WHAT TO EXPECT.
THEY STEPPED INTO ANOTHER WORLD...AND YOU SURPRISED THEM.
THAT'S HOW I'LL BEAT THEM.
NO MATTER WHAT...I'LL FIGURE OUT A WAY...
...TO TAKE THEM BY SURPRISE.
THEY'VE TAKEN A FEW SHOTS...
...BUT THEY'VE BEEN HIDDEN AWAY SO LONG...
...THEY DON'T KNOW WHO THEY'RE DEALING WITH.

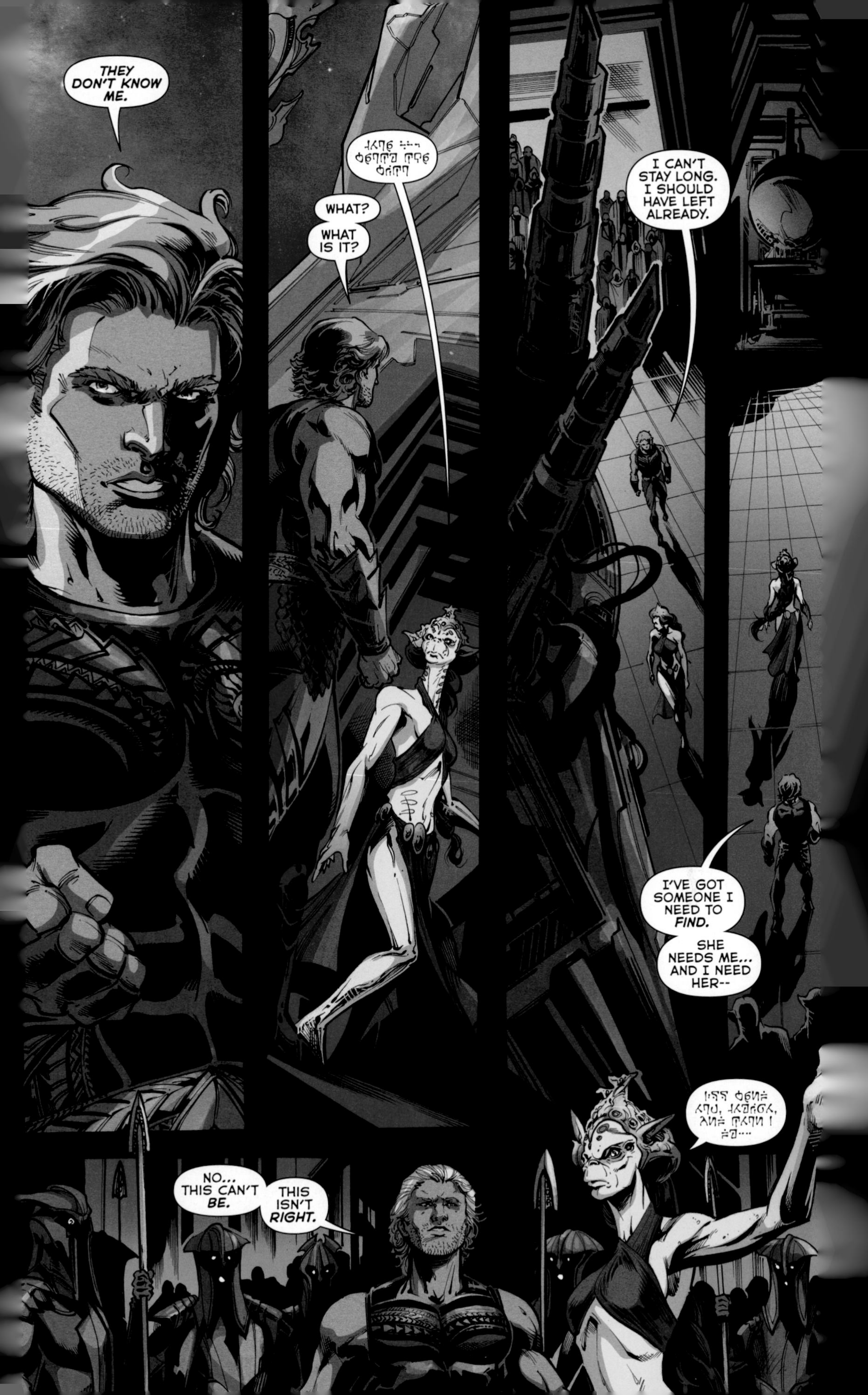
THEY DON'T KNOW ME.
WHAT?
WHAT IS IT?
I CAN'T STAY LONG. I SHOULD HAVE LEFT ALREADY.
I'VE GOT SOMEONE I NEED TO FIND.
SHE NEEDS ME... AND I NEED HER--
NO... THIS CAN'T BE.
THIS ISN'T RIGHT.

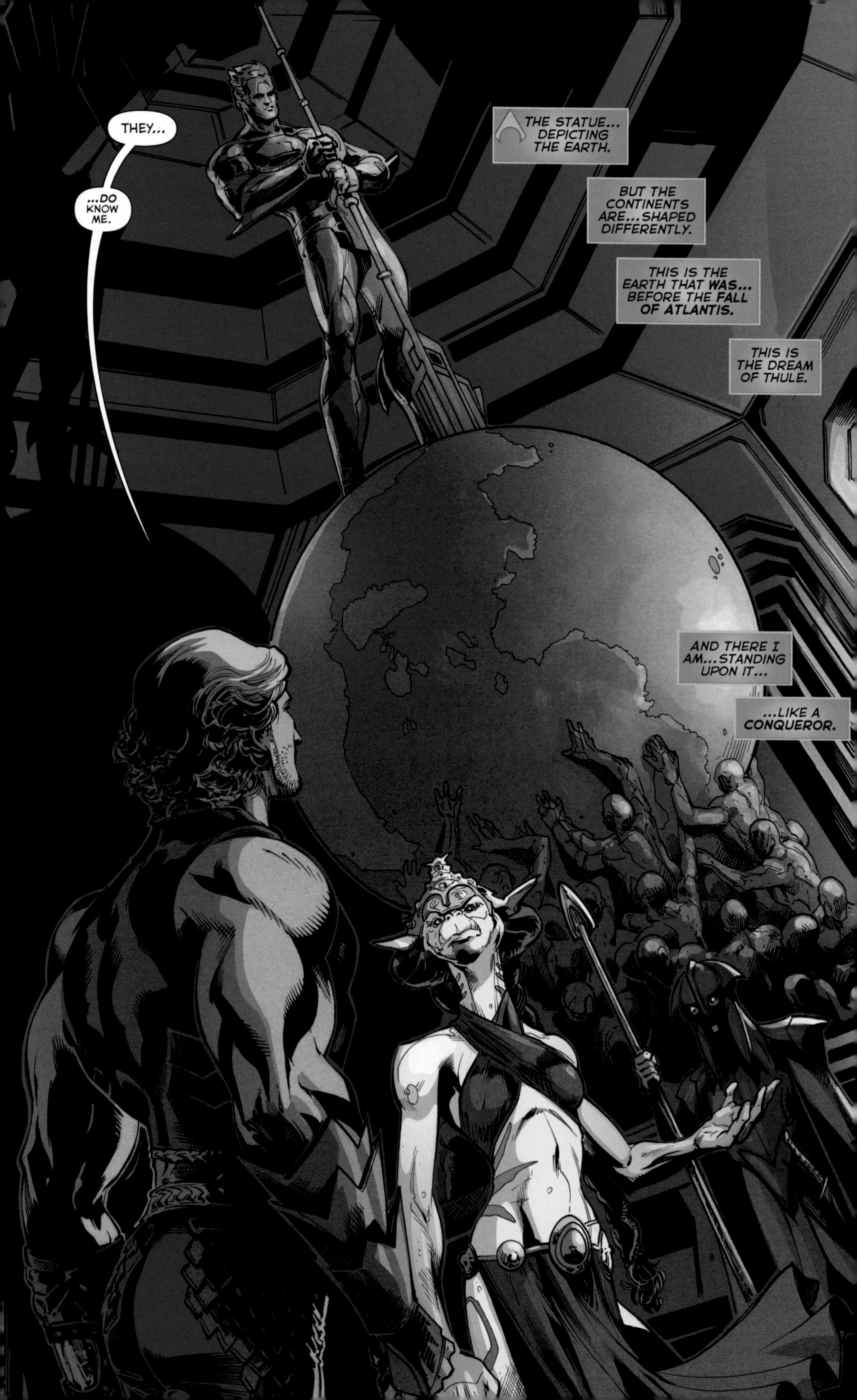
THEY...
...DO KNOW ME.
THE STATUE... DEPICTING THE EARTH.
BUT THE CONTINENTS ARE...SHAPED DIFFERENTLY.
THIS IS THE EARTH THAT WAS... BEFORE THE FALL OF ATLANTIS.
THIS IS THE DREAM OF THULE.
AND THERE I AM...STANDING UPON IT...
...LIKE A CONQUEROR.

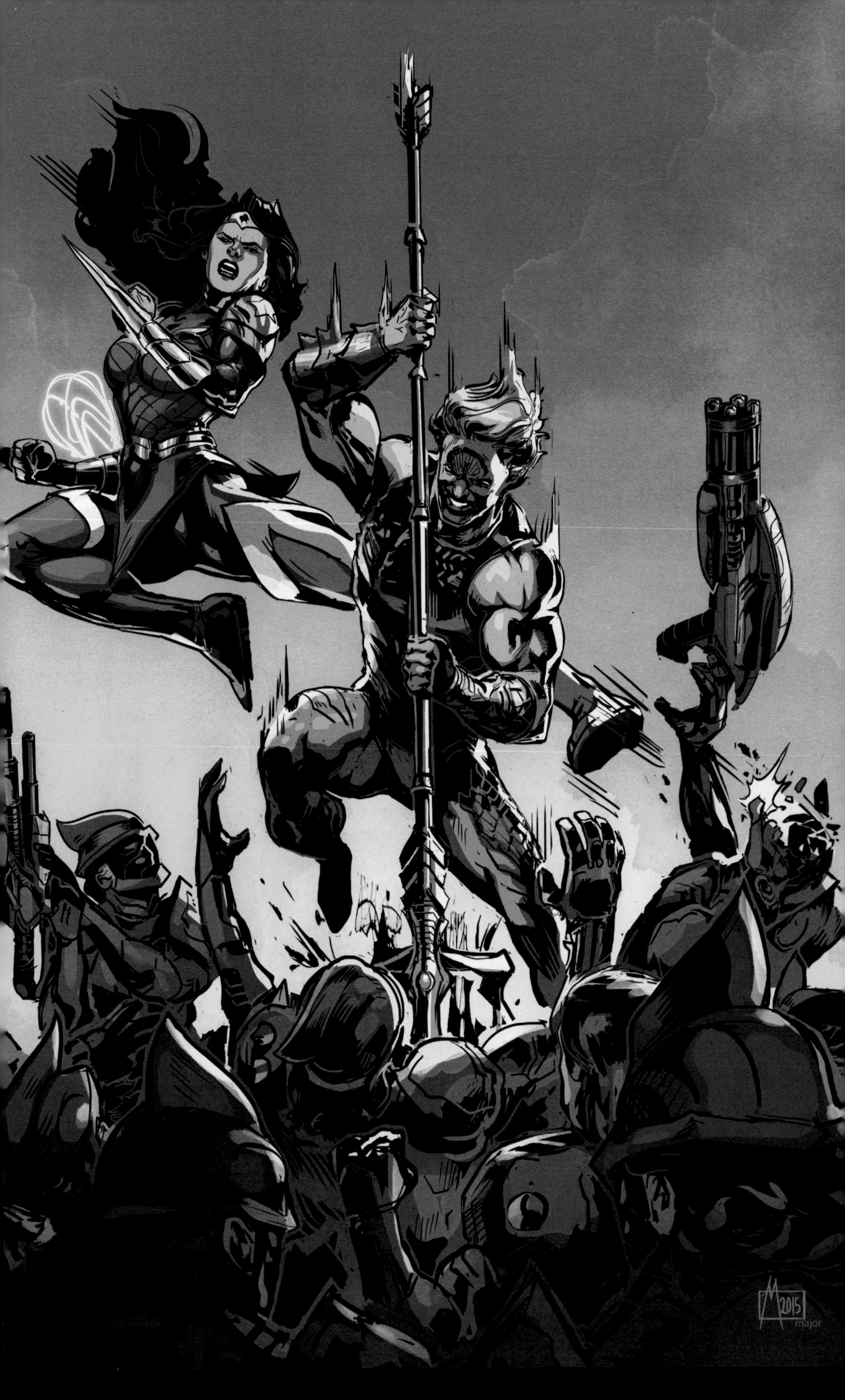
2015
major

AMAZON IN THE AMAZON

CULLEN BUNN writer **VICENTE CIFUENTES** penciller **JOHN DELL, JOHN LIVESAY, MARC DEERING** inkers **GUY MAJOR** colorist **TOM NAPOLITANO** letterer
TREVOR MCCARTHY cover art

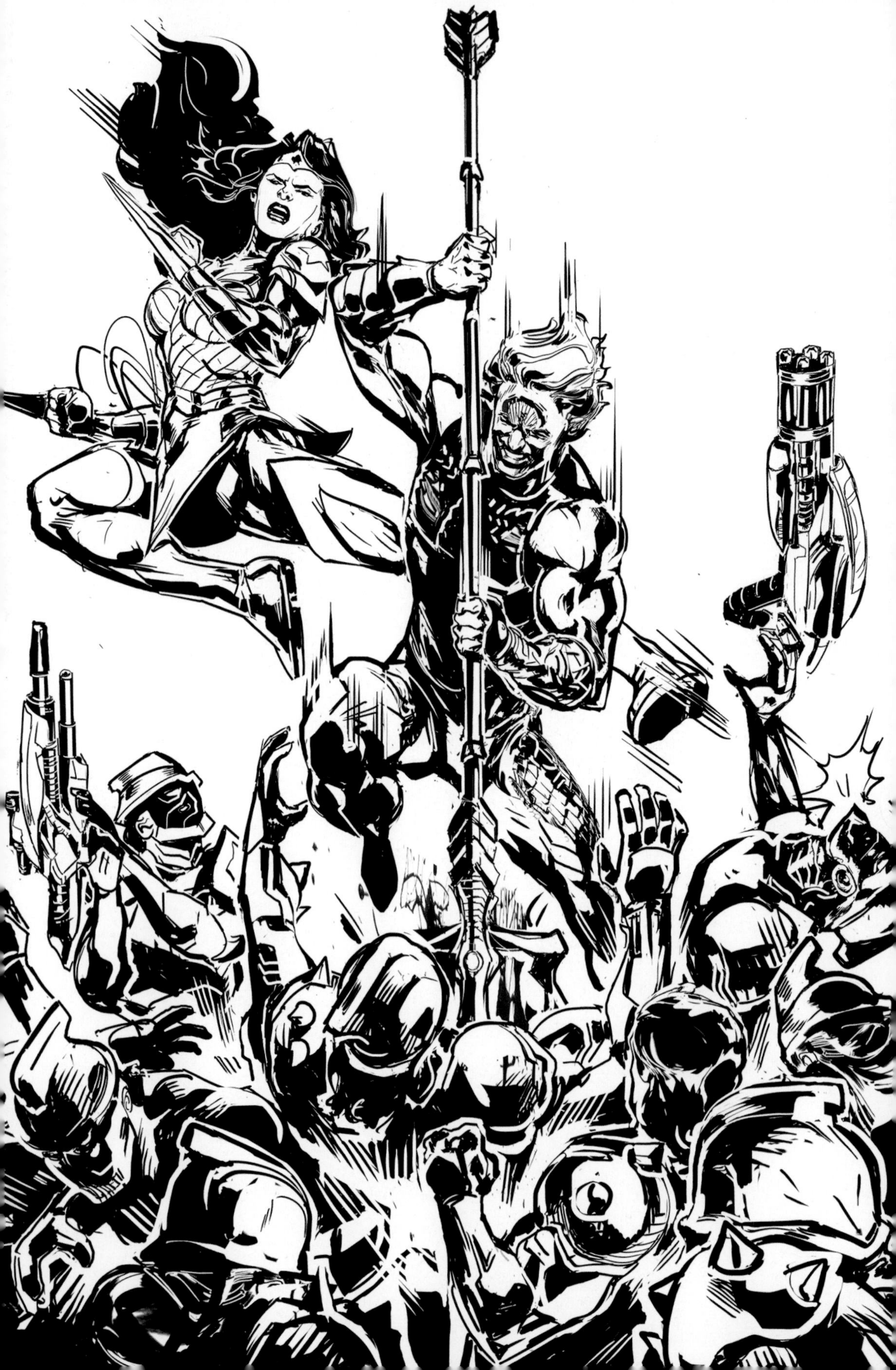

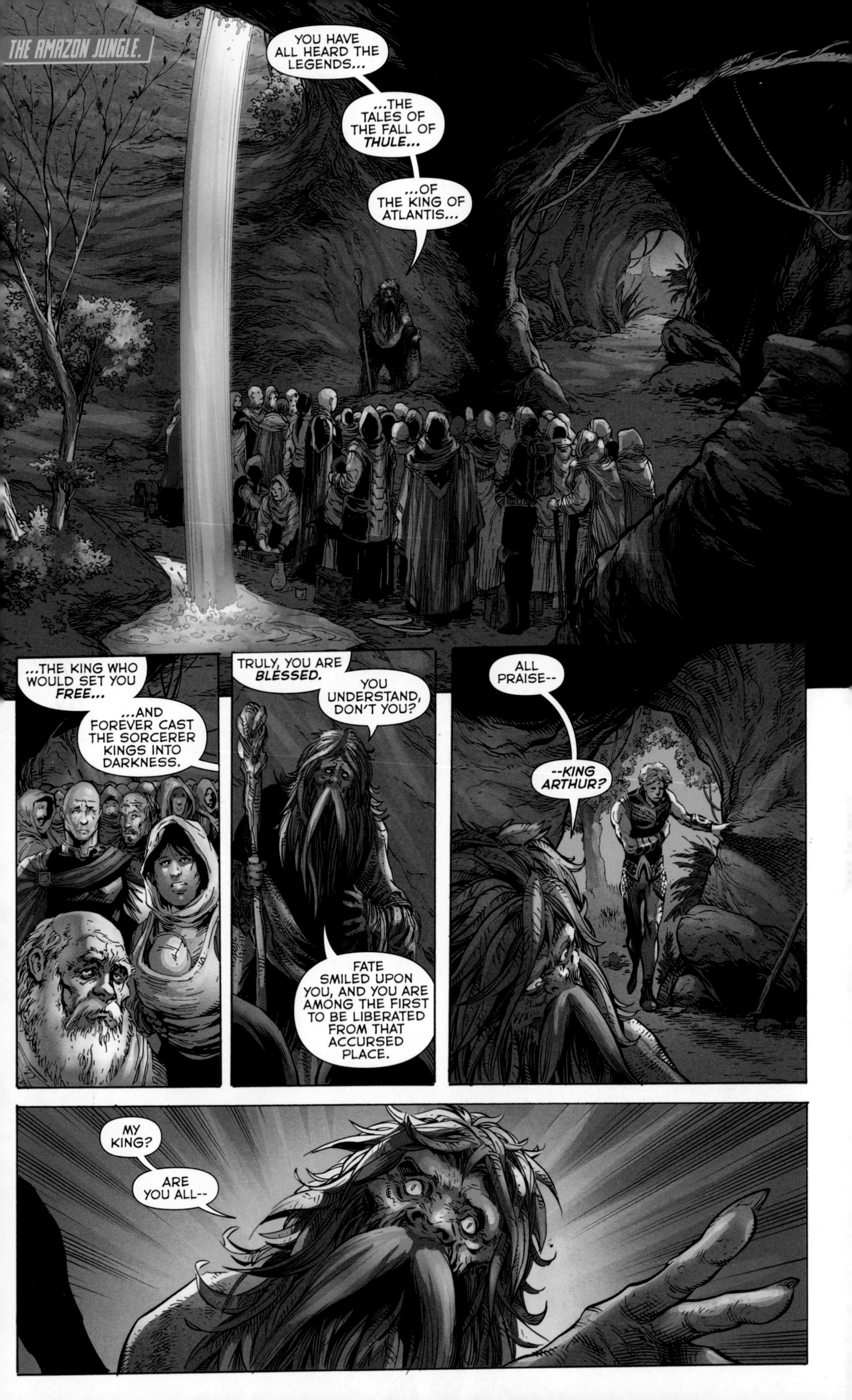
THE AMAZON JUNGLE.
YOU HAVE ALL HEARD THE LEGENDS...
...THE TALES OF THE FALL OF THULE...
...OF THE KING OF ATLANTIS...
...THE KING WHO WOULD SET YOU FREE...
...AND FOREVER CAST THE SORCERER KINGS INTO DARKNESS.
TRULY, YOU ARE BLESSED.
YOU UNDERSTAND, DON'T YOU?
FATE SMILED UPON YOU, AND YOU ARE AMONG THE FIRST TO BE LIBERATED FROM THAT ACCURSED PLACE.
ALL PRAISE--
--KING ARTHUR?
MY KING?
ARE YOU ALL--

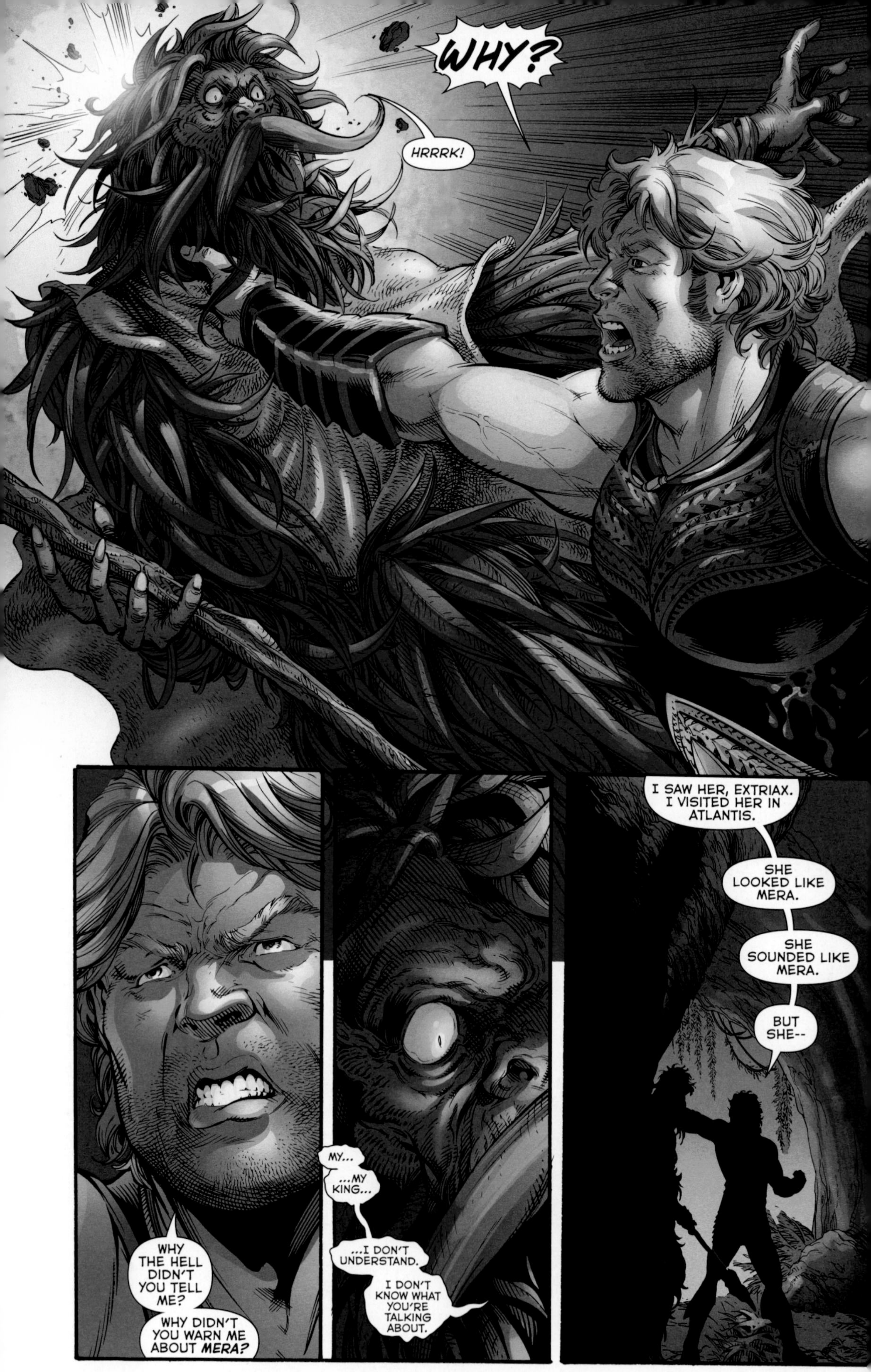
WHY?
HRRRK!
WHY THE HELL DIDN'T YOU TELL ME?
WHY DIDN'T YOU WARN ME ABOUT *MERA?*
MY...
...MY KING...
...I DON'T UNDERSTAND.
I DON'T KNOW WHAT YOU'RE TALKING ABOUT.
I SAW HER, EXTRIAX. I VISITED HER IN ATLANTIS.
SHE LOOKED LIKE MERA.
SHE SOUNDED LIKE MERA.
BUT SHE--

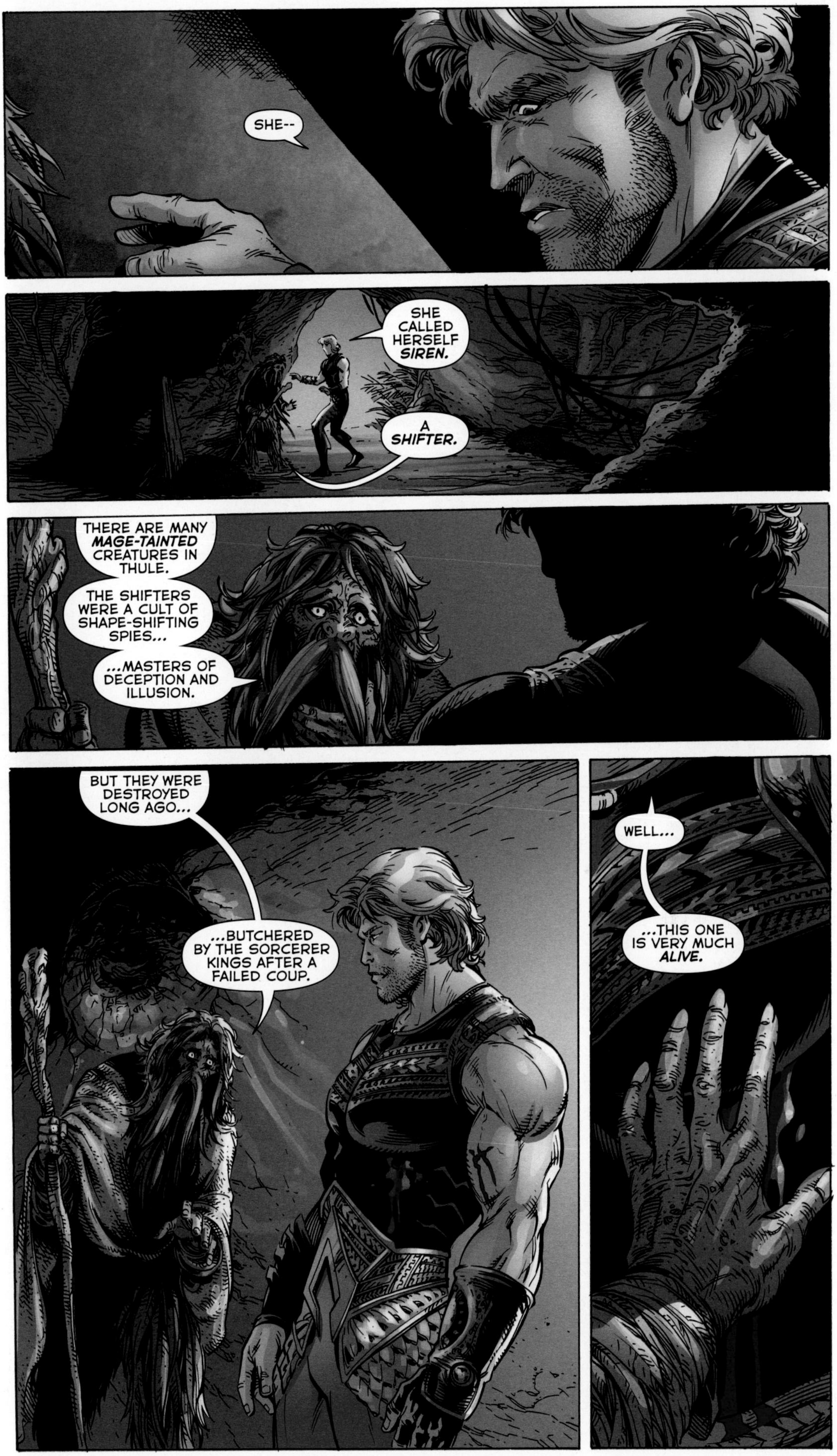
SHE--
SHE CALLED HERSELF SIREN.
A SHIFTER.
THERE ARE MANY MAGE-TAINTED CREATURES IN THULE.
THE SHIFTERS WERE A CULT OF SHAPE-SHIFTING SPIES...
...MASTERS OF DECEPTION AND ILLUSION.
BUT THEY WERE DESTROYED LONG AGO...
...BUTCHERED BY THE SORCERER KINGS AFTER A FAILED COUP.
WELL...
...THIS ONE IS VERY MUCH ALIVE.

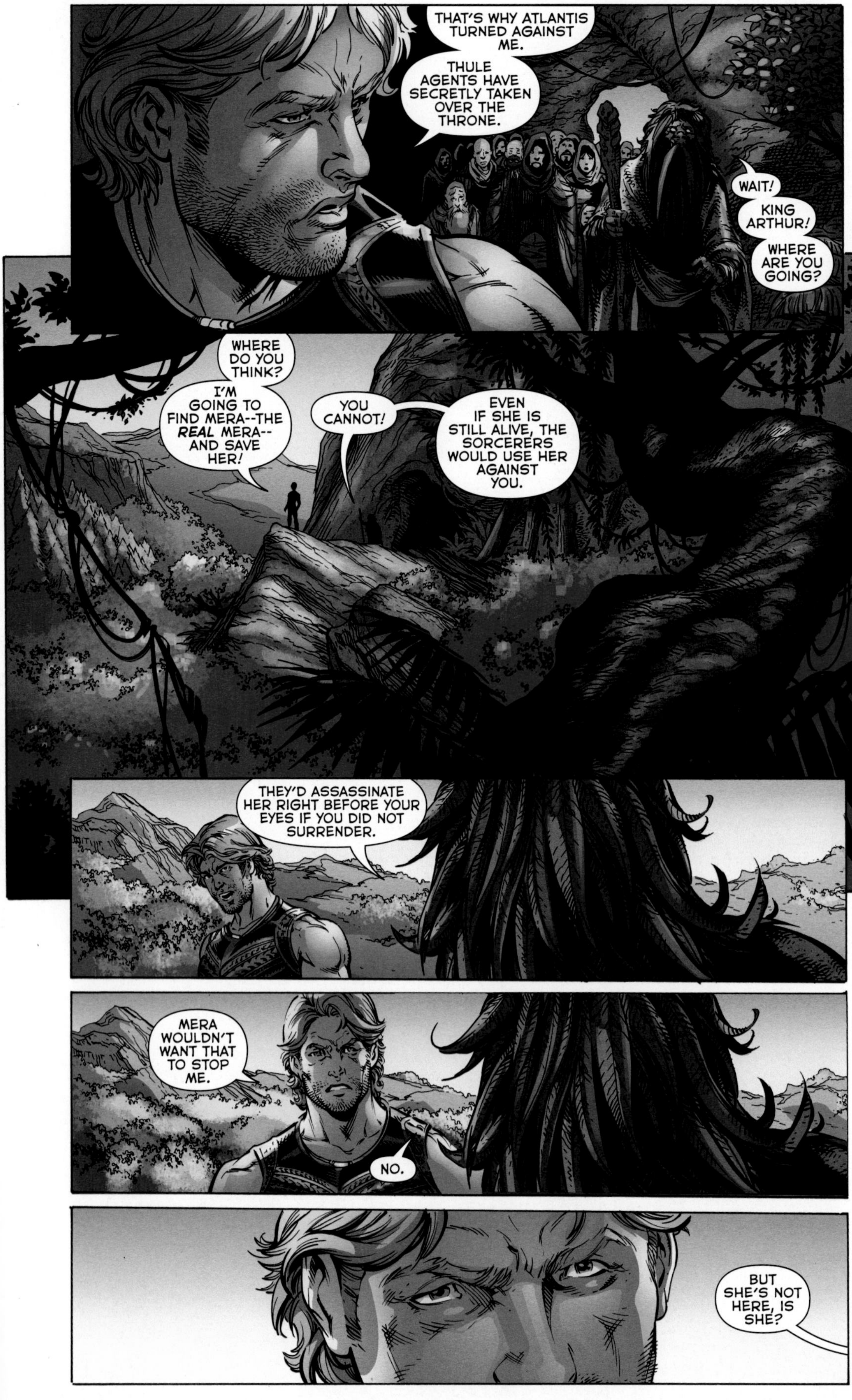
THAT'S WHY ATLANTIS TURNED AGAINST ME.
THULE AGENTS HAVE SECRETLY TAKEN OVER THE THRONE.
WAIT!
KING ARTHUR!
WHERE ARE YOU GOING?
WHERE DO YOU THINK?
I'M GOING TO FIND MERA--THE *REAL* MERA--AND SAVE HER!
YOU CANNOT!
EVEN IF SHE IS STILL ALIVE, THE SORCERERS WOULD USE HER AGAINST YOU.
THEY'D ASSASSINATE HER RIGHT BEFORE YOUR EYES IF YOU DID NOT SURRENDER.
MERA WOULDN'T WANT THAT TO STOP ME.
NO.
BUT SHE'S NOT HERE, IS SHE?

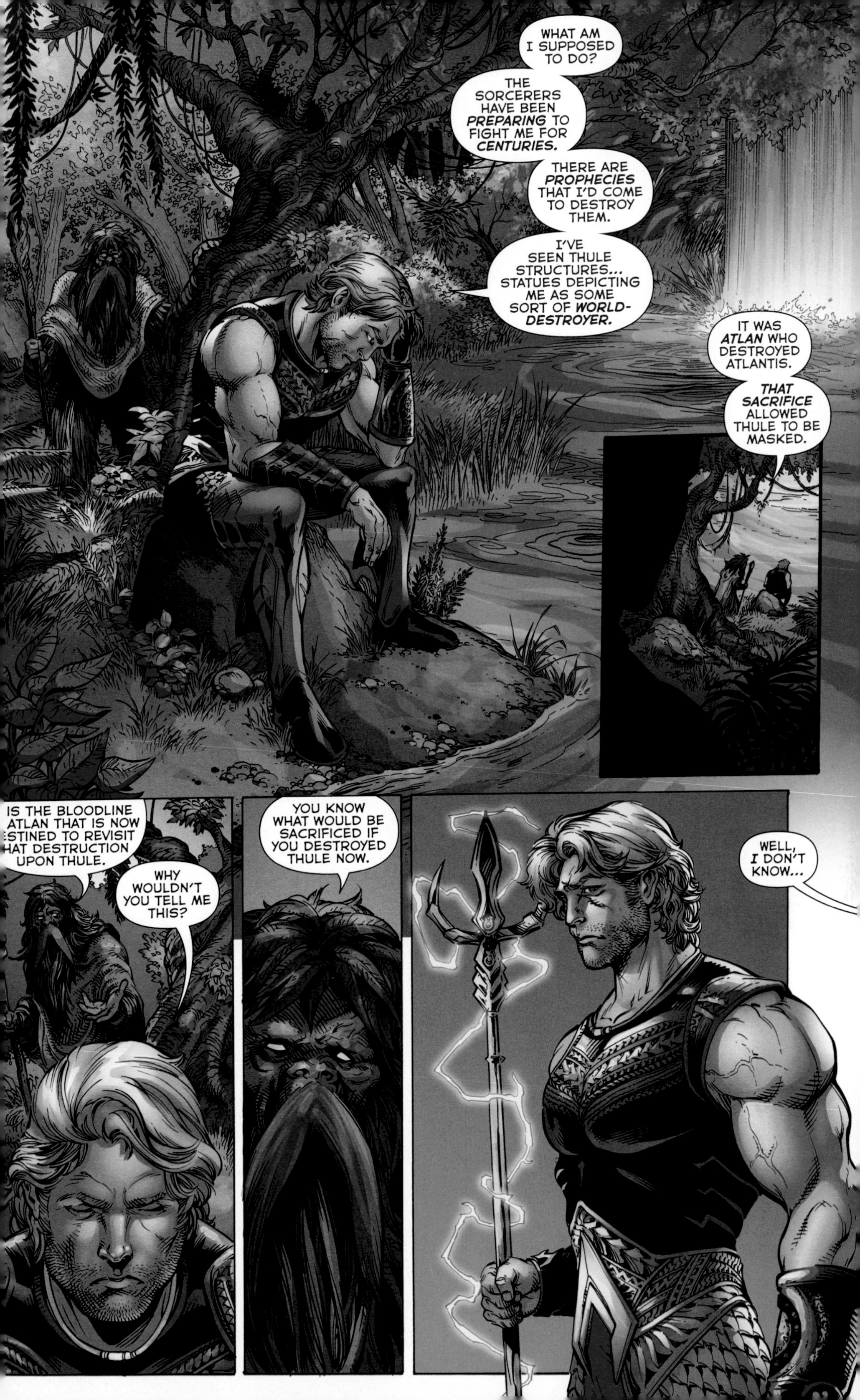
WHAT AM I SUPPOSED TO DO?
THE SORCERERS HAVE BEEN PREPARING TO FIGHT ME FOR CENTURIES.
THERE ARE PROPHECIES THAT I'D COME TO DESTROY THEM.
I'VE SEEN THULE STRUCTURES... STATUES DEPICTING ME AS SOME SORT OF WORLD-DESTROYER.
IT WAS ATLAN WHO DESTROYED ATLANTIS.
THAT SACRIFICE ALLOWED THULE TO BE MASKED.
IS THE BLOODLINE ATLAN THAT IS NOW ESTINED TO REVISIT HAT DESTRUCTION UPON THULE.
WHY WOULDN'T YOU TELL ME THIS?
YOU KNOW WHAT WOULD BE SACRIFICED IF YOU DESTROYED THULE NOW.
WELL, I DON'T KNOW...

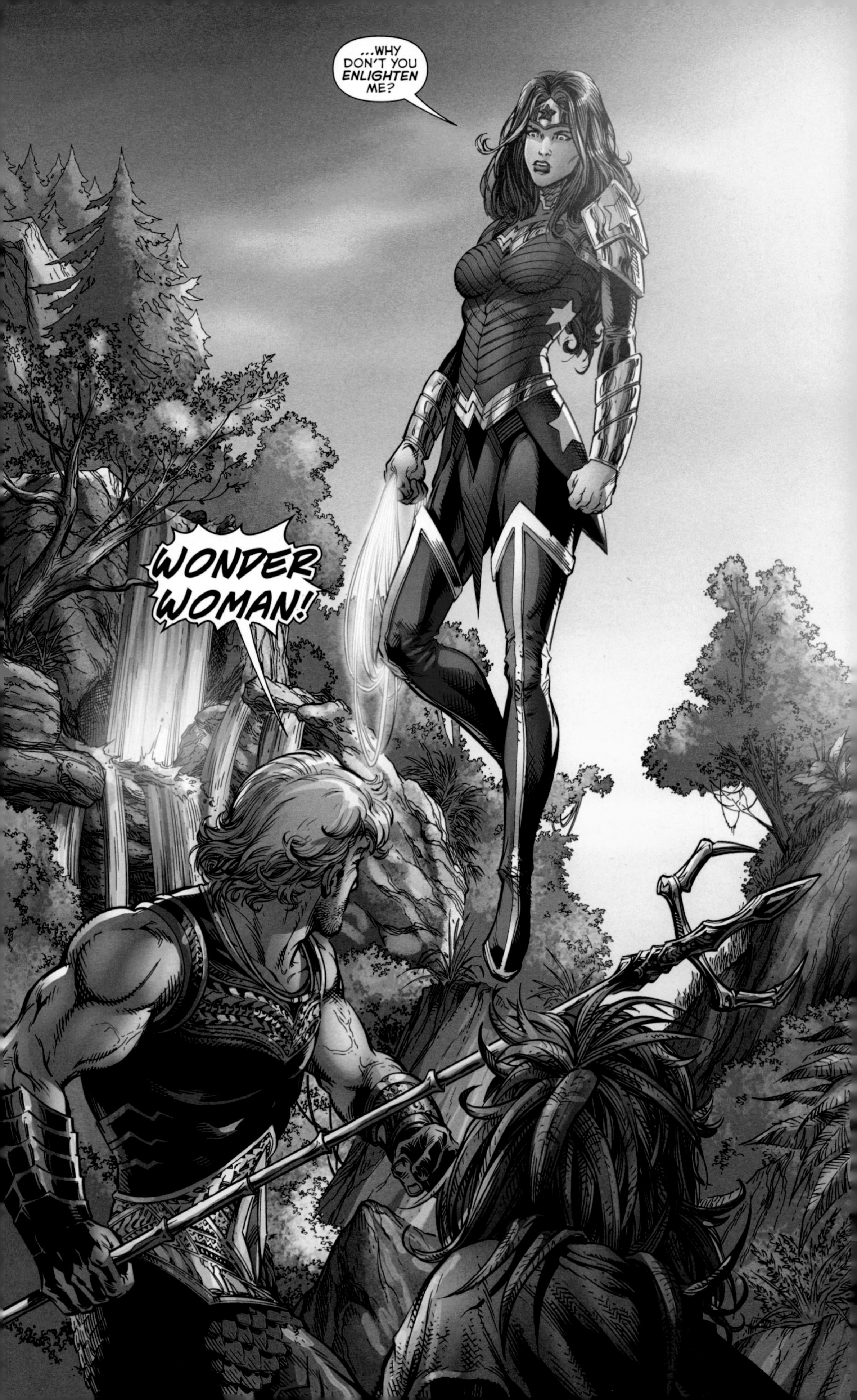
...WHY DON'T YOU ENLIGHTEN ME?
WONDER WOMAN!

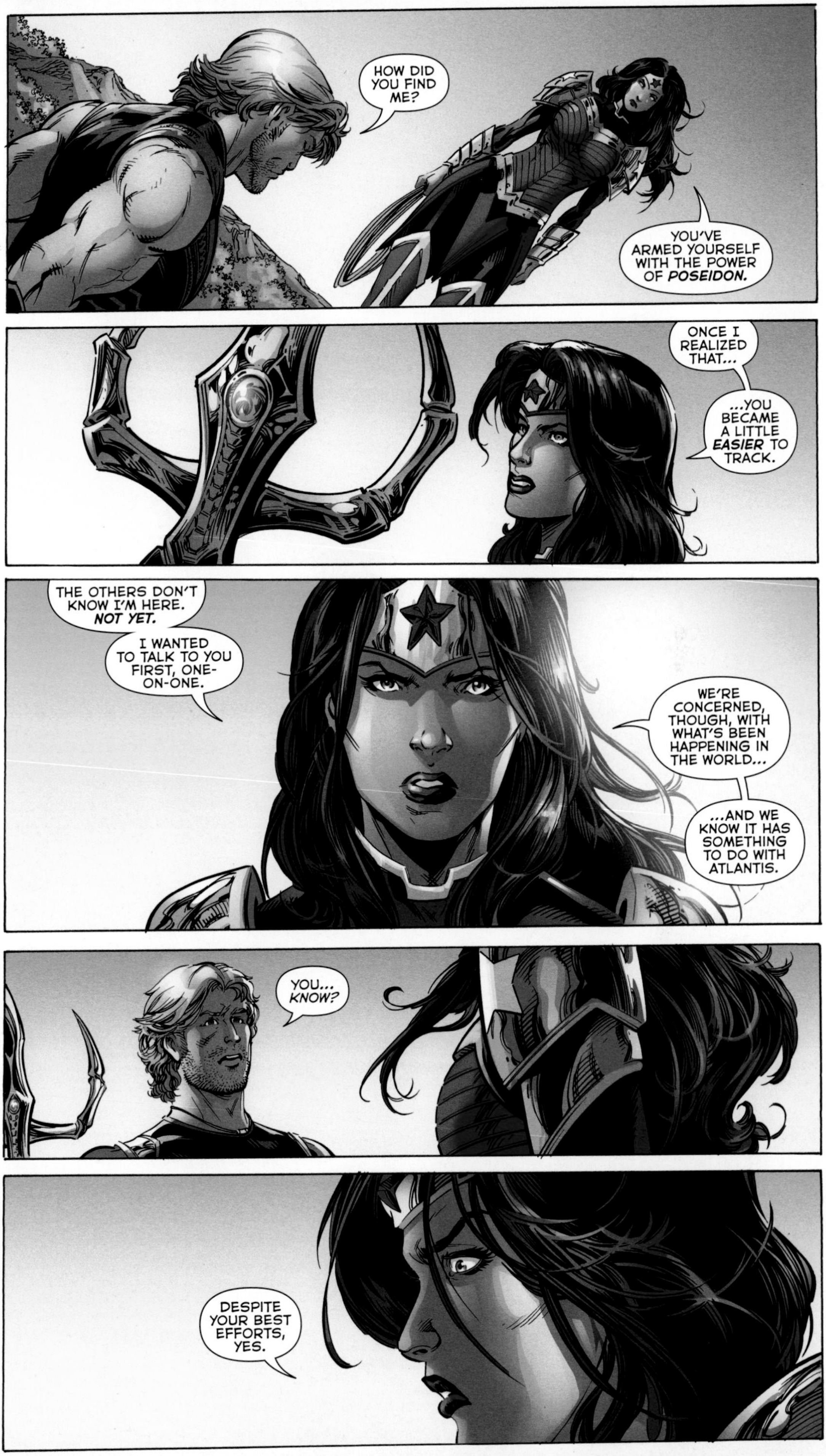

HOW DID YOU FIND ME?
YOU'VE ARMED YOURSELF WITH THE POWER OF *POSEIDON.*
ONCE I REALIZED THAT...
...YOU BECAME A LITTLE *EASIER* TO TRACK.
THE OTHERS DON'T KNOW I'M HERE. *NOT YET.*
I WANTED TO TALK TO YOU FIRST, ONE-ON-ONE.
WE'RE CONCERNED, THOUGH, WITH WHAT'S BEEN HAPPENING IN THE WORLD...
...AND WE KNOW IT HAS SOMETHING TO DO WITH ATLANTIS.
YOU... *KNOW?*
DESPITE YOUR BEST EFFORTS, YES.

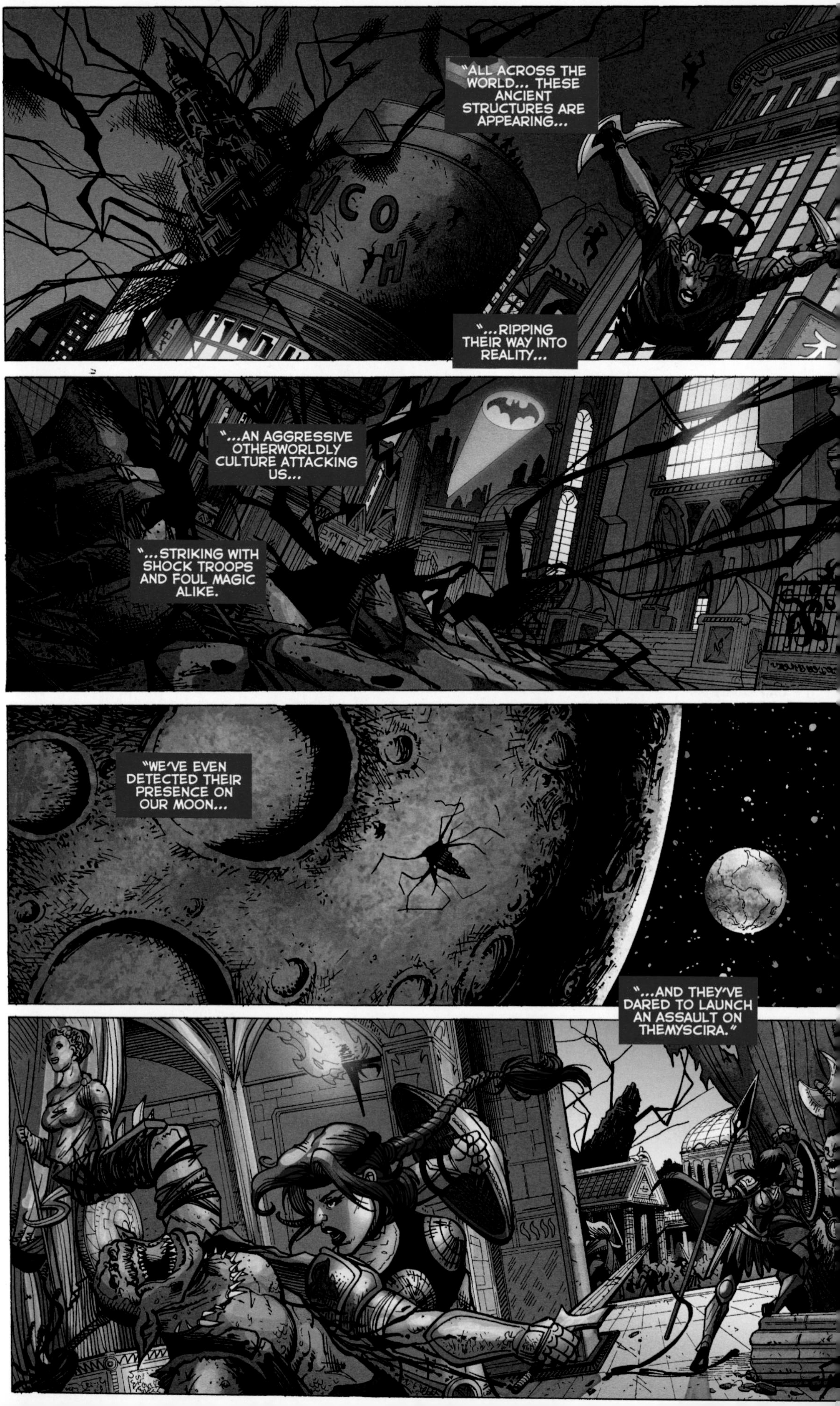
"ALL ACROSS THE WORLD... THESE ANCIENT STRUCTURES ARE APPEARING...
"...RIPPING THEIR WAY INTO REALITY...
"...AN AGGRESSIVE OTHERWORLDLY CULTURE ATTACKING US...
"...STRIKING WITH SHOCK TROOPS AND FOUL MAGIC ALIKE.
"WE'VE EVEN DETECTED THEIR PRESENCE ON OUR MOON...
"...AND THEY'VE DARED TO LAUNCH AN ASSAULT ON THEMYSCIRA."

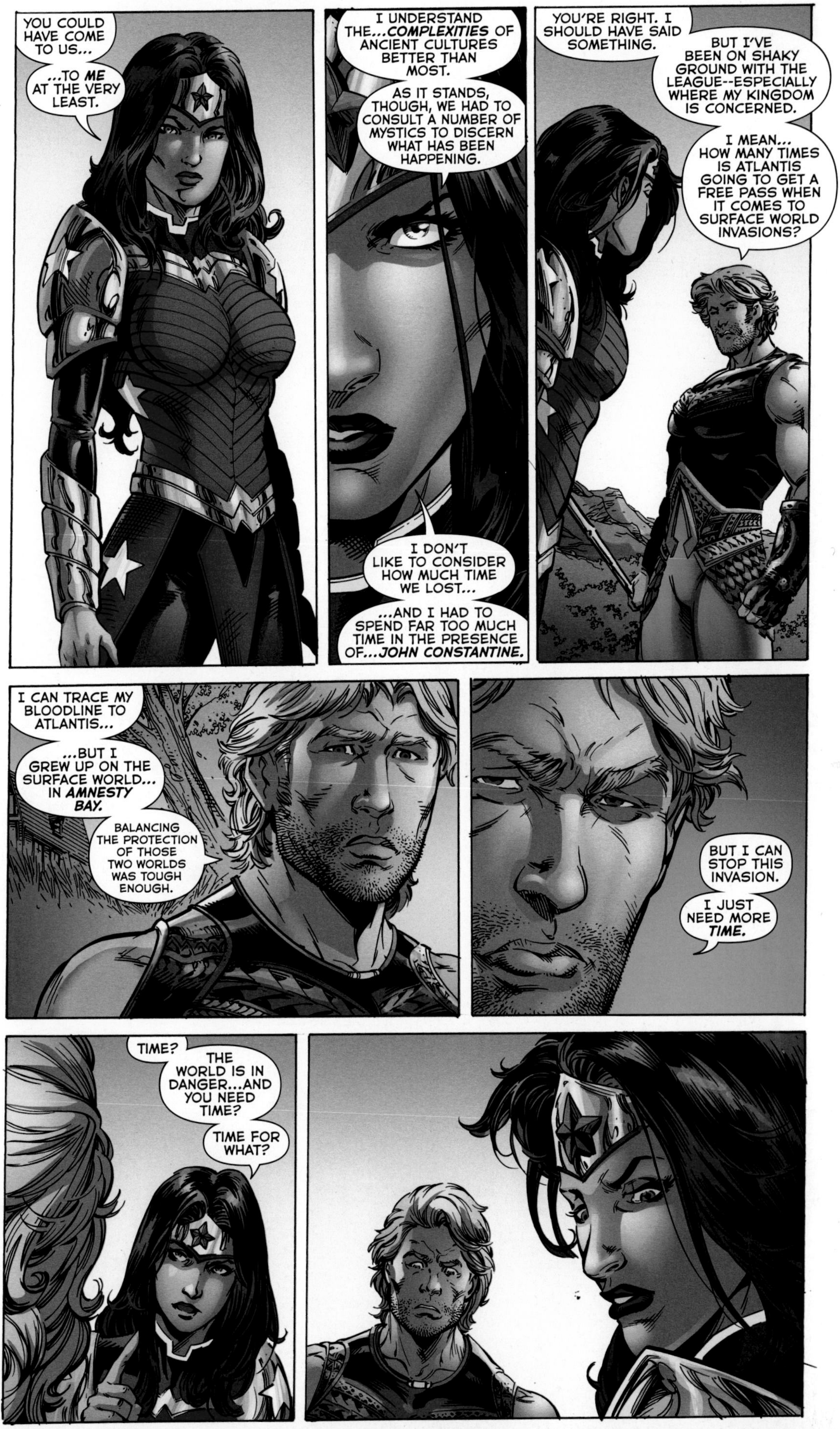

YOU COULD HAVE COME TO US...
...TO *ME* AT THE VERY LEAST.
I UNDERSTAND THE...*COMPLEXITIES* OF ANCIENT CULTURES BETTER THAN MOST.
AS IT STANDS, THOUGH, WE HAD TO CONSULT A NUMBER OF MYSTICS TO DISCERN WHAT HAS BEEN HAPPENING.
I DON'T LIKE TO CONSIDER HOW MUCH TIME WE LOST...
...AND I HAD TO SPEND FAR TOO MUCH TIME IN THE PRESENCE OF...*JOHN CONSTANTINE.*
YOU'RE RIGHT. I SHOULD HAVE SAID SOMETHING.
BUT I'VE BEEN ON SHAKY GROUND WITH THE LEAGUE--ESPECIALLY WHERE MY KINGDOM IS CONCERNED.
I MEAN... HOW MANY TIMES IS ATLANTIS GOING TO GET A FREE PASS WHEN IT COMES TO SURFACE WORLD INVASIONS?
I CAN TRACE MY BLOODLINE TO ATLANTIS...
...BUT I GREW UP ON THE SURFACE WORLD... IN *AMNESTY BAY.*
BALANCING THE PROTECTION OF THOSE TWO WORLDS WAS TOUGH ENOUGH.
BUT I CAN STOP THIS INVASION.
I JUST NEED MORE *TIME.*
TIME?
THE WORLD IS IN DANGER...AND YOU NEED TIME?
TIME FOR WHAT?

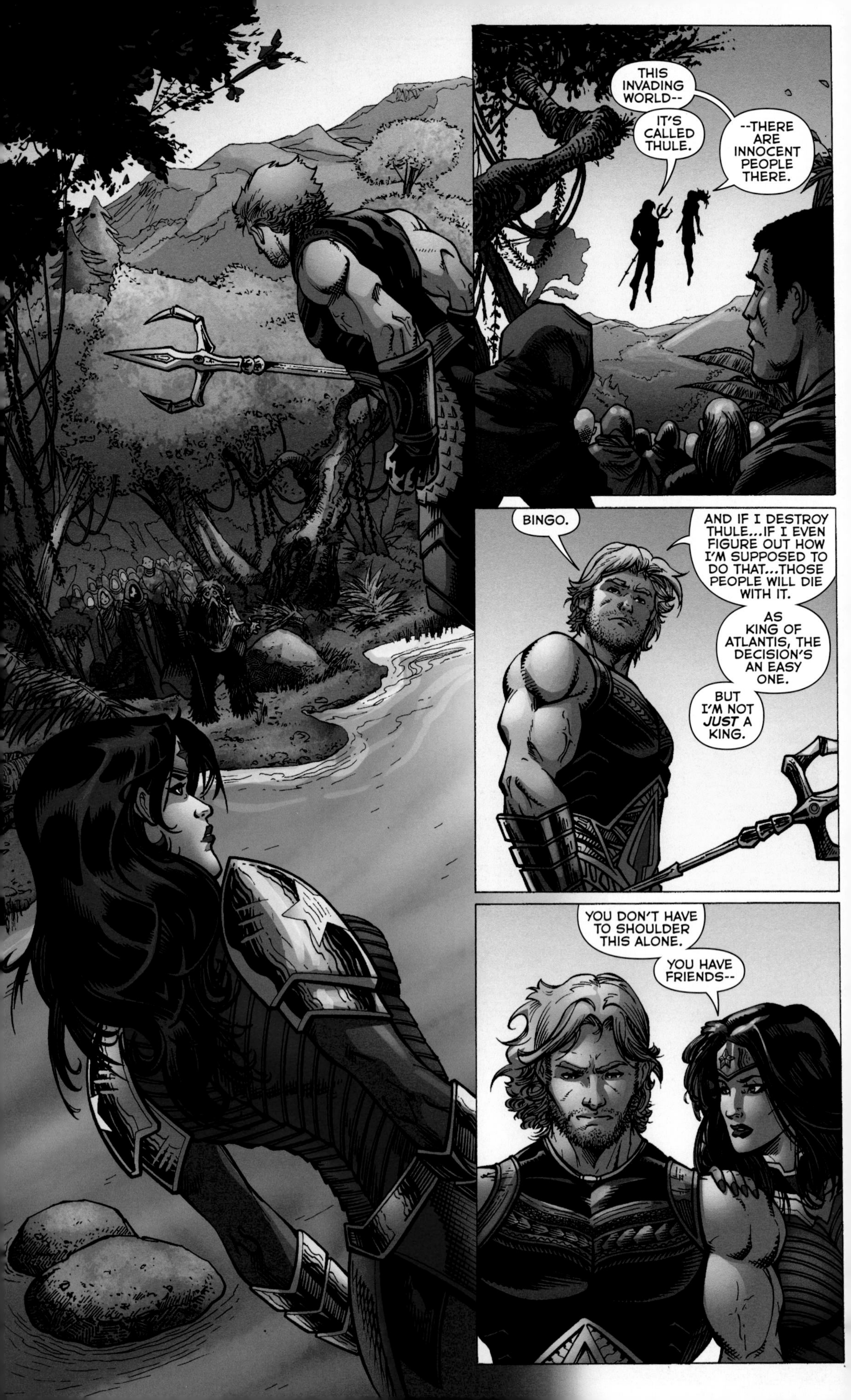
THIS INVADING WORLD--
IT'S CALLED THULE.
--THERE ARE INNOCENT PEOPLE THERE.
BINGO.
AND IF I DESTROY THULE...IF I EVEN FIGURE OUT HOW I'M SUPPOSED TO DO THAT...THOSE PEOPLE WILL DIE WITH IT.
AS KING OF ATLANTIS, THE DECISION'S AN EASY ONE.
BUT I'M NOT *JUST* A KING.
YOU DON'T HAVE TO SHOULDER THIS ALONE.
YOU HAVE FRIENDS--

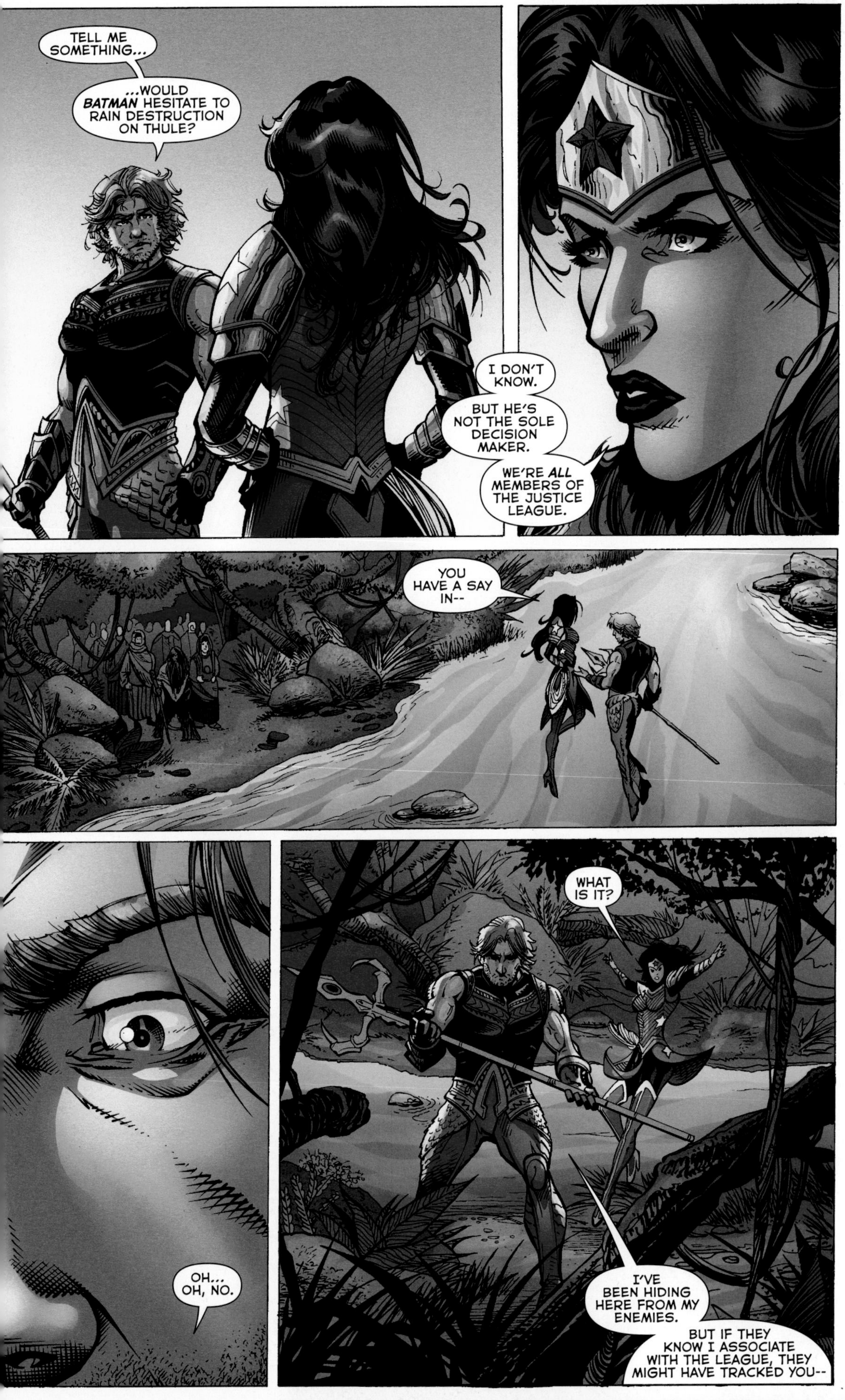
TELL ME SOMETHING...
...WOULD BATMAN HESITATE TO RAIN DESTRUCTION ON THULE?
I DON'T KNOW.
BUT HE'S NOT THE SOLE DECISION MAKER.
WE'RE ALL MEMBERS OF THE JUSTICE LEAGUE.
YOU HAVE A SAY IN--
OH... OH, NO.
WHAT IS IT?
I'VE BEEN HIDING HERE FROM MY ENEMIES.
BUT IF THEY KNOW I ASSOCIATE WITH THE LEAGUE, THEY MIGHT HAVE TRACKED YOU--

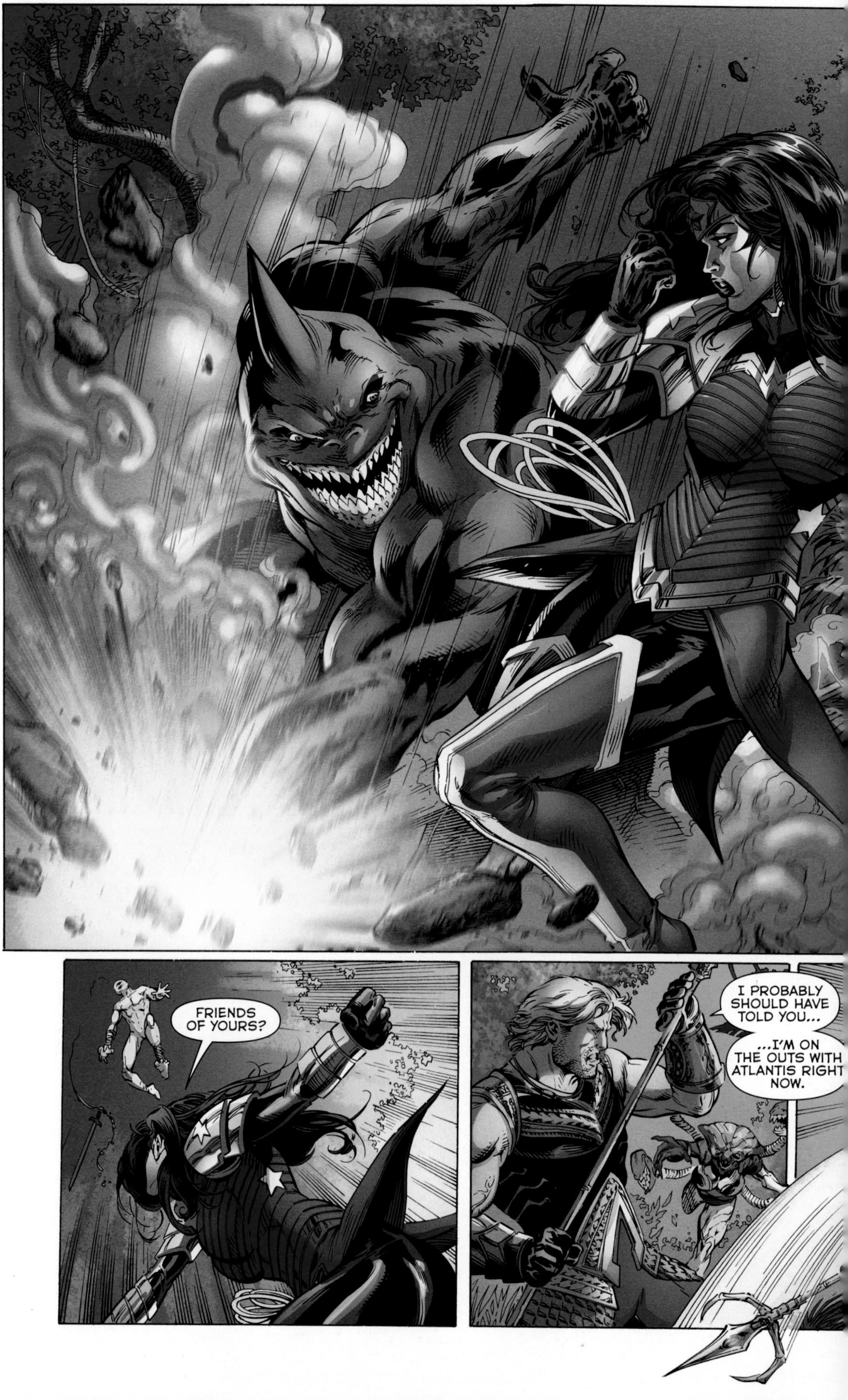
FRIENDS
OF YOURS?
I PROBABLY
SHOULD HAVE
TOLD YOU...
...I'M ON
THE OUTS WITH
ATLANTIS RIGHT
NOW.

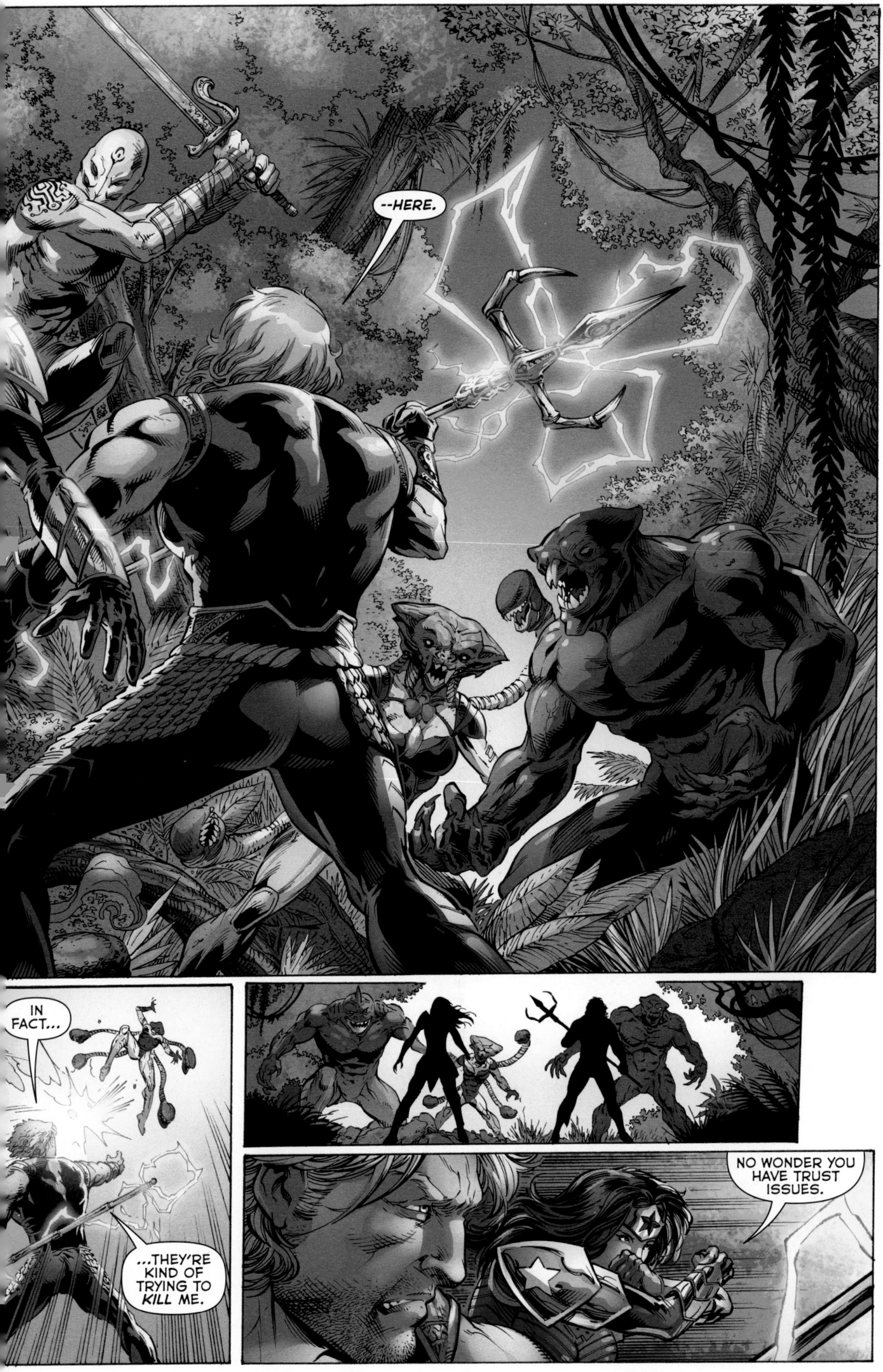
--HERE.
IN FACT...
...THEY'RE KIND OF TRYING TO KILL ME.
NO WONDER YOU HAVE TRUST ISSUES.

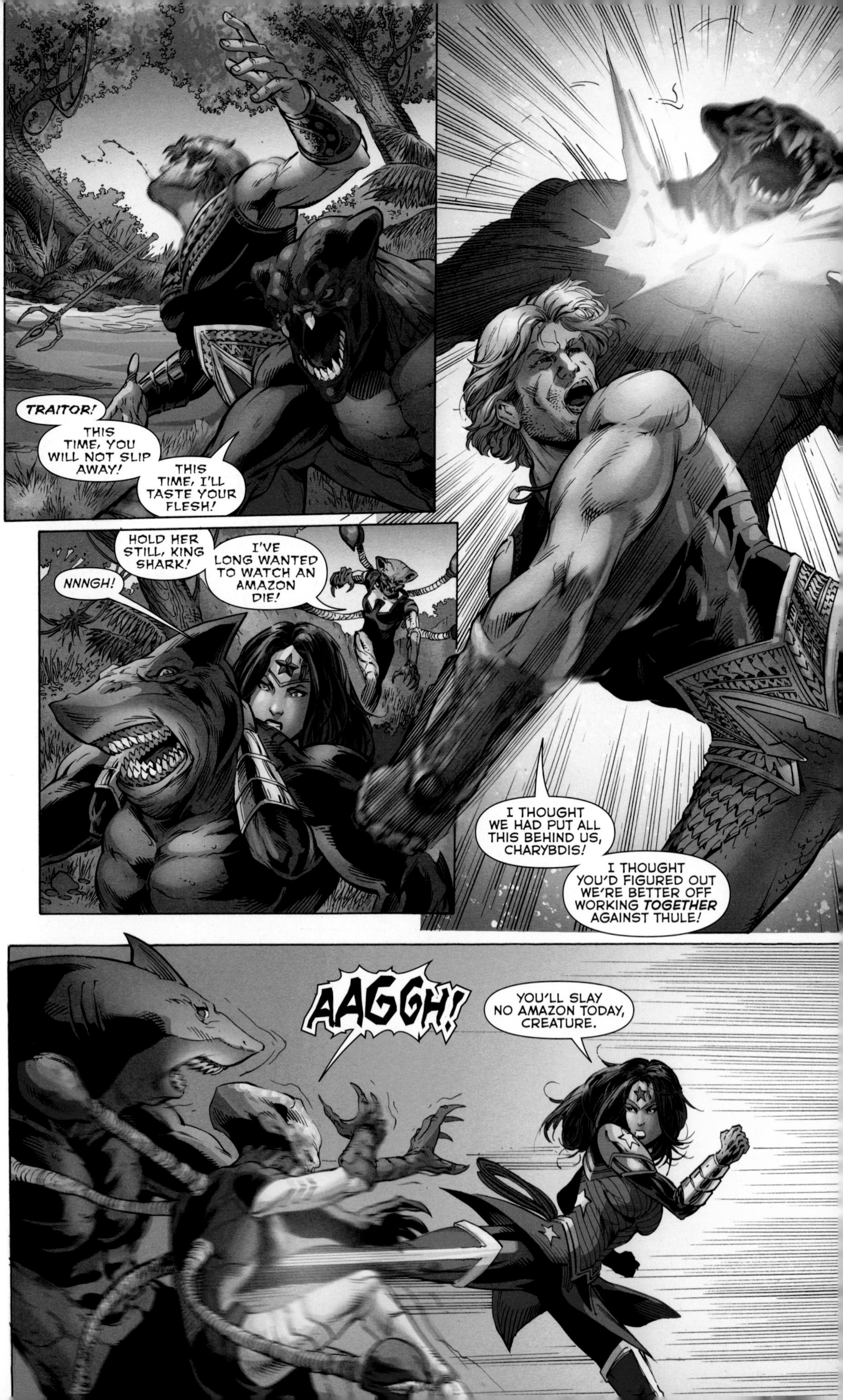
TRAITOR!
THIS TIME, YOU WILL NOT SLIP AWAY!
THIS TIME, I'LL TASTE YOUR FLESH!
I THOUGHT WE HAD PUT ALL THIS BEHIND US, CHARYBDIS!
I THOUGHT YOU'D FIGURED OUT WE'RE BETTER OFF WORKING TOGETHER AGAINST THULE!
HOLD HER STILL, KING SHARK!
NNNGH!
I'VE LONG WANTED TO WATCH AN AMAZON DIE!
AAGGH!
YOU'LL SLAY NO AMAZON TODAY, CREATURE.

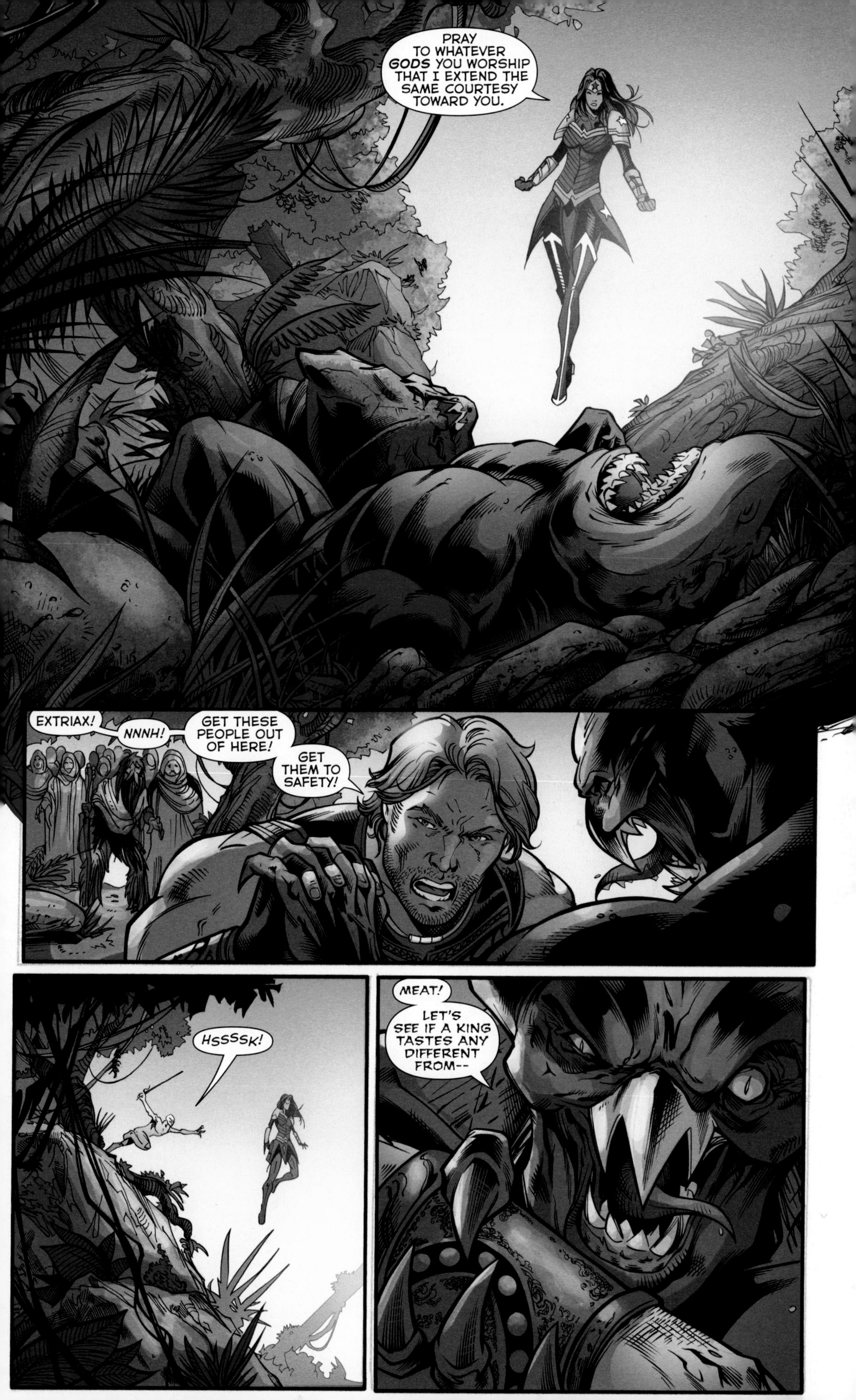
PRAY TO WHATEVER GODS YOU WORSHIP THAT I EXTEND THE SAME COURTESY TOWARD YOU.
EXTRIAX!
NNNH!
GET THESE PEOPLE OUT OF HERE!
GET THEM TO SAFETY!
HSSSSK!
MEAT!
LET'S SEE IF A KING TASTES ANY DIFFERENT FROM--

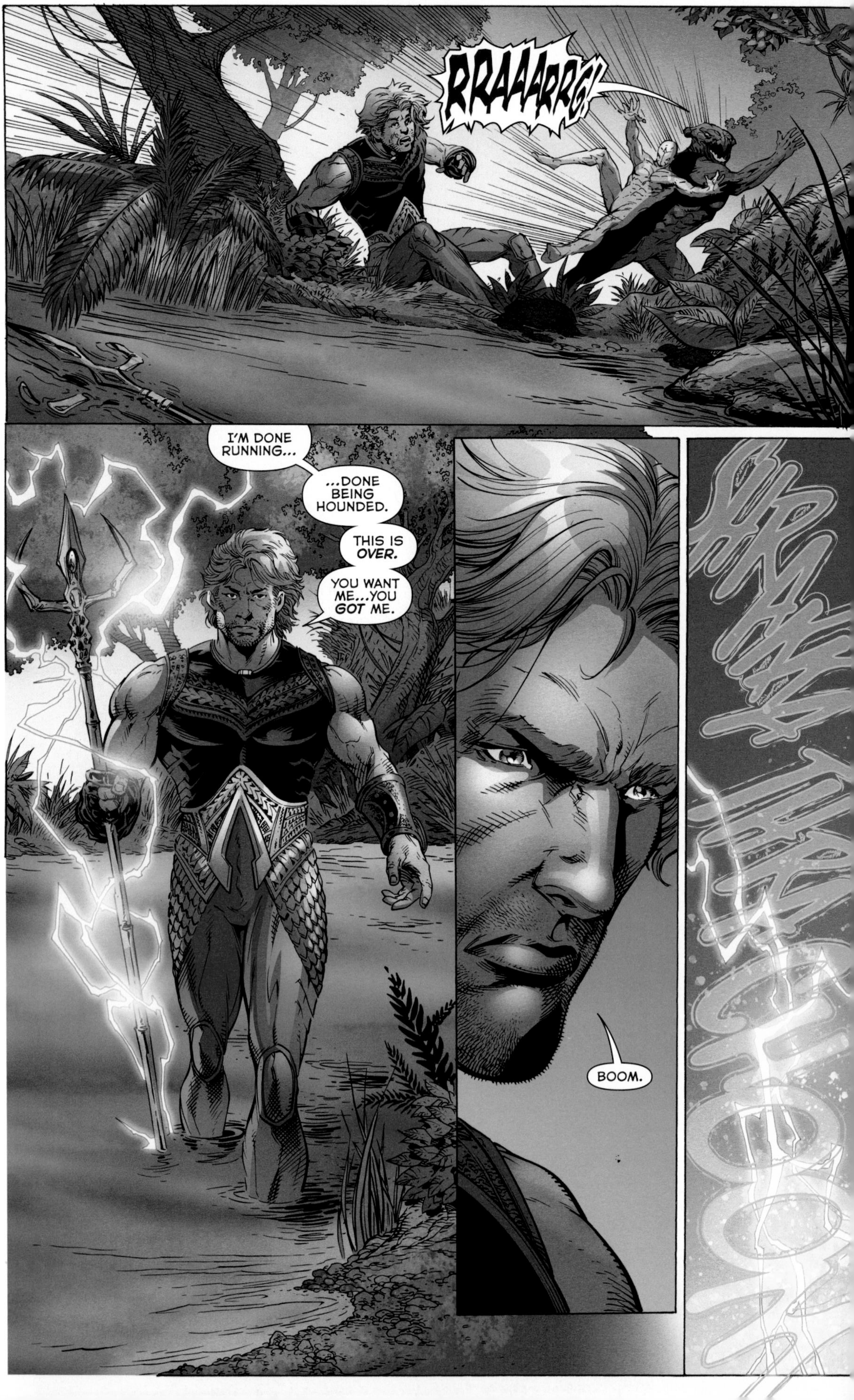
RRAAARRG!
I'M DONE RUNNING...
...DONE BEING HOUNDED.
THIS IS OVER.
YOU WANT ME...YOU GOT ME.
BOOM.

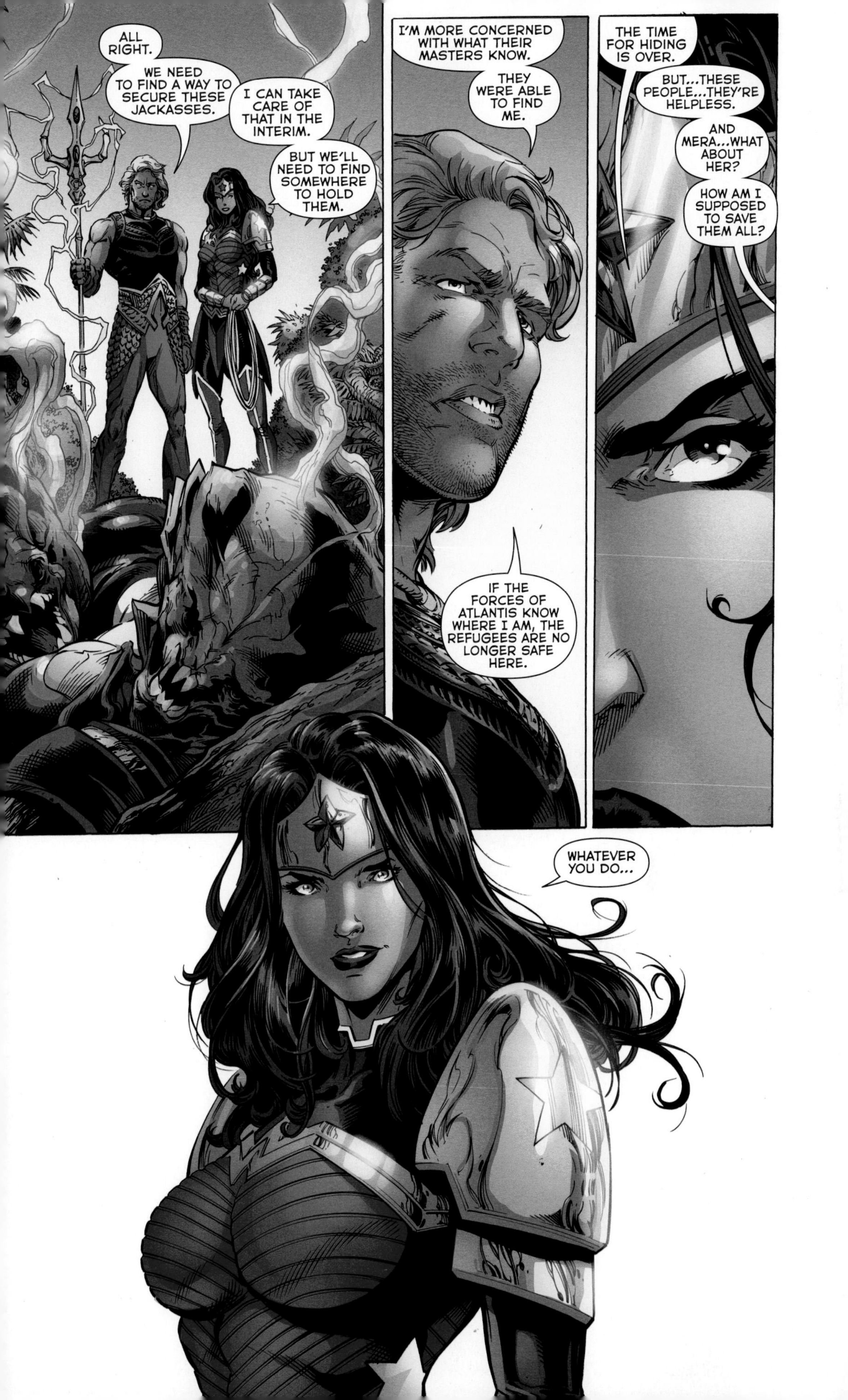
ALL RIGHT.
WE NEED TO FIND A WAY TO SECURE THESE JACKASSES.
I CAN TAKE CARE OF THAT IN THE INTERIM.
BUT WE'LL NEED TO FIND SOMEWHERE TO HOLD THEM.
I'M MORE CONCERNED WITH WHAT THEIR MASTERS KNOW.
THEY WERE ABLE TO FIND ME.
IF THE FORCES OF ATLANTIS KNOW WHERE I AM, THE REFUGEES ARE NO LONGER SAFE HERE.
THE TIME FOR HIDING IS OVER.
BUT...THESE PEOPLE...THEY'RE HELPLESS.
AND MERA...WHAT ABOUT HER?
HOW AM I SUPPOSED TO SAVE THEM ALL?
WHATEVER YOU DO...

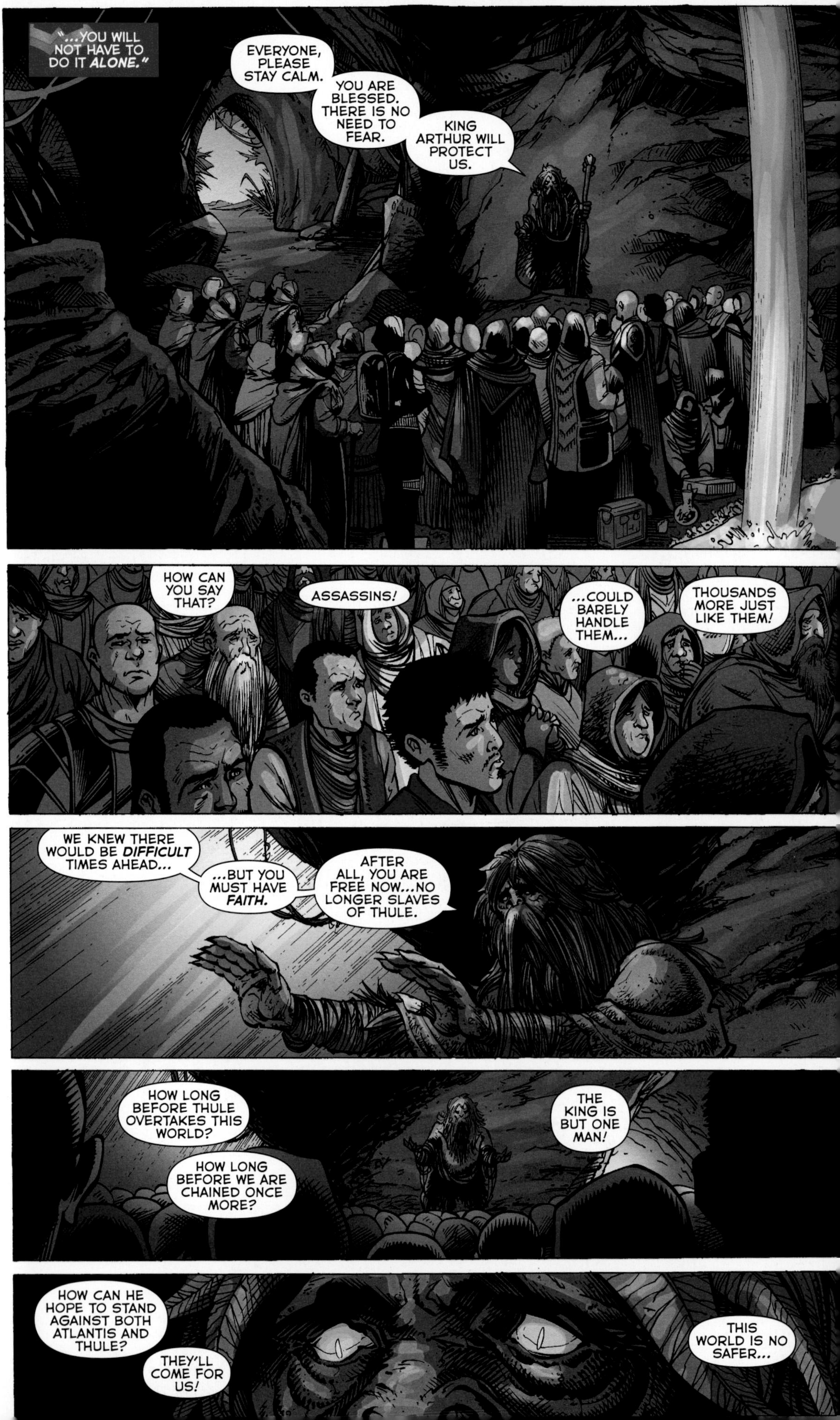
"...YOU WILL NOT HAVE TO DO IT *ALONE*."
EVERYONE, PLEASE STAY CALM.
YOU ARE BLESSED. THERE IS NO NEED TO FEAR.
KING ARTHUR WILL PROTECT US.
HOW CAN YOU SAY THAT?
ASSASSINS!
...COULD BARELY HANDLE THEM...
THOUSANDS MORE JUST LIKE THEM!
WE KNEW THERE WOULD BE *DIFFICULT* TIMES AHEAD...
...BUT YOU MUST HAVE *FAITH*.
AFTER ALL, YOU ARE FREE NOW...NO LONGER SLAVES OF THULE.
HOW LONG BEFORE THULE OVERTAKES THIS WORLD?
HOW LONG BEFORE WE ARE CHAINED ONCE MORE?
THE KING IS BUT ONE MAN!
HOW CAN HE HOPE TO STAND AGAINST BOTH ATLANTIS AND THULE?
THEY'LL COME FOR US!
THIS WORLD IS NO SAFER...

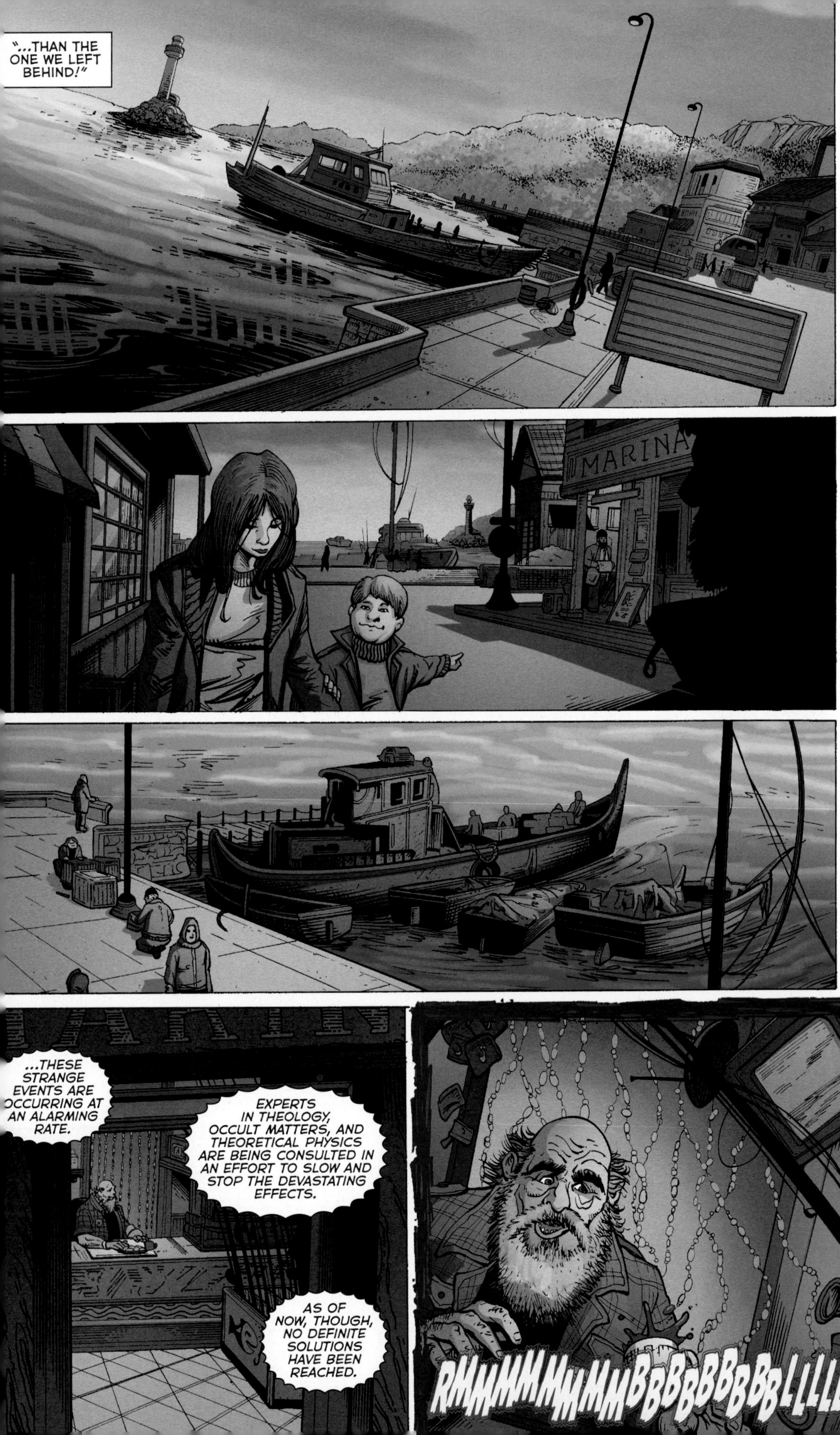
"...THAN THE ONE WE LEFT BEHIND!"
MARINA
...THESE STRANGE EVENTS ARE OCCURRING AT AN ALARMING RATE.
EXPERTS IN THEOLOGY, OCCULT MATTERS, AND THEORETICAL PHYSICS ARE BEING CONSULTED IN AN EFFORT TO SLOW AND STOP THE DEVASTATING EFFECTS.
AS OF NOW, THOUGH, NO DEFINITE SOLUTIONS HAVE BEEN REACHED.
RMMMMMMMMMBBBBBBBBLLLLE

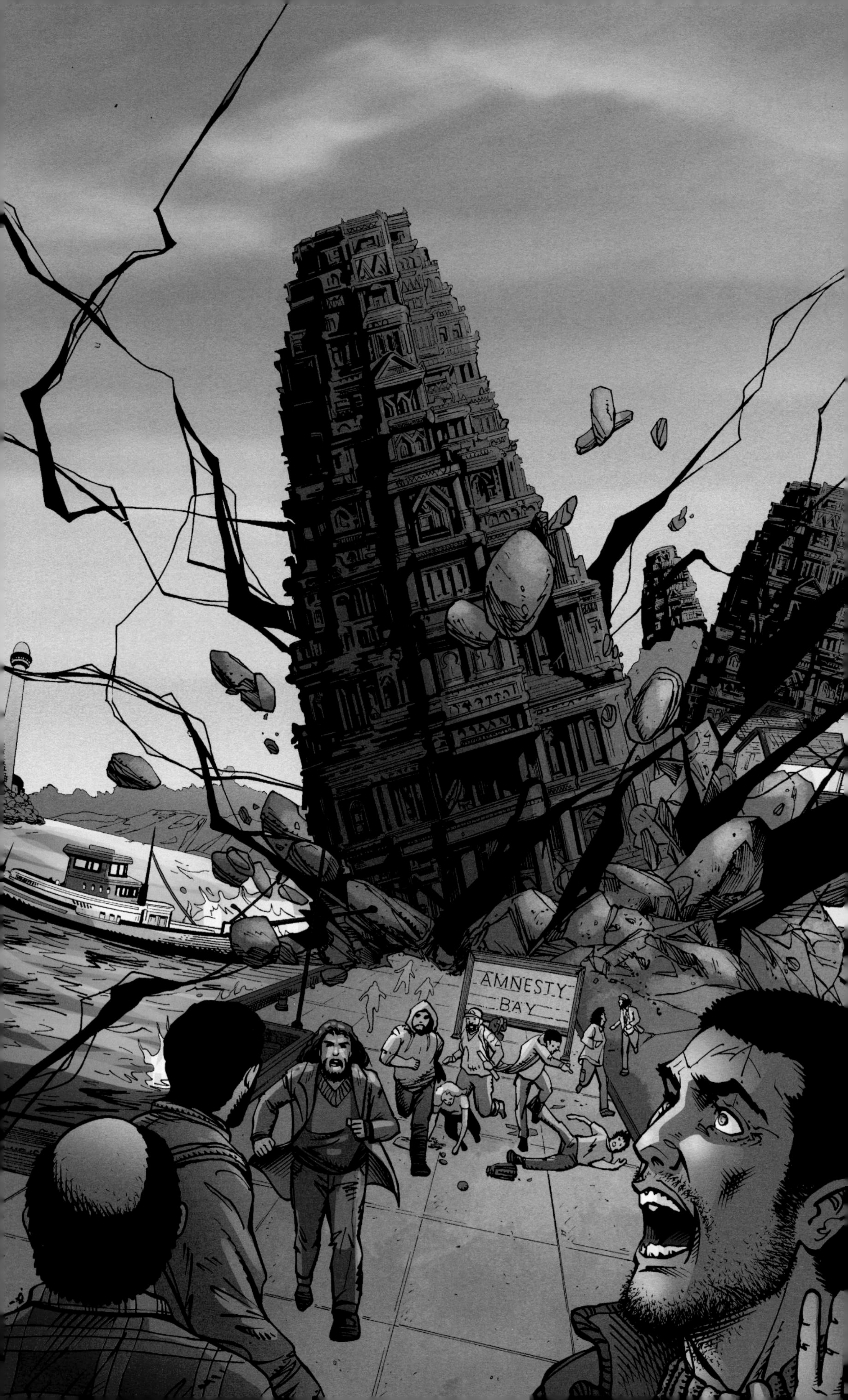
AMNESTY
BAY

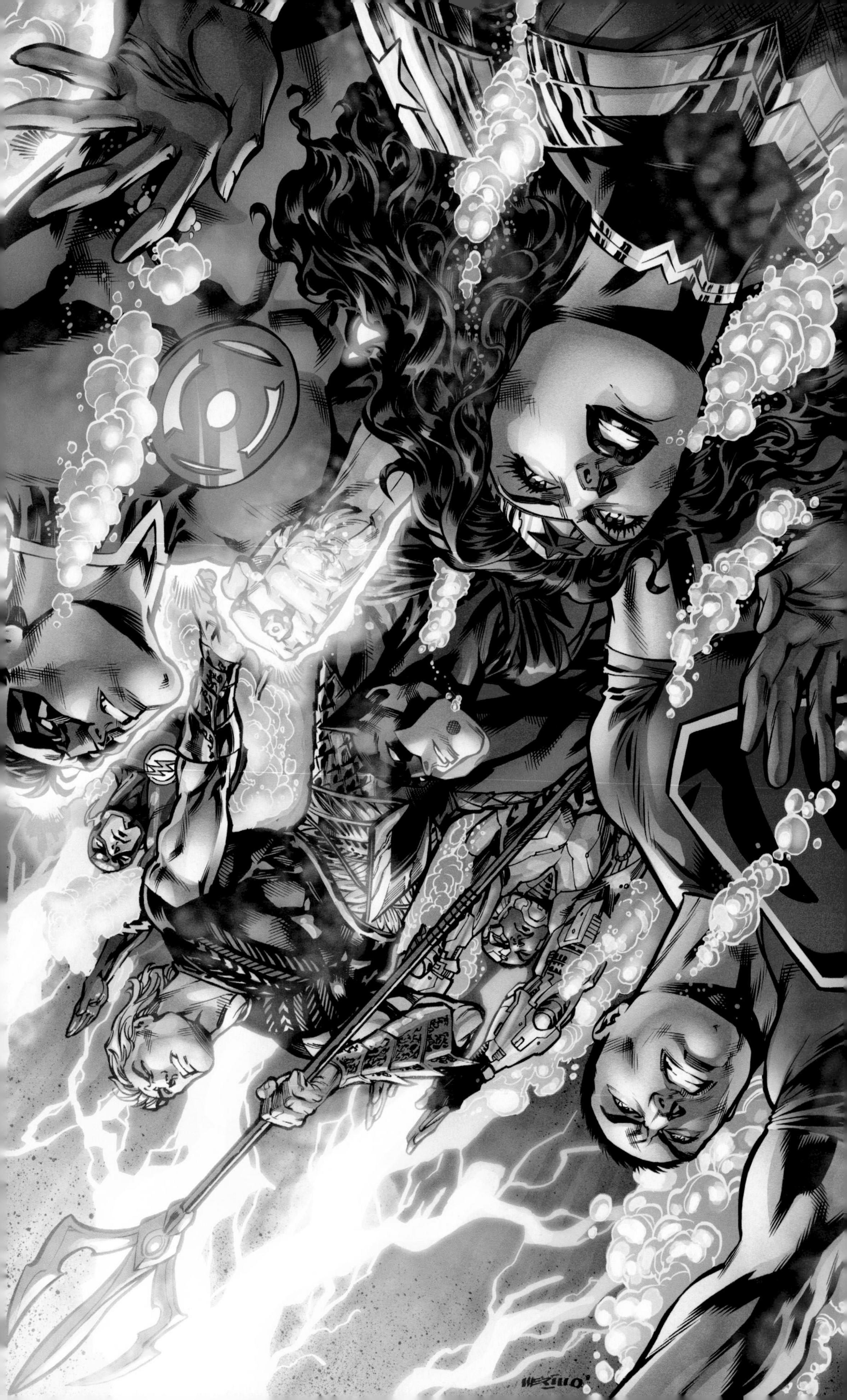

LEAGUES BELOW, A LEAGUE ABOVE

CULLEN BUNN writer **VICENTE CIFUENTES** penciller **JOHN DELL, DON HO, MARK IRWIN, VICENTE CIFUENTES** inkers **GUY MAJOR** colorist **TOM NAPOLITANO** letterer
JESUS MERINO and **GUY MAJOR** cover art

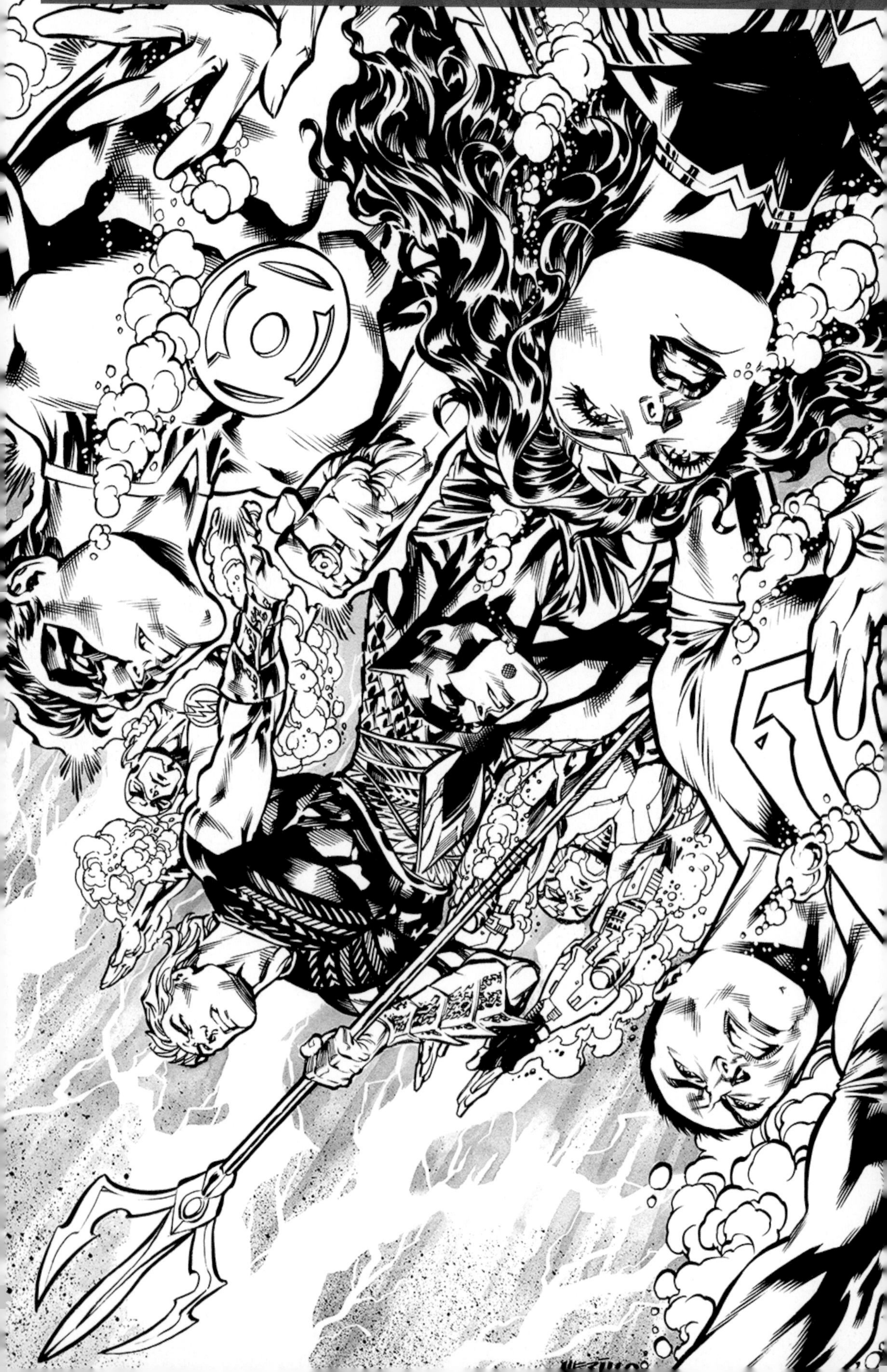

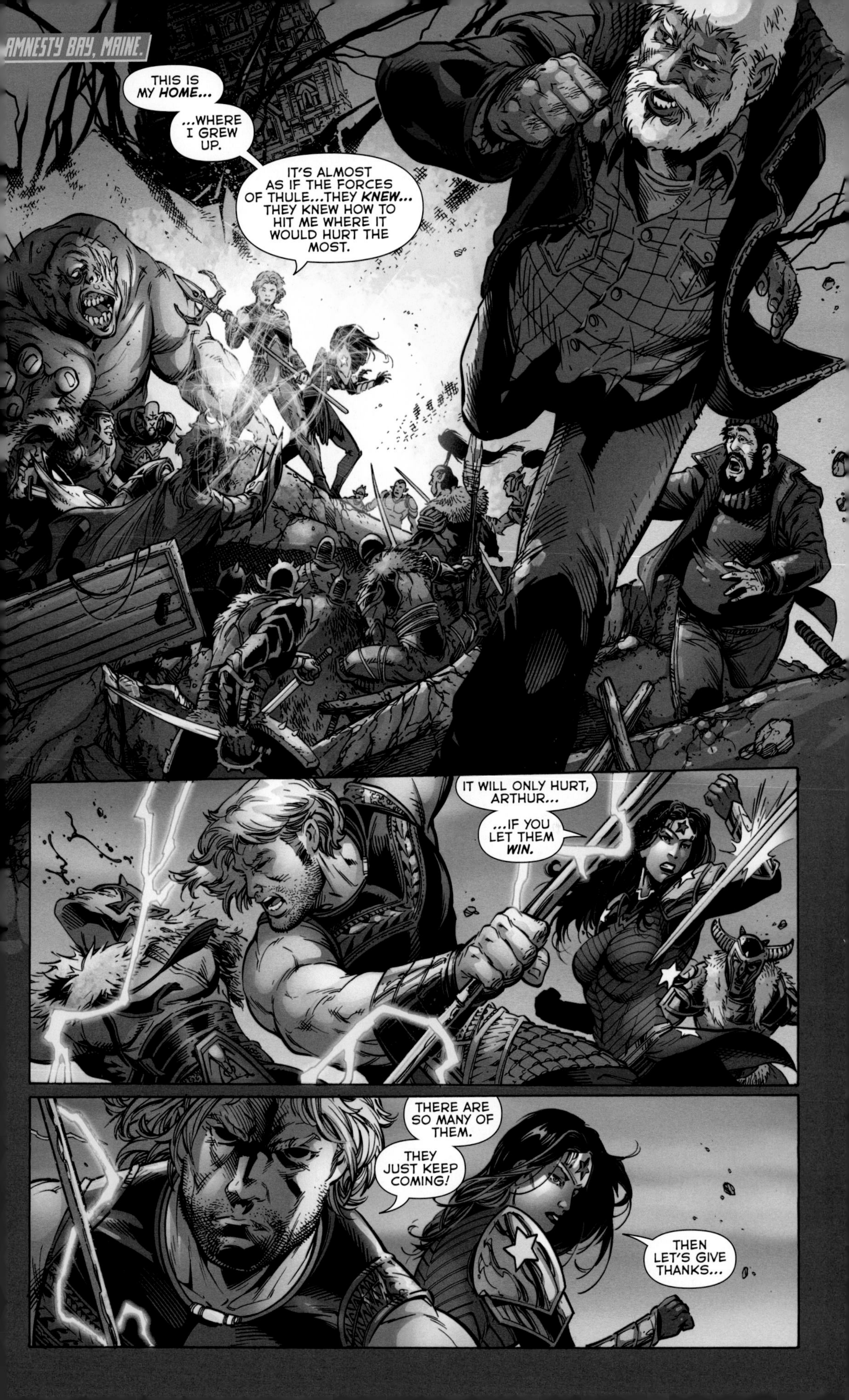
AMNESTY BAY, MAINE.
THIS IS MY HOME...
...WHERE I GREW UP.
IT'S ALMOST AS IF THE FORCES OF THULE...THEY KNEW... THEY KNEW HOW TO HIT ME WHERE IT WOULD HURT THE MOST.
IT WILL ONLY HURT, ARTHUR...
...IF YOU LET THEM WIN.
THERE ARE SO MANY OF THEM.
THEY JUST KEEP COMING!
THEN LET'S GIVE THANKS...

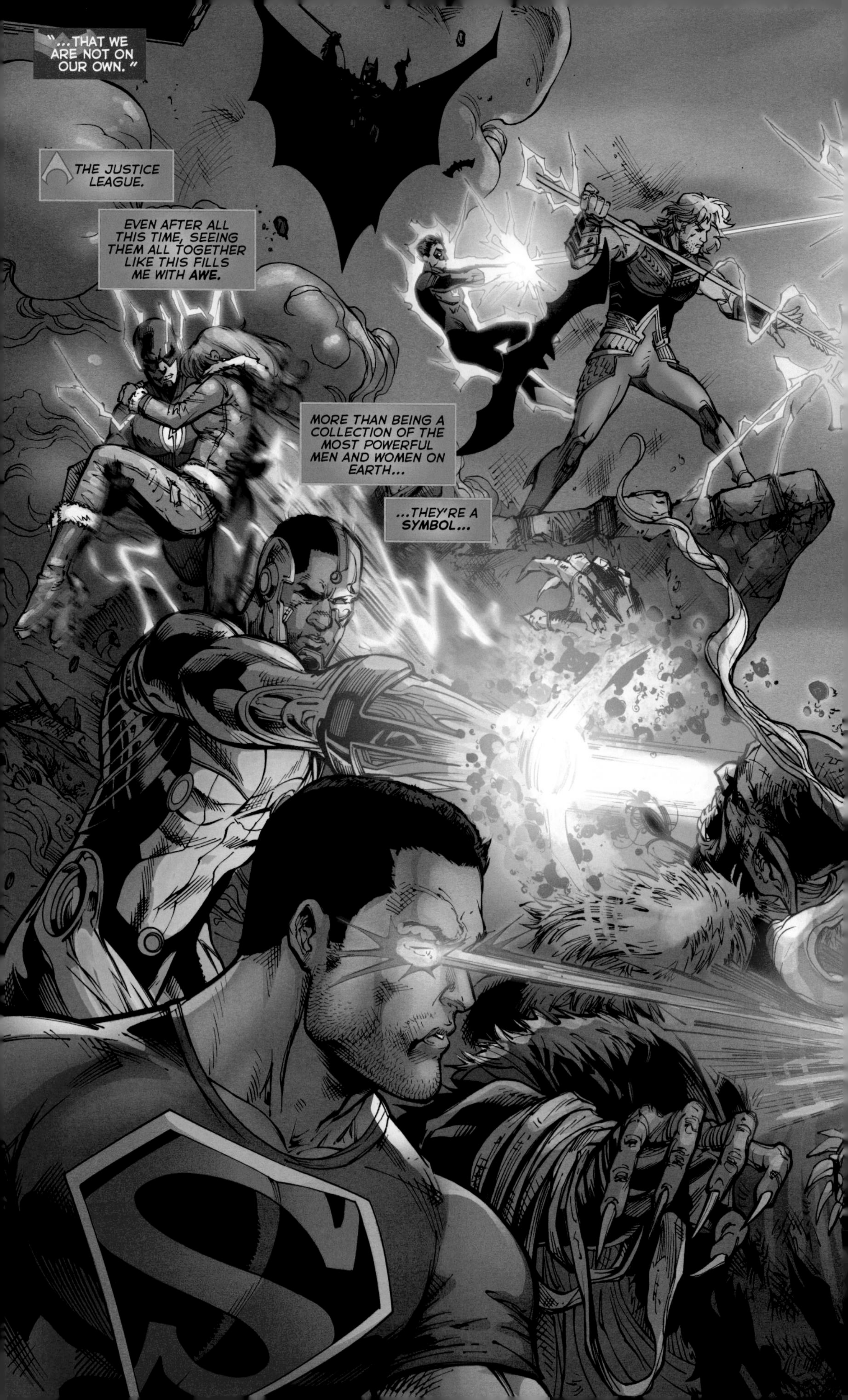
"...THAT WE ARE NOT ON OUR OWN."
THE JUSTICE LEAGUE.
EVEN AFTER ALL THIS TIME, SEEING THEM ALL TOGETHER LIKE THIS FILLS ME WITH AWE.
MORE THAN BEING A COLLECTION OF THE MOST POWERFUL MEN AND WOMEN ON EARTH...
...THEY'RE A SYMBOL...

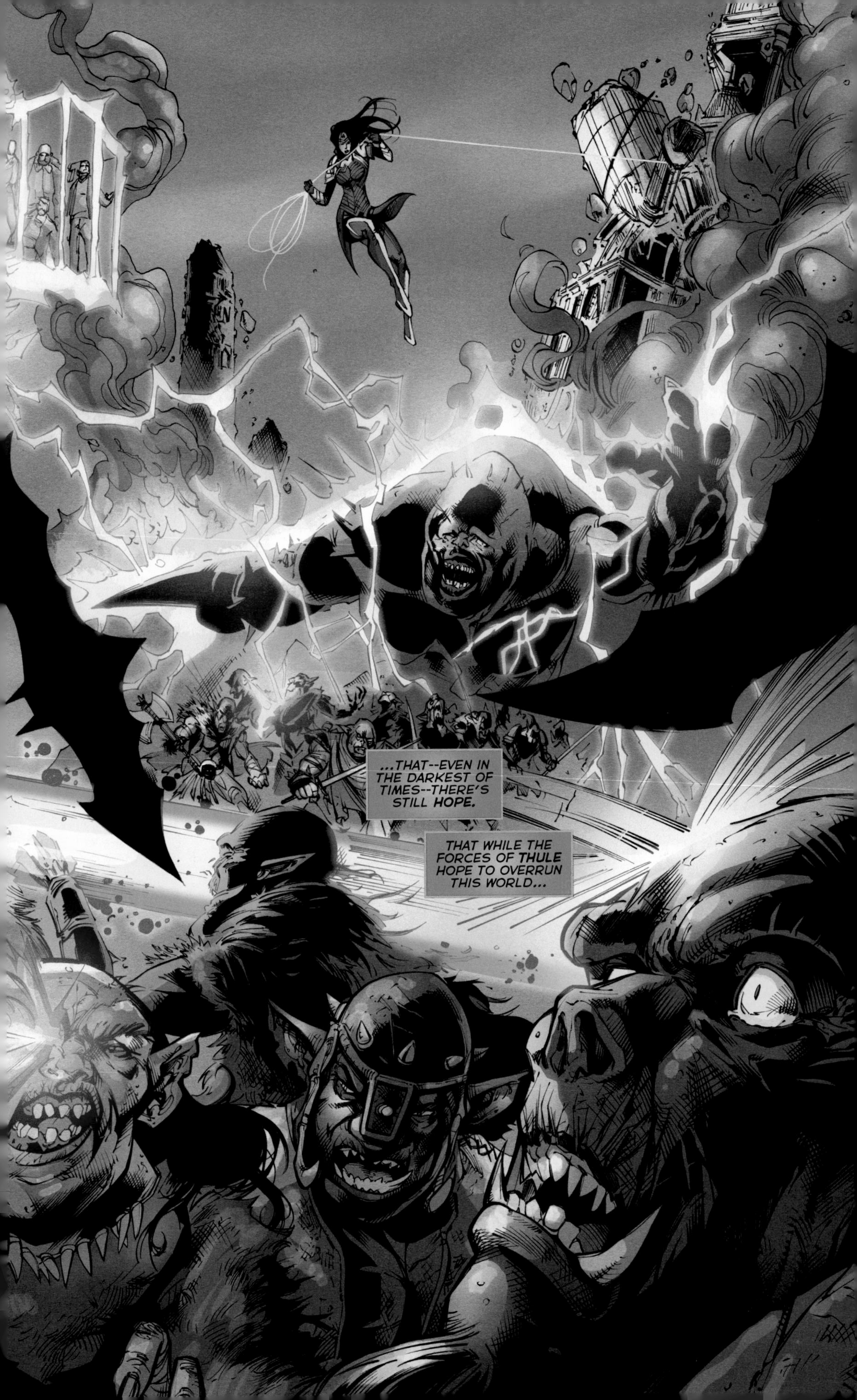
...THAT--EVEN IN THE DARKEST OF TIMES--THERE'S STILL HOPE.
THAT WHILE THE FORCES OF THULE HOPE TO OVERRUN THIS WORLD...

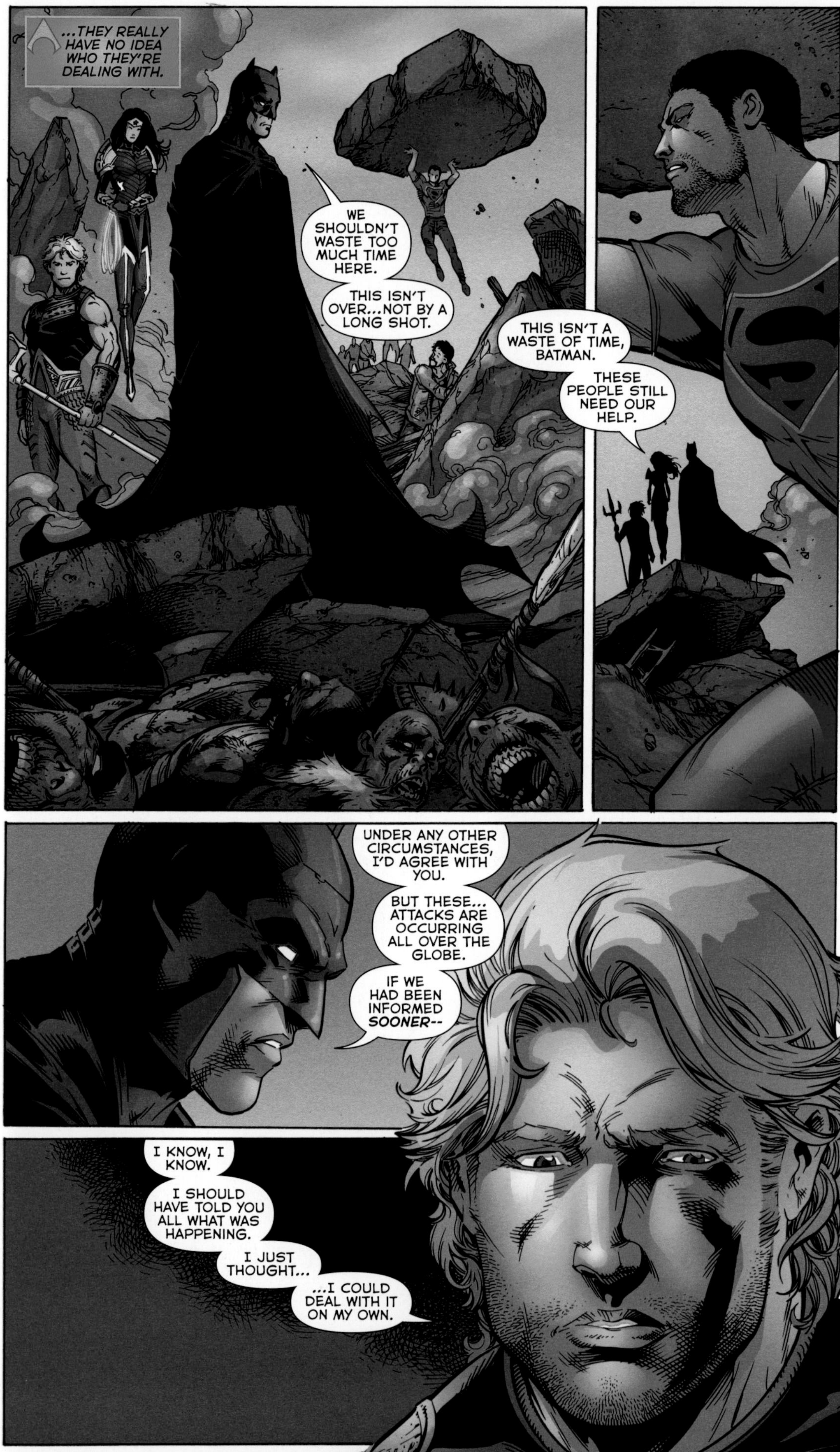
...THEY REALLY HAVE NO IDEA WHO THEY'RE DEALING WITH.
WE SHOULDN'T WASTE TOO MUCH TIME HERE.
THIS ISN'T OVER...NOT BY A LONG SHOT.
THIS ISN'T A WASTE OF TIME, BATMAN.
THESE PEOPLE STILL NEED OUR HELP.
UNDER ANY OTHER CIRCUMSTANCES, I'D AGREE WITH YOU.
BUT THESE... ATTACKS ARE OCCURRING ALL OVER THE GLOBE.
IF WE HAD BEEN INFORMED SOONER--
I KNOW, I KNOW.
I SHOULD HAVE TOLD YOU ALL WHAT WAS HAPPENING.
I JUST THOUGHT...
...I COULD DEAL WITH IT ON MY OWN.

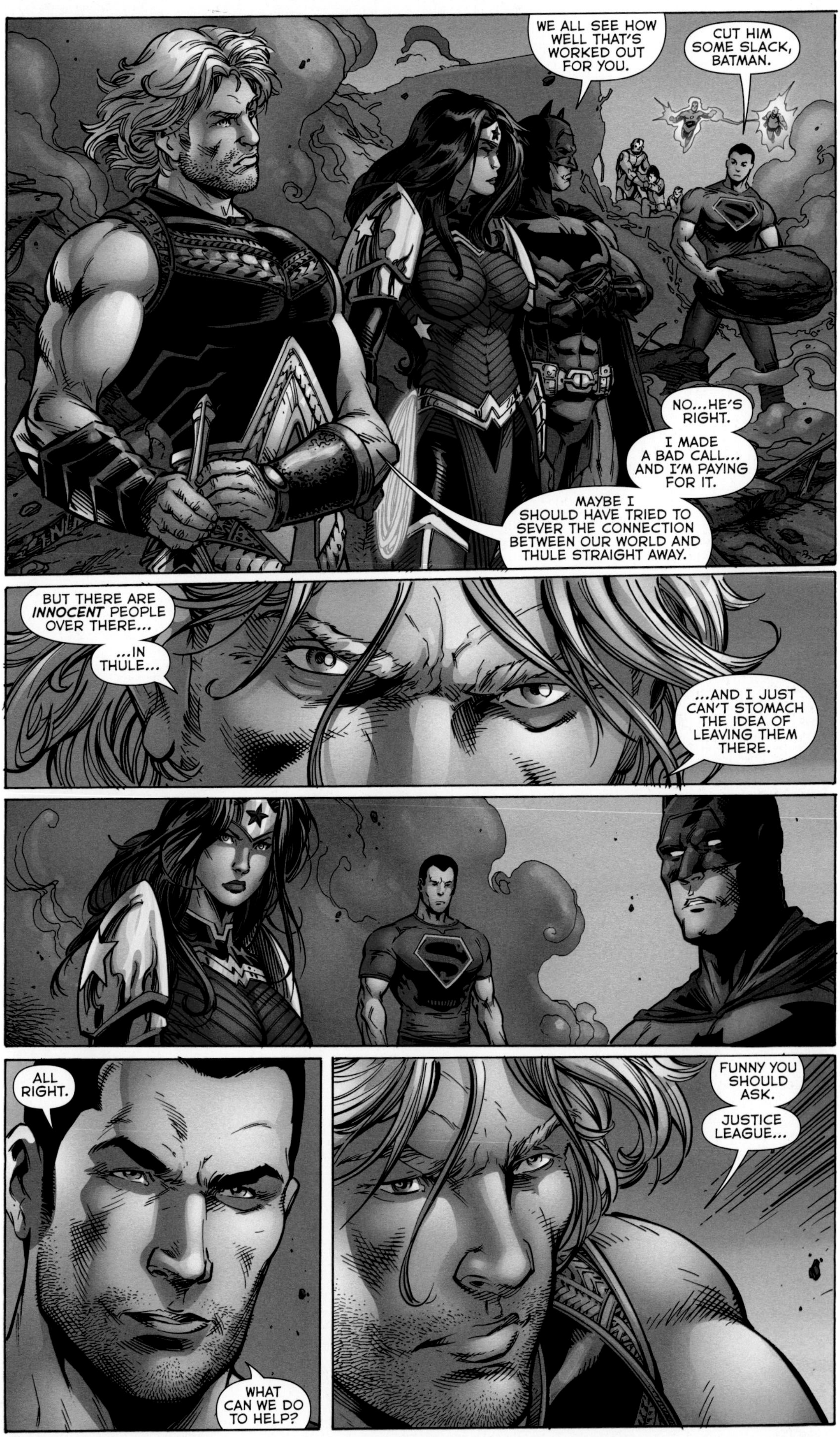
WE ALL SEE HOW WELL THAT'S WORKED OUT FOR YOU.
CUT HIM SOME SLACK, BATMAN.
NO...HE'S RIGHT.
I MADE A BAD CALL... AND I'M PAYING FOR IT.
MAYBE I SHOULD HAVE TRIED TO SEVER THE CONNECTION BETWEEN OUR WORLD AND THULE STRAIGHT AWAY.
BUT THERE ARE *INNOCENT* PEOPLE OVER THERE...
...IN THULE...
...AND I JUST CAN'T STOMACH THE IDEA OF LEAVING THEM THERE.
ALL RIGHT.
WHAT CAN WE DO TO HELP?
FUNNY YOU SHOULD ASK.
JUSTICE LEAGUE...

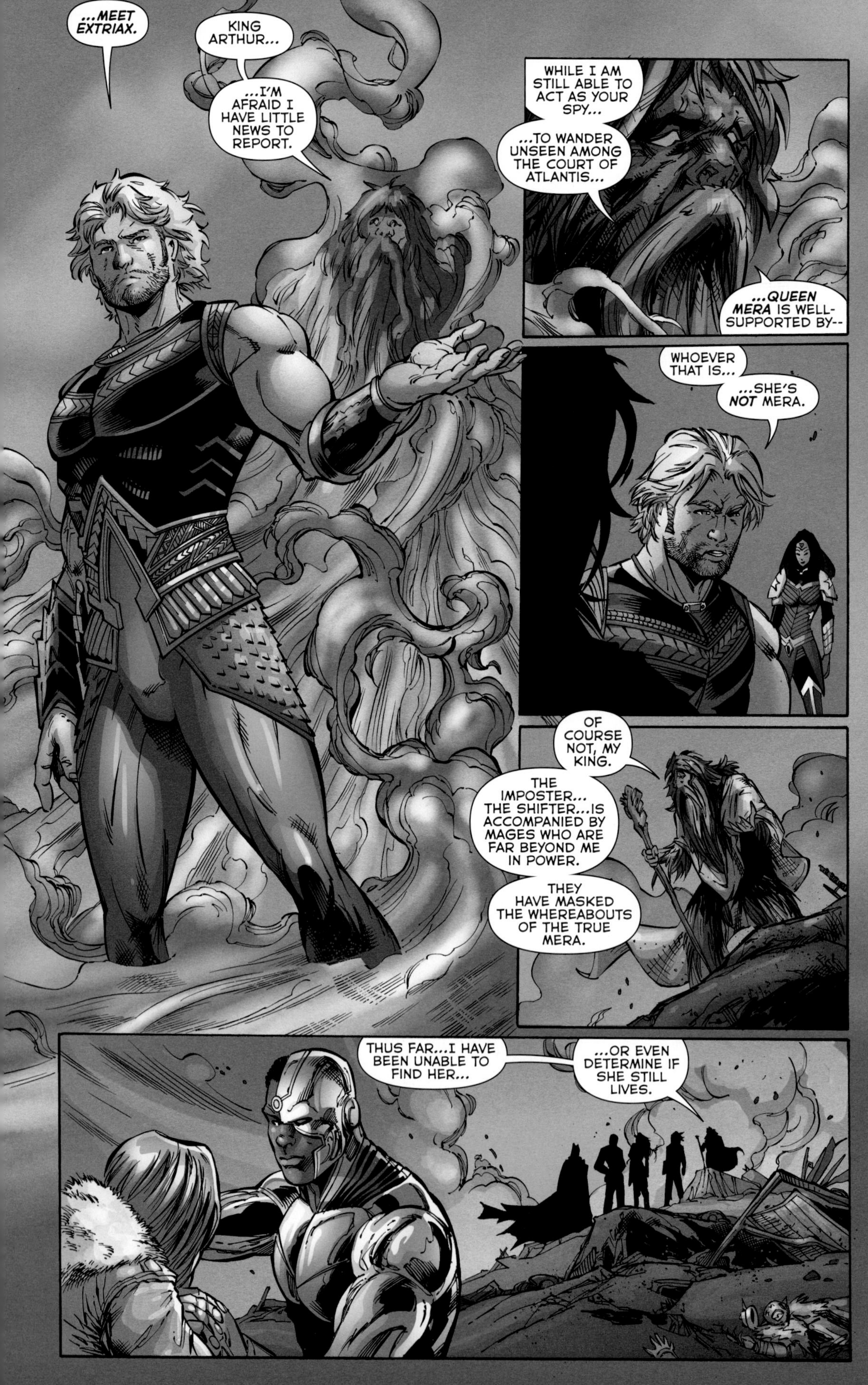
...MEET EXTRIAX.
KING ARTHUR...
...I'M AFRAID I HAVE LITTLE NEWS TO REPORT.
WHILE I AM STILL ABLE TO ACT AS YOUR SPY...
...TO WANDER UNSEEN AMONG THE COURT OF ATLANTIS...
...QUEEN MERA IS WELL-SUPPORTED BY--
WHOEVER THAT IS...
...SHE'S NOT MERA.
OF COURSE NOT, MY KING.
THE IMPOSTER... THE SHIFTER...IS ACCOMPANIED BY MAGES WHO ARE FAR BEYOND ME IN POWER.
THEY HAVE MASKED THE WHEREABOUTS OF THE TRUE MERA.
THUS FAR...I HAVE BEEN UNABLE TO FIND HER...
...OR EVEN DETERMINE IF SHE STILL LIVES.

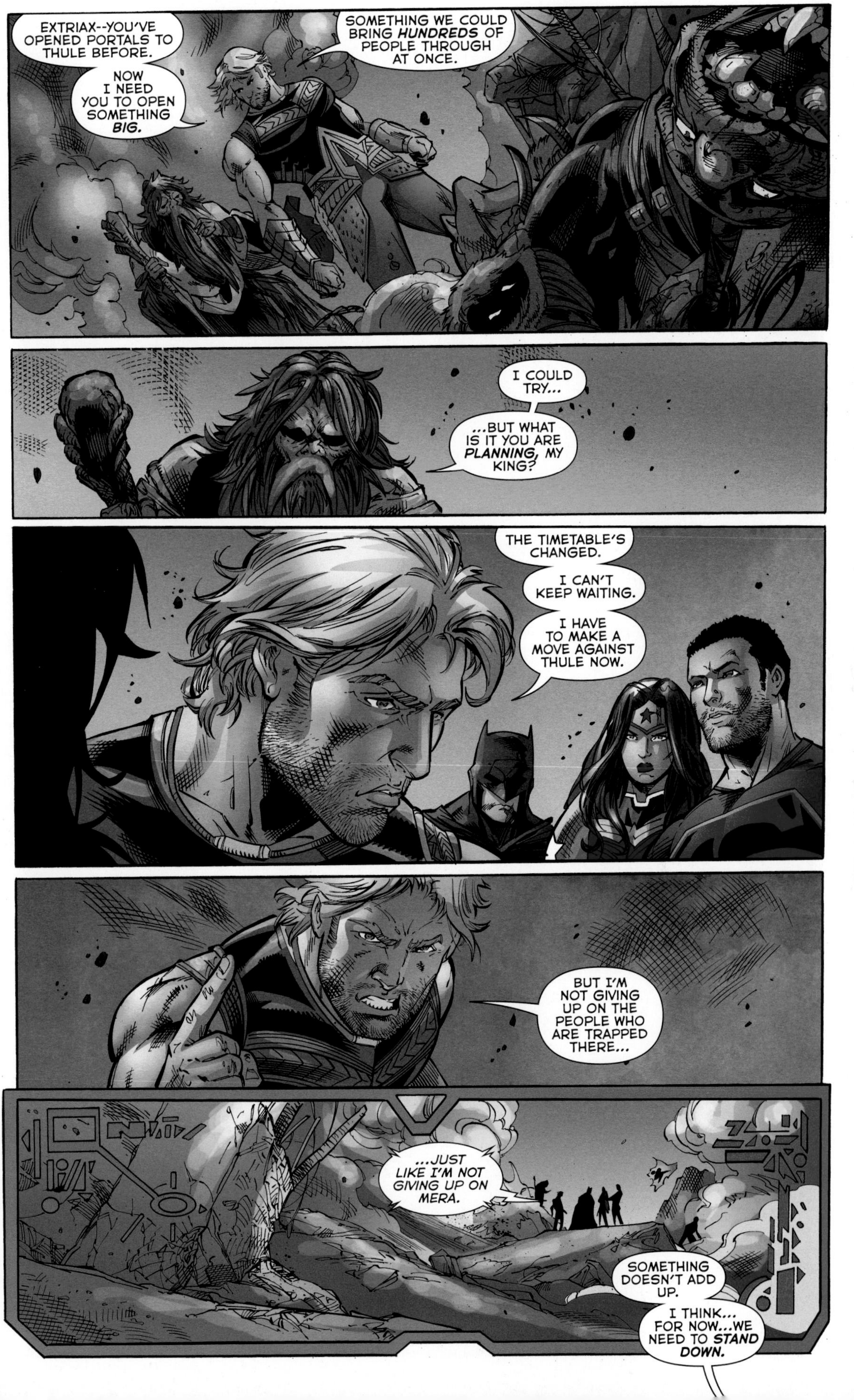

EXTRIAX--YOU'VE OPENED PORTALS TO THULE BEFORE.
NOW I NEED YOU TO OPEN SOMETHING *BIG.*
SOMETHING WE COULD BRING *HUNDREDS* OF PEOPLE THROUGH AT ONCE.
I COULD TRY...
...BUT WHAT IS IT YOU ARE *PLANNING,* MY KING?
THE TIMETABLE'S CHANGED.
I CAN'T KEEP WAITING.
I HAVE TO MAKE A MOVE AGAINST THULE NOW.
BUT I'M NOT GIVING UP ON THE PEOPLE WHO ARE TRAPPED THERE...
...JUST LIKE I'M NOT GIVING UP ON MERA.
SOMETHING DOESN'T ADD UP.
I THINK... FOR NOW...WE NEED TO *STAND DOWN.*

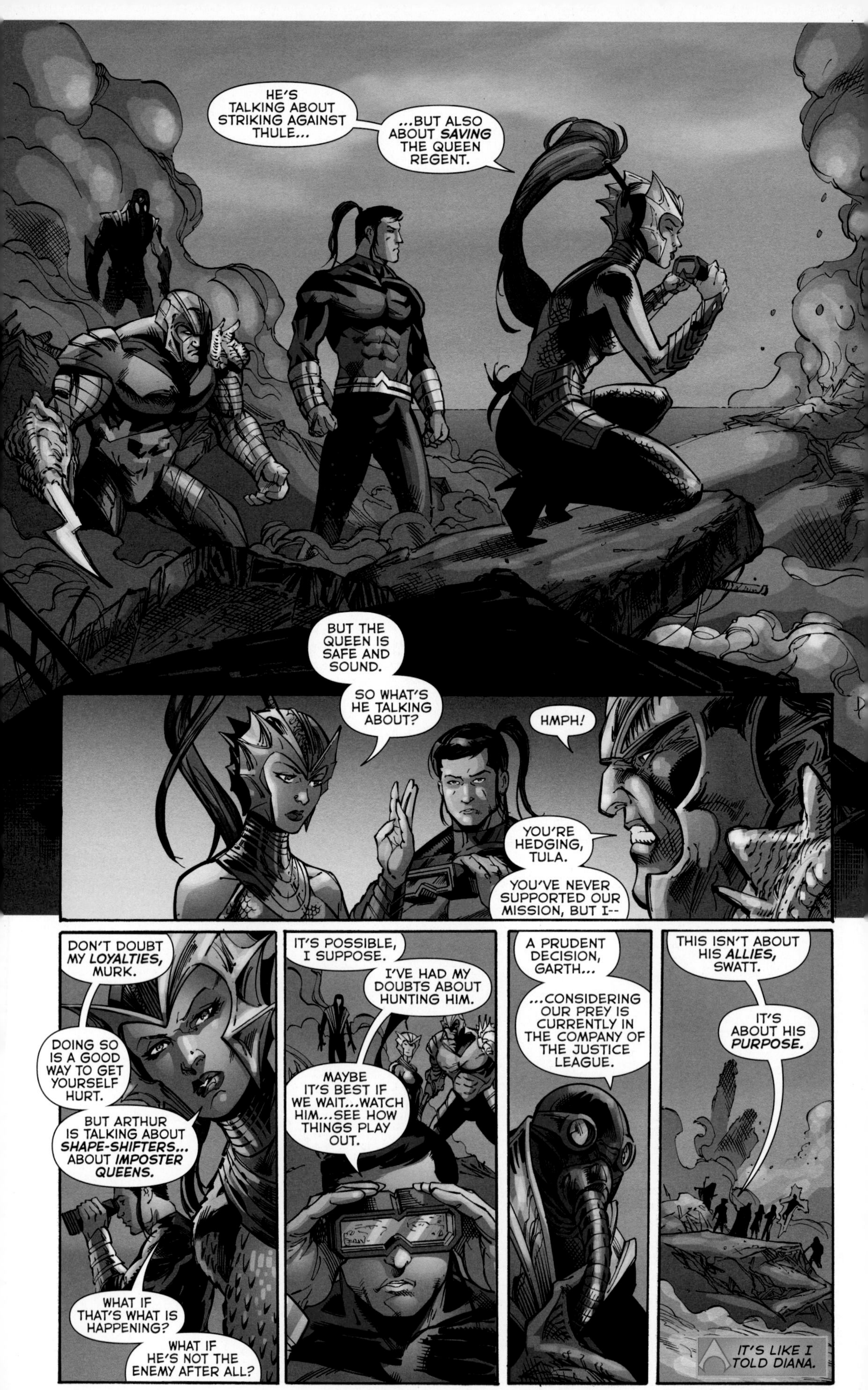
HE'S TALKING ABOUT STRIKING AGAINST THULE...
...BUT ALSO ABOUT SAVING THE QUEEN REGENT.
BUT THE QUEEN IS SAFE AND SOUND.
SO WHAT'S HE TALKING ABOUT?
HMPH!
YOU'RE HEDGING, TULA.
YOU'VE NEVER SUPPORTED OUR MISSION, BUT I--
DON'T DOUBT MY LOYALTIES, MURK.
DOING SO IS A GOOD WAY TO GET YOURSELF HURT.
BUT ARTHUR IS TALKING ABOUT SHAPE-SHIFTERS... ABOUT IMPOSTER QUEENS.
WHAT IF THAT'S WHAT IS HAPPENING?
WHAT IF HE'S NOT THE ENEMY AFTER ALL?
IT'S POSSIBLE, I SUPPOSE.
I'VE HAD MY DOUBTS ABOUT HUNTING HIM.
MAYBE IT'S BEST IF WE WAIT...WATCH HIM...SEE HOW THINGS PLAY OUT.
A PRUDENT DECISION, GARTH...
...CONSIDERING OUR PREY IS CURRENTLY IN THE COMPANY OF THE JUSTICE LEAGUE.
THIS ISN'T ABOUT HIS ALLIES, SWATT.
IT'S ABOUT HIS PURPOSE.
IT'S LIKE I TOLD DIANA.

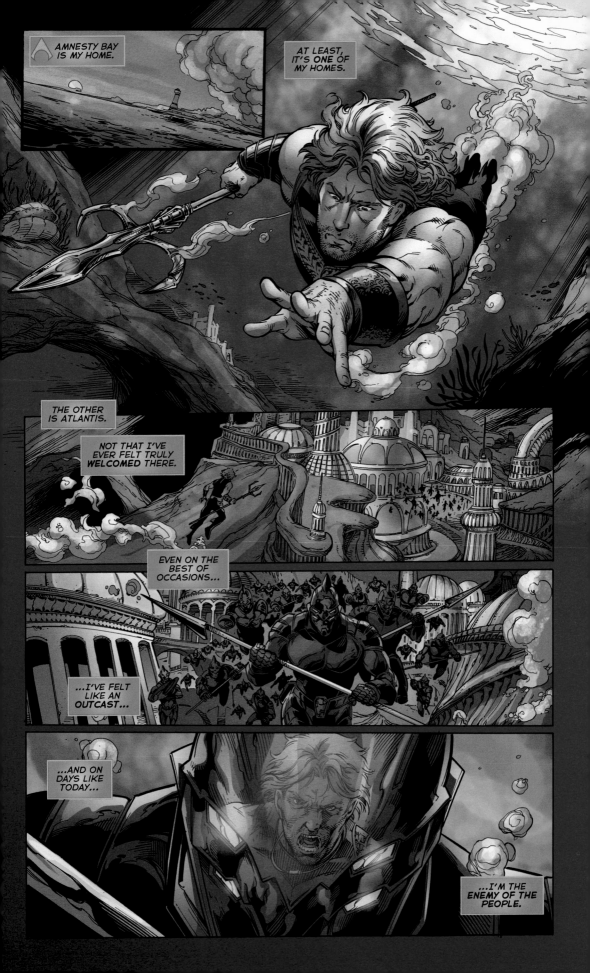

AMNESTY BAY IS MY HOME.

AT LEAST, IT'S ONE OF MY HOMES.

THE OTHER IS ATLANTIS.

NOT THAT I'VE EVER FELT TRULY WELCOMED THERE.

EVEN ON THE BEST OF OCCASIONS...

...I'VE FELT LIKE AN OUTCAST...

...AND ON DAYS LIKE TODAY...

...I'M THE ENEMY OF THE PEOPLE.

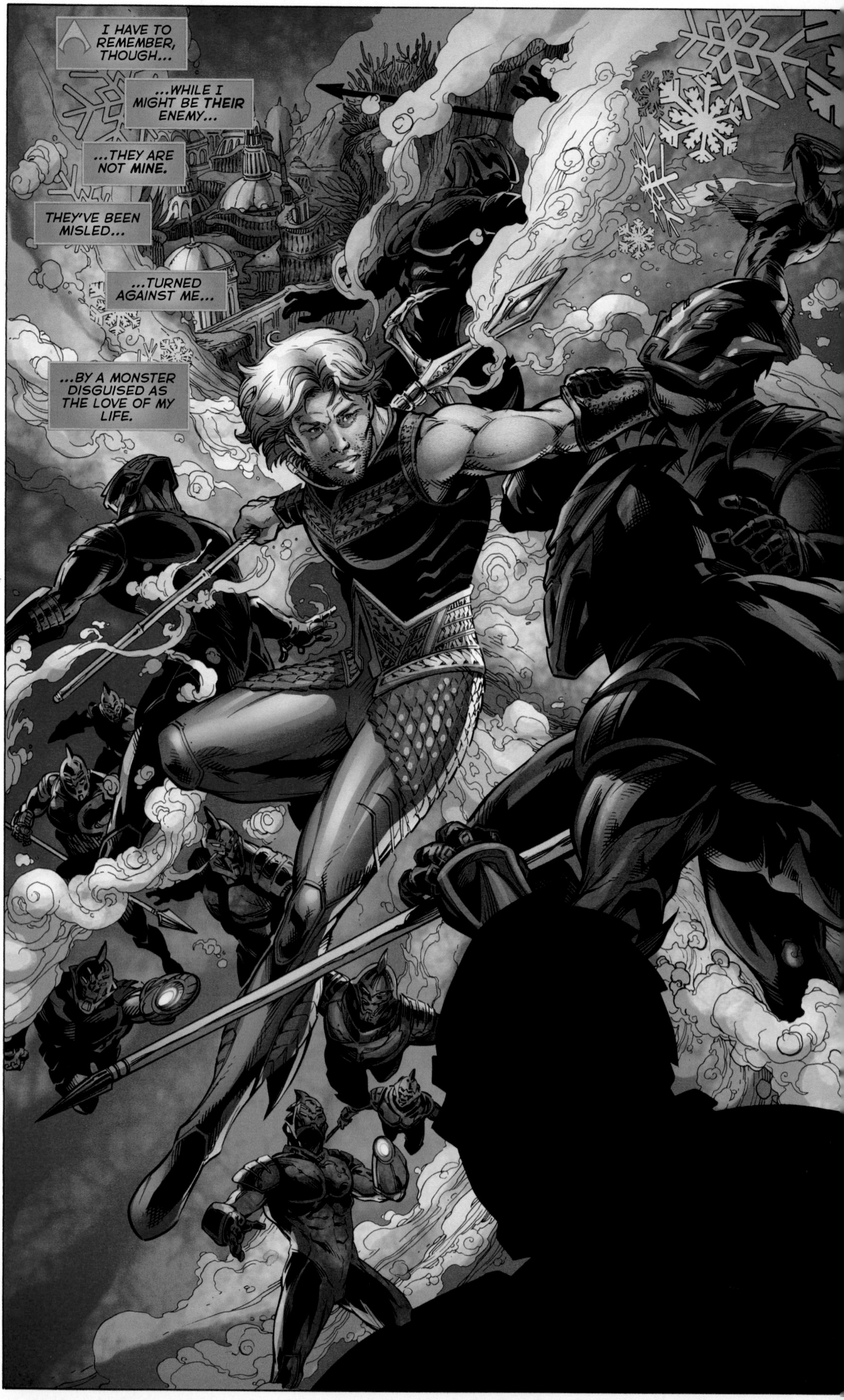
I HAVE TO REMEMBER, THOUGH...
...WHILE I MIGHT BE THEIR ENEMY...
...THEY ARE NOT MINE.
THEY'VE BEEN MISLED...
...TURNED AGAINST ME...
...BY A MONSTER DISGUISED AS THE LOVE OF MY LIFE.

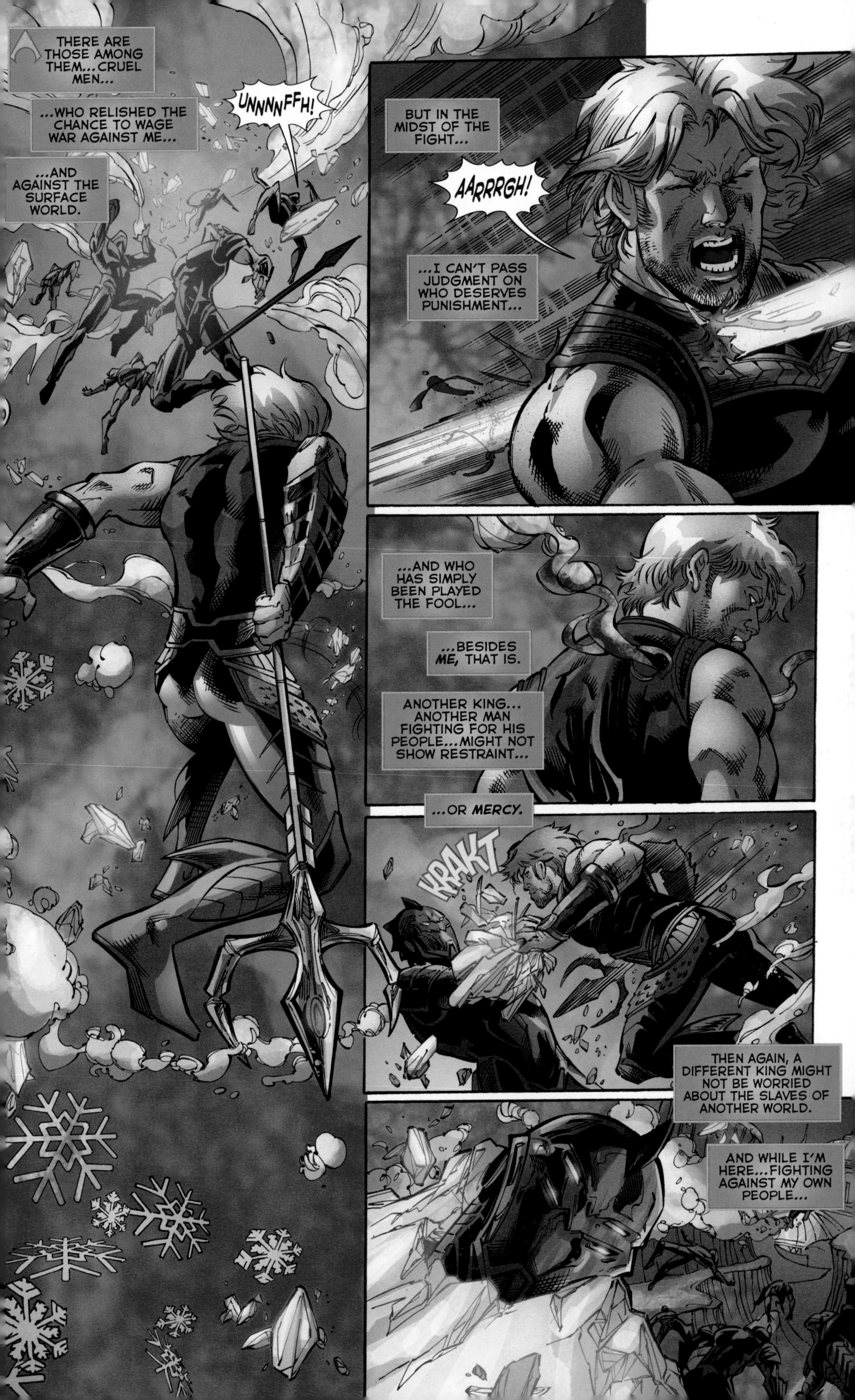
THERE ARE THOSE AMONG THEM...CRUEL MEN...
...WHO RELISHED THE CHANCE TO WAGE WAR AGAINST ME...
...AND AGAINST THE SURFACE WORLD.
UNNNNFFH!
BUT IN THE MIDST OF THE FIGHT...
AARRRGH!
...I CAN'T PASS JUDGMENT ON WHO DESERVES PUNISHMENT...
...AND WHO HAS SIMPLY PLAYED THE FOOL...
...BESIDES ME, THAT IS.
ANOTHER KING... ANOTHER MAN FIGHTING FOR HIS PEOPLE...MIGHT NOT SHOW RESTRAINT...
...OR MERCY.
KRAKT
THEN AGAIN, A DIFFERENT KING MIGHT NOT BE WORRIED ABOUT THE SLAVES OF ANOTHER WORLD.
AND WHILE I'M HERE...FIGHTING AGAINST MY OWN PEOPLE...

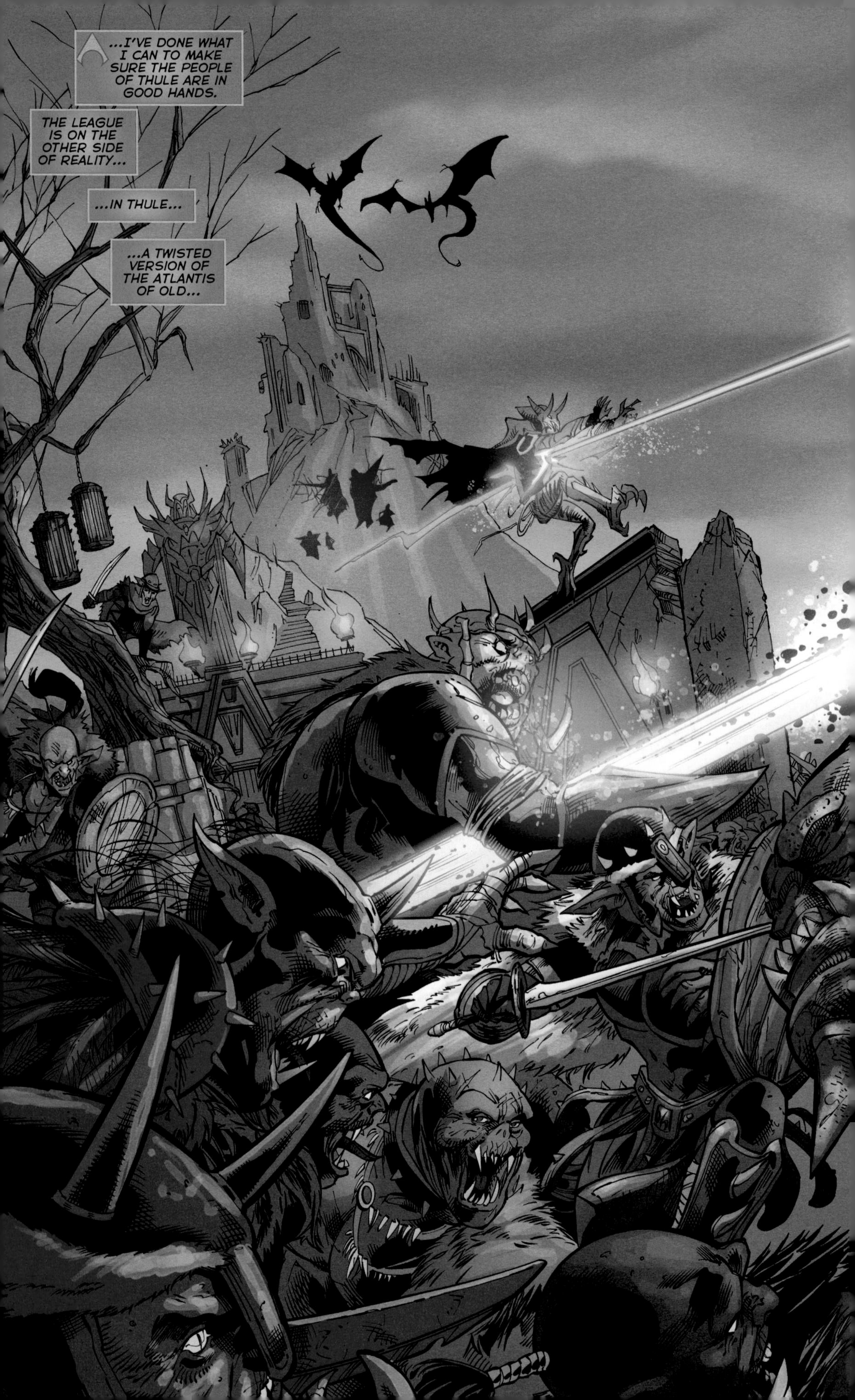
...I'VE DONE WHAT I CAN TO MAKE SURE THE PEOPLE OF THULE ARE IN GOOD HANDS.
THE LEAGUE IS ON THE OTHER SIDE OF REALITY...
...IN THULE...
...A TWISTED VERSION OF THE ATLANTIS OF OLD...

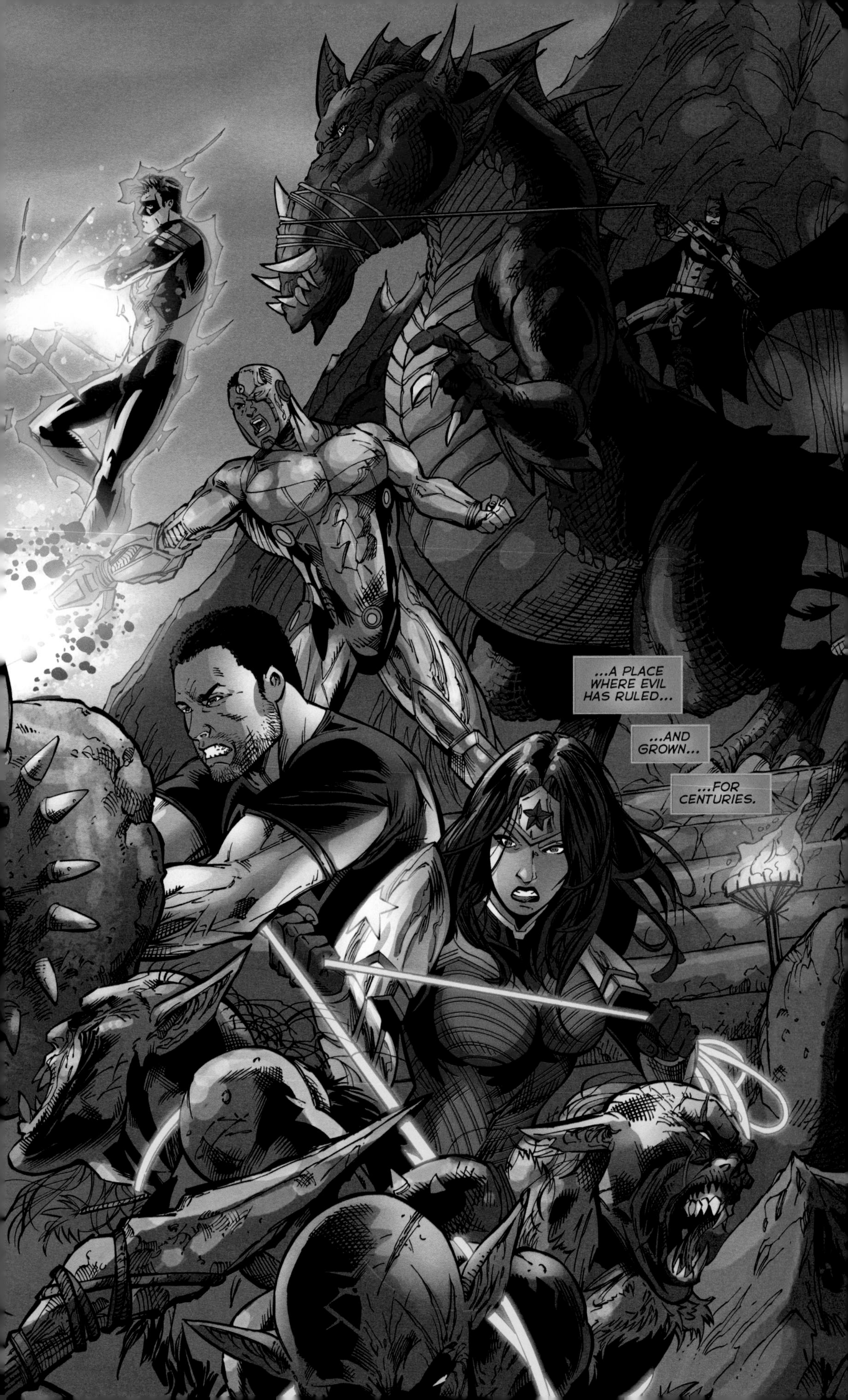
...A PLACE WHERE EVIL HAS RULED...
...AND GROWN...
...FOR CENTURIES.

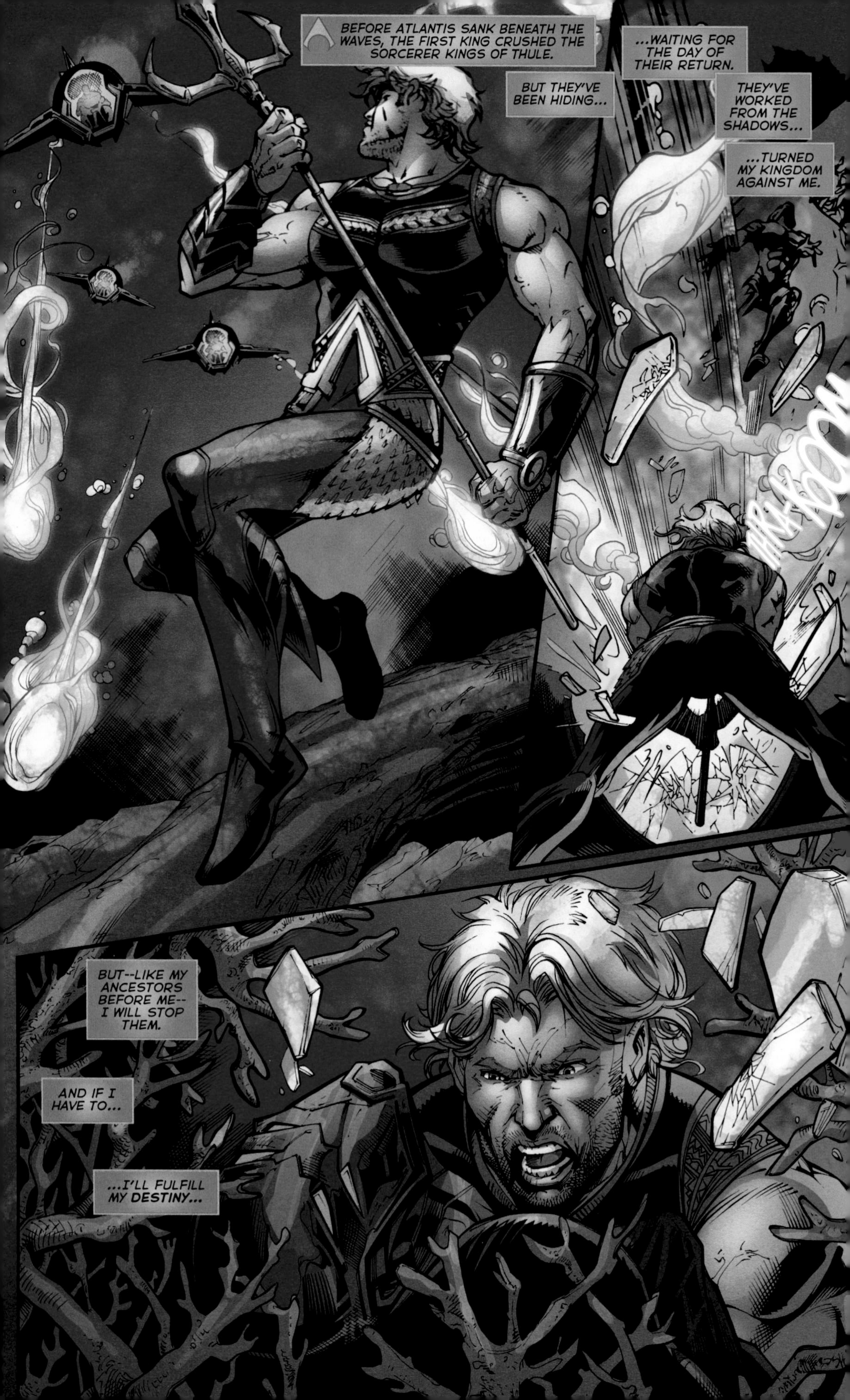

BEFORE ATLANTIS SANK BENEATH THE WAVES, THE FIRST KING CRUSHED THE SORCERER KINGS OF THULE.
BUT THEY'VE BEEN HIDING...
...WAITING FOR THE DAY OF THEIR RETURN.
THEY'VE WORKED FROM THE SHADOWS...
...TURNED MY KINGDOM AGAINST ME.
THRA-KOOOM
BUT--LIKE MY ANCESTORS BEFORE ME--I WILL STOP THEM.
AND IF I HAVE TO...
...I'LL FULFILL MY DESTINY...

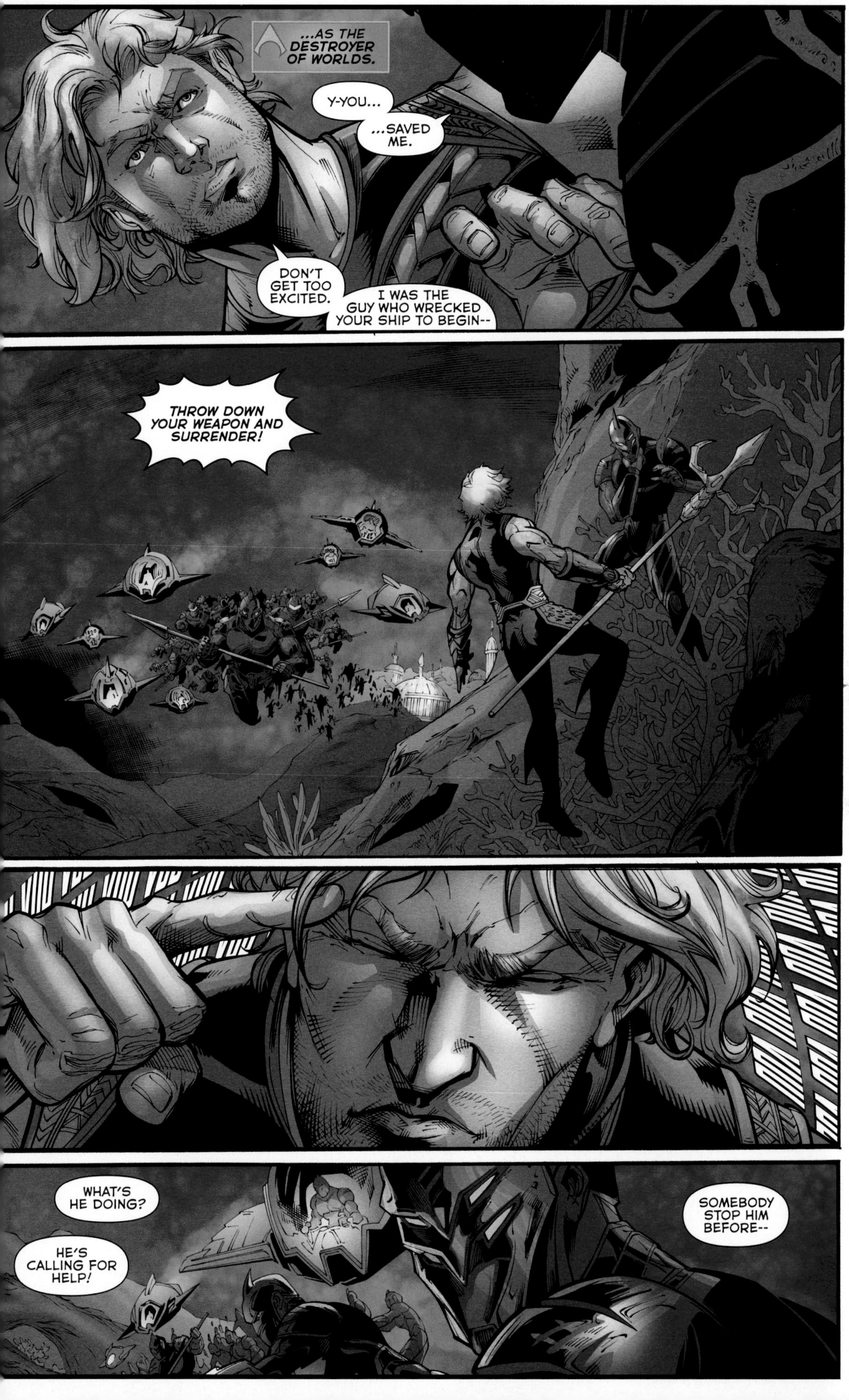
...AS THE DESTROYER OF WORLDS.
Y-YOU...
...SAVED ME.
DON'T GET TOO EXCITED.
I WAS THE GUY WHO WRECKED YOUR SHIP TO BEGIN--
THROW DOWN YOUR WEAPON AND SURRENDER!
WHAT'S HE DOING?
HE'S CALLING FOR HELP!
SOMEBODY STOP HIM BEFORE--

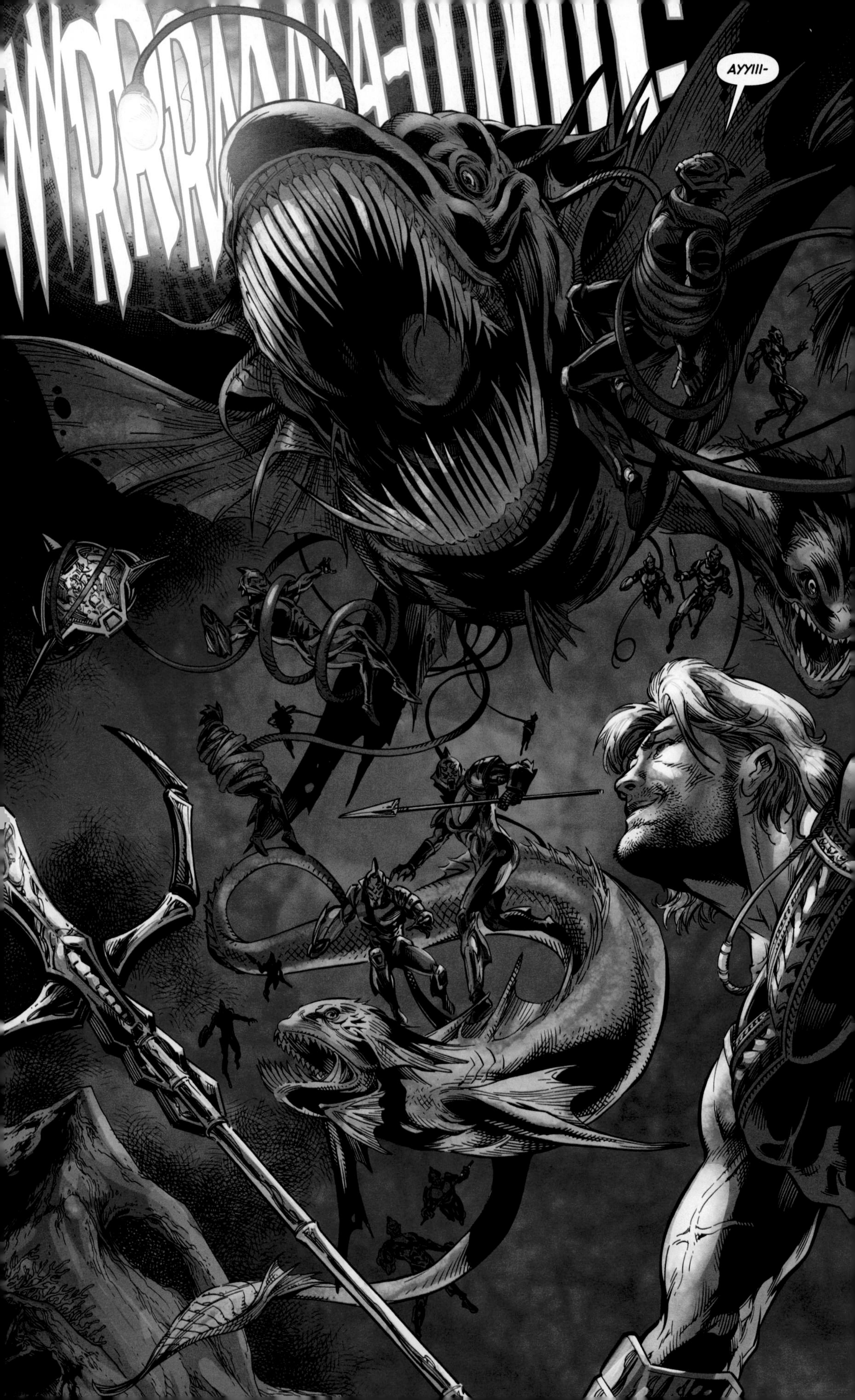
AYYIII-

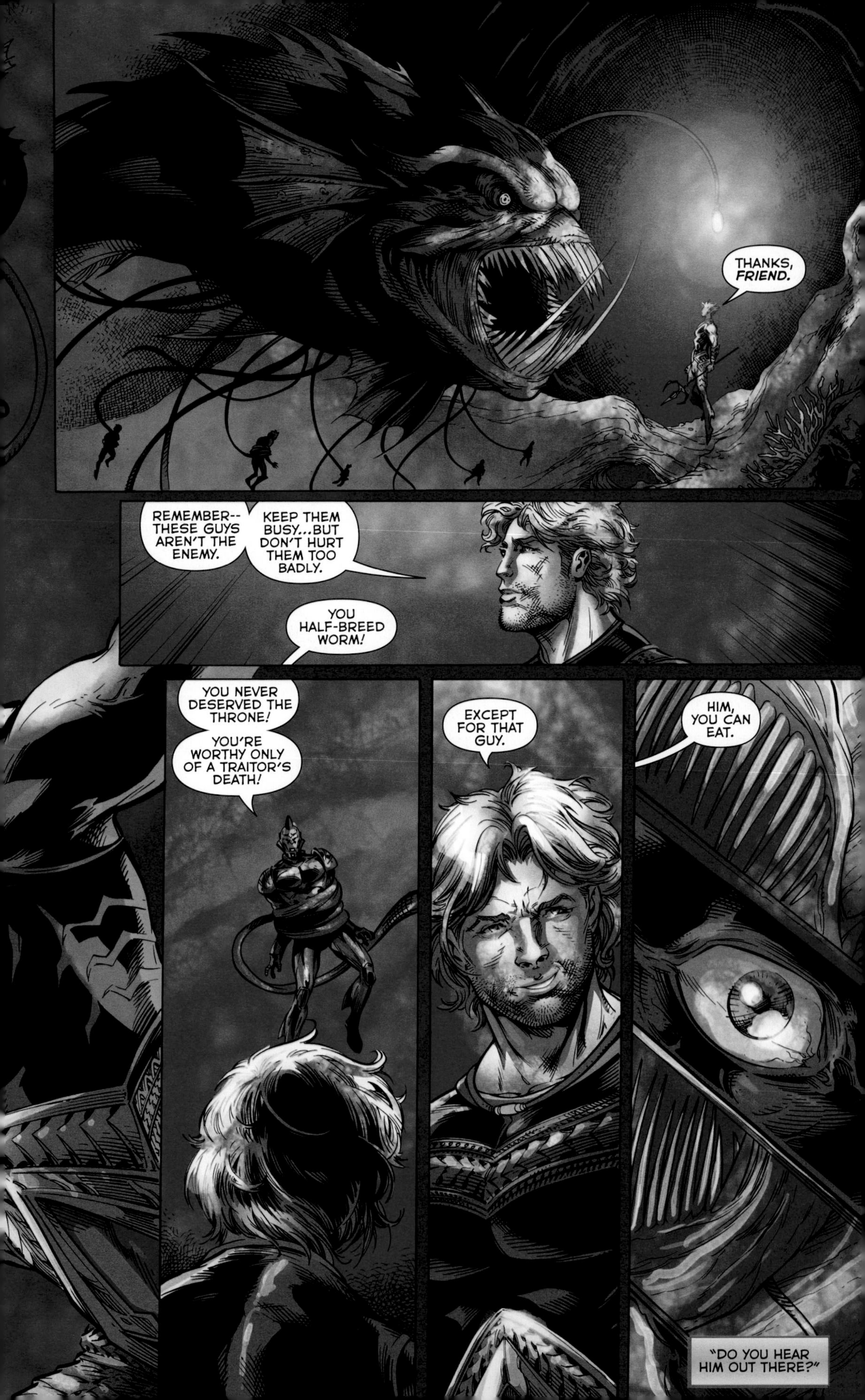
THANKS, FRIEND.
REMEMBER-- THESE GUYS AREN'T THE ENEMY.
KEEP THEM BUSY...BUT DON'T HURT THEM TOO BADLY.
YOU HALF-BREED WORM!
YOU NEVER DESERVED THE THRONE!
YOU'RE WORTHY ONLY OF A TRAITOR'S DEATH!
EXCEPT FOR THAT GUY.
HIM, YOU CAN EAT.
"DO YOU HEAR HIM OUT THERE?"

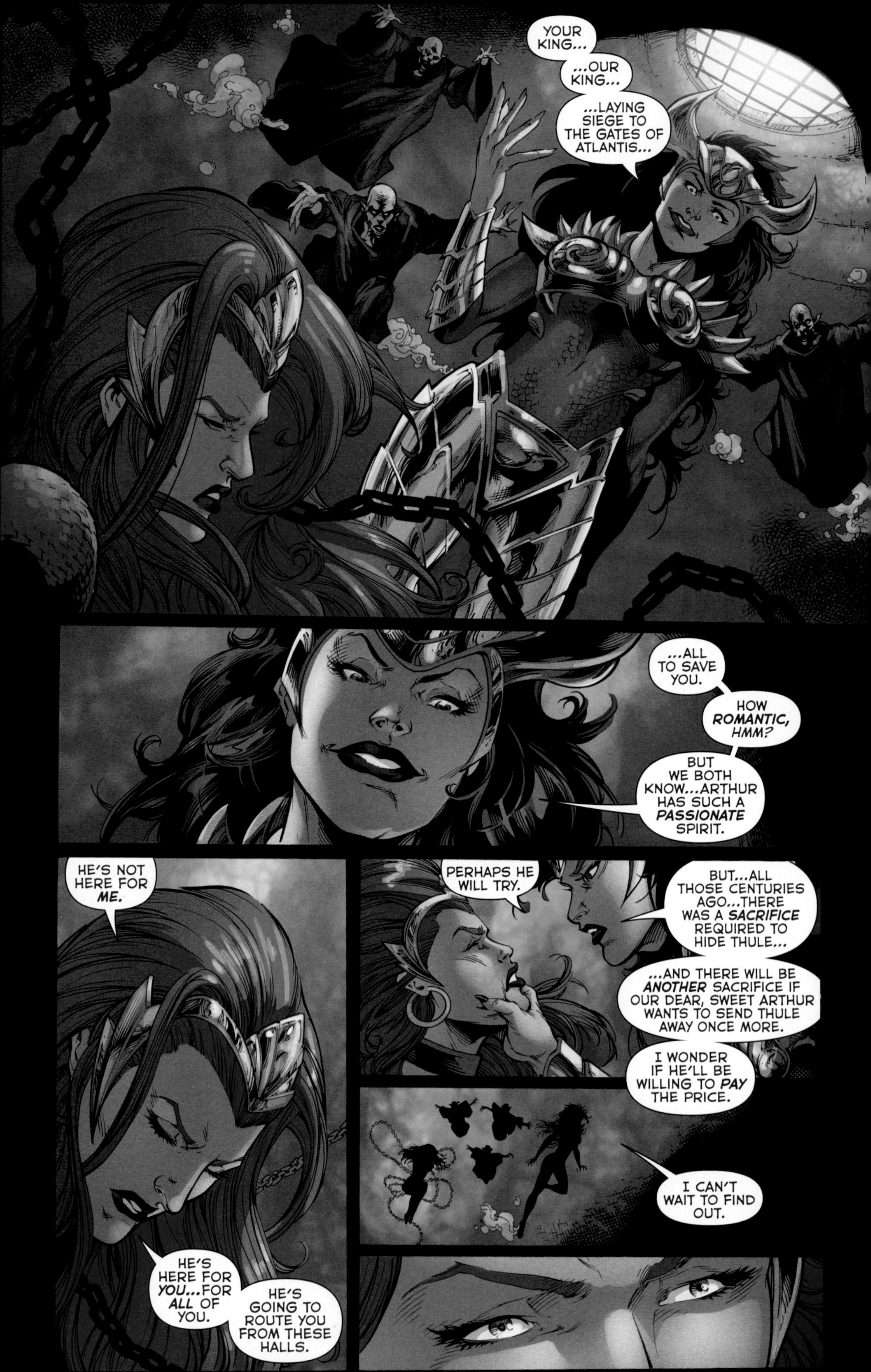
YOUR KING...
...OUR KING...
...LAYING SIEGE TO THE GATES OF ATLANTIS...
...ALL TO SAVE YOU.
HOW ROMANTIC, HMM?
BUT WE BOTH KNOW...ARTHUR HAS SUCH A PASSIONATE SPIRIT.
HE'S NOT HERE FOR ME.
HE'S HERE FOR YOU...FOR ALL OF YOU.
HE'S GOING TO ROUTE YOU FROM THESE HALLS.
PERHAPS HE WILL TRY.
BUT...ALL THOSE CENTURIES AGO...THERE WAS A SACRIFICE REQUIRED TO HIDE THULE...
...AND THERE WILL BE ANOTHER SACRIFICE IF OUR DEAR, SWEET ARTHUR WANTS TO SEND THULE AWAY ONCE MORE.
I WONDER IF HE'LL BE WILLING TO PAY THE PRICE.
I CAN'T WAIT TO FIND OUT.

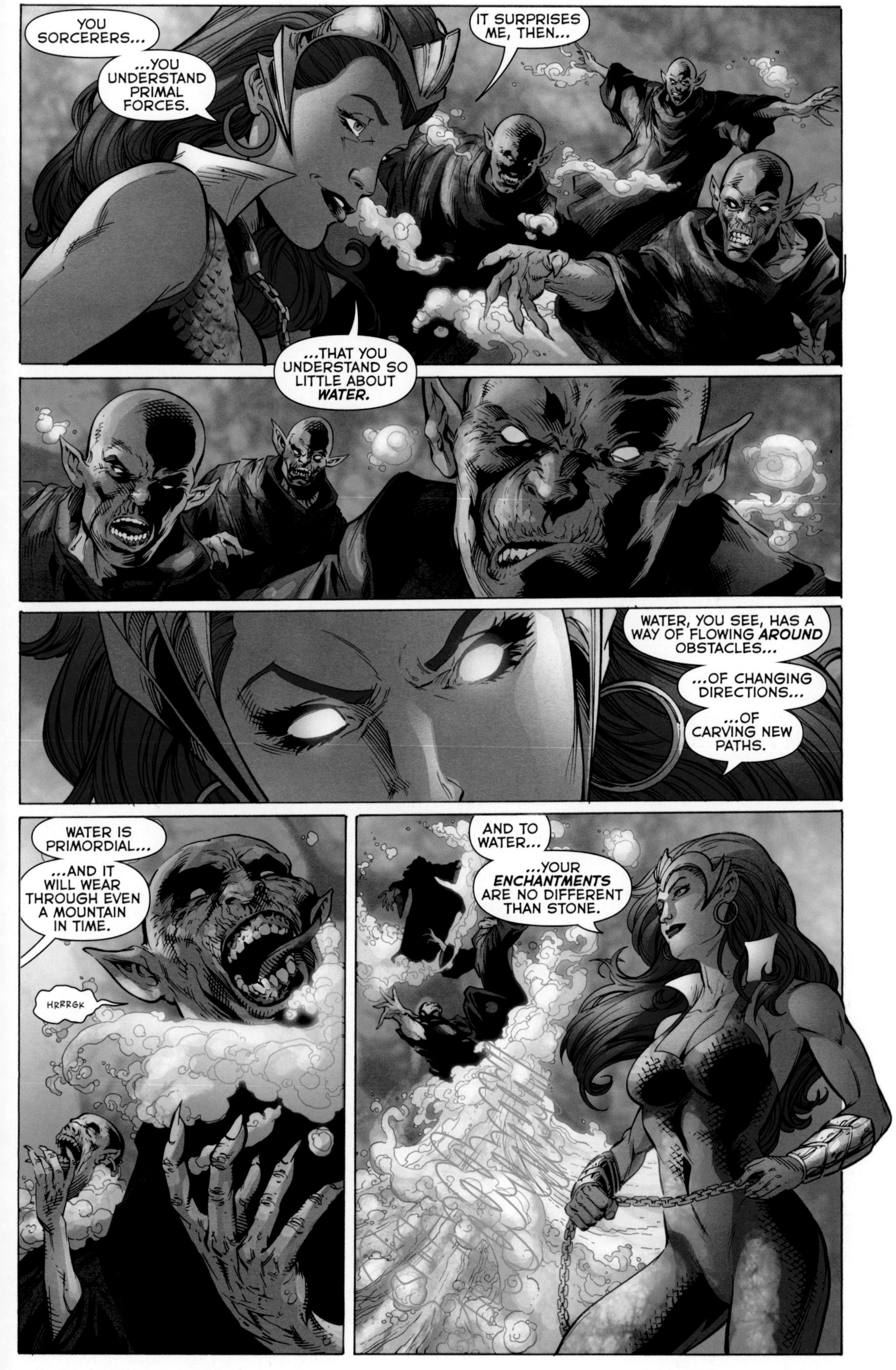

YOU SORCERERS...
...YOU UNDERSTAND PRIMAL FORCES.
IT SURPRISES ME, THEN...
...THAT YOU UNDERSTAND SO LITTLE ABOUT *WATER.*
WATER, YOU SEE, HAS A WAY OF FLOWING *AROUND* OBSTACLES...
...OF CHANGING DIRECTIONS...
...OF CARVING NEW PATHS.
WATER IS PRIMORDIAL...
...AND IT WILL WEAR THROUGH EVEN A MOUNTAIN IN TIME.
HRRRGK
AND TO WATER...
...YOUR *ENCHANTMENTS* ARE NO DIFFERENT THAN STONE.

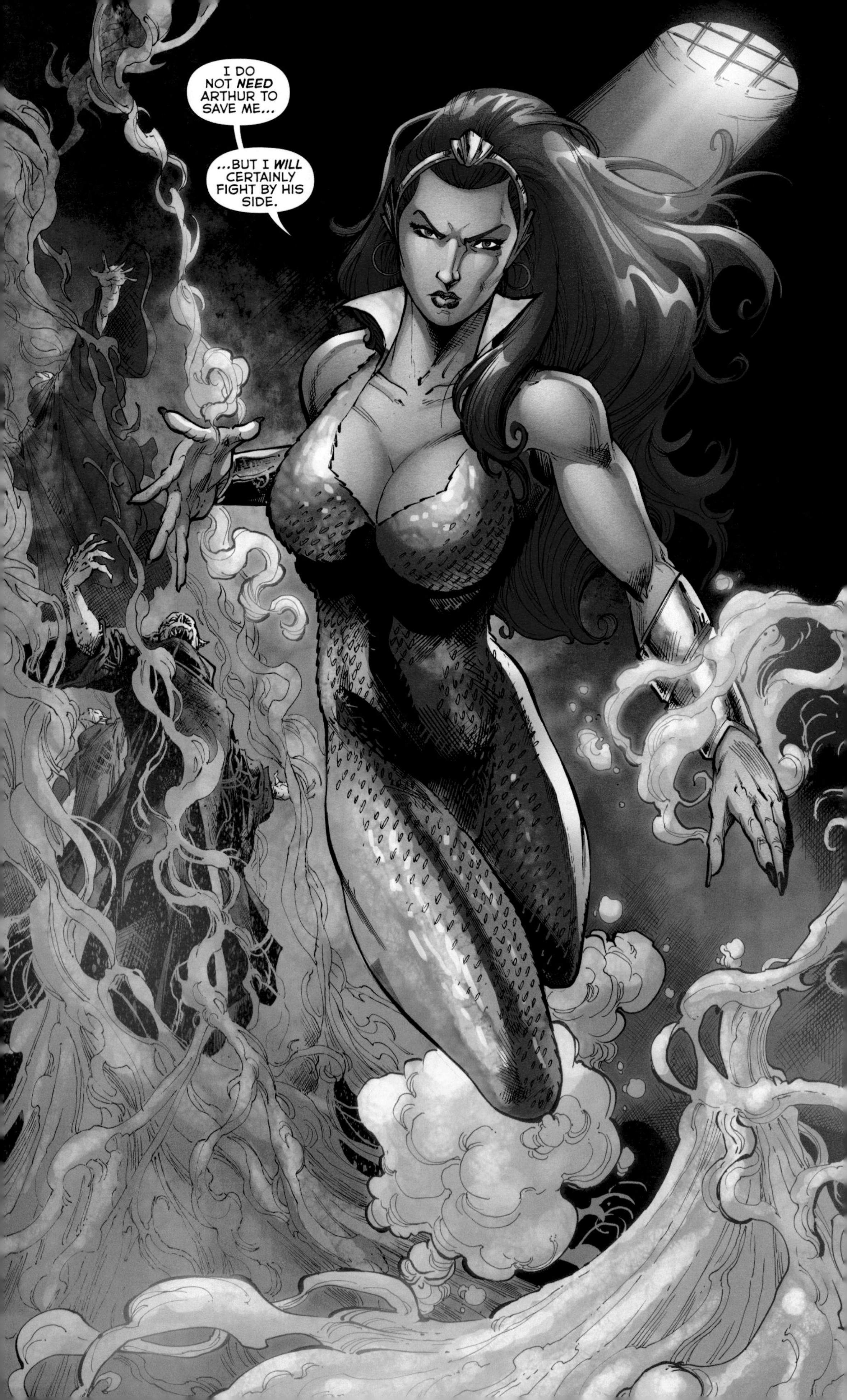
I DO NOT NEED ARTHUR TO SAVE ME...
...BUT I WILL CERTAINLY FIGHT BY HIS SIDE.

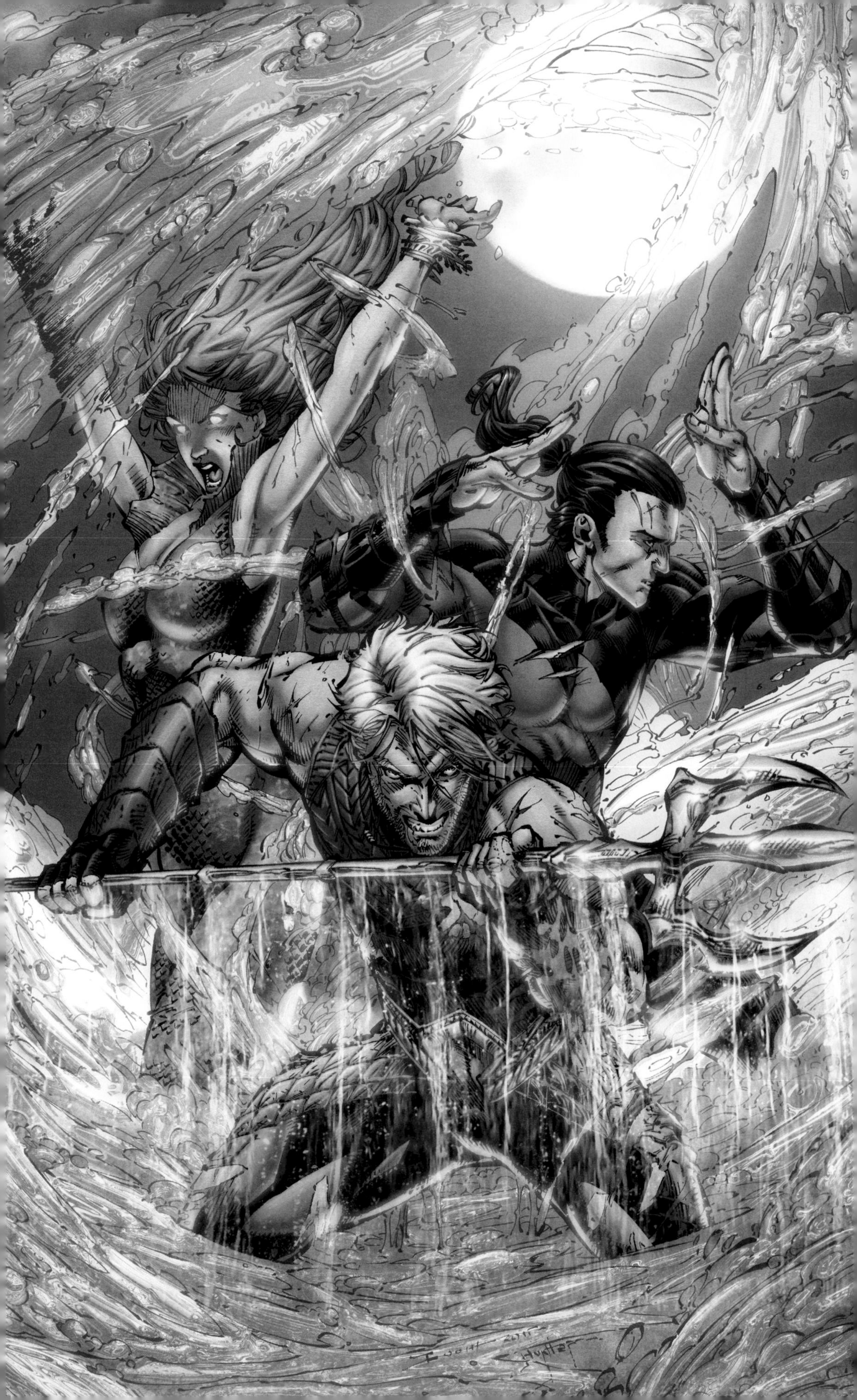

RETURN OF THE KING

CULLEN BUNN writer **VICENTE CIFUENTES** penciller **JOHN DELL, JUAN CASTRO, VICENTE CIFUENTES** inkers **GUY MAJOR** colorist **TOM NAPOLITANO** letterer
BRETT BOOTH, NORM RAPMUND and **ANDREW DALHOUSE** cover art

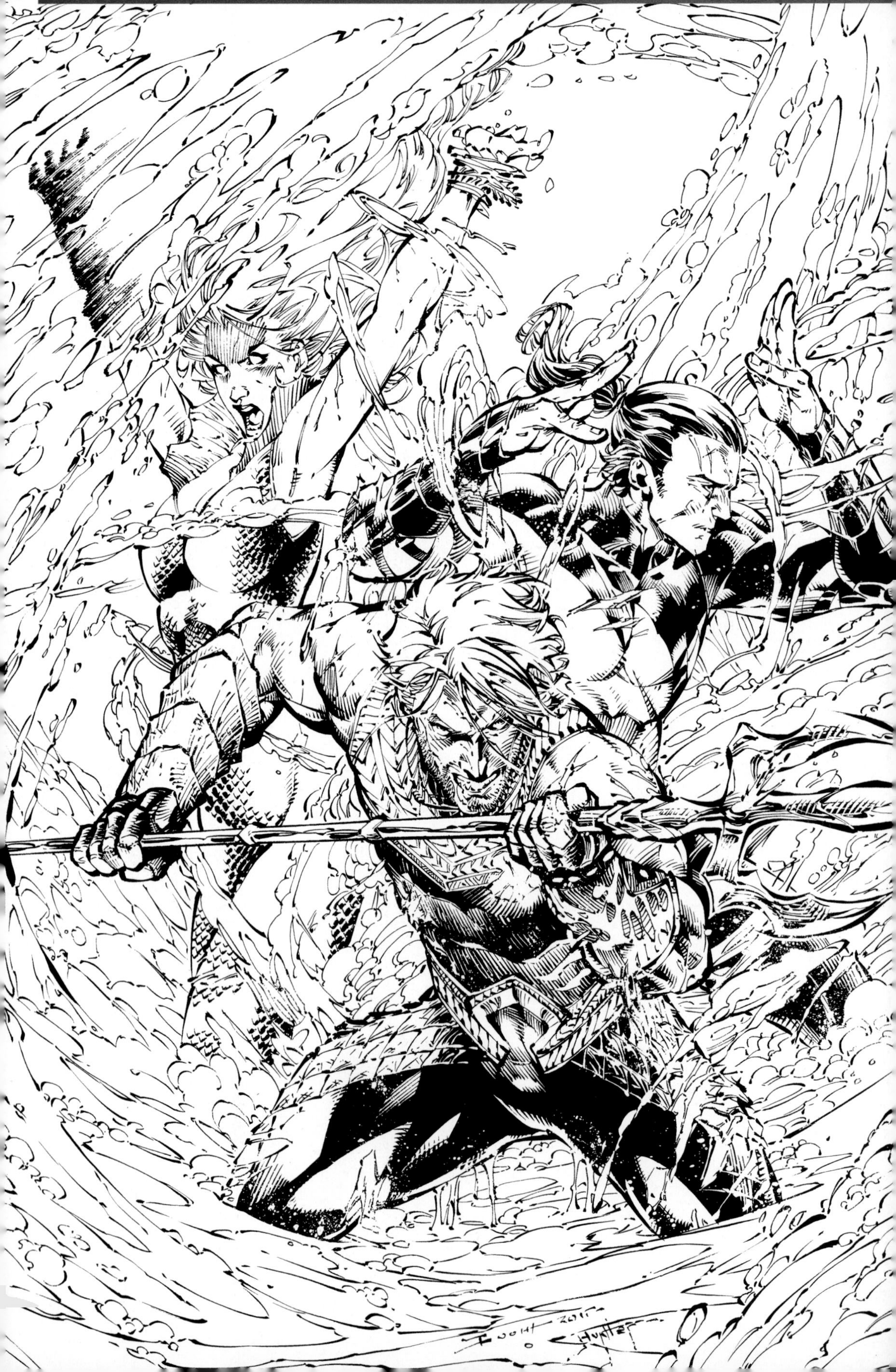

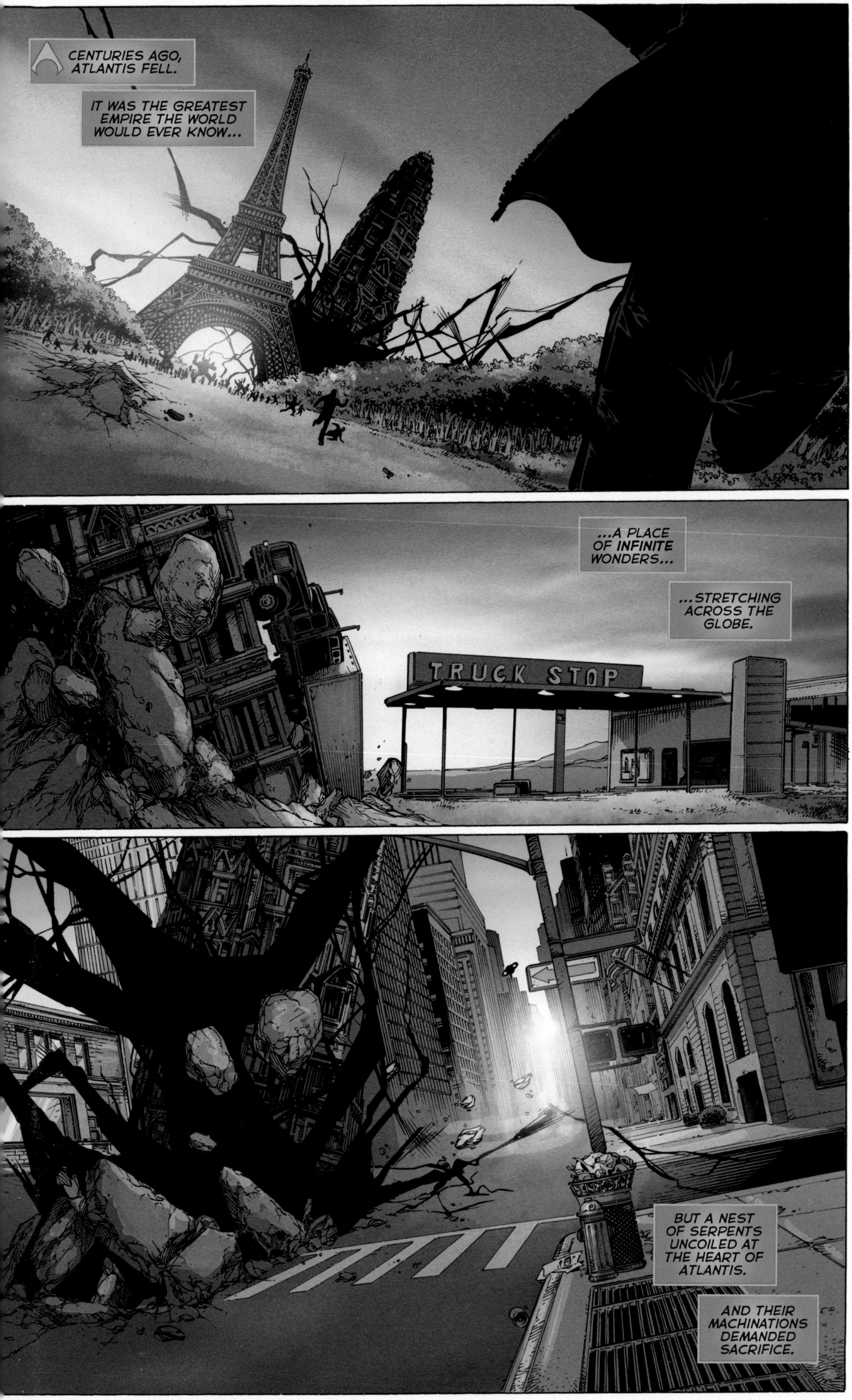
CENTURIES AGO, ATLANTIS FELL.
IT WAS THE GREATEST EMPIRE THE WORLD WOULD EVER KNOW...
...A PLACE OF INFINITE WONDERS...
...STRETCHING ACROSS THE GLOBE.
TRUCK STOP
BUT A NEST OF SERPENTS UNCOILED AT THE HEART OF ATLANTIS.
AND THEIR MACHINATIONS DEMANDED SACRIFICE.

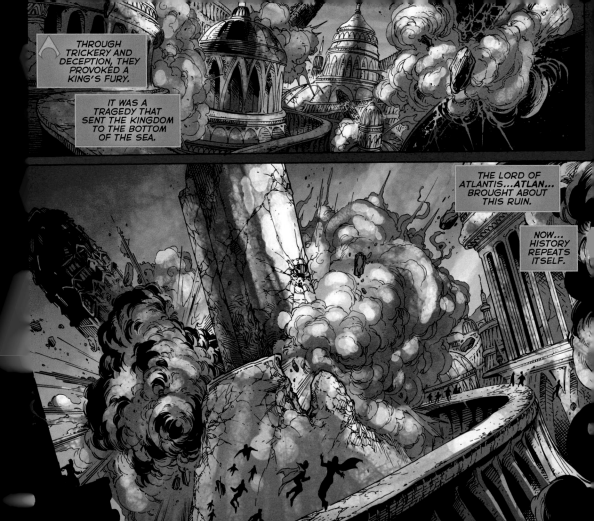

THROUGH TRICKERY AND DECEPTION, THEY PROVOKED A KING'S FURY.

IT WAS A TRAGEDY THAT SENT THE KINGDOM TO THE BOTTOM OF THE SEA.

THE LORD OF ATLANTIS...ATLAN... BROUGHT ABOUT THIS RUIN.

NOW... HISTORY REPEATS ITSELF.

THE KING ONCE AGAIN RAINS DESTRUCTION ON HIS PEOPLE.

ONLY...IN THE DAYS OF ATLAN... CALAMITY WAS BIRTHED FROM RAGE.

TODAY, THE KING...AND THAT WOULD BE ME...

...TRIES TO TELL HIMSELF THAT THIS IS FOR THE GREATER GOOD.

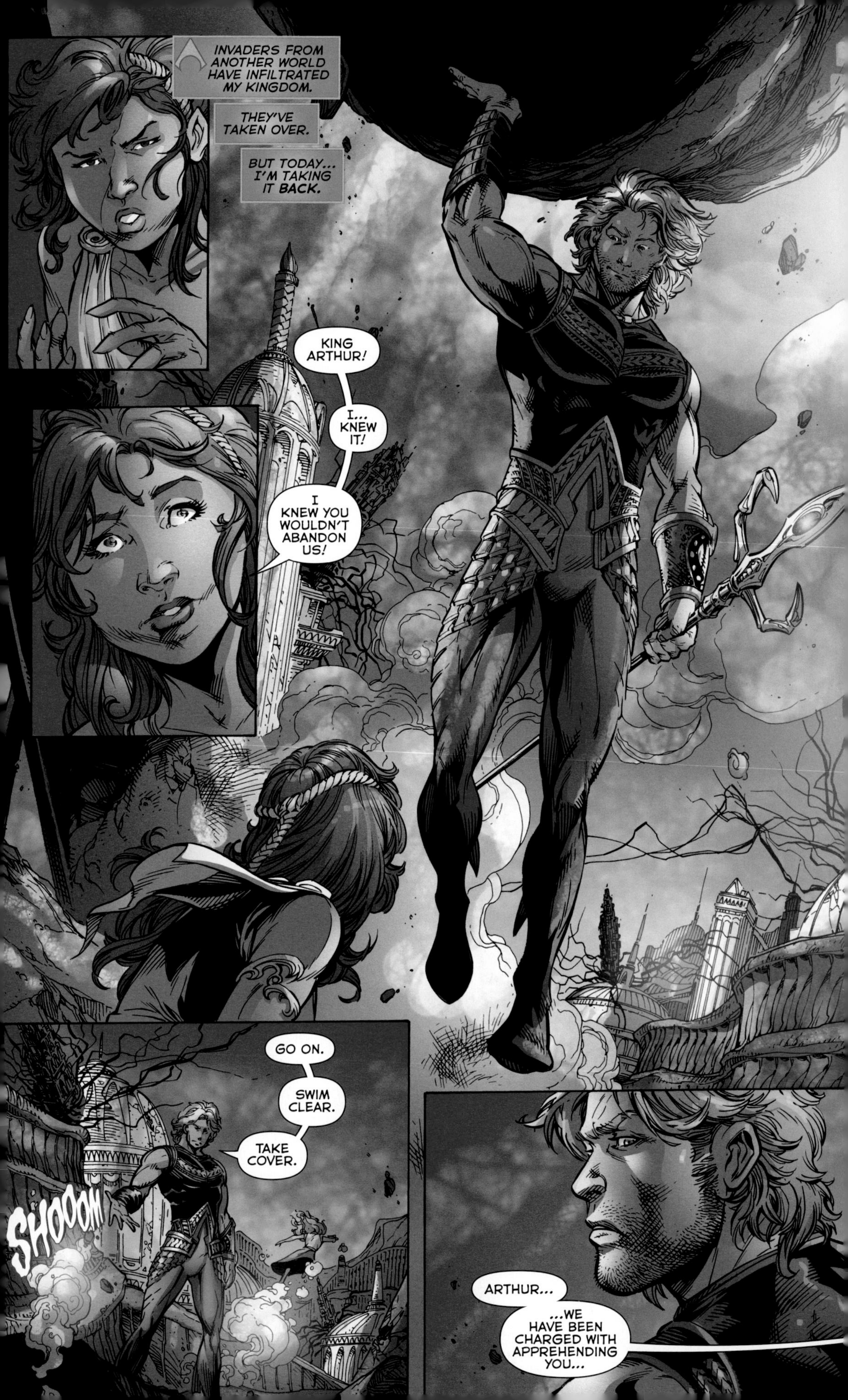
INVADERS FROM ANOTHER WORLD HAVE INFILTRATED MY KINGDOM.
THEY'VE TAKEN OVER.
BUT TODAY... I'M TAKING IT BACK.
KING ARTHUR!
I... KNEW IT!
I KNEW YOU WOULDN'T ABANDON US!
GO ON.
SWIM CLEAR.
TAKE COVER.
SHOOOM
ARTHUR...
...WE HAVE BEEN CHARGED WITH APPREHENDING YOU...

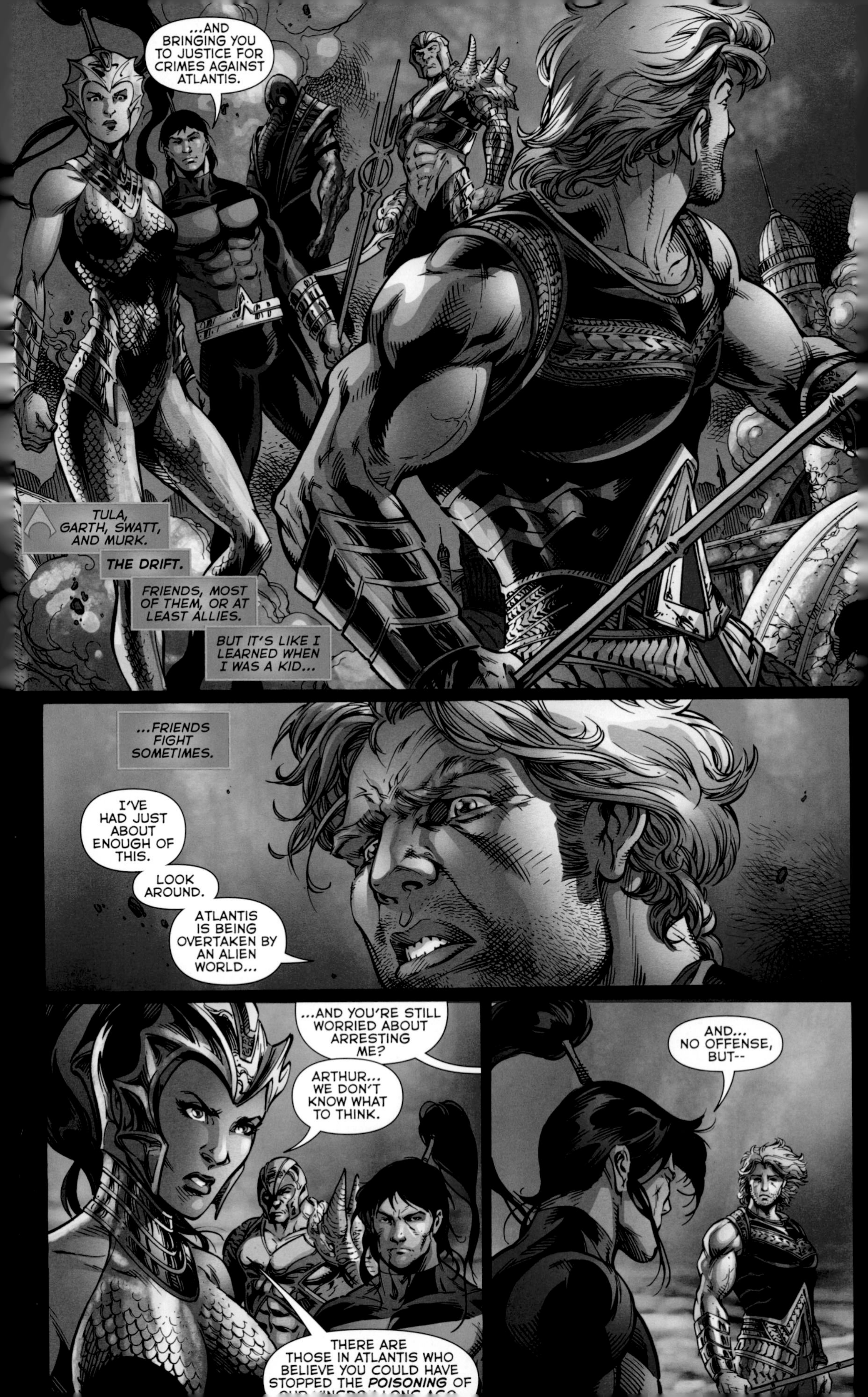
...AND BRINGING YOU TO JUSTICE FOR CRIMES AGAINST ATLANTIS.
TULA, GARTH, SWATT, AND MURK.
THE DRIFT.
FRIENDS, MOST OF THEM, OR AT LEAST ALLIES.
BUT IT'S LIKE I LEARNED WHEN I WAS A KID...
...FRIENDS FIGHT SOMETIMES.
I'VE HAD JUST ABOUT ENOUGH OF THIS.
LOOK AROUND.
ATLANTIS IS BEING OVERTAKEN BY AN ALIEN WORLD...
...AND YOU'RE STILL WORRIED ABOUT ARRESTING ME?
ARTHUR... WE DON'T KNOW WHAT TO THINK.
THERE ARE THOSE IN ATLANTIS WHO BELIEVE YOU COULD HAVE STOPPED THE POISONING OF
AND... NO OFFENSE, BUT--

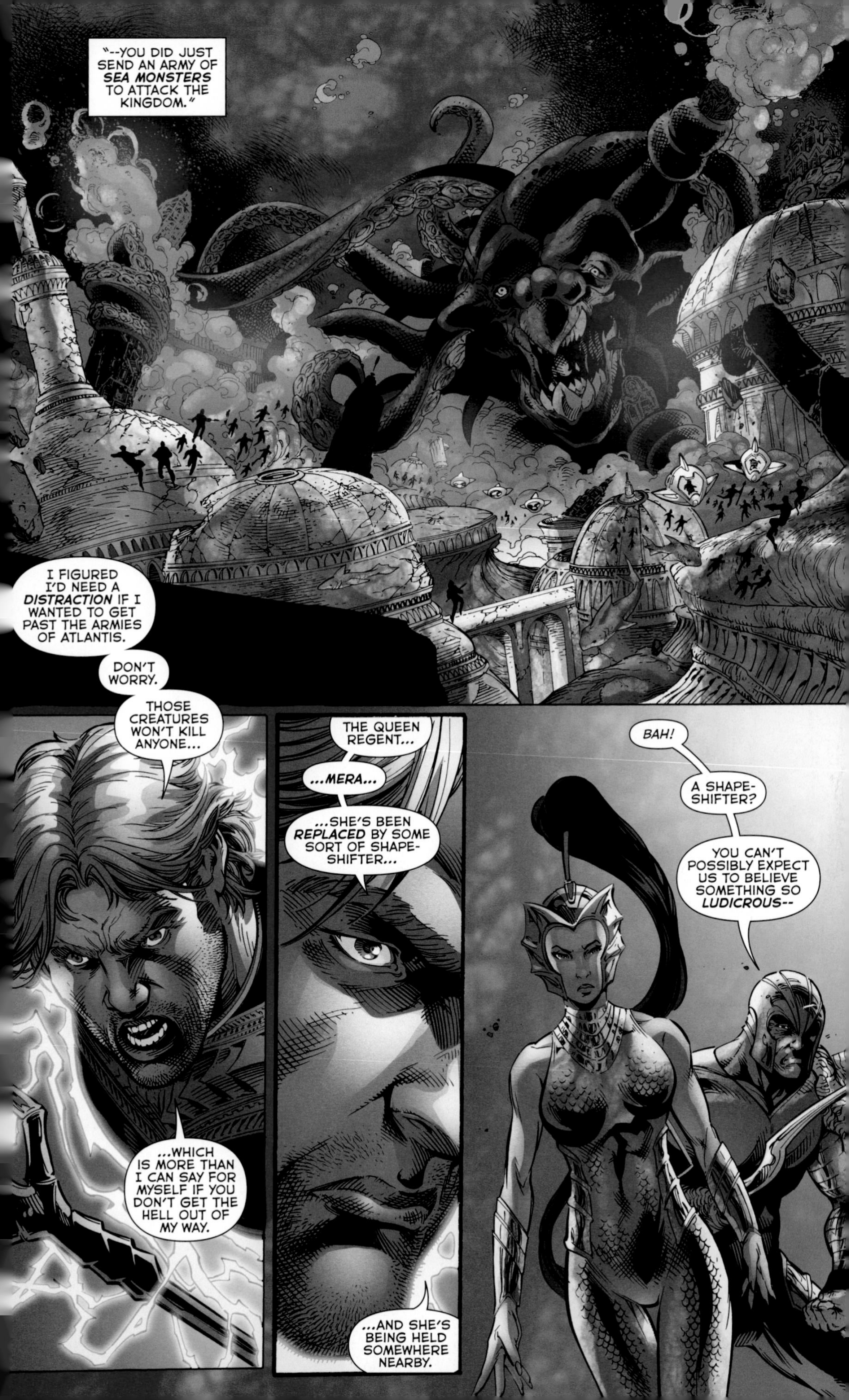
"--YOU DID JUST SEND AN ARMY OF *SEA MONSTERS* TO ATTACK THE KINGDOM."
I FIGURED I'D NEED A *DISTRACTION* IF I WANTED TO GET PAST THE ARMIES OF ATLANTIS.
DON'T WORRY.
THOSE CREATURES WON'T KILL ANYONE...
...WHICH IS MORE THAN I CAN SAY FOR MYSELF IF YOU DON'T GET THE HELL OUT OF MY WAY.
THE QUEEN REGENT...
...MERA...
...SHE'S BEEN *REPLACED* BY SOME SORT OF SHAPE-SHIFTER...
...AND SHE'S BEING HELD SOMEWHERE NEARBY.
BAH!
A SHAPE-SHIFTER?
YOU CAN'T POSSIBLY EXPECT US TO BELIEVE SOMETHING SO *LUDICROUS*--

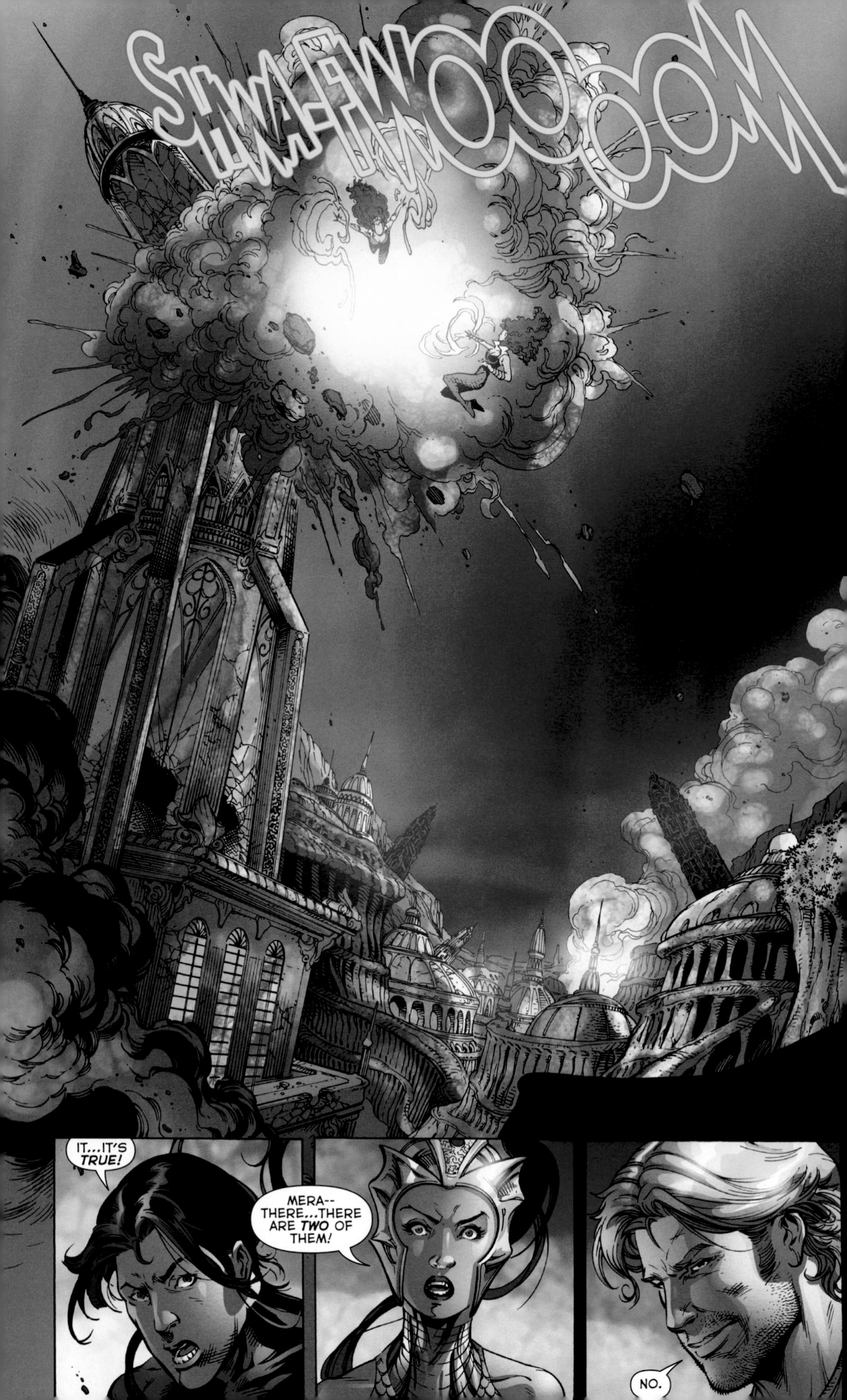
IT...IT'S TRUE!
MERA-- THERE...THERE ARE TWO OF THEM!
NO.

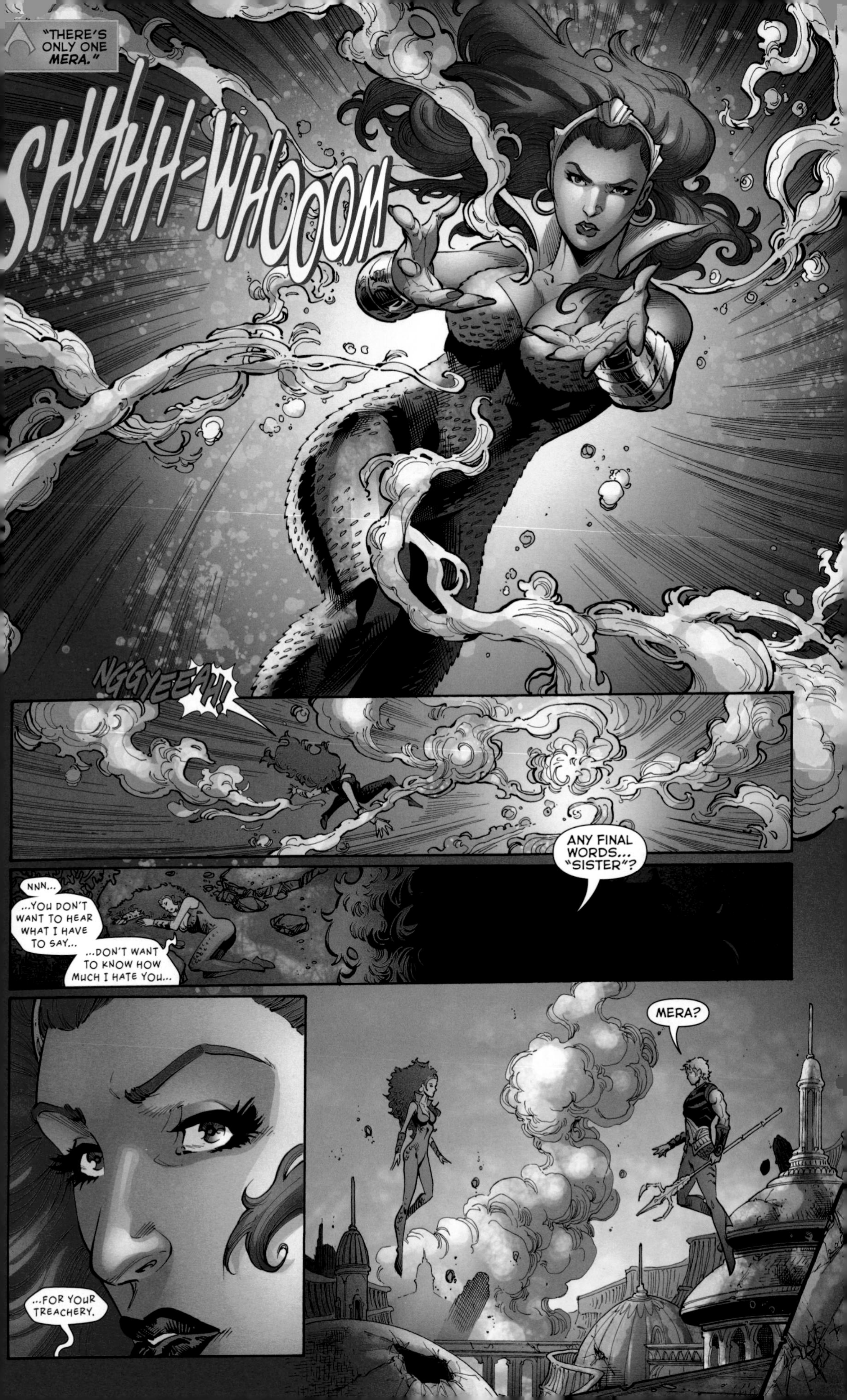
"THERE'S ONLY ONE MERA."
SHHHH-WHOOOM
NGGYEEAH!
ANY FINAL WORDS... "SISTER"?
NNN...
...YOU DON'T WANT TO HEAR WHAT I HAVE TO SAY...
...DON'T WANT TO KNOW HOW MUCH I HATE YOU...
...FOR YOUR TREACHERY.
MERA?

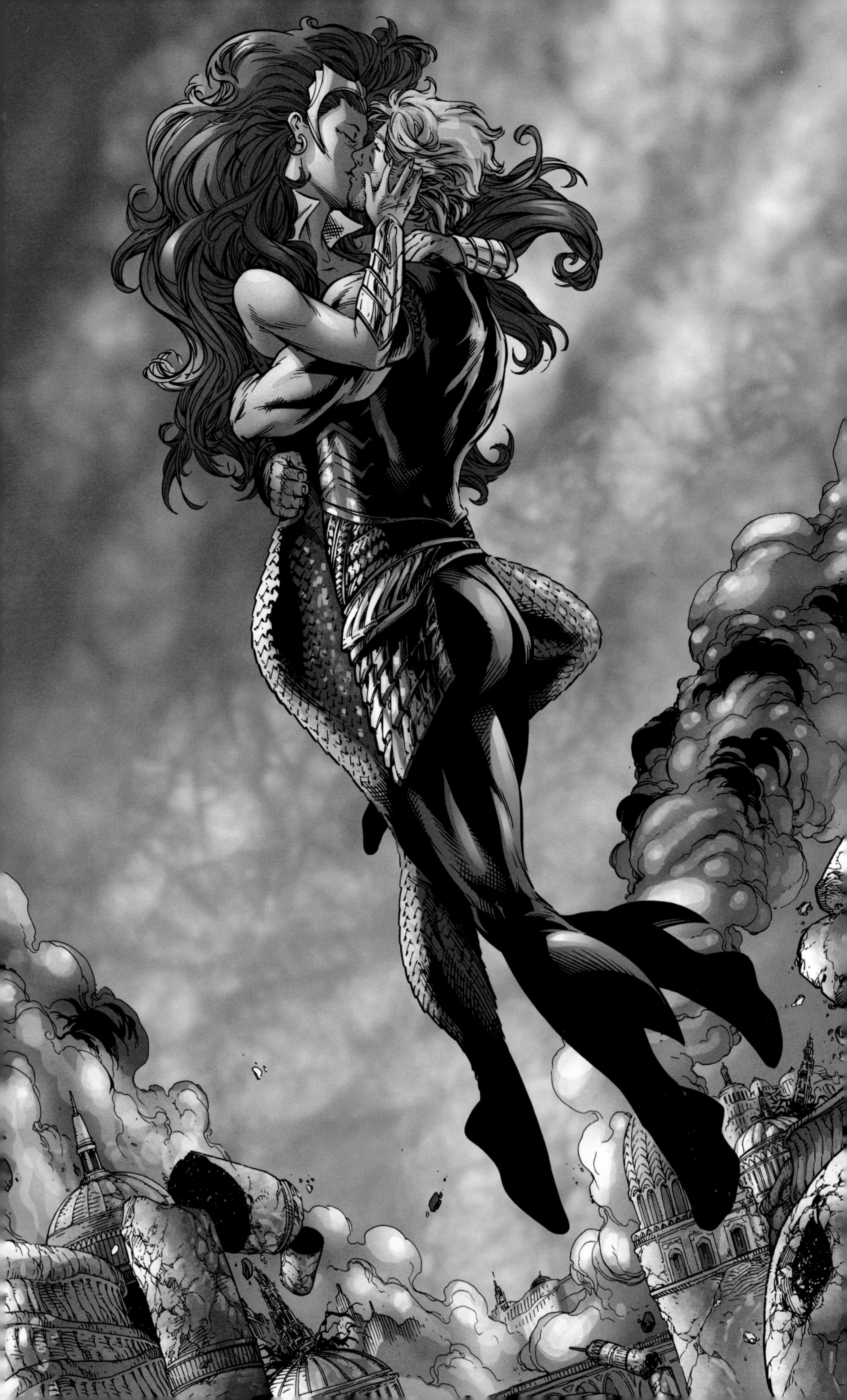

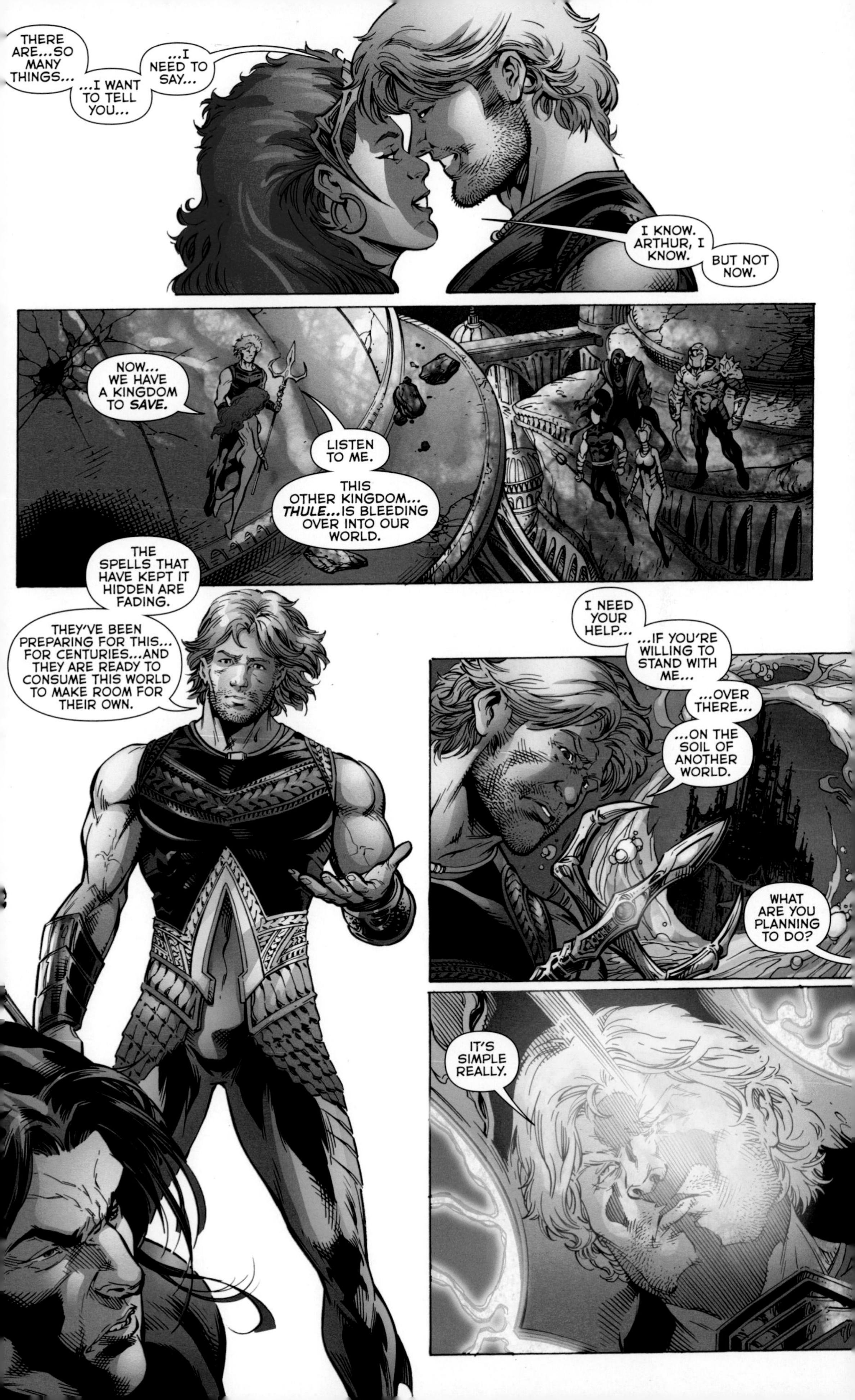
THERE ARE...SO MANY THINGS...
...I WANT TO TELL YOU...
...I NEED TO SAY...
I KNOW. ARTHUR, I KNOW.
BUT NOT NOW.
NOW... WE HAVE A KINGDOM TO SAVE.
LISTEN TO ME.
THIS OTHER KINGDOM... THULE...IS BLEEDING OVER INTO OUR WORLD.
THE SPELLS THAT HAVE KEPT IT HIDDEN ARE FADING.
THEY'VE BEEN PREPARING FOR THIS... FOR CENTURIES...AND THEY ARE READY TO CONSUME THIS WORLD TO MAKE ROOM FOR THEIR OWN.
I NEED YOUR HELP...
...IF YOU'RE WILLING TO STAND WITH ME...
...OVER THERE...
...ON THE SOIL OF ANOTHER WORLD.
WHAT ARE YOU PLANNING TO DO?
IT'S SIMPLE REALLY.

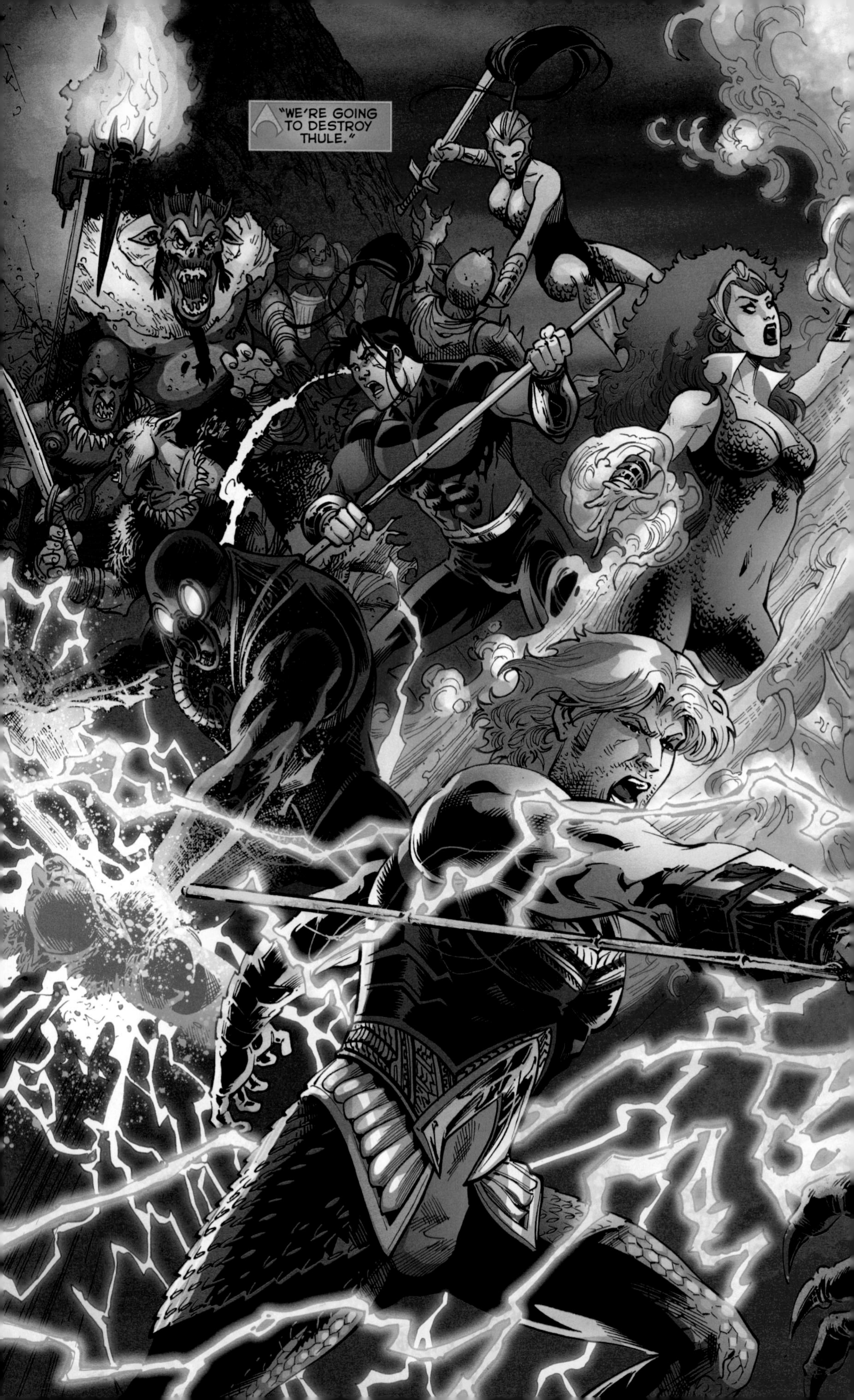
"WE'RE GOING TO DESTROY THULE."

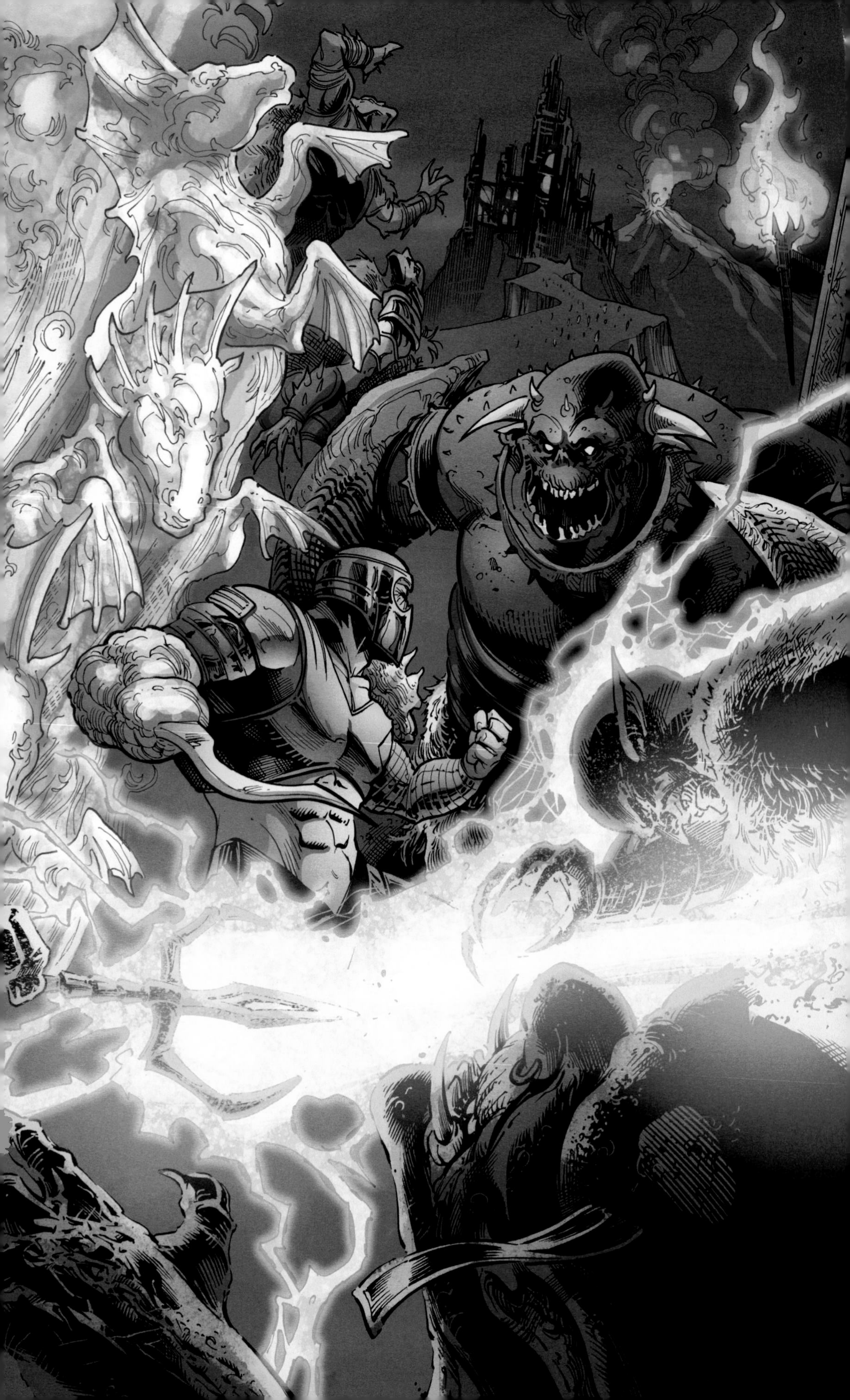

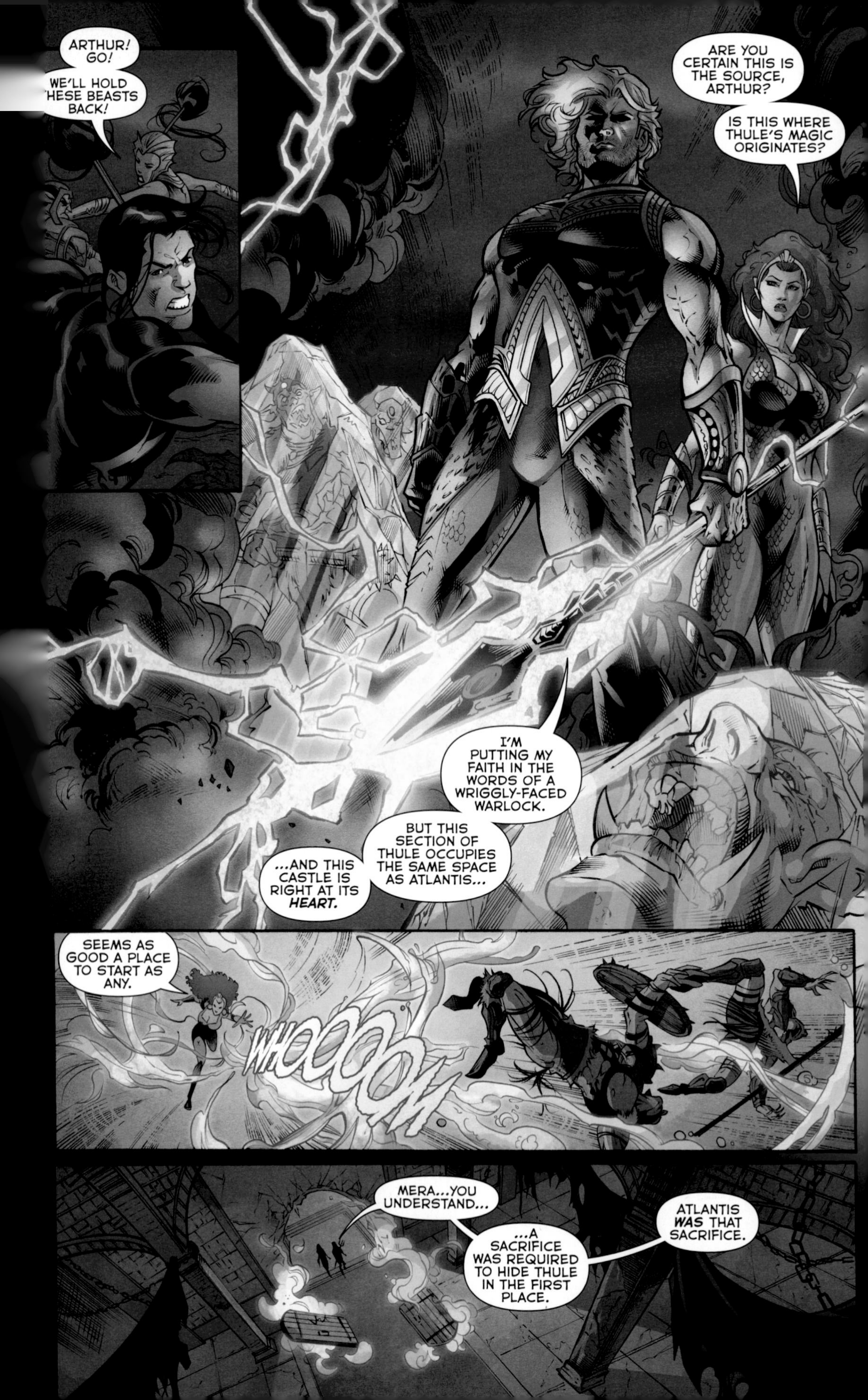
ARTHUR! GO!
WE'LL HOLD THESE BEASTS BACK!
ARE YOU CERTAIN THIS IS THE SOURCE, ARTHUR?
IS THIS WHERE THULE'S MAGIC ORIGINATES?
I'M PUTTING MY FAITH IN THE WORDS OF A WRIGGLY-FACED WARLOCK.
BUT THIS SECTION OF THULE OCCUPIES THE SAME SPACE AS ATLANTIS...
...AND THIS CASTLE IS RIGHT AT ITS HEART.
SEEMS AS GOOD A PLACE TO START AS ANY.
WHOOOOOM
MERA...YOU UNDERSTAND...
...A SACRIFICE WAS REQUIRED TO HIDE THULE IN THE FIRST PLACE.
ATLANTIS WAS THAT SACRIFICE.

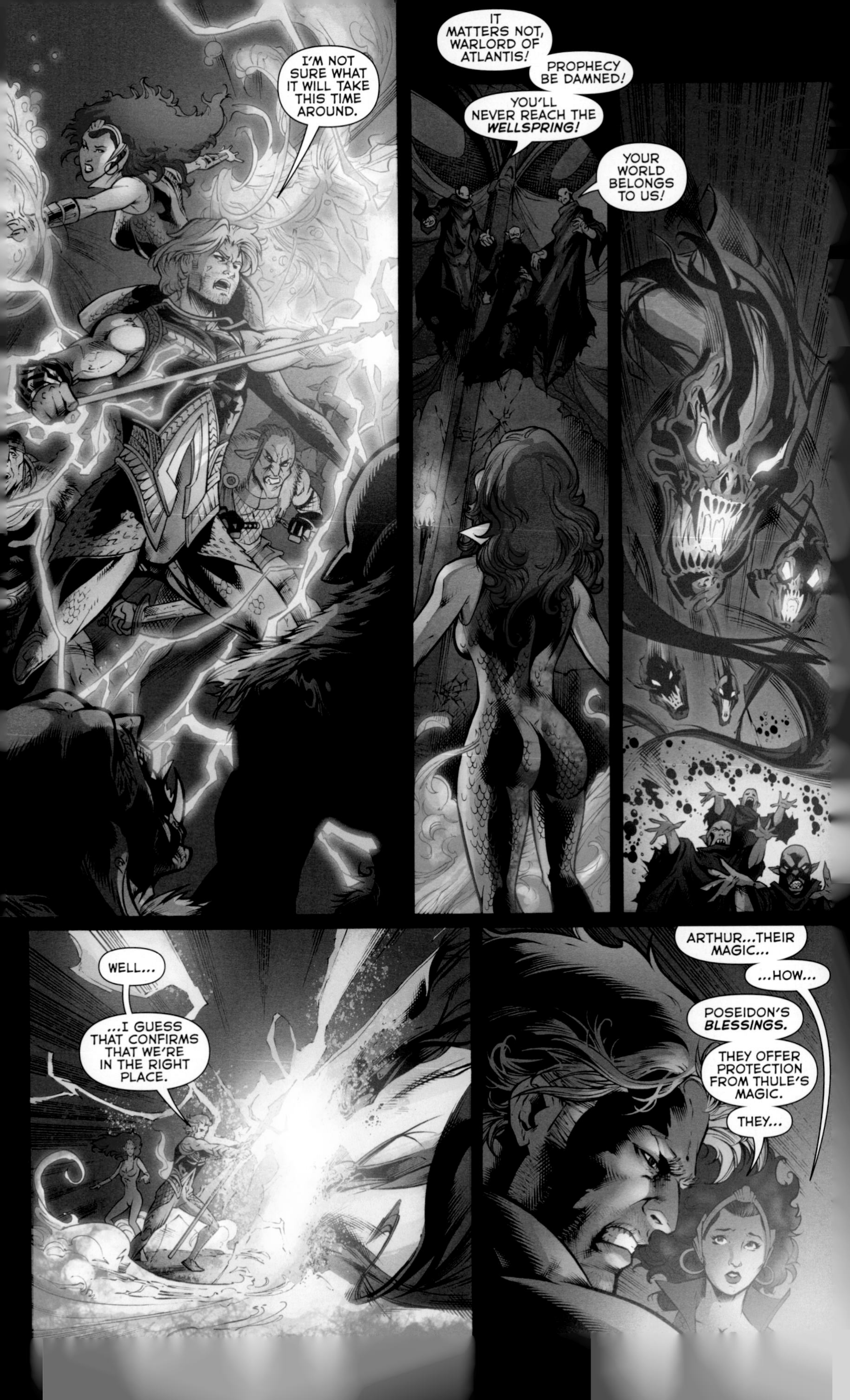
I'M NOT SURE WHAT IT WILL TAKE THIS TIME AROUND.
IT MATTERS NOT, WARLORD OF ATLANTIS!
PROPHECY BE DAMNED!
YOU'LL NEVER REACH THE **WELLSPRING!**
YOUR WORLD BELONGS TO US!
WELL...
...I GUESS THAT CONFIRMS THAT WE'RE IN THE RIGHT PLACE.
ARTHUR...THEIR MAGIC...
...HOW...
POSEIDON'S **BLESSINGS.**
THEY OFFER PROTECTION FROM THULE'S MAGIC.
THEY...

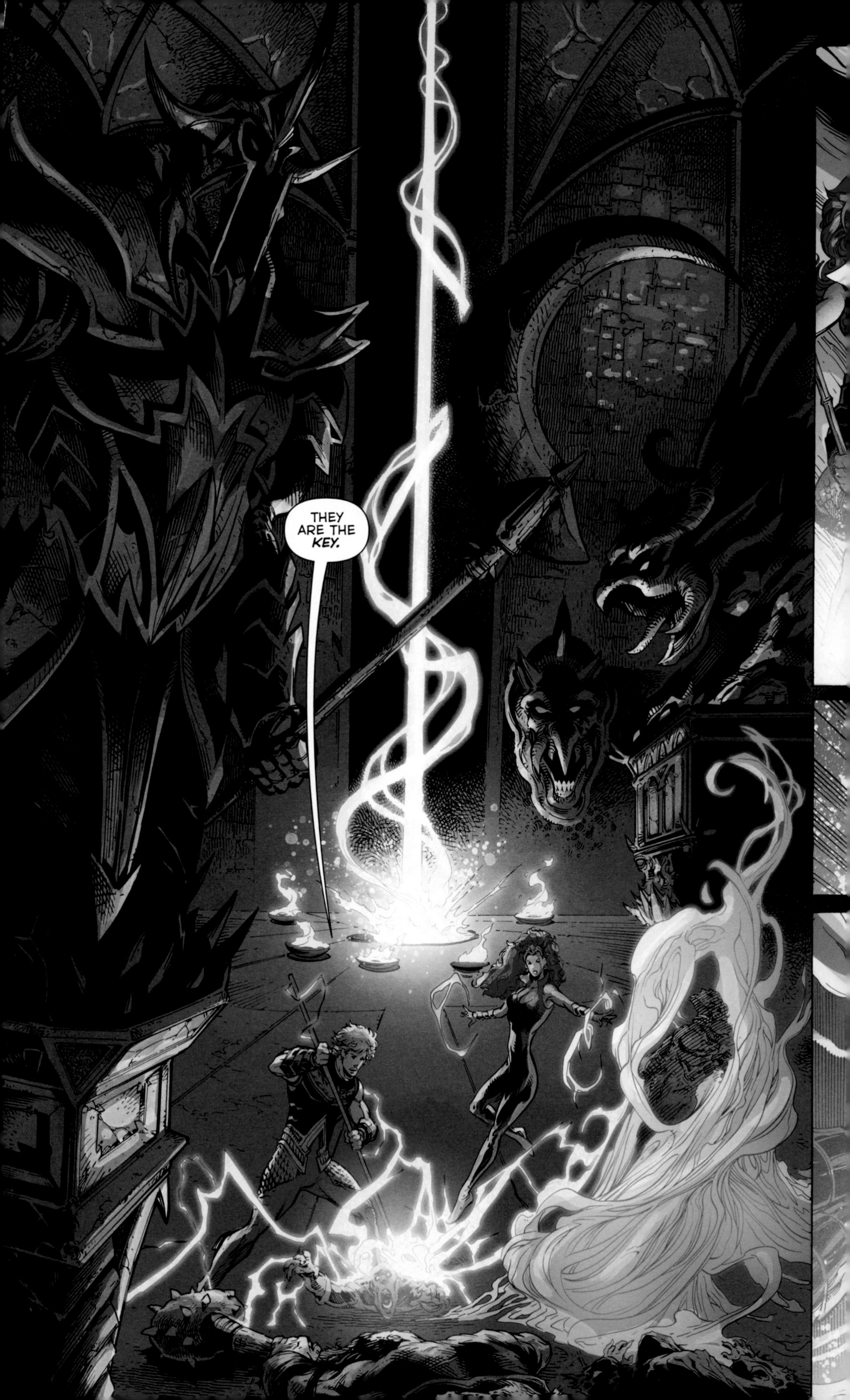
THEY ARE THE KEY.

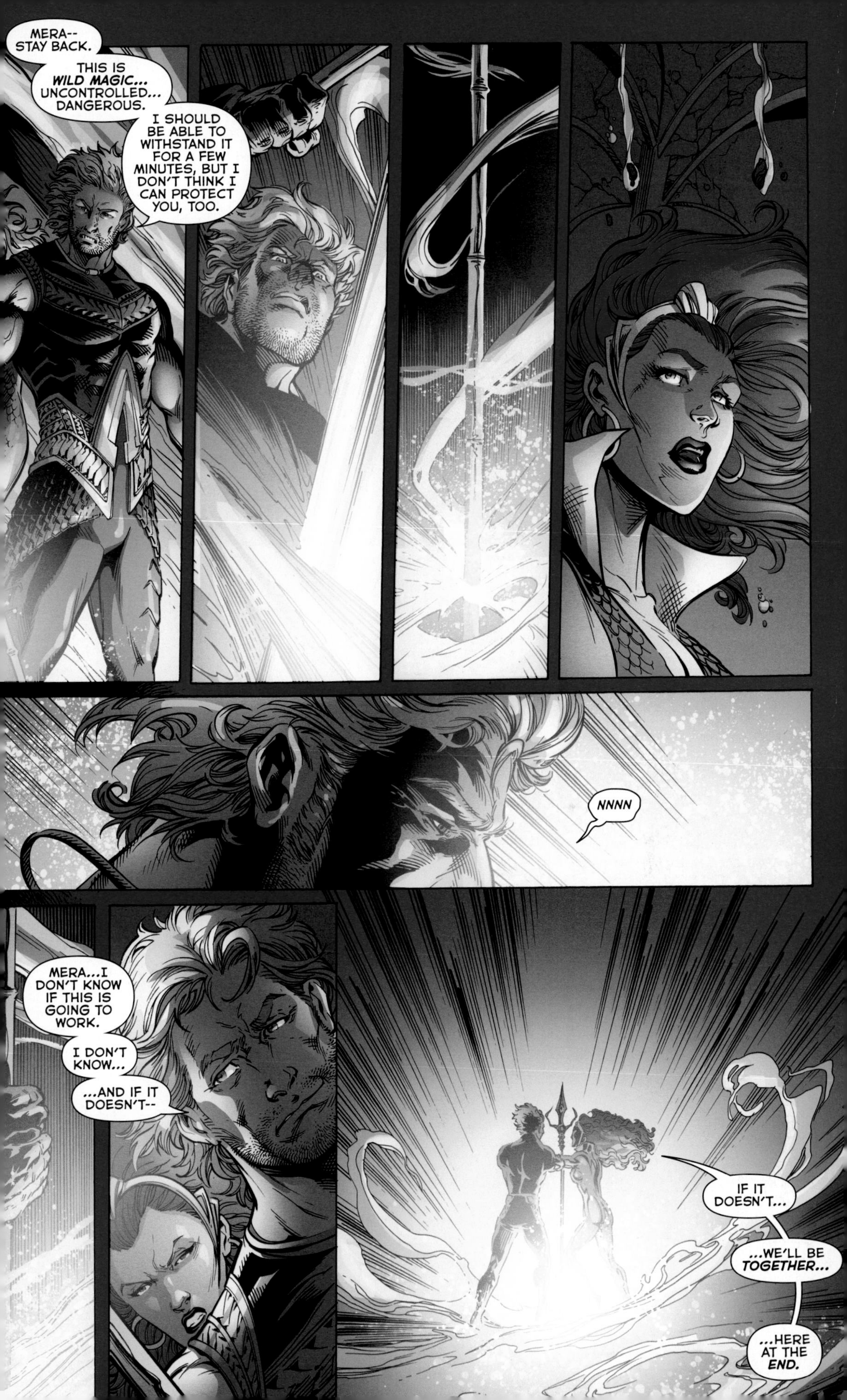
MERA--
STAY BACK.
THIS IS *WILD MAGIC...* UNCONTROLLED... DANGEROUS.
I SHOULD BE ABLE TO WITHSTAND IT FOR A FEW MINUTES, BUT I DON'T THINK I CAN PROTECT YOU, TOO.
NNNN
MERA...I DON'T KNOW IF THIS IS GOING TO WORK.
I DON'T KNOW...
...AND IF IT DOESN'T--
IF IT DOESN'T...
...WE'LL BE *TOGETHER...*
...HERE AT THE *END.*

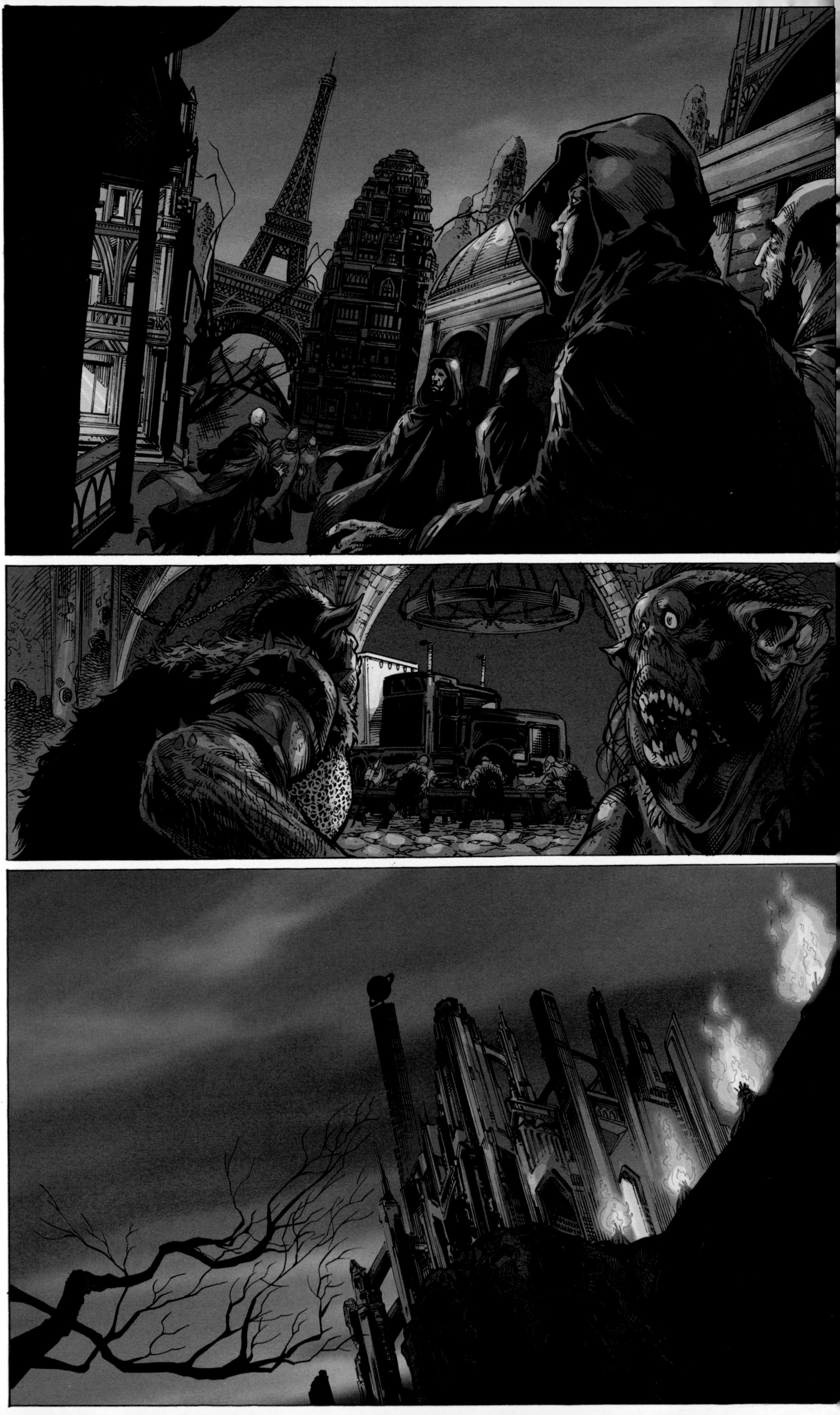

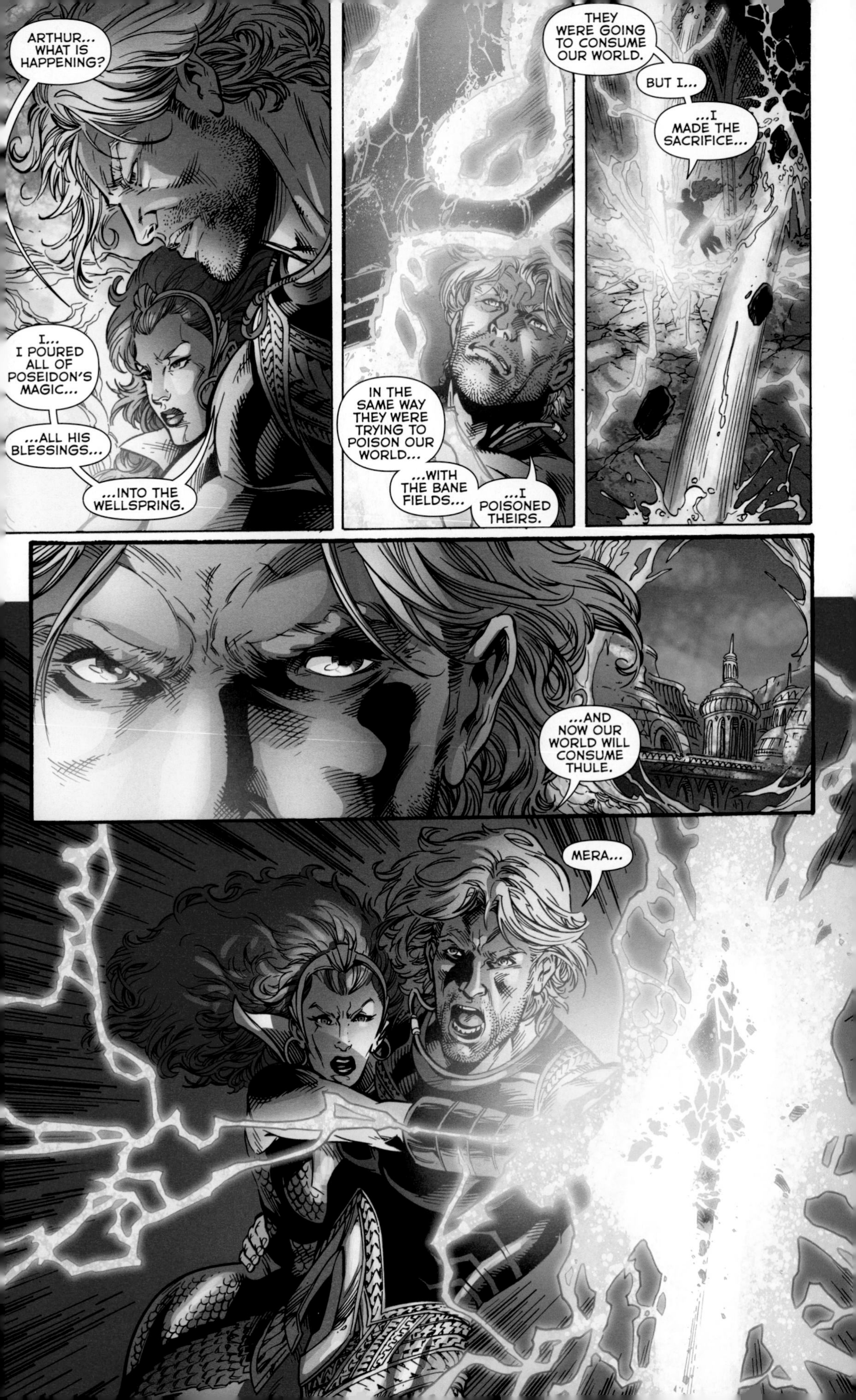
ARTHUR... WHAT IS HAPPENING?
I... I POURED ALL OF POSEIDON'S MAGIC...
...ALL HIS BLESSINGS...
...INTO THE WELLSPRING.
IN THE SAME WAY THEY WERE TRYING TO POISON OUR WORLD...
...WITH THE BANE FIELDS...
...I POISONED THEIRS.
THEY WERE GOING TO CONSUME OUR WORLD.
BUT I...
...I MADE THE SACRIFICE...
...AND NOW OUR WORLD WILL CONSUME THULE.
MERA...

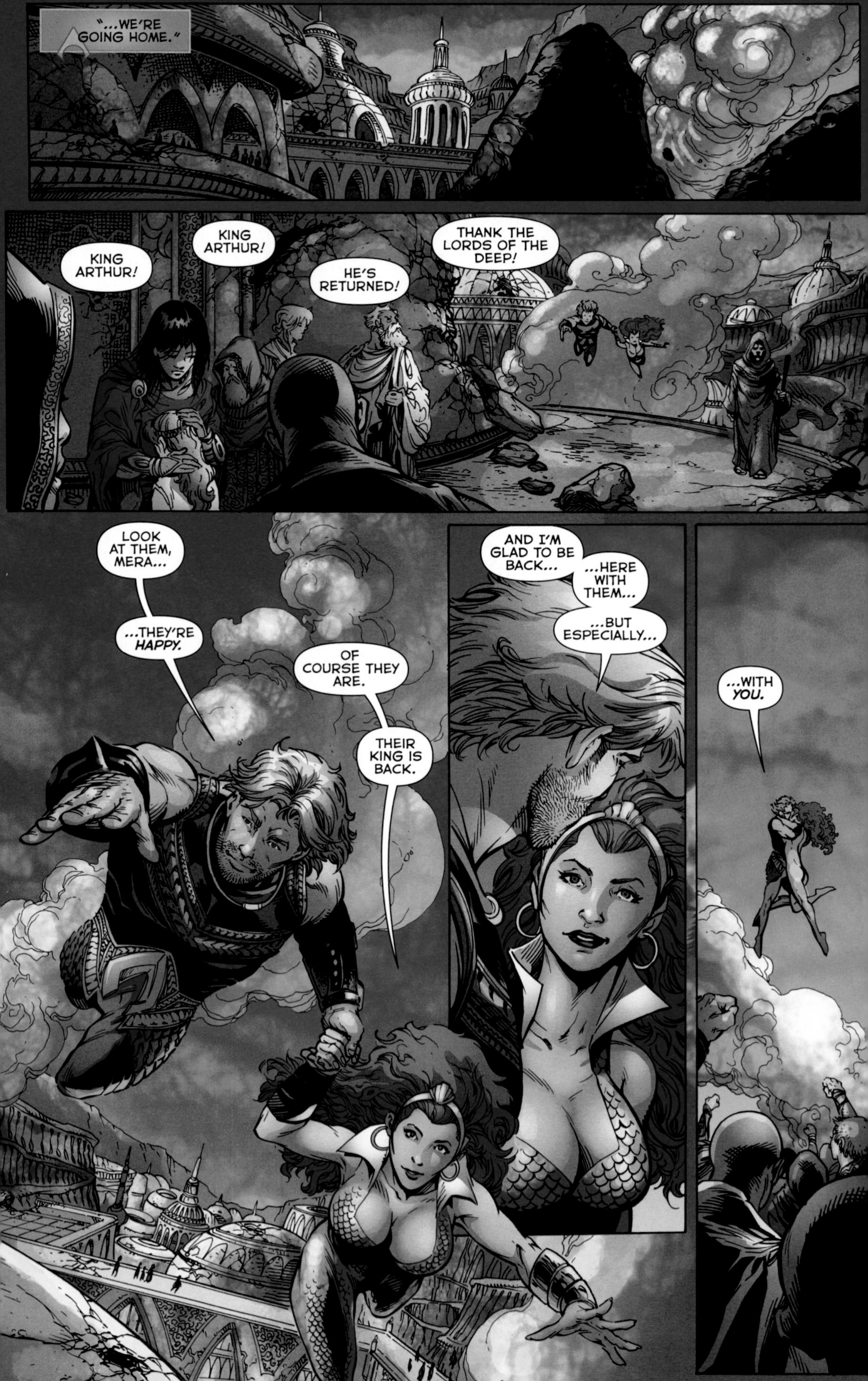
"...WE'RE GOING HOME."
KING ARTHUR!
KING ARTHUR!
HE'S RETURNED!
THANK THE LORDS OF THE DEEP!
LOOK AT THEM, MERA...
...THEY'RE *HAPPY.*
OF COURSE THEY ARE.
THEIR KING IS BACK.
AND I'M GLAD TO BE BACK...
...HERE WITH THEM...
...BUT ESPECIALLY...
...WITH *YOU.*

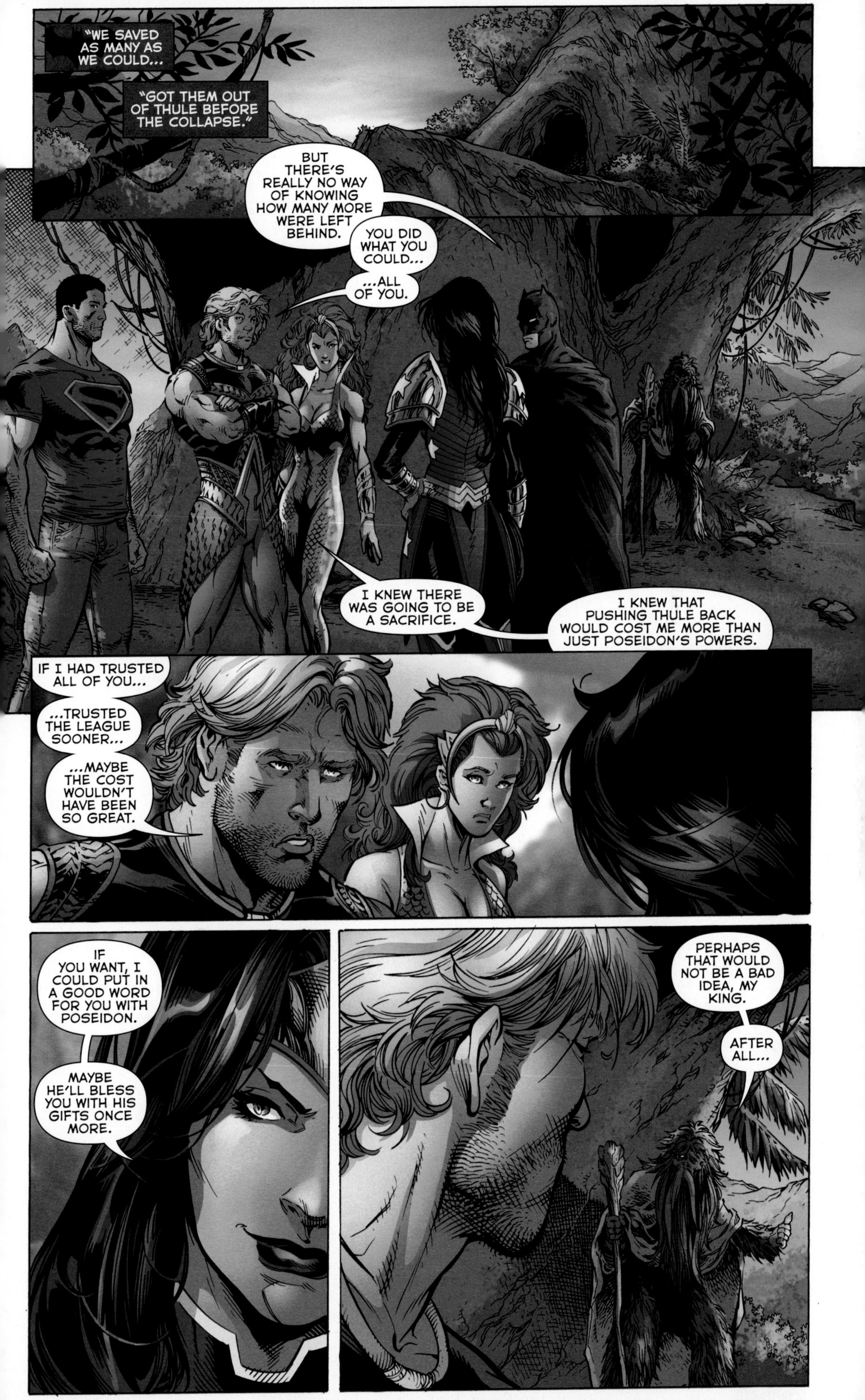
"WE SAVED AS MANY AS WE COULD...
"GOT THEM OUT OF THULE BEFORE THE COLLAPSE."
BUT THERE'S REALLY NO WAY OF KNOWING HOW MANY MORE WERE LEFT BEHIND.
YOU DID WHAT YOU COULD...
...ALL OF YOU.
I KNEW THERE WAS GOING TO BE A SACRIFICE.
I KNEW THAT PUSHING THULE BACK WOULD COST ME MORE THAN JUST POSEIDON'S POWERS.
IF I HAD TRUSTED ALL OF YOU...
...TRUSTED THE LEAGUE SOONER...
...MAYBE THE COST WOULDN'T HAVE BEEN SO GREAT.
IF YOU WANT, I COULD PUT IN A GOOD WORD FOR YOU WITH POSEIDON.
MAYBE HE'LL BLESS YOU WITH HIS GIFTS ONCE MORE.
PERHAPS THAT WOULD NOT BE A BAD IDEA, MY KING.
AFTER ALL...

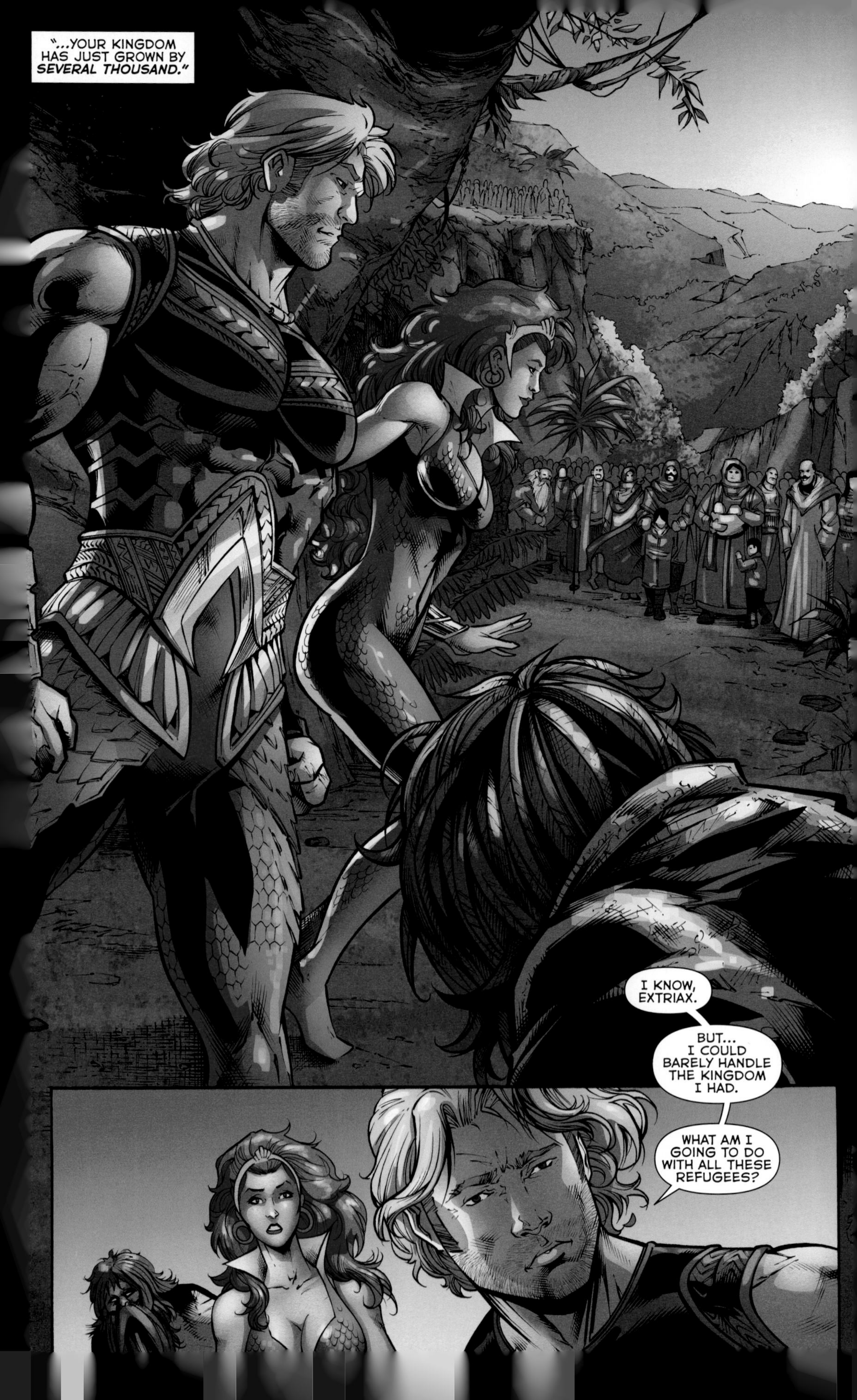
"...YOUR KINGDOM HAS JUST GROWN BY *SEVERAL THOUSAND.*"
I KNOW, EXTRIAX.
BUT... I COULD BARELY HANDLE THE KINGDOM I HAD.
WHAT AM I GOING TO DO WITH ALL THESE REFUGEES?

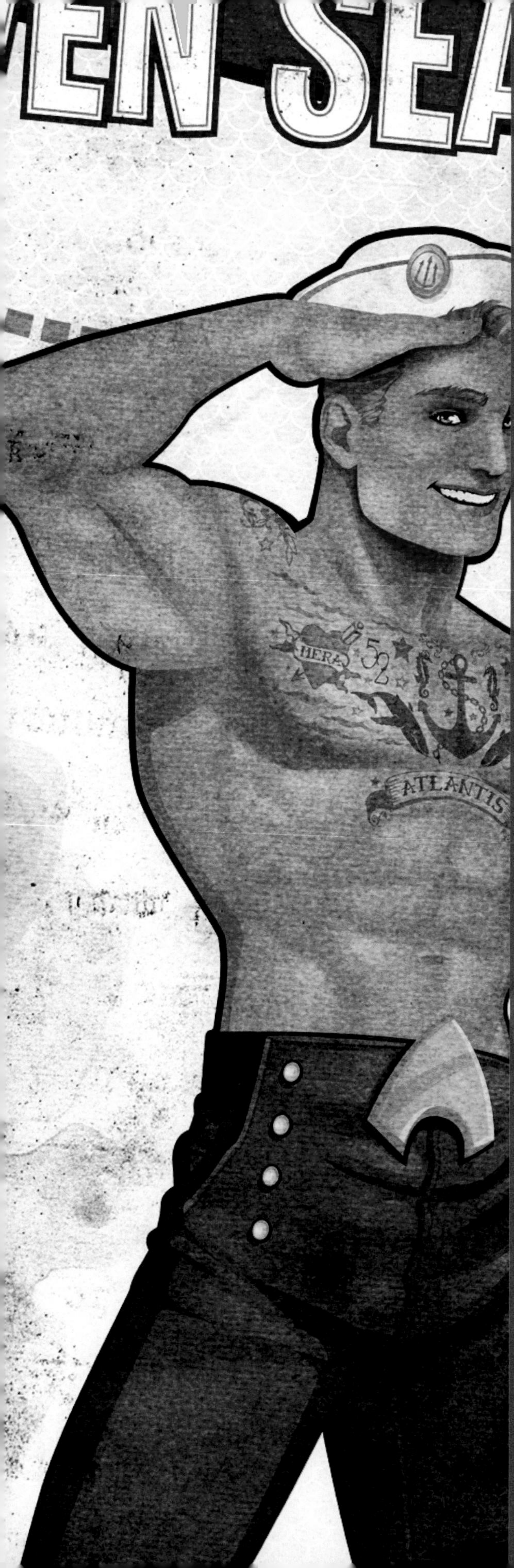
MERA
52
ATLANTIS

VARIANT COVER GALLERY

AQUAMAN #41
VARIANT COVER BY
WALT SIMONSON AND
LAURA MARTIN

AQUAMAN #42
TEEN TITANS GO!
VARIANT COVER BY
CRAIG ROUSSEAU

AQUAMAN #43
BOMBSHELLS VARIANT COVER BY
ANT LUCIA

AQUAMAN #44
GREEN LANTERN
75TH ANNIVERSARY
VARIANT COVER BY
FRANCIS MANAPUL

AQUAMAN #45
MONSTER VARIANT COVER
BY MICHAEL GOLDEN

AQUAMAN #46
LOONEY TUNES
VARIANT COVER BY
IVAN REIS, BRAD ANDERSON
AND SPIKE BRANDT

AQUAMAN #48
COLORING BOOK
VARIANT COVER BY
ANDY KUHN

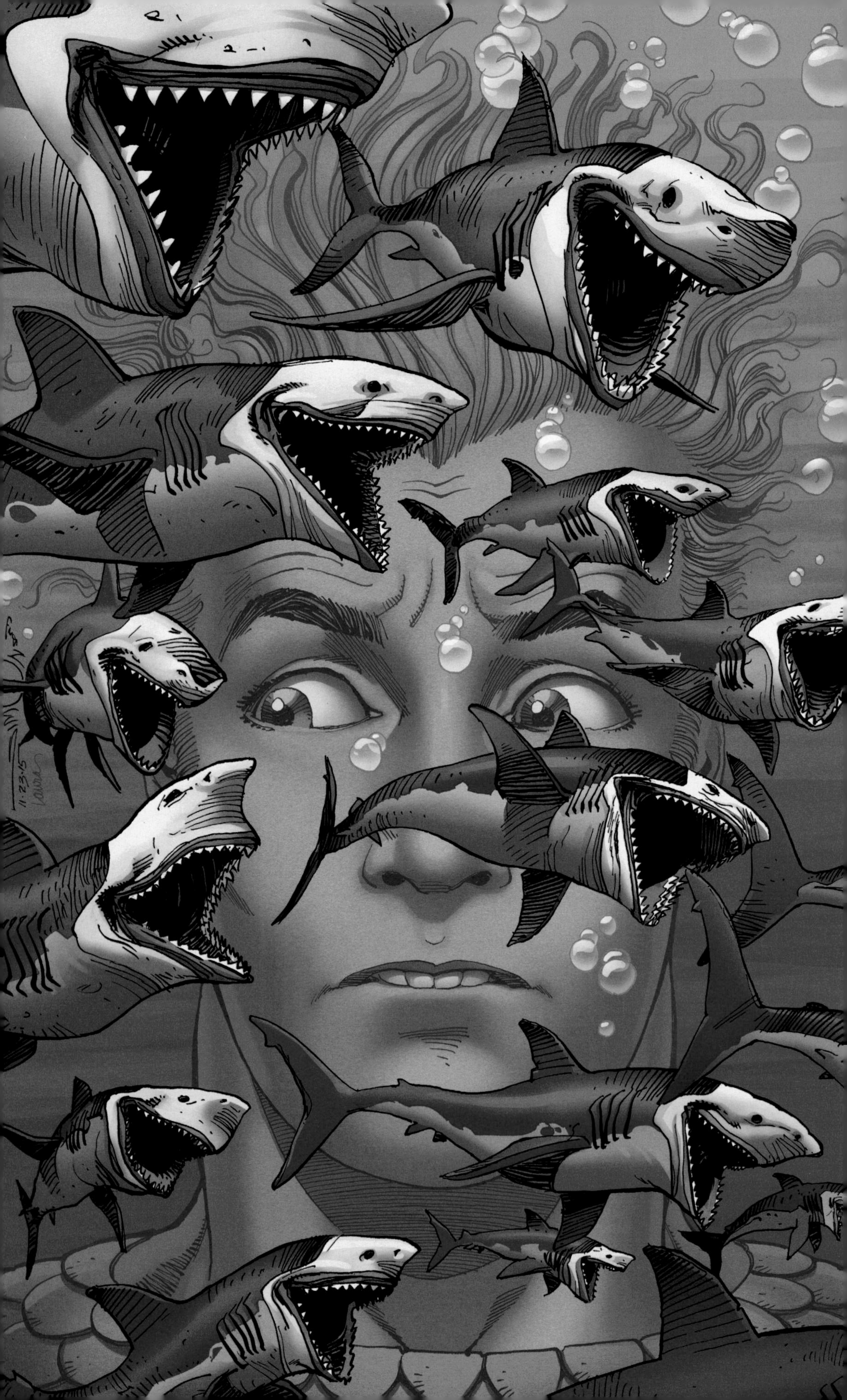

11·23·15
Laura

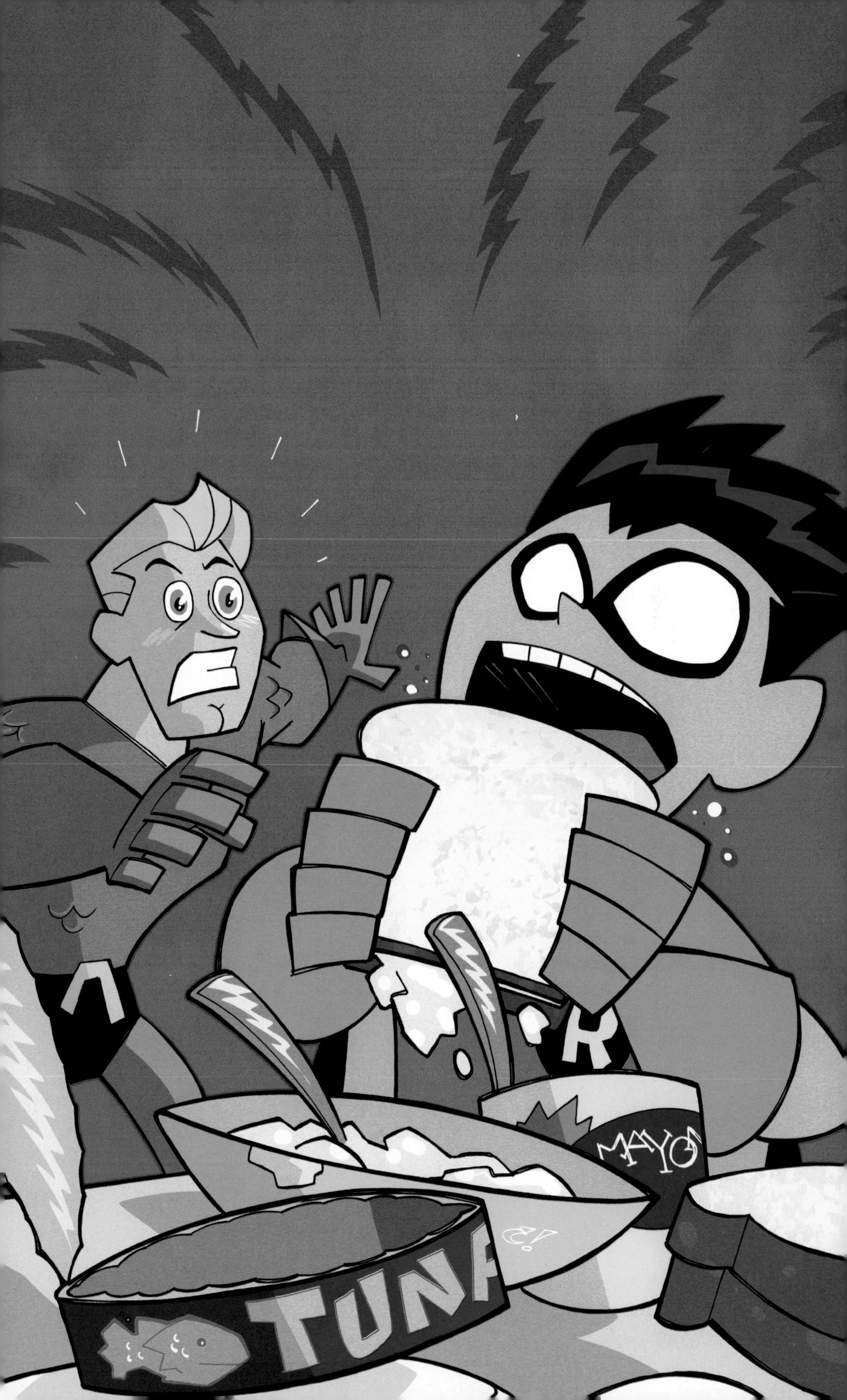
MAYO
TUNA

Tour
THE SEVEN SEAS
With
AQUAMAN
Captain of the S.S. Atlantis!
Spot sea horses, dolphins
and many other
aquatic creatures!
Call 555-FISH

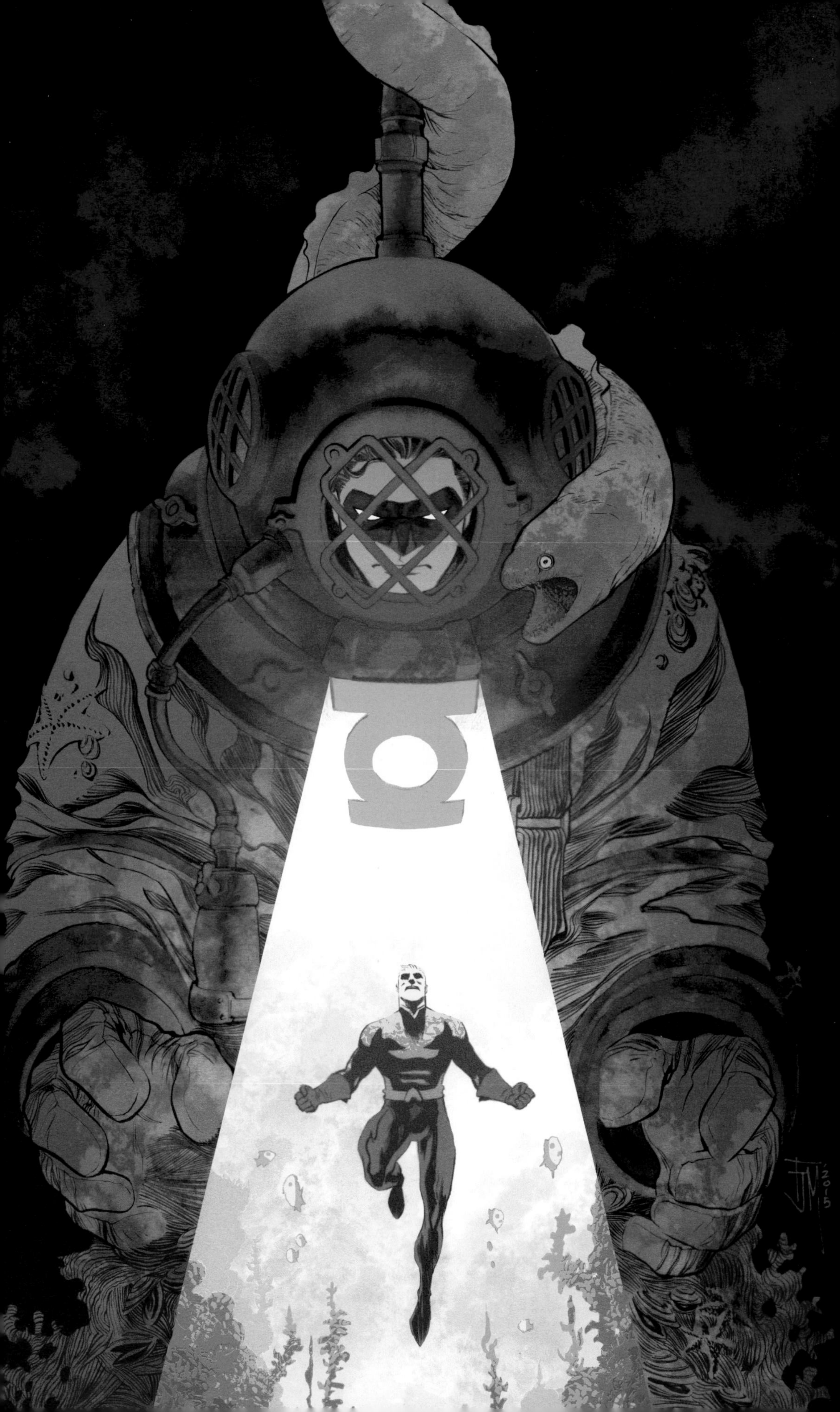

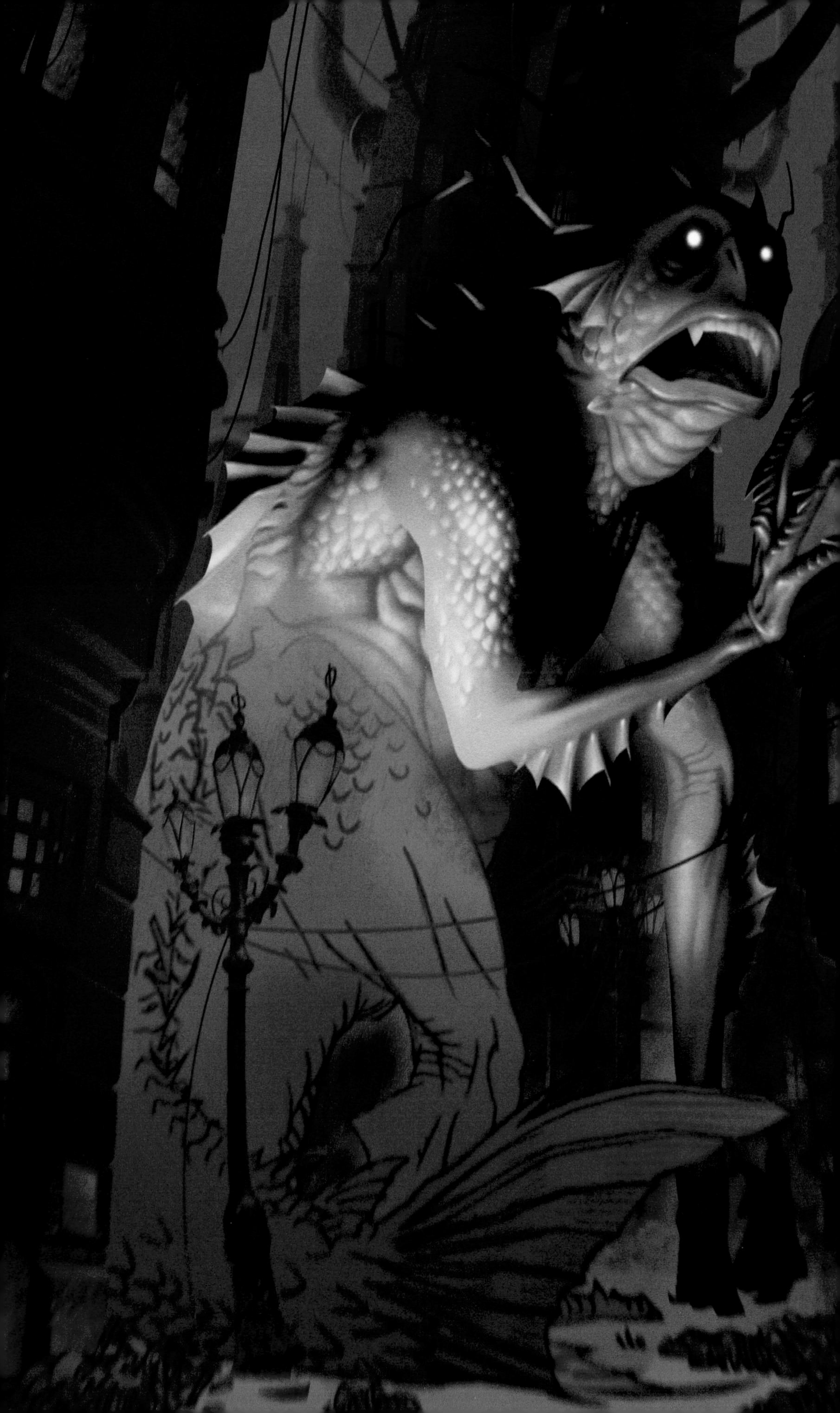

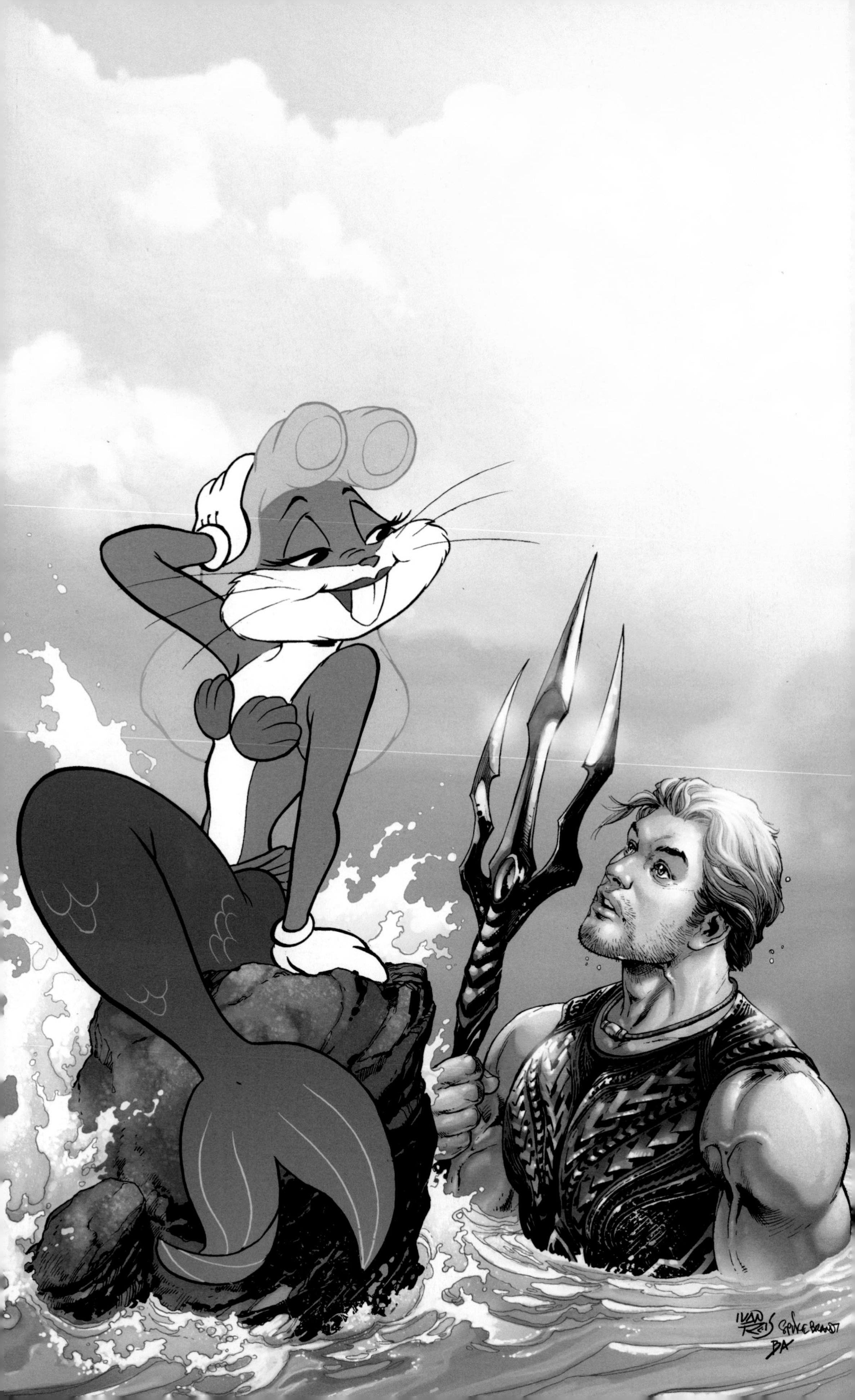

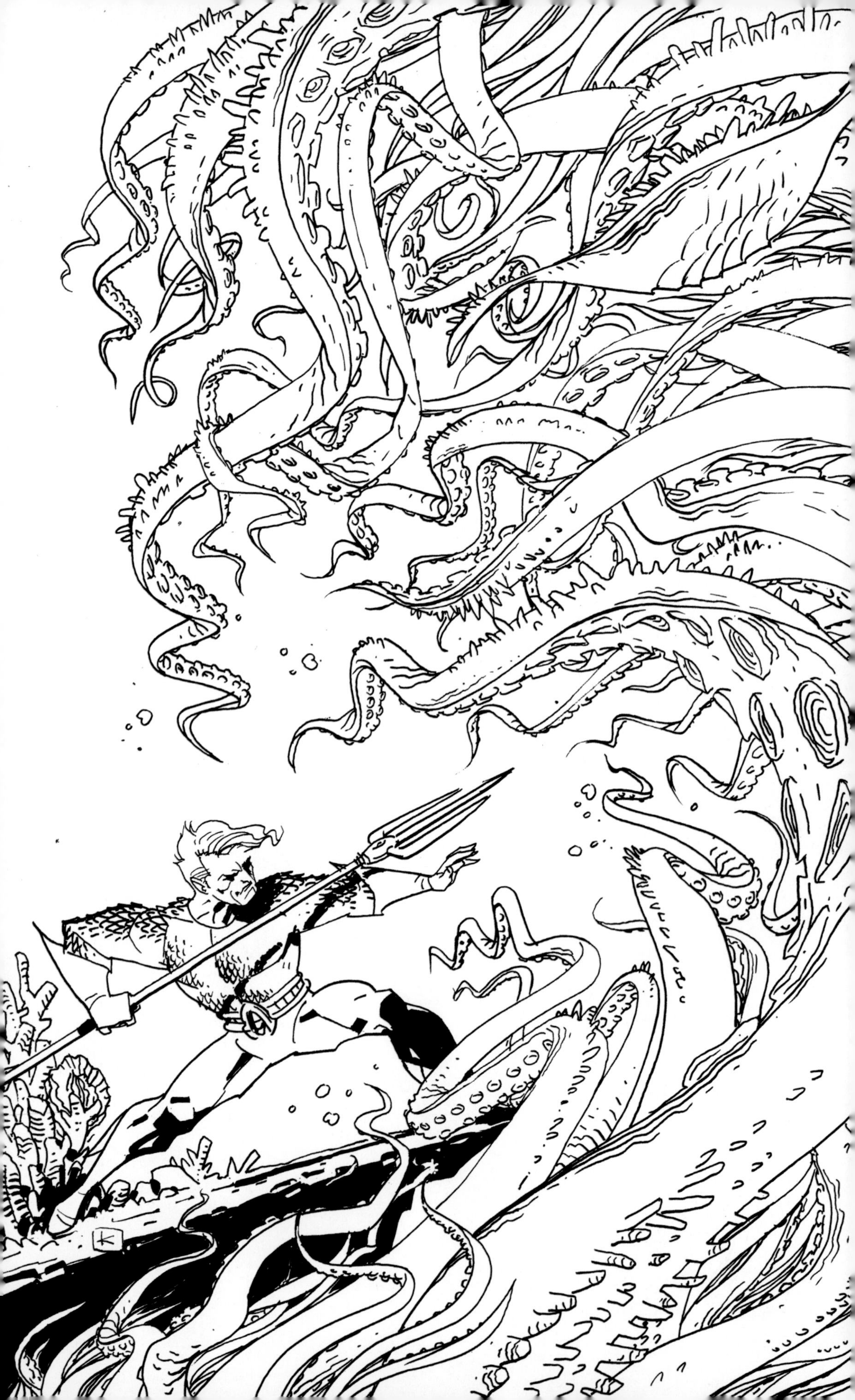

AQUAMAN #44
COVER ROUGHS BY TREVOR MCCARTHY

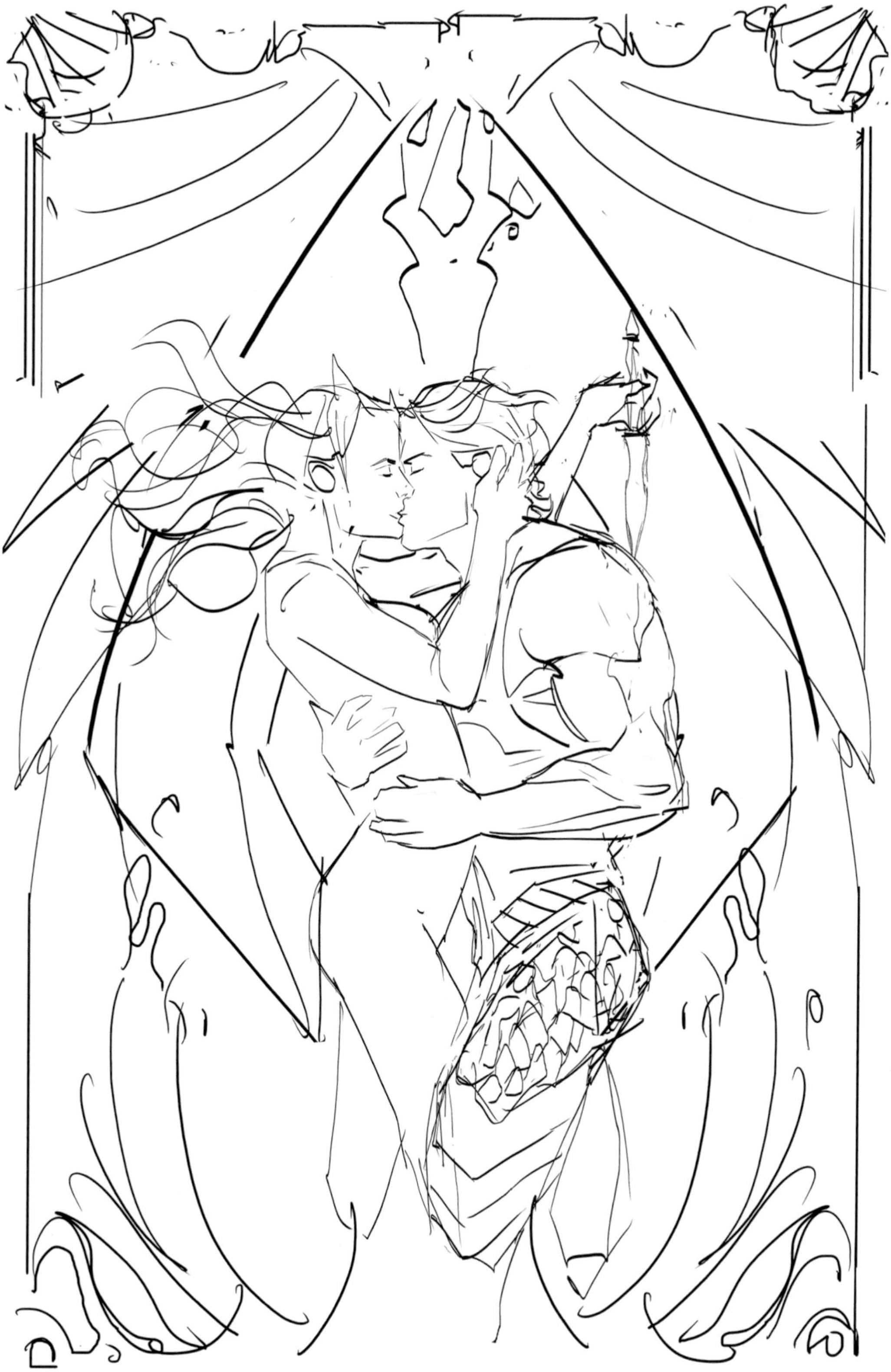

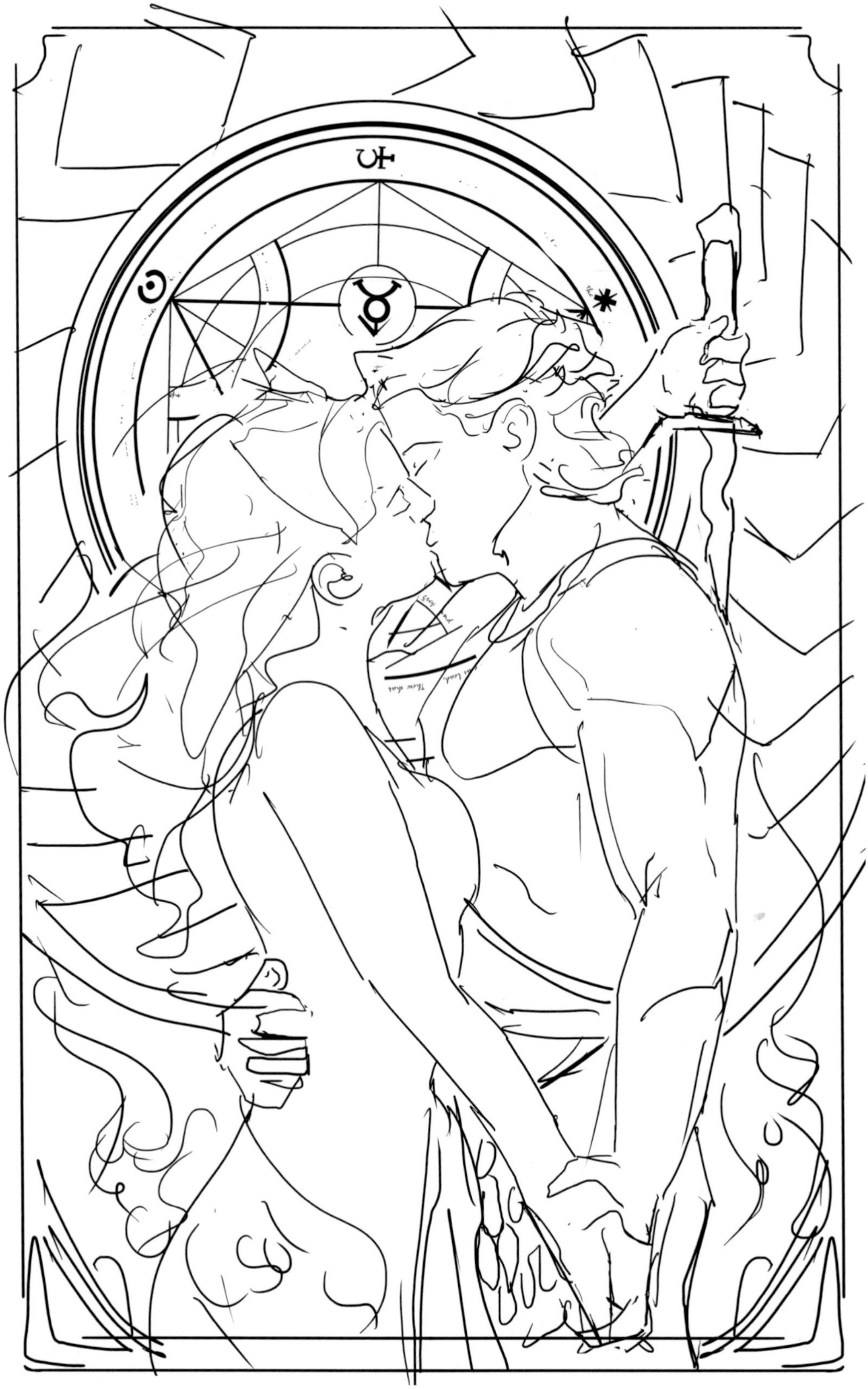

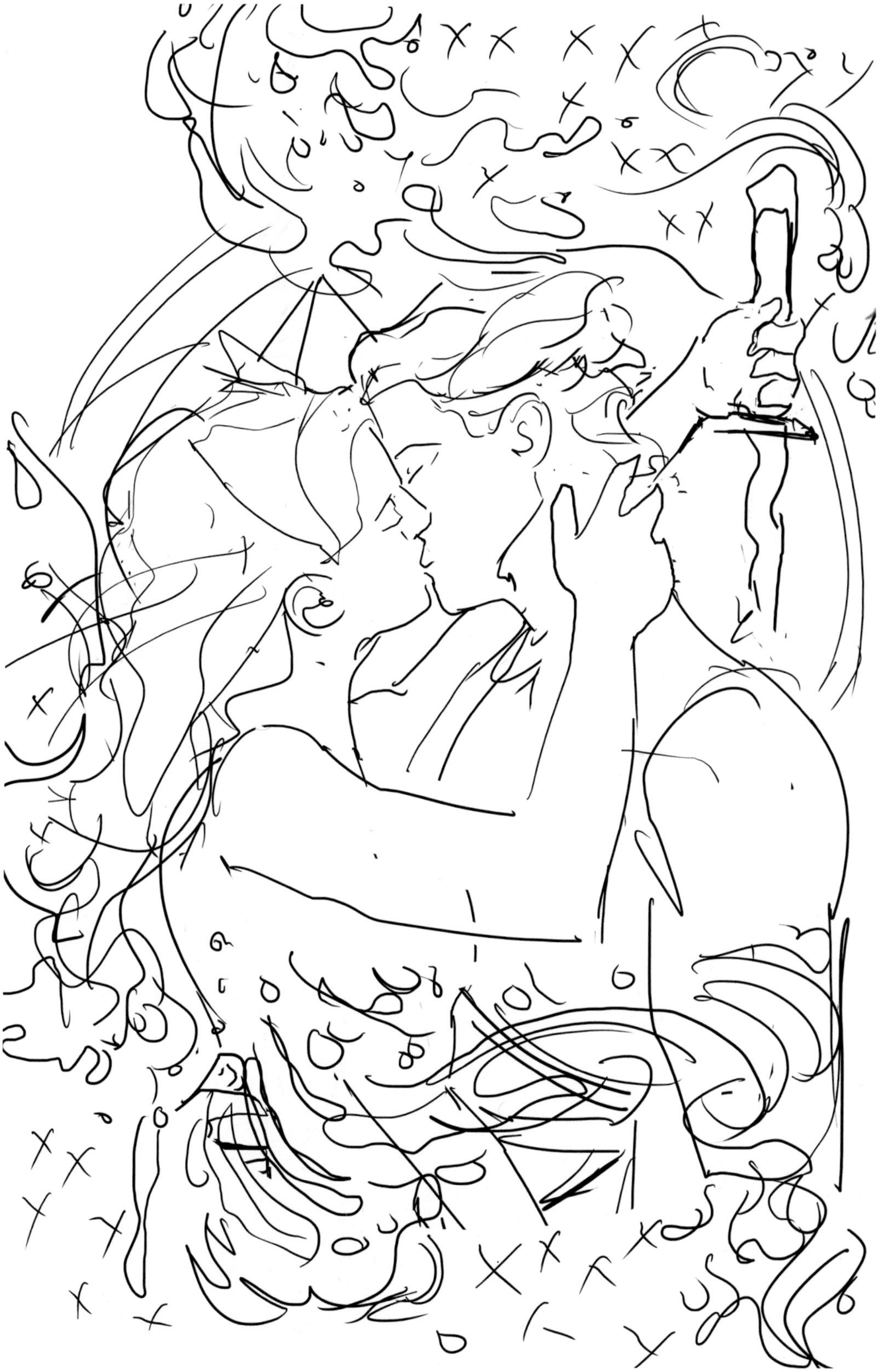

START AT THE BEGINNING!
AQUAMAN
VOLUME 1: THE TRENCH
GEOFF JOHNS and IVAN REIS

AQUAMAN VOL. 2: THE OTHERS

AQUAMAN VOL. 3: THE THRONE OF ATLANTIS

JUSTICE LEAGUE VOL. 3: THE THRONE OF ATLANTIS

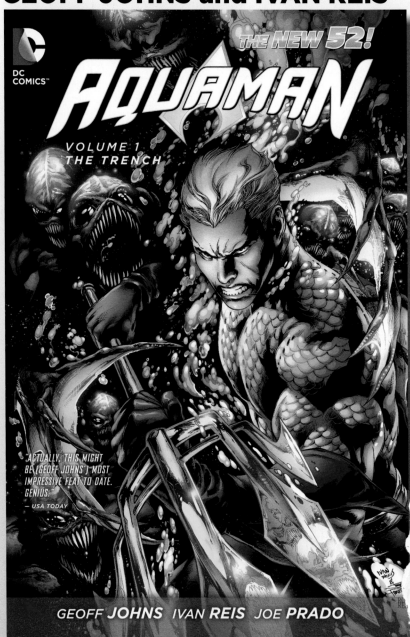

THE NEW 52!

AQUAMAN

VOLUME 1
THE TRENCH

"ACTUALLY, THIS MIGHT BE [GEOFF JOHNS'] MOST IMPRESSIVE FEAT TO DATE. GENIUS."
— USA TODAY

GEOFF **JOHNS** IVAN **REIS** JOE **PRADO**